Data Dictionary/Directory Systems

Administration, Implementation and Usage

BELKIS W. LEONG-HONG

Department of Defense
Washington, D.C.

BERNARD K. PLAGMAN

The Plagman Group, Inc.
New York, New York

A WILEY-INTERSCIENCE PUBLICATION

JOHN WILEY & SONS

New York   Chichester   Brisbane   Toronto   Singapore

Copyright ©1982 by John Wiley & Sons, Inc.

All rights reserved. Published simultaneously in Canada.

Reproduction or translation of any part of this work beyond that permitted by Section 107 or 108 of the 1976 United States Copyright Act without the permission of the copyright owner is unlawful. Requests for permission or further information should be addressed to the Permissions Department, John Wiley & Sons, Inc.

This publication is designed to provide accurate and authoritative information in regard to the subject matter covered. It is sold with the understanding that the publisher is not engaged in rendering legal, accounting, or other professional service. If legal advice or other expert assistance is required, the services of a competent professional person should be sought. *From a Declaration of Principles jointly adopted by a Committee of the American Bar Association and a Committee of Publishers.*

Library of Congress Cataloging in Publication Data:

Leong-Hong, Belkis.
  Data dictionary/directory systems.

  "A Wiley-Interscience publication."
  Includes bibliographical references and index.
  1. Data base management. 2. Data dictionaries.
I. Plagman, Bernard K. II. Title.
QA76.9.D3L46   001.64   81-21875
ISBN 0-471-05164-0   AACR2

Printed in the United States of America

10 9 8 7 6 5 4 3 2 1

Data Dictionary/Directory Systems

To Ken and Denise
for their love, patience, support,
and encouragement.

To the blessed memory of my father,
Herman Plagman,
my source of inspiration and perseverance.

Preface

Decision making at all levels of management requires complete, accurate, and timely information. The increasing use of computers and information processing technology in all enterprises has heightened management's awareness of the advantages of utilizing *data as a resource* in producing this information. Management awareness has increased interest in developing tools and methodologies to facilitate the management of data as a resource. The Data Dictionary/Directory System (DD/DS) is one such tool.

The DD/DS is a software tool that provides for logical centralization of information about an enterprise's data resources. As such, this tool plays a key role in aiding the management and control of the enterprise's data resources. The DD/DS is useful in all aspects of an enterprise's data processing environment, including database-related applications and non-database-related applications.

The dictionary and directory technology is relatively young. The first commercial DD/DS package appeared around 1970. Since then, seventeen commercial DD/DSs have appeared in the marketplace, and four more are in various stages of development. This is testimony to the increasing awareness of the usefulness of this tool in the management of data as an enterprise resource. Because this tool is relatively young, the literature on data dictionary/directory systems is sparse.

The purpose of this book is to share with data processing and other relevant professions our understanding and experience regarding data dictionary/directory systems. The topic is gaining acceptance in the profession as the concept of Data Resources Management matures. We are confident that our effort will contribute further in the evolution of tools and techniques to support the management of data as an enterprise resource. This book comprehensively describes a DD/DS from several perspectives: conceptual, functional use, design, implementation, and administration.

from several perspectives: conceptual, functional use, design, implementation, and administration.

The book is intended for a wide audience, but it is aimed primarily at those concerned with the management and effective utilization of data resources, such as data administrators, database administrators, system developers, designers, analysts, and programmers.

Data administration and database administration personnel will find the entire book interesting. The first chapter provides a broad conceptual treatment of the topic. The second chapter discusses the DD/DS from a functional viewpoint and addresses the use of the DD/DS in an information system development life cycle framework. Chapters 3 to 7 provide insight into DD/DS design and, in particular, into the evaluation of commercial DD/DS software design and implementation. Chapter 8 specifically describes a selection methodology. Chapter 9 presents a detailed treatment of the data administration aspects of dealing with a DD/DS, from the user's perspective. This chapter emphasizes the use of the DD/DS as a data administration tool. Chapter 10 discusses the DD/DS from the perspective of the emerging technology: distributed database processing. Chapter 11 is written as a stand-alone chapter, and it emphasizes the use of the DD/DS as a tool for audit and control. Chapter 12 concludes with a look at the future of data dictionary/directory systems.

System analysts and designers will find the greatest value in reading Chapters 1, 2, 8, 9, 10, 11, and 12, while those in systems management would find Chapters 1, 2, 9, and 12 most informative. Persons most concerned with programming and implementation would be most concerned with Chapters 1 and 2. Developers and vendors of software should be concerned with issues raised in the entire book. Nevertheless, the material in Chapters 1, 2, 3, 4, 5, 6, 7, and 12 is most pertinent. General auditors and EDP auditors would find Chapters 1 and 11 most interesting and informative.

The effort to write this book has been shared jointly by its co-authors. Each of us is indebted to the other for the prodding, perseverance, encouragement, and patience required to bring this effort to successful completion.

We gratefully acknowledge the excellent cooperation of the DD/DS vendors in providing us with necessary technical documentation for our analysis. We also wish to thank our editor, John Mahaney, and our reviewers for their helpful advice, comments, and criticism. In particular, a number of individuals deserve special thanks. These are Marshall Abrams, Gene Altshuler, Herman C. Kocks, and Herman Roos. And last but not least we wish to thank our typists Brenda Croson and Ginger Keyser.

BELKIS W. LEONG-HONG
BERNARD K. PLAGMAN

March 1982

Contents

1   BASIC PRINCIPLES OF DATA DICTIONARY/
    DIRECTORY SYSTEMS

    1.1 Concept: Data Is a Resource   2
        1.1.1 Information Hierarchy   *4*
        1.1.2 Information Is Derived from Data   *6*
        1.1.3 Why so Late?   *7*
    1.2 Concept: Metadata   8
        1.2.1 Characteristics of Metadatabases   *10*
        1.2.2 Similarities Between Database Management and Metadatabase Management   *10*
    1.3 Management and Control of Metadata   11
        1.3.1 Establishing Lines of Responsibility and Authority   *12*
        1.3.2 Common Formats and Conventions for Data Definition   *13*
        1.3.3 Common Procedures for Collection, Update and Maintenance of the Metadata   *14*
        1.3.4 Common Procedures for Access Control to Metadata   *15*
    1.4 The Data Dictionary/Directory System – Definition   16
        1.4.1 General DD/DS Functions   *16*
        1.4.2 Spectrum of DD/DSs   *17*
        1.4.3 Types of Metadata in the DD/DS   *17*
    1.5 Distinction Between Dictionary and Directory Metadata   18
        1.5.1 Dictionary Metadata   *18*

		1.5.2 Directory Metadata	19
		1.5.3 Relationship Between Dictionary and Directory Metadata	19
	1.6	Active Versus Passive DD/DS	20
		1.6.1 Active DD/DS	21
		1.6.2 Passive and Potentially Active DD/DSs	22
	1.7	Summary	23
		References	23
2	**THE USE OF THE DATA DICTIONARY/DIRECTORY SYSTEM AS A TOOL**		**25**
	2.1	An Information System Development Life Cycle	26
	2.2	DD/DS: A Tool for System Planning	27
		2.2.1 Assess the Current Environment	27
		2.2.2 Analyze Current Usage and Determine Future Requirements	28
		2.2.3 DD/DS Supports System Planning Activities	28
		2.2.4 Benefits of Using a DD/DS During System Planning	32
		2.2.5 What the Last National Bank Did	33
	2.3	DD/DS: A Tool for Requirements Definition and Analysis	34
		2.3.1 Requirements Definition: Describe Functions and Data	34
		2.3.2 Requirements Analysis: Manipulate Functions and Detailed Conceptual Model	41
		2.3.3 DD/DS Supports Requirements Definition and Analysis Activities	41
		2.3.4 What the Last National Bank Did	44
	2.4	DD/DS: A Tool for Design, Implementation, Testing, Operation and Maintenance	46
		2.4.1 Design Phase	46
		2.4.2 Programming Phase	47
		2.4.3 DD/DS Supports All SDLC Activities	48
		2.4.4 What the Last National Bank Did	48
	2.5	DD/DS: A Tool for Documentation and Standards	49
		2.5.1 Application Systems Documentation	50
		2.5.2 Program Documentation	50

	2.5.3 Data Documentation	*51*
	2.5.4 Standards	*51*
	2.5.5 What the Last National Bank Did	*52*
2.6	DD/DS: A Tool for Operational Control Through Metadata Generation and Metadata Audit Trail	*53*
	2.6.1 Operational Control	*54*
	2.6.2 Audit Trail Aid	*55*
	2.6.3 What the Last National Bank Did	*55*
2.7	DD/DS: A Tool to Support the Distributed Database Environment	*56*
2.8	DD/DS: A Tool for End-User Support	*57*
2.9	Summary	*58*
	References	*59*

3 FOUNDATIONS FOR DESIGN OF THE DATA DICTIONARY/DIRECTORY SYSTEM *61*

3.1	DD/DS Design Philosophy	*62*
	3.1.1 Use of the Database Approach	*63*
	3.1.2 Foundation for Metadatabase Design	*64*
	3.1.3 Input/output and Generation Facilities Design	*65*
3.2	Conceptual Design of the Metadatabase	*65*
	3.2.1 Metadata Entities	*66*
	3.2.2 Metasystem Entities	*68*
	3.2.3 Meta-Environment Entities	*68*
	3.2.4 Representing Physical/Logical Views	*68*
	3.2.5 Meta-Entity Data Structure	*69*
3.3	Summary	*73*
	References	*74*

4 META-ENTITIES AND ATTRIBUTES *75*

4.1	Meta-Entity	*76*
	4.1.1 Nonstandard Nomenclature	*76*
	4.1.2 Classification of Meta Entities	*77*

	4.2 Attributes	*80*
	4.2.1 Identification Attributes	*82*
	4.2.2 Representation Attributes	*82*
	4.2.3 Relationship Attributes	*83*
	4.2.4 Statistical Attributes	*83*
	4.2.5 Control Attributes	*84*
	4.2.6 Physical Attributes	*85*
	4.2.7 User-Defined Attributes	*85*
	4.2.8 Using Attributes Across Entities	*86*
	4.3 The Expansibility Concept for the Metadatabase	*86*
	4.3.1 Adding Entities and Attributes	*88*
	4.3.2 Guidelines for Using Expansibility	*88*
	4.4 Summary	*90*
	References	*90*
5	**INPUT AND OUTPUT FACILITIES**	*93*
	5.1 Input Facilities for the DD/DS	*94*
	5.1.1 The Language for Defining Metadata	*94*
	5.1.2 Types of DDL Format	*96*
	5.1.3 Standards for DD/DSs	*100*
	5.2 Inputting of Metadata	*101*
	5.2.1 Batch Versus Online Input	*102*
	5.2.2 Special Input Features	*103*
	5.3 Metadata Integrity	*104*
	5.3.1 Quality of Metadata	*105*
	5.3.2 Security and Control of Metadata	*106*
	5.3.3 Backup and Recovery	*107*
	5.4 Output Facilities	*107*
	5.4.1 Output Requirements	*108*
	5.4.2 Batch Versus Online Output	*108*
	5.4.3 Characteristics of DD/DS Output	*109*
	5.4.4 Ad Hoc Output	*112*
	5.5 Summary	*112*
	References	*113*

6 AUTOMATED INTERFACES FOR METADATA GENERATION — 115

6.1 Metadata Generation and the Active DD/DS — 116
- 6.1.1 Spectrum of DD/DS Activity — 117
- 6.1.2 Active DD/DSs and "Binding" — 117
- 6.1.3 Benefits of an Active DD/DS — 118

6.2 Metadata Generation for Application Programs — 121
- 6.2.1 Metadata Needs — 121
- 6.2.2 DD/DS Provides Consistent Metadata — 121
- 6.2.3 Degree of Activity with Respect to Application Programs — 123
- 6.2.4 Copy Library — 126
- 6.2.5 Source Program Library — 127
- 6.2.6 Benefits of Using an Active DD/DS — 128

6.3 Metadata Generation for End-User Facilities — 128
- 6.3.1 Report Generators and Screen Generators — 129
- 6.3.2 Query Language Processors — 136
- 6.3.3 Benefits — 138

6.4 Metadata Generation for Integrity Functions — 139
- 6.4.1 Edit and Validation — 139
- 6.4.2 Access Control — 140
- 6.4.3 Benefits — 142

6.5 Metadata Generation for Database Management Software — 142
- 6.5.1 DBMS — 142
- 6.5.2 Benefits — 144

6.6 Metadata Generation for Special-Purpose Utilities — 144
- 6.6.1 Database Design Aid — 145
- 6.6.2 Database Performance Simulators — 147
- 6.6.3 Test Data Generator — 147
- 6.6.4 Audit Software — 148
- 6.6.5 Conversion Software — 148
- 6.6.6 Operating System – JCL — 149
- 6.6.7 Benefits — 149

6.7 Generalized (Multi-Purpose) Metadata Generation Interface — 149
6.8 Summary — 149
References — 150

7 STRATEGIES FOR BUILDING A DD/DS — 153

7.1 Strategies for Implementing Metadatabase Sharing — 154
    7.1.1 Parallel Sharing — 156
    7.1.2 Serial Sharing — 159

7.2 Software Management of the Metadatabase — 162
    7.2.1 Database Management Requirements of the Metadatabase — 162
    7.2.2 Database Management Services for the Metadatabase — 164

7.3 Dependent DD/DSs — 166

7.4 Independent DD/DSs — 167

7.5 The Subsumed DD/DS Implementation Approach — 169

7.6 Strategies for Implementation of User Interfaces for the DD/DS — 170
    7.6.1 Requirements for the User Interface — 170
    7.6.2 Strategies for the User Interface — 172

7.7 Summary — 173

References — 174

8 CLASSIFICATION AND SELECTION METHODOLOGY FOR DD/DSs — 175

8.1 Classification of Commercially Available DD/DSs — 176
    8.1.1 The Metadata Generation Characteristic — 176
    8.1.2 The Metadata Management Characteristic — 176
    8.1.3 A Taxonomy for Classification of DD/DSs — 177

8.2 An Evaluation and Selection Methodology for DD/DS Package Acquisition — 178
    8.2.1 Appointing a Selection Team — 178
    8.2.2 Establishing Requirements for Selection — 179
    8.2.3 Establish Methdology for Selection — 179

8.3 Selection Criteria for DD/DSs — 182
    8.3.1 Data Description Facility — 184
    8.3.2 Data Documentation Support — 185
    8.3.3 Metadata Generation — 185

CONTENTS xv

    8.3.4 Security Support *186*
    8.3.5 Integrity Support *186*
    8.3.6 User Interface/Output *186*
    8.3.7 Ease of Use/Flexibility *187*
    8.3.8 Resource Utilization *188*
    8.3.9 Vendor Support *188*

8.4 Selection Considerations *189*

    8.4.1 Active Versus Passive DD/DS *189*
    8.4.2 Independent Versus Dependent DD/DS *189*
    8.4.3 Special Cases *189*

8.5 The Make-Versus-Buy Issue *191*

8.6 Summary *193*

    References *194*

9 IMPLEMENTATION OF THE DD/DS IN USER ORGANIZATIONS *195*

9.1 Common Problems Users Face in Implementing DD/DS *196*

    9.1.1 Coordination Among Users *196*
    9.1.2 Technical Integration *197*

9.2 Implementation Planning *198*

    9.2.1 Authority and Responsibility for Data Resources *199*
    9.2.2 Requirements Statement *201*
    9.2.3 Assumptions and Constraints *201*
    9.2.4 Implementation Strategy *201*
    9.2.5 Schedule and Milestones *202*

9.3 Integration of the DD/DS into the System Development Life Cycle *202*

    9.3.1 Support of the Database Effort *202*
    9.3.2 SDLC for Database Development *203*
    9.3.3 DD/DS-Supported SDLC Reduces Common Problems *205*

9.4 The Data Administration/Database Administration Function *207*

    9.4.1 Historical Development of the Function *207*
    9.4.2 Functions of the DA/DBA *209*

9.5 Using the DD/DS to Support the DB/DBA Function *213*

	9.5.1 The DA/DBAs Indispensable Tool	214
	9.5.2 Implementation Sequence of the DD/DS Versus the DA/DBA Function	214
	9.5.3 Administration of the DD/DS	216
	9.5.4 Using the DD/DS as a DA/DBA Tool to Mitigate Coordination Problems	217
9.6	Data Description Standards	217
	9.6.1 Standards for the Description Process	217
	9.6.2 Standard Formats for Meta-Entities	219
	9.6.3 Data Description Standards Help Solve User Coordination Problems	220
9.7	Planning for the Population of the DD/DS	221
	9.7.1 Cost Factors in DD/DS Population	221
	9.7.2 Alternative Strategies for DD/DS Population	222
	9.7.3 Cost Reduction Tools for DD/DS Population	223
	9.7.4 Planning for DD/DS Population Can Help Solve User Coordination Problems	223
9.8	Planning for the Security of the Metadatabase	224
9.9	Planning for Support of Software Interfaces	225
9.10	Summary	226
	References	227

10 THE DD/DS IN A DISTRIBUTED DATABASE ENVIRONMENT 229

10.1	Functional Requirements of a DD/DS in a Distributed Database Environment	232
	10.1.1 The Functional Requirement to Locate Data	232
	10.1.2 Coordination of Distribution Alternatives for Databases and Metadatabases	233
	10.1.3 The Functional Requirement of Data Translation	235
10.2	Special Features of a DD/DS for Distributed Environments	236
	10.2.1 A New Meta-Entity: Node	236
	10.2.2 Metadata Migration Features	237
	10.2.3 Data Translation Features	240
10.3	Distribution Strategies for Metadata	240
	10.3.1 Replication of Metadata	241

CONTENTS xvii

      10.3.2 *Partitioning Metadata*   242
      10.3.3 *Hybrid Allocation of Metadata*   242

  10.4 DA/DBA Considerations   243

      10.4.1 *The DA in a Distributed Environment*   244
      10.4.2 *The DBA in a Distributed Environment*   244

  10.4 Summary   245

  References   246

11 CONTROL AND AUDITING TECHNIQUES USING THE DD/DS   249

  11.1 Control and Audit-Related Functions of the DD/DS: Documentation of Data and Systems   250

      11.1.1 *Automation of Metadata*   252
      11.1.2 *Active DD/DS*   252

  11.2 Control and Audit-Related Functions of the DD/DS: Audit Trail at the Type Level   254

      11.2.1 *Transaction Impact Analysis*   256
      11.2.2 *Correction of Valid but Incorrect Updates*   256

  11.3 Control Through Metadata Generation   257

      11.3.1 *Control on Development and Maintenance*   258
      11.3.2 *Control on Program Execution*   258

  11.4 Control Concerns Addressed by the DD/DS   259

  11.5 Summary   260

  References   260

12 THE FUTURE OF DATA DICTIONARY/ DIRECTORY SYSTEMS   261

  12.1 Future User Requirements for DD/DSs   262

      12.1.1 *General Aspects of the Future Environment*   262
      12.1.2 *A Tool for Data Resource Management*   265
      12.1.3 *Support for the DA/DBA Function*   266
      12.1.4 *A Tool for Audit and Control*   266

  12.2 DD/DS Features and Capabilities to Support Future Requirements   266

      12.2.1 *Support for SDLC and Project Control Activities*   267

	12.2.2	*More Comprehensive Metadata Generation*	*269*
	12.2.3	*Dynamic Collection and Reflection of Metadata*	*271*
	12.2.4	*User-Friendly Interfaces*	*271*
12.3	DD/DS Technology Trends		*272*
	12.3.1	*Architectural Placement of the DD/DS*	*272*
	12.3.2	*Reliance on DBMS for Support*	*273*
	12.3.3	*External Technological Trends*	*274*
12.4	DD/DS Trends in the Commercial Market		*276*
	12.4.1	*DBMS-Dependent DD/DSs*	*276*
	12.4.2	*DBMS-Independent Vendors*	*278*
	12.4.3	*Small Computer System Vendors*	*278*
12.5	Summary		*279*
	Appendix: Hypothetical Case Study		*281*
	Glossary		*317*
	Index		*325*

Data Dictionary/Directory Systems

1
Basic Principles of Data Dictionary/Directory Systems

Data as an important corporate resource is a relatively new concept, but one which is gaining increasing acceptance. In this introductory chapter, the concept of data as a resource is presented as a fundamental prerequisite to the principles of Data Dictionary/Directory Systems (DD/DSs).

To treat data as a resource requires the same degree of administration and control as is involved in the management of other resources. Data resources are managed through the administration and control of the data that describes and defines the data, or the *metadata*. Administration and control of metadata requires coordinated rules and procedures to maintain control over the integrity of the metadata. The primary tool that provides support for the administration and control of metadata is the Data Dictionary/Directory System. It supports in a comprehensive manner the logical centralization of metadata.

The DD/DS supports the administration and control of two types of metadata: "dictionary" and "directory" metadata. In theory, these two types of metadata differ in the information each provides: Dictionary metadata provides information which describes what the data is, what it means, and what exists; directory metadata describes where the data is located, and how it can be accessed. Current DD/DSs contain both types of metadata, and some hybrid forms. Closely related to the kind of information a DD/DS contains is the architectural framework in which it functions. The two strategies that will be discussed in this book are an *active* DD/DS and a *passive* DD/DS.

An *active* DD/DS exercises a greater degree of control over metadata usage than its *passive* counterpart. A DD/DS is considered active with respect to a program or a process *if and only if* that program or process is fully dependent upon the DD/DS to obtain its metadata.

1.1 CONCEPT: DATA IS A RESOURCE

Data has been an important ingredient in the operation of an enterprise throughout history. Through the timely use of information derived from reliable data, many critical decisions have been made, some of which have left indelible marks in history. However, it is not until recent years, with the introduction of computer technology, that the value of data as a resource has been fully recognized.

To recognize that data is a resource is to realize that data has certain properties, much like other more commonly known resources, such as human, financial, and material resources. All these more commonly recognized resources share the characteristics of cost and value to an enterprise. Data resources also have cost and value.

Resources are managed efficiently to optimize their utilization. To manage resources means to plan for, allocate, maintain and conserve, prudently exploit, effectively employ, and integrate those resources [NOLA 74]. To do all this properly, it is necessary to utilize information to understand the resource fully (see Figure 1.1).

Money is probably the best known resource of all, and one which affects everyone — whether in day-to-day individual activities or in big business institutions. Money is managed. In an enterprise, there are extensive budgetary plans for allocating the money available for expenses; there are extensive fiscal policies to conserve financial resources; there are investment policies and financial forecasting used to effectively employ and exploit all the financial resources available.

To manage money as a resource, it is necessary to understand the resource — know what is available, what has been used, the sources of the money, and the destination. The financial officer — the person responsible for the management of money — uses a tool to support the administration of the money resources: the general ledger or the balance sheet which provides summary information about the money resource. Supplemented by budget reviews, which help determine how the money has been used, where it went, what has been used, and what is available, the financial officer can make decisions based on the information about the resource.

Like money, material (e.g., any or all of the raw materials used for producing a product) is a resource. Managing material resources follows the same procedures as managing money — the only distinction is that the environment is different. The financial officer's counterpart is the warehouseman or the production manager. This person is responsible for overseeing that there is enough raw material for manufacturing the

CONCEPT: DATA IS A RESOURCE

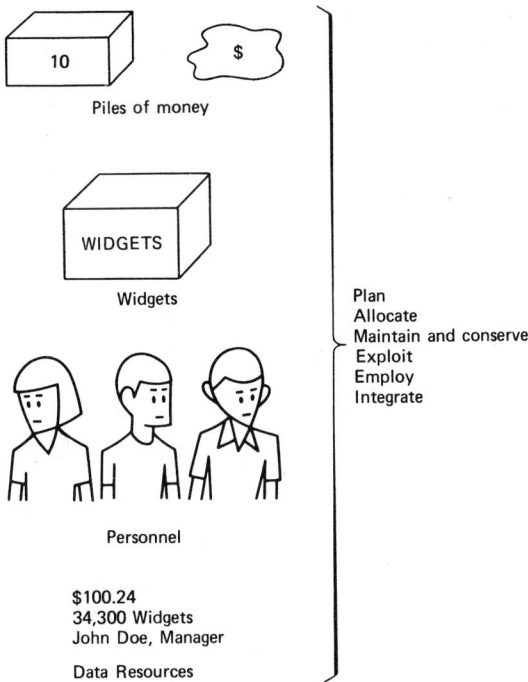

Figure 1.1 Management of resources.

"widget" and that the proper raw material goes to the right department. The warehouseman must know what material is available, where the material goes, the sources of the different kinds of raw materials, the prices, and the appropriate timing for ordering. To support these functions, the warehouseman uses an inventory control sheet, which provides information on the exact quantity of each type of raw material ordered, used, remaining, and scheduled for reorder. In order to control the effective use of the resource, the warehouseman must be well aware of the *Economic Order Quantity,* and of the right time during the production cycle for ordering. The need for information about inventory is essential.

Still other very commonly known resources are personnel, or human resources. For this resource, there is also a person responsible for its management. In most enterprises, the responsible person is the personnel officer. Information about an enterprise's human resources are kept in personnel files. These files contain information about the number of people in the enterprise, their skills, their salaries, their location within the enterprise, their relative position with respect to the enterprise. Via personnel reviews, it is possible to determine the past contributions of the people involved, their potential with respect to the organization, current position, promotion potentials, and so forth. The personnel officer needs information to make decisions concerning personnel actions.

The information required to manage any or all of these enterprise resources is derived from data. Thus, by derivation, data itself is also a resource. Data must be understood, conserved, exploited, employed, and integrated. In understanding the data, it is necessary to learn about its nature and characteristics, how it is used, what it is used for, where it resides, where it comes from, and so forth.

Thus in order to manage the data effectively as a resource, it is necessary to obtain as much data about the data resource as is possible. Data about data can be conserved, if there are stringent procedures for collecting, maintaining, and using the data resource. To exploit the data resource, it is necessary to learn about its utilization in the entire enterprise, and how it may be manipulated to suit the enterprise needs. Once this information is collected, it is possible to effectively employ data resources throughout the enterprise to produce the information necessary to manage other resources. As more segments of the enterprise use the data resources, redundancy can be avoided in the different usage of data resources by integrating information about the data resource into a centralized repository, which all segments of the enterprise can access. An added advantage is that this resource can be centrally coordinated to achieve common enterprise goals.

Recognizing that data is a resource entails the realization that there are many similarities between data resources and other more commonly recognized resources, such as money, people, and raw material. It is essential to realize that the most important bond among the different kinds of resources (data and otherwise) is information used to manage the enterprise. Information about the resources is needed to manage these resources. And in fact, timely and reliable information is an essential element in decision making at all levels of management.

1.1.1 Information Hierarchy

Information used in managing the enterprise can be described as belonging to three levels of a hierarchy [PLAG 77] (see Figure 1.2). On the first level is the repetitive, predictable, routine, frequently produced, and frequently accessed information. This type of information is used for day-to-day operation by first-level management, such as the accounting, payroll, and credit departments. This is known as *operational information*. As the basic building blocks for the information hierarchy, operational information is the most amenable to automation in an organization.

On the next level is the *functional information*. At this level, similar information types are grouped together into functional units, with the

CONCEPT: DATA IS A RESOURCE

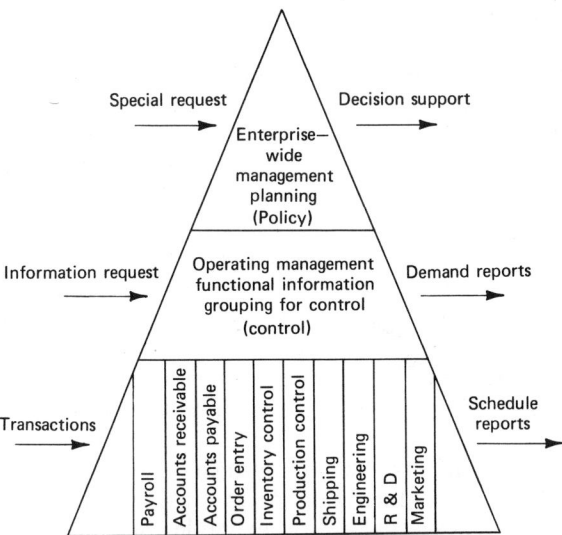

Figure 1.2 The information system hierarchy.

objective of providing operating management with a certain degree of control and a broader scope of information about the business operation. For example, the personnel officer may require summary information about all the employees in the enterprise, regardless of skills, department affiliation, or salary range. Based on this information, the personnel officer can determine the enterprise's total people resources, the need for hiring, or the need for distribution. Functional information is predictable, recurring, and not as frequently required as the operational information. Functional information appears to be more summarized than the operational type, and its reports are produced on demand. With the aid of automation, functional information can be more accurately and promptly produced.

At the apex of this information pyramid is *enterprise-level,* or *executive-level, information.* This high-level information is designed to provide management with information that will support enterprisewide policy-making activities and high level planning.

Enterprise-level information is characterized by a high degree of summarization. Reports and other informational output are produced on request, which makes this highly unpredictable, nonrecurring, and infrequent. Operational and functional information are manipulated to produce executive-level information. Often information at this level appears in succinct but complete summary form. Automation at this level of information enables sophisticated manipulation of available information, higher degrees of integration in the enterprise data resources, and more complex analytical reports, on a more timely basis.

1.1.2 Information is Derived from Data

Information at each level is derived from data. Data can be thought of as raw material which is processed to produce the finished product: information. Data is manipulated so that meaning and context are assigned to it, thereby transforming it into information. Looking at data from the other end of the spectrum, information includes the semantics of the data.

At the operational level, information is found on regularly scheduled automated output, such as reports and online screens, and is derived from operational data, such as payroll data, accounting data, accounts payable data, and engineering data. After manipulation, operational data is transformed into meaningful information on such accounting reports as *Year-To-Date Accrual Reports,* and *Unliquidated Obligations Reports.*

Functional-level information is produced by further processing the operational data, by summarizing, or by providing a different context to previously processed data. For example, accounting reports produced for operational usage are grouped by departments and summarized to produce a *Quarterly Expenses Report,* or *Expense Report by Departments.*

Management on the corporate level requires information that contains yet a higher degree of summarization. The original operational data is processed further to produce the desired result, by assigning different meaning and different context to that data. For example, the accounting data used previously must be transformed into cost, benefit, and profit reports.

With this hierarchy of information needs in an enterprise, the same raw data is shared by different groups of users, and this same data can be used for different purposes. To insure integrity and consistency it is imperative that the source of raw data be consistent, accurate, and efficiently managed. If the resulting information is derived from uncoordinated raw data sources, there is a higher probability of it being inconsistent, inaccurate, and inefficient, than if the data sources were coordinated at all levels.

Coordinating raw data usage to produce information requires that data be established as an important resource. Like other resources, data must be administered and controlled to insure proper handling, proper access and proper utilization. Data must rely in part on human procedures and methodologies for its management and control. Nevertheless, whenever possible, it can and does utilize automated facilities. The human function responsible for the administration, control, and coordination of all data-related activities is called the *Data Administration* (DA) function. Thus the DA function is analogous to the financial officer, warehouseman, and personnel officer. Because of the impor-

CONCEPT: DATA IS A RESOURCE   7

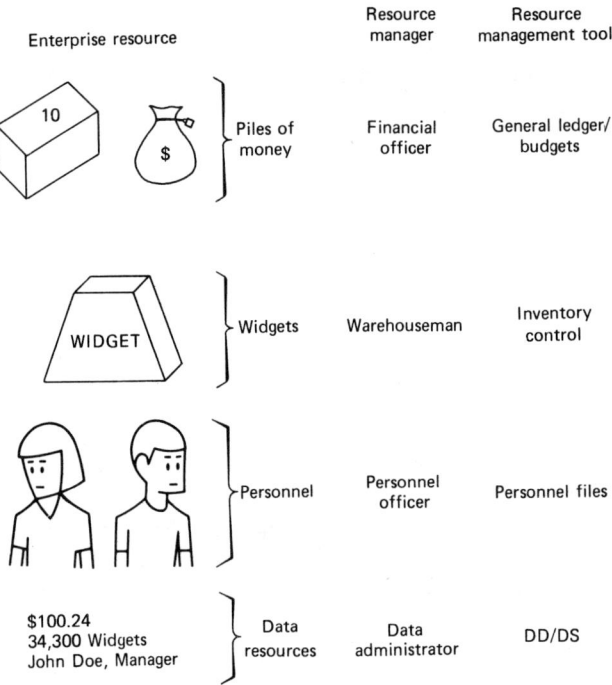

Figure 1.3 Management of enterprise resources.

tance of the DA function to the management of data as a resource, this function will be discussed in greater detail in Chapter 9.

The Data Dictionary/Directory System is an automated facility that supports the data administration function in managing data as a resource. The DD/DS provides a logically centralized repository of definitive information about the relevant data in an enterprise, including characteristics, relationships, usage, and responsibilities [LEON 77]. Thus, the DD/DS as a resource management tool for the Data Administrator is analogous to the general ledger for the financial officer, to inventory control for the warehouseman, and to personnel files for the personnel officer (see Figure 1.3).

1.1.3 Why so Late?

A common concern regarding the concept of managing data as a resource is the fact that data has been neglected as a resource for many years. A pervasive question remains: "Why is it that only recently there is increasingly greater recognition of data and its potential as a resource?"

Although data has some common characteristics with other corporate resources, data does not have all the same basic characteristics of such other corporate resources as money, goods, and people. Specifically, the more common resources share two additional characteristics: they are scarce, and allocable. Data resources, on the other hand, are not relatively scarce, and they are not inherently allocable. However, the data resource, like its more tangible counterparts, does have value. The value of the data derives from the fact that the entire enterprise depends on its availability for the proper management of all the other resources of the enterprise. Without current and reliable data to produce required information, it is possible to slow down and considerably impair the operation of the enterprise.

All data has value, even "bad" data. Bad data has *negative* value. For example, if the data collected by the U.S. Census Bureau were unreliable, projections made on the basis of this bad data could have far reaching, adverse effects. For, if unreliable data were used to determine population shift, the result could be changes in congressional representation and in revenue sharing between Federal, state, and local governments.

This partially explains why organizations are now just beginning to treat data as a resource, and emphasizes the need for establishing conscious effort to implement a program that supports the management and control of the data resources. Without this conscious effort it is more than likely that, since data does not inherently possess all the characteristics of other resources, it will not be managed as a resource. The management and control of data resources begins with a disciplined definition and description of the data.

1.2 CONCEPT: METADATA

In order to manage data as a resource that is shared by users at all levels in an enterprise, it is essential that data about data be clearly specified, easily accessible, and well controlled. The first step in this process is to identify and describe those data objects that exist in the "real world" of the enterprise, such as the customer, account, salesman, and orders. These objects are called *entities*. Descriptions of these objects are identified and converted to computer-readable form, so that they can be stored, processed, and made available to various user groups in the enterprise. In the data processing or database environment, these entities are represented in the form of data objects such as data elements, records, files, or databases. These data objects are called *metadata entities*.

The data used to describe metadata entities are called *metadata*, that is, data about the data. A collection of related metadata, when

CONCEPT: METADATA

managed and controlled as a unit, is a metadata database. It is referred to as *metadatabase*.

Metadata should not be confused with *user data*. The former is used to identify, define, and describe the characteristics of the latter. That is, metadata is used to describe user data. Metadata is the essential ingredient in the management and control of data as a resource. Figure 1.4 illustrates the differences between user data and metadata.

An example of the metadata for a "data element" in the "customer database" follows:

> *Name of metadata entity:* data element
> *Identification:* CUSTNAME
> *Narrative description:* customer's name is entered as last name first, first initial, and middle initial. This is a required data element for the customer database, and should be linked to a customer ID.
> *Length/size:* 32 characters, only alphanumeric characters allowed.
> *Relationship/usage:* this entity is used in the files:
>   ACCTREC, CRED, ... , and in the programs BALDUE, REGCUS, . . .

An *occurrence* of a metadata entity is a *type* of the user data entity. Thus, CUSTOMER RECORD in Figure 1.4 is both a metadata 'data' entity occurrence, (i.e., an instance of the metadata entity, *record*), and a userdata data-entity type (i.e., customer record).

This example has shown that metadata is one level of abstraction higher than the actual data used in the processing of operational data.

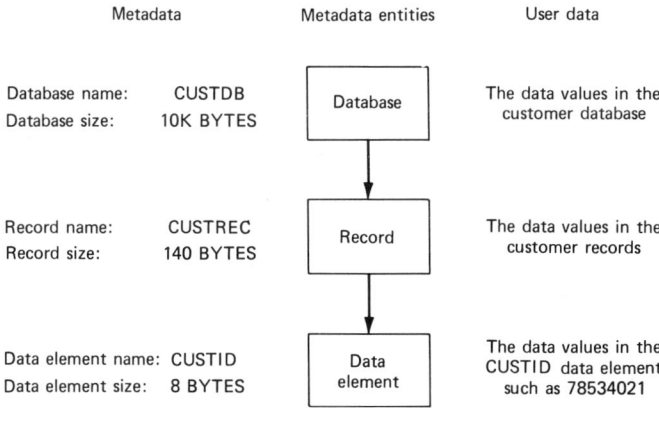

Figure 1.4 Metadata versus user data.

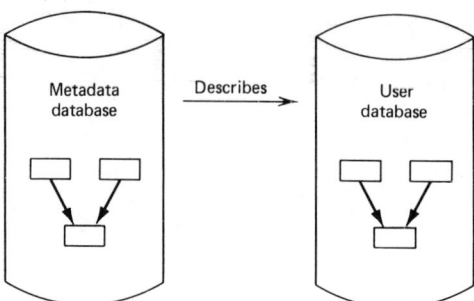

Figure 1.5 The metadata database describes the user database.

That is, the metadatabase consists of a database that contains descriptive information and definitional information about the user database (see Figure 1.5).

1.2.1 Characteristics of Metadatabases

A basic principle in this book is that a metadatabase has many of the same characteristics as those of a user database. First, the metadatabase can be shared among many of the same user groups that share the userdatabase, such as the data administrator, the database designer, casual users, and system designers. In addition, a metadatabase can also be shared among processes and automated systems such as the DD/DS, the database management system (DBMS), report generators, and query processors.

Metadatabases also have other characteristics of user databases. These include: data sharing, data integrity, and data independence. *Data sharing* is the ability of various users to access common data with different logical views from one physical representation. The ability to share data helps in reducing unwanted duplication, in reducing storage requirements, and in facilitating processing. *Data integrity* is the ability to preserve the currency and accuracy of the data without unintentional changes, to produce results that are correct to a predefined level, and to maintain data availability. *Data independence* is seen as the ability of various users or applications to have different views of the same data. Specifically, the way the data is logically defined and utilized does not depend on a specific application, storage structure, or access strategy.

1.2.2 Similarities Between Database Management and Metadatabase Management

Like its user data counterpart, the metadata requires a set of software to define the metadata, to organize it, and to access and control it. In short, it needs a *metadatabase management system,* just as the user

MANAGEMENT AND CONTROL OF METADATA

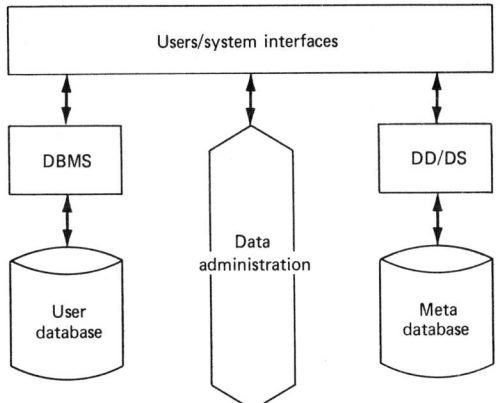

Figure 1.6 A conceptual view of a database environment.

data needs a database management system for organization, access, and control.

In a similar fashion, the administration and control of the metadata require restrictions and control measures that are similar to but more stringent than those used for the user data. Examples of these control measures are: standards definitions, access control procedures, standard procedures for metadata acquisition, and security procedures to protect the metadata. Thus, it is logical that, with so many similarities between user data and metadata, the database approach should be used also for the administration and control of metadata. This implies that the basic elements of a database environment must exist: a database, a database management system to organize, access and control that database, a data administration function, and user/system interfaces. Indeed, each of these elements is present in the case of the metadata: there is a metadatabase, mapping directly into the user database above; there is a metadatabase management system, which is the Data Dictionary/Directory System; there is a data administration function; and finally, the user/system interfaces also exist. Thus, it is possible and highly desirable to manage the metadatabase using known techniques and procedures of database technology (see Figure 1.6).

1.3 MANAGEMENT AND CONTROL OF METADATA

Earlier in the chapter, it was established that there is need to manage and control data as a resource. Since metadata is the key element in gaining control over the data resources, then it follows logically that the metadata itself is also to be managed and controlled. A critical aspect of

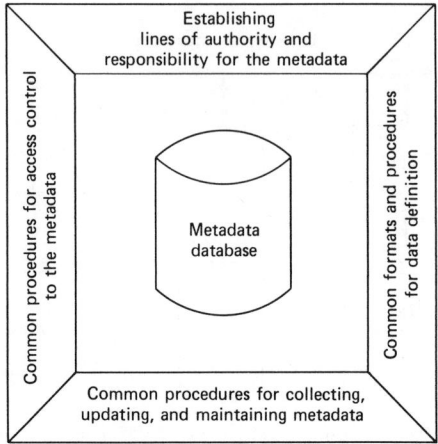

Figure 1.7 Common rules and procedures must surround the metadatabase to insure effective management control.

managing metadata is planning for the design, implementation, maintenance, utilization, and control of the metadatabase. Planning requires the cooperation and support of all levels of the enterprise. Most of all, planning requires management's decision to participate and support the sharing of the data, and to contribute their understanding of how the metadata describes the enterprise's data resources.

This implies that an overall framework must be established in which such management and control activities are fostered (see Figure 1.7). Under this framework, it is necessary to establish lines of responsibility for the metadata; to establish formal rules and detailed procedures to guide metadata-related activities, such as: establishing common formats and conventions for data definition; establishing common procedures for collection, update, and maintenance of the metadata; and establishing common procedures for access control to the metadata.

1.3.1 Establishing Lines of Responsibility and Authority

Management and technical issues that arise as a result of the collection, definition, and description of the metadata often require mediation and compromise before actual resolution. In this framework, lines of authority and responsibility must be well defined, so that management and technical issues may be satisfactorily resolved.

Stringent rules and detailed procedures need to be established to aid in maintaining control of the integrity of the metadatabase, and to maintain control over the access to the metadatabase. These procedures are designed to aid in understanding, maintaining, developing, using, and integrating the metadatabase. User-friendly tools that help in these processes should be selected and their use encouraged in management and technical activities.

An important aspect of metadata management is the fact that authority and responsibility is shifted from an "owner" of the data to a function that is responsible for all the enterprise's metadata. This function is usually vested in a data administration function. The DA may assume sole responsibility over the consistent definition of the metadata, for controlling access to the metadatabase, for the integrity of the metadatabase, and for consistent usage of the metadata.

1.3.2 Common Formats and Conventions for Data Definition

Metadata management requires establishing common formats and conventions for the definition and description of data. Establishing these conventions is equally important in large enterprises as in small companies, especially when the metadatabase is meant for sharing among different and diverse groups of users within the enterprise. When various segments of the enterprise have the ability to define and describe their own data requirements, it is imperative that generally accepted rules regarding common formats and conventions be established and used. These conventions help in coordinating multiple sources of inputs and in controlling the metadatabase by identifying redundancies that occur during development of applications in different functional areas. Furthermore, it is a technical reality that data may be stored redundantly. When plausible reasons are found for this (e.g., that the data is actually needed in different places), then metadata management should coordinate this to insure consistency.

Existence of common formats and conventions can help in resolving conflicts. Of course, each "owner" of the data in dispute would prefer one particularly applicable set of conventions. It would be rather difficult to identify, let alone resolve, the brewing conflict without enterprise-wide common formats and conventions for defining and describing the metadata. In this context, data administration will play an important role.

With common conventions, data sharing is facilitated and may be more widespread. Users in various segments of the enterprise use the same rules and conventions for describing and using the data. Most common examples are conventions for identifying, naming, and describing metadata entities. Data-element naming conventions may involve prefixes, keywords, or phrases. For example, an enterprise may stipulate that all data related to financial resources shall have a three-character prefix, such as FIN. People responsible for defining and using financial data would then know that any such data element would have the FIN prefix, instead of FINANCE, or FI, or 123. These conventions are useful to the person using the data, as well as to the person responsible for defining the data. All concerned would be able to refer to the same set of rules.

1.3.3 Common Procedures for Collection, Update and Maintenance of the Metadata

Common procedures are required for collecting the metadata at its source in order to help coordinate and control the metadata that is to be stored in the metadatabase. These procedures insure completeness by describing in detail the type of metadata that are required, and the sources from which the metadata should be collected. Such procedures contribute to timeliness, by specifying when, and how often the metadata must be collected. The procedures also help ensure the accuracy of the metadata collected by capturing it at the source, as opposed to collecting it from already processed information.

Examples of common procedures are those that establish *where, when, what,* and *by whom* the metadata is to be recorded. For example, one such common procedure might establish that *system analysts* must define and describe data elements during the *Requirements Definition* stage, and that *database designers* must write the database design specifications during *detailed design.*

Another aspect of metadata management involves the establishment of procedures for ongoing maintenance of the metadata. It is not sufficient to control the metadata at the time of metadata design and collection but, once the metadatabase is established, it must be carefully maintained to insure the currency, the timeliness, and the integrity of the metadata.

Maintenance procedures contribute to the ongoing coordination and control of metadata usage. One way in which maintenance procedures can be effective is to insure that any changes made in the metadata are made only by authorized people, and that they are accurately and timely reflected. Since metadata is intended to be shared, it is important that the integrity of the metadatabase be maintained. Procedures that assure this integrity would also assure that there is continued accuracy and timeliness in the metadata.

Migration of bad metadata into the operational metadatabase from an uncontrolled external source would be highly counterproductive, because the bad metadata would degrade the integrity of the operational metadatabase. The bad metadata could be propagated further, and the entire metadatabase could become suspect. Moreover, reliance on metadata management for the enterprise would be suspect, at best. Thus, it is highly critical that control measures and other procedures

MANAGEMENT AND CONTROL OF METADATA 15

be established to prevent bad metadata from being inserted into the operational metadatabase.

One such control measure is to specify that only changes that have been previously authorized should be incorporated into the metadatabase. Maintenance procedures should specify when, how, and by whom changes are to be recorded. For example, such a procedure might establish that when new data elements are recommended by a systems analyst, they must be approved by a user committee, which is headed by a DBA (database administrator), and inserted by the DBA at the beginning of each week during a regular update cycle. Critical elements might be inserted in an emergency situation, but only in test mode, so that there would be minimal effect on the operational metadatabase. Furthermore, such procedures might include a stipulation that database design changes be prepared by the DBA, and can only be installed during a test period, when all possible ramifications can be determined.

1.3.4 Common Procedures for Access Control to Metadata

Further, to insure that the metadata is timely and accurate, procedures and techniques are required to control access to the metadatabase. These procedures and techniques insure authorized accessibility and availability of the metadata. Access control is required both to insure that only properly authorized users are allowed to update, maintain, and gain access to the metadatabase while the more general access control mechanism insures that a system analyst or end-user can browse and find relevant data elements. Automated mechanisms can serve as a deterrent to an unauthorized person attempting to modify the metadatabase. In general, access control techniques to the metadatabase work both ways: they restrict modification to the metadatabase, but they allow browsing — for example, the query capability enables an end-user to find the meaning of a data element appearing on a terminal. Thus, access procedures and techniques both restrict and enable the use of the metadatabase.

The automated system that supports the management and control of the metadata is the Data Dictionary/Directory System. The DD/DS provides within its scope the metadatabase management function as well as some of the user/system interface functions, such as report generation and query processing required for metadata usage. Furthermore, many of the administration and control activities required for metadata management can be supported by the DD/DS.

The following paragraphs introduce and define the Data Dictionary/ Directory System (DD/DS).

1.4 THE DATA DICTIONARY/DIRECTORY SYSTEM-DEFINITION

Discussions in the previous sections have established the need for administration and control procedures and for facilities to harness the enterprise's data resources. The Data Dictionary/Directory System (DD/DS) is the primary tool that can be used to support this objective. The following is provided as a working definition (see Figure 1.8).

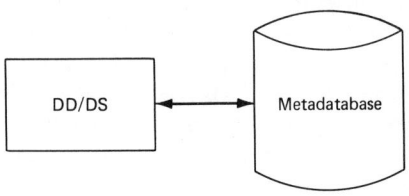

A Data Dictionary/Directory System – DD/DS is a system that is designed to support comprehensively the logical centralization of data about data (metadata).

Figure 1.8 The DD/DS defined.

Logical centralization means that the user's perception of the DD/DS is that it provides a centralized repository for the metadata. This does not preclude, however, the possibility or the desirability of physical distribution of the metadata, as may be with the case of distributed processing. Logical centralization also suggests that there is enterprise-wide coordination and control of the metadata, a key requirement for integrated metadatabase management.

Further, comprehensive support implies that there is a wide range of facilities and capabilities provided by the DD/DS. Each of these facilities is designed to support a facet of metadata management. For example, the DD/DS's data definition facilities can be used as the central mechanism for data description and definition throughout the enterprise. This would ensure that the metadata collected will be clearly, concisely, and consistently defined. The DD/DS's maintenance facilities can be used to insure that the metadata will be updated consistently for applications using the metadata, and that only proper and authorized changes will be incorporated.

1.4.1 General DD/DS Functions

Retrieval facilities in the DD/DS provide the capability for disseminating information about the metadatabase to interested users, and provide documentation about the enterprise's data resources. Through the

THE DATA DICTIONARY/DIRECTORY SYSTEM-DEFINITION

access control facilities of the DD/DS, the database administrator can effectively control usage of the metadatabase by providing various capabilities to different kinds of users. For example, the DBA can allow the database designer to have complete access to the metadatabase, including the ability to update, and maintain the metadatabase; on the other hand, the DBA may not allow the operations manager of a department to change any data definitions, but only to browse, and to obtain information about the metadata. For the system analyst, the DD/DS would provide analytical support in the design process. For example, a system analyst designing a new application can use the DD/DS to determine what data is available, where it is located, and how it can be used. However, such an analyst would be precluded from updating the DD/DS's metadatabase.

1.4.2 Spectrum of DD/DSs

A DD/DS can be different things to different people, and can take different forms. In its implemented form, the DD/DS may range from a simple set of programs that produce solely a listing of existing data elements, to a very sophisticated data resources management and control tool. Both in theory and in practice, a DD/DS may vary from a manual system consisting of 3 X 5 index cards to a highly complex automated system that performs complex analytical functions.

Thus, the DD/DS can be a very sophisticated and versatile tool. Its primary use is for management and control of the data resources, although innovative application specialists have used the DD/DS to suit their own application environments while capitalizing on the main features of the DD/DS.

The DD/DS can be implemented as an independent system, or as a dependent system on a specific DBMS. It can assume a passive role by merely producing documentation about the database, or it can actively manage and control the data resources by forcing all other software to depend on the DD/DS for the definition and description of the data. The DD/DS can exercise general control over the enterprise's data resources, or just over the data elements. If a DD/DS contains only metadata about data elements, then it is considered a *Data Element Dictionary (DED)*. Since data elements are but one of many different kinds of metadata entities, the DED is in essence a limited DD/DS. In fact, many DEDs that begin as a limited tool evolve into fully developed DD/DSs.

1.4.3 Types of Metadata in the DD/DS

The kinds of metadata that reside in a DD/DS are descriptive data. For example, they would include size, value range, type of characters, and relationship to other data entities. In short, metadata is *data about data*.

Metadata falls into two general categories: (a) *what* the data is or *what* it means and (b) *where* the data can be found, and *how* it can be accessed. These two categories in fact are the main differences between the dictionary and the directory content of a DD/DS [LEON 77, PLAG 78]. The dichotomy is discussed further in the following paragraphs.

1.5 DISTINCTION BETWEEN DICTIONARY AND DIRECTORY METADATA

The DD/DS contains data that describes both what the data is, and where and how the data is available. Strictly speaking, the Data Dictionary/Directory System has dual functionality. The dictionary function of the DD/DS answers to such questions as: "What data is available in the enterprise? What is the meaning of the data used?". The directory function of the DD/DS answers to such questions as: "Where is the data located? How can it be accessed?" In general, dictionary users of the DD/DS are humans, while directory users are usually system components.

To take this distinction further, it is possible to think in terms of "Dictionary metadata" and "Directory metadata." However, the two kinds of metadata are typically not mutually exclusive. In fact, the relative independence of the two types of metadata residing in the DD/DS will be an important issue in our later discussion concerning architectural implementation alternatives for the DD/DS.

1.5.1 Dictionary Metadata

In essence, dictionary metadata contains the characteristics about meta entities. Dictionary metadata describes what data means, what data exists in the enterprise, and what the structure of the entity is. Typical dictionary metadata includes identification of the data to be described, and the various names that may be used to refer to the entity, such as NAME, ID, and PSEUDONYM.

Dictionary metadata also includes descriptions or a short narrative about the data, explaining unique properties or characteristics of a data entity; the source of the data, or where a data entity comes from; the type of data — that is, whether it is quantitative or qualitative — for example, codes, names, amounts, and dates; use of the data, including processes and reports that use the elements.

Dictionary metadata describes the logical aspect of the data, that is, the way that the data is perceived by the user, the way the user sees it, and the way that the data is used in generating information.

DISTINCTION BETWEEN DICTIONARY AND DIRECTORY METADATA

Dictionary data is important in the management of data as a resource. It provides descriptions of what data exists and provides logical context to the data resource. The *primary* users of dictionary metadata are the human end-users, and end-user processes.

1.5.2 Directory Metadata

Directory metadata describes where the data is stored, how the data is to be accessed, and how the data is internally represented. Directory metadata provides a logical and/or physical address for the data being described, that is, it tells where the data can be found: for instance, data element EMP-COMP resides in user database PAYROLL, on DISKB. Furthermore, it describes how the data can be accessed; for example, by giving an access key, such as the identifying data elements for retrieving the desired data. In addition, directory metadata also includes internal representation of the data entity such as the physical characteristics of the data — internal length, character types, value range, internal justification, and compaction rules. If the data has multiple-access methods for storage and retrieval optimization, these algorithms could also be described or named as part of the directory metadata. In essence, the directory metadata describes the physical aspect of the data resources — how data is actually stored and accessed physically. Directory metadata is used to process and manipulate physical representations. Directory metadata is important to metadata management because it provides context to the physical attributes of the data resources. It enables the user to find the physical location of the data. The primary users of directory metadata are the programs and processes requiring physical access to user data.

1.5.3 Relationship Between Dictionary and Directory Metadata

The relationship between the dictionary and directory metadata fall into one of these categories:

Directory metadata is a subset of dictionary metadata.
Directory and dictionary metadata are mutually exclusive.
Directory and dictionary metadata are mutually interdependent.

In the first instance, the directory metadata actually becomes a subset of the dictionary metadata. This translates to mean that the physical view of the metadata is a subset of the logical view of the metadata.

By contrast, when there is mutual exclusivity, the dictionary and the directory metadata are completely independent of each other. In this case, the physical view is totally separate from the logical view. It

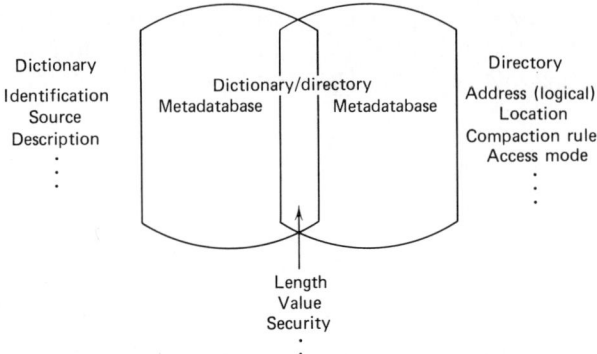

Figure 1.9 Dictionary and directory metadata.

should be noted that this case is virtually nonexistent in the current technology, and appears to be only a theoretical possibility.

Current technology suggests that the two extremes are impractical to implement. In reality, dictionary and directory metadata are mutually interdependent, resulting in partial independence (or partial dependence), with some metadata falling into both categories (see Figure 1.9). The overlapping metadata is used both physically and logically. For example, among this shared metadata is the description of length, value, security, etc.

With DD/DS technology as it exists today, it is neither practical nor desirable to separate the dictionary and the directory metadata in the context of metadatabase implementation, for various reasons. These include:

1. the introduction of redundancy, since it may be necessary to duplicate part or all the metadata from the dictionary or the directory;
2. with the duplication of metadata, the potential for introducing inconsistent metadata is a high risk; and
3. there is need to coordinate the database design to support physical and logical mappings of metadata.

Thus, current commercially available DD/DSs support this hybrid view of the metadata, with partial independence between the dictionary and the directory metadata.

1.6 ACTIVE VERSUS PASSIVE DD/DS

The underlying reason for implementing a DD/DS is to gain greater control over the enterprise's data resources. To achieve this, a proper implementation strategy must be selected for integrating the DD/DS

ACTIVE VERSUS PASSIVE DD/DS

into the operating environment. An important aspect of this implementation strategy is the selection of a system architecture framework under which the DD/DS can function. Two basic architectural alternatives, an *active* DD/DS, and a *passive* DD/DS, are introduced in this section, but will be discussed in greater detail in Chapter 6.

1.6.1 Active DD/DS

Data Dictionary/Directory Systems can be used to actively control the use of the metadata, (see Figure 1.10) and by extension, can also actively control the data (base) processing environment. All processing systems, whether application software or system software, require metadata to operate. For example, a DBMS requires metadata to operate. The DBMS metadata is known as the *schema,* or database definition. Application programs written in COBOL require metadata in the form of their File Definition (FD) section, and/or subschema. System software such as the Operating System (OS) require metadata in the context of the Job Control Language (JCL). In effect, by controlling their metadata, it is possible to control the processing programs themselves.

The definition of an *active* DD/DS is based upon the *scope* of control exercised through metadata management. This can be measured by the

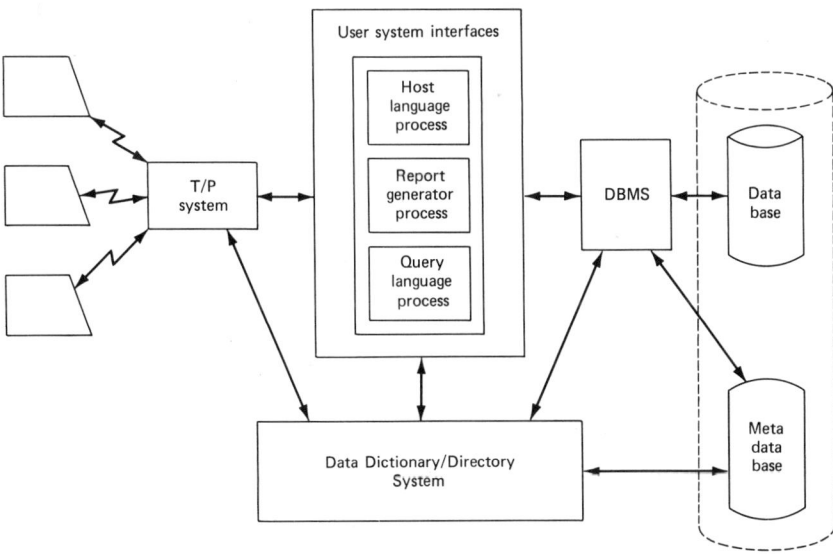

Figure 1.10 Active control of the metadata. The program construction function, implied by the arrow between the user system interface and the DD/DS, may in effect use a "program library system."

number of processes or systems components that depend solely on the DD/DS for their source of metadata. *A DD/DS is said to be active with respect to a program or process if and only if that program or process is fully dependent upon the DD/DS for its metadata* [PLAG 78]. Therefore, a DD/DS is active with respect to a database management system (DBMS) if and only if the DBMS is solely dependent on the DD/DS for its schema definition. A DD/DS is active with respect to a report generation program if and only if the program is totally dependent on the DD/DS for its file definition. And, a DD/DS is active with respect to an application program if and only if the program is totally dependent on the DD/DS for its data description. This is equally true for OS, and other processes, when the only source of metadata is in the DD/DS.

1.6.2 Passive and Potentially Active DD/DSs

By contrast, definition of a *passive* DD/DS is based upon the relative *lack of active control* that is exercised through metadata management. A passive DD/DS does not require that the processes or system components depend on the DD/DS for their metadata. In fact, the program or process may obtain its metadata from other sources. The completely passive DD/DS simply registers the metadata for programs and processes such as DBMS, programs, and systems on an after-the-fact basis, as a documentation facility. There is no direct link maintained with any other components or processes through the metadata maintained by the DD/DS.

If the DD/DS has the *capability of producing* the metadata for a given program or process, then such a DD/DS is said to be *potentially active*. A potentially active DD/DS can be made more active through supportive administrative procedures. Examples of such procedures include procedures to control metadata definition and metadata collection, and directives establishing that only metadata generated by the DD/DS can be used in processes and application development. Thus, this would insure that accesses to the user database can only be through the DD/DS. When these procedures are established and enforced, then potentially active DD/DS can be viewed as having been implemented in *active mode*. The extent of control that the DD/DS exercises on the processing environment is not total; therefore, such a DD/DS cannot be considered fully active. Currently, many of the commercially available DD/DSs are of this latter, potentially active type.

The two architectural alternatives, active and passive, and the intermediate possibilities will be discussed further in Chapter 6.

1.7 SUMMARY

This chapter has served to establish a set of basic principles to serve as foundation in further discussion of Data Dictionary/Directory Systems (DD/DS). The most important concept presented is specifically related to the management of data as a resource. In summary, the fundamental principles of DD/DSs include the following:

1. A DD/DS is a tool for administration and control of an enterprise-wide policy of managing data as a resource.
2. Metadata is used to describe the data resource of an enterprise.
3. Metadatabase management is required to achieve the goals of managing data as a resource.
4. A DD/DS is the primary tool for metadatabase management.
5. Both dictionary and directory metadata are required to achieve these goals.
6. Active DD/DSs can better serve the goals of managing data as a resource than can passive DD/DSs.

REFERENCES

[LEON 77] Leong-Hong, B. and B. Marron, "Technical Profile of Seven Data Element Dictionary/Directory Systems," National Bureau of Standards Special Publication 500-3, February 1977.

[NOLA 74] Nolan, R., *Managing the Data Resources Function,* West Publishing Co., 1974.

[PLAG 77] Plagman, B. K., "Data Dictionary/Directory System: A Tool for Data Administration and Control," in Auerbach Data Base Management Series, Portfolio 22-01-02, 1977.

[PLAG 78] Plagman, B. K. and C. Moss, "Alternative Architecture for Active Data Dictionary/Directory Systems," in Auerbach Data Base Management Series, Portfolio 22-04-02, 1978.

2

The Use of the Data Dictionary/Directory System as a Tool

The Data Dictionary/Directory System is a software tool whose usefulness has extended far beyond its original scope. Originally intended as a documentation aid for data management, the DD/DS has been found useful in many other areas of computer processing and data resource management. In this chapter, the usages of the DD/DS are explored. In particular, the benefits that can be derived from the use of the DD/DS are emphasized.

The hypothetical case study of Last National Bank, presented in the Appendix, is used to illustrate the advantages of using a DD/DS in various application situations.

The usage of the DD/DS is considered from seven functional perspectives:

1. Information systems planning.
2. Information requirements definition and analysis.
3. Systems and application development and conversion.
4. Documentation and standards enforcement.
5. Operational control of the environment.
6. Distributed databases.
7. End-user support.

These application situations are explored in subsequent sections. In particular, the earlier stages of the SDLC (System Development Life Cycle) are described in depth, explaining the activities that take place, and showing how the DD/DS can be used to assist in those activities. In addition, Chapter 11 explores an eighth functional area that utilizes a DD/DS, in audit, and control.

2.1 AN INFORMATION SYSTEM DEVELOPMENT LIFE CYCLE

Information services are the result of a great amount of thought and careful planning. From the time the need for a service is first perceived to the time that an information system is actually delivered, there are many activities that take place. Among these are:

1. Detailed planning for the development of such a system.
2. Analysis of its feasibilities.
3. Analysis of its cost and benefit trade-offs
4. Determination of functional, data, and other requirements.
5. Design of a system to perform the required functions.
6. Coding of programs which comprise the system.
7. Test and validation to insure that the programs of the new system perform the functions intended.
8. Incorporate the information system in a controlled operation.

These activities are collectively known as the *system development life cycle (SDLC)* for an information system.

It is unfortunate that, in our industry, there is no common definition for the phases of a system development life cycle. In our case study (see appendix), the Last National Bank (LNB) has its own system development life cycle (SDLC). LNB's life-cycle phases are not identical to the ones defined here, although the sequence of activities does correspond loosely to the ones presented here: feasibility (which loosely corresponds to our systems planning phase); systems requirements (corresponding to our requirements definition and analysis phase); systems development (which loosely corresponds to three of our phases: design, implementation, and testing); and implementation (which corresponds to our operation and maintenance phase). Detailed activities throughout each phase may differ in duration and order, depending on individual circumstances. For the purpose of this book, the following phases of the SDLC will be used [NBS 76]:

1. System planning phase or initiation phase.
2. Requirements definition and analysis phase.
3. Design phase.
4. Implementation phase, incorporating coding.
5. Testing phase.
6. Operation and maintenance phase.

In this high-level categorization, there is no clear beginning and end for each activity. Nevertheless, a recognized, ordered progression of activi-

DD/DS: A TOOL FOR SYSTEM PLANNING

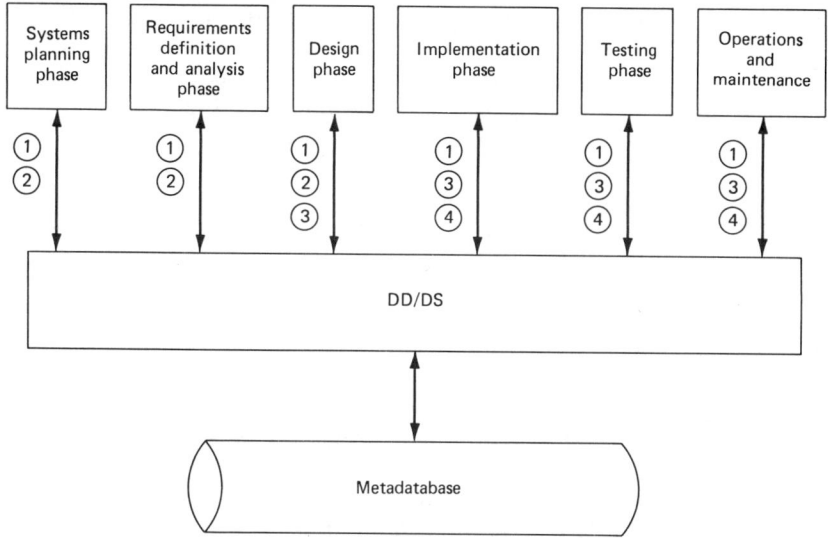

Figure 2.1 Use of a DD/DS during the System Development Life Cycle. DD/DS usage categories are: ① documentation support; ② design aid; ③ metadata generation; 4 change control.

ties does take place: for instance, requirements must be clearly and accurately defined, and carefully analyzed before the design activities can begin. In this chapter, the primary concern is over SDLC activities in which the DD/DS can be a useful tool (see Figure 2.1). The first of these is the planning activity.

2.2 DD/DS: A TOOL FOR SYSTEM PLANNING

System planning is necessary for any information system, but especially for large systems with enterprise-wide applicability. The purpose of this planning activity is to determine the feasibility and the technical and economic trade-offs for a planned system, based on an assessment of the current environment and an analysis of current use and future requirements.

The planning activity does not cease at the end of the first SDLC phase. On the contrary, it continues throughout the active life of an information system. Only the focus of the planning activity varies with each phase of the SDLC. The focus of the system planning phase is strategic in nature.

2.2.1 Assess the Current Environment

Planning for information services requires an initial assessment of the current environment. This includes determining the data that is available and analyzing the information requirements. These activities are closely related to each other, and are used in determining the data needed to produce an information product, the data that is already available, the potential conflicts and redundancies, the impact on existing systems, and the potential users of the system.

The extent and scope of this assessment varies with respect to the scope of the system being planned. For example, if the system is planned for enterprise-wide use, then the assessment process must extend to the entire enterprise and may require the cooperation of diverse user groups within the organization. In this situation it is important to determine the data available throughout the enterprise and to analyze how the planned information service may affect currently available systems. The DD/DS plays an important role in these initial activities, especially for recording and coordinating information needs from various segments of the enterprise, and for retrieving information about the data that already exists.

2.2.2 Analyze Current Usage and Determine Future Requirements

Performing this planning phase does not require detailed knowledge of all of the enterprise's systems, files, records, down to the data element level. It does require, however, learning how information is actually used to perform specific business functions, how the data underlying this information is related to other data entities and to other components, as well as to learn about the dependencies of these data on other entities and processes.

The necessity to determine the data that is required for producing specific information products means that it is necessary to determine the kinds of information products desired, to perform specific business functions e.g., reports, tables, and charts. This planning process is business-function-driven. Furthermore, data currently available must be evaluated against data required to perform the information service. In essence, included in this plan is a strategy that describes how to produce the specified information products, with the currently available data.

2.2.3 DD/DS Supports System Planning Activities

Planning for an information service is a continuous activity, and one which requires a high degree of consistency and coordination over a period of time. Many of the tasks performed during this stage are tedious and error prone, when performed manually. With the aid of an automated tool, such as the DD/DS, the tasks may be simplified, reliability may be increased, and consistency may be maintained, while facilitating coordination of these planning activities.

DD/DS: A TOOL FOR SYSTEM PLANNING

When information requirements change for the planned service, it is important that these changes be reflected in the plan. These activities should be coordinated over time, in order to ensure consistency and currency of the critical elements in the planning activity.

The DD/DS can be used as a support tool for information services planning. It provides coordinated and consistent functional support for documenting the plan and its subsequent use as a control mechanism over development and operation since the DD/DS contains data about the enterprise's operational data, that is, it is an inventory of currently available data. Further, the DD/DS contains information about how the data is used, its relationship to other data entities, occurrences, dependencies, and constraints. Thus, with a DD/DS fully operational, its use during the planning phase can increase control over developmental and operational aspects of the organization.

The use of the DD/DS in support of the information systems planning and modeling process can be accomplished by applying the DD/DS to the following five steps of the planning procedure (see Figure 2.2):

Steps in information systems planning	Use of DD/DS
Definition of business functions	Document business functions and input/output
Definition of data clusters	Document data clusters and identify redundancy
Definition of data cluster usage	Document usage and perform analysis
Definition and analysis of transactions	Document transactions and perform analysis
Development of a conceptual data model	Document data structure and perform impact analysis

Figure 2.2 DD/DS support for systems planning.

1. Definition of business functions.
2. Definition of data clusters.
3. Definition of data cluster usage.
4. Definition and analysis of transactions.
5. Development of a conceptual data model (global conceptual data structure).

The following paragraphs briefly describe how the DD/DS can be used in each of these five procedural steps of information systems planning and modeling. It should be noted, however, that this discussion is

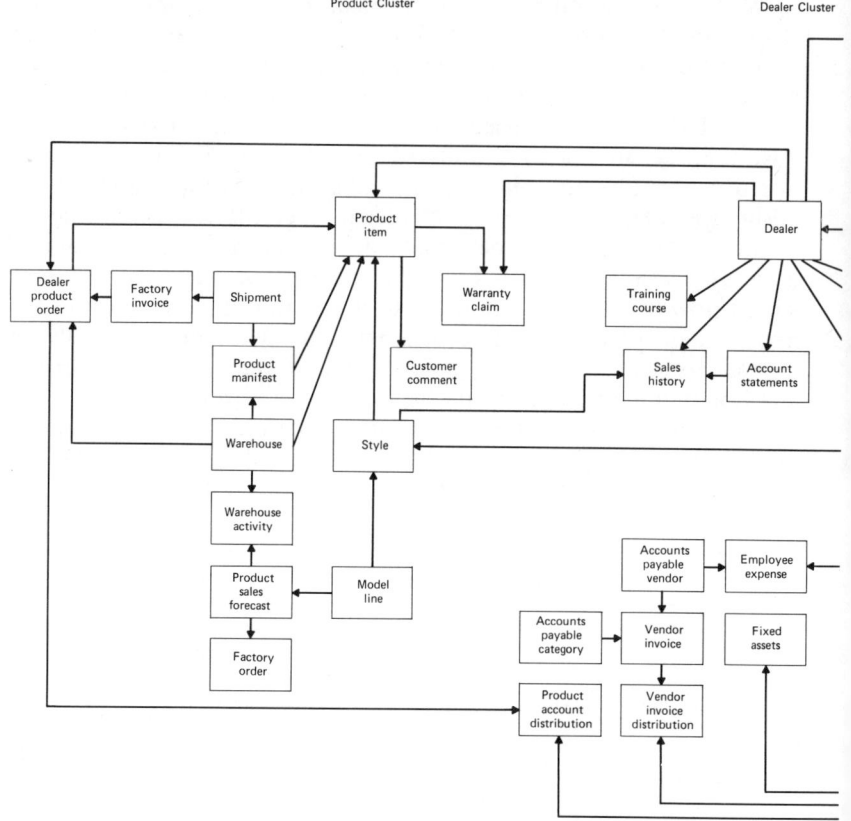

Figure 2.3 Sample conceptual data model.

not intended as a treatise on the procedures for information systems planning. Enough detail is included just to show how the DD/DS can be useful.

2.2.3.1 Definition of Business Functions

As previously mentioned, system planning must be based on a clear understanding of the underlying business functions. These business functions are defined in hierarchically arranged terms defining the information required as input and output for each business activity within the defined scope. The DD/DS should be used to document (in standard formats) each of these business functions together with their associated inputs and outputs.

DD/DS: A TOOL FOR SYSTEM PLANNING

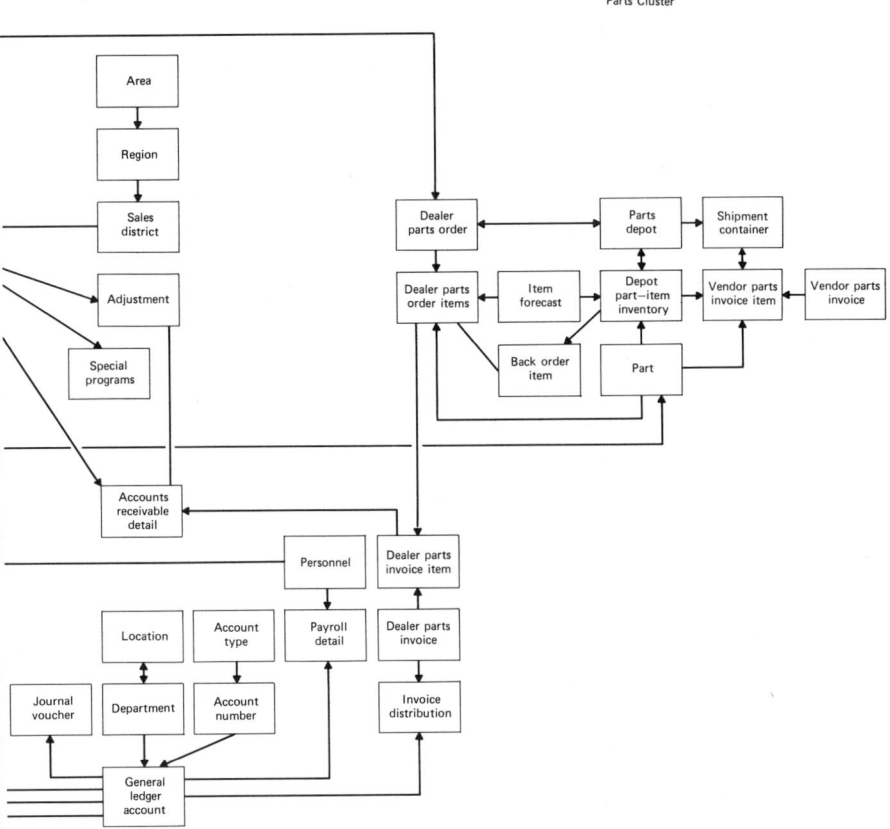

Used by permission of Peat, Marwick, Mitchell & Co.

2.2.3.2 Definition of Data Clusters

Planning for information services should not depend on the details of data elements. Instead, it should concentrate on aggregates of data required to produce the information specified in the previous step as required input and output of specific business functions. These data aggregates are referred to as *data clusters*.

A data cluster revolves around an entity in the real world which requires description in order to perform business functions (see Figure 2.3). For example, the dealer is an entity in the real world involved in the sales business functions. The *Dealer Data Cluster* is the data aggregate that includes all the data required to describe a parts dealer for the specific business functions of an auto dealership enterprise.

These data clusters must be defined. The DD/DS can be used to document (in standard formats) each of these data clusters.

In this task, as in the previous one, the DD/DS can be invaluable in assessing redundantly defined business functions and data clusters. The use of keyword searching and the analysis features of the DD/DS can support this activity based upon new and existing metadata content of the DD/DS.

2.2.3.3 Definition of Data Cluster Usage

Having defined the business functions and their related data clusters, the next step focuses on how the data clusters are used by business functions. Analysis is performed to ascertain the extent and nature of data sharing across business functions.

The DD/DS should be used to document (using standard formats) how the business functions use data clusters. The manipulative capabilities of the DD/DS can help in the analysis.

2.2.3.4 Definition and Analysis of Transactions

A transaction represents an aggregate of data which describes an event in the real world. However, all events are not relevant; only those events which cause a business function to have an impact (retrieval or update) on a data cluster are relevant.

The definition and analysis of these transactions is the next step in the planning process and should be documented and supported by the DD/DS. Much of the analysis performed is tedious and laborious and can be greatly alleviated by using a DD/DS.

2.2.3.5 Development of a Conceptual Data Model

The *conceptual data model* is a model of the data required to support the business functions of an enterprise [BCS 77]. It is referred to as *conceptual schema* by the ANSI/X3/SPARC Database Study Group [TSICH 77]. A sample of such a data model is shown in Figure 2.3 and can be documented in the DD/DS. Definition and analysis of subsequent information requirements (and eventually, database design) will be dependent upon this data model.

2.2.4 Benefits of Using a DD/DS During System Planning

To recapitulate, use of the DD/DS during the system planning phase assists the analysts in developing an initial (global) conceptual model of the enterprise. High-level descriptions of business functions, when stored in the DD/DS, can be used for determining relationships between systems and programs. Data clusters are defined at this level as *blocks* of input and output data used by the functions above, that is, data cluster usages. Transactions, whenever possible, are defined and analyzed at this point.

When the DD/DS is already used to support existing systems, the DD/DS allows one to determine readily if any of the required data already exists in a database or some file. It will reveal how that data is currently being used, how it can be accessed, and its relationship to other entities. Further, it facilitates recording other data not already in the system, but required for the planning process.

By using the DD/DS, coordination and consistency is provided through the metadatabase, since a single authoritative source of data definition is found, common definitions and interpretations are enforced, and each iteration of a plan can be coordinated. The DD/DS provides the analyst information about related systems and programs that also use the required data, and provides information on the potential impact of adding one more relationships or new data entities on existing systems. The use of the DD/DS provides greater visibility to potential redundancies, thus enabling the analyst to make use of existing resources. The use of the DD/DS enables the developing team to gain early control of the system development process, by creating a structured framework and establishing global perspective.

The DD/DS's Keyword-In-Context (KWIC) feature provides greater visibility to potential redundancy. This capability allows for the retrieval of similar DD/DS entries based upon the keywords used in the Description and/or Name attribute. Thus, if the buyer of services in a business were referred to as *customer* and as *client,* the potential redundancy would be visible based upon the keywords *buyer of services* which would appear in a KWIC listing that the DD/DS can produce after scanning the descriptions for both entries.

Without a DD/DS, it is more difficult to complete a comprehensive, integrated system plan. The documentation of the business functions and of the enterprise model alone would require much painstaking effort, and it could result in a less than complete description of the real world. The analysis may not be as thorough as with a DD/DS, and the control over the development process may not be perceptible.

2.2.5 What the Last National Bank Did

In our case study, the Last National Bank (LNB) is planning a massive conversion of its automated data systems to the database environment. LNB chose as its pilot application for conversion the retail Demand Deposit Account (DDA) system. The DDA system is fully described in the Appendix. Briefly, the DDA system has four major functions:

1. Nondollar status maintenance: Provides information on the status of an account, such as whether the account is new, closed or has changed.

2. Financial transaction posting: Provides financial transaction information, including posting of credits, debits, and interests.
3. Inquiry: Provides online information regarding status, balance, and stops and holds.
4. Marketing summary processing: Provides marketing staff with information regarding LNB's customer base, use of LNB's services, and activity and profitability of services.

In the case study, LNB did not go through a formal systems planning phase for two reasons: (1) it was converting from an existing DDA application, and perhaps more significant, (2) LNB does not have, as yet, established procedures for this phase. Projects are initiated by directives. LNB has decided, however, to implement an EDP planning function, after the DDA system is converted.

2.3 DD/DS: A TOOL FOR REQUIREMENTS DEFINITION AND ANALYSIS

The use of the DD/DS in requirements definition and analysis is critical. The DD/DS provides a framework in which the end-user and the analyst can communicate with each other using common terminology and definitions. Communication between the end-user and the analysts, between the analyst and the designer, and between the designer and the developer is essential in building a system. By maintaining consistency in the data used, potentially disastrous conditions caused by inexact or inconsistent data can be averted.

The activities collectively known as requirements definition and analysis begin where the conceptual planning stage left off. For our purposes of discussion, this stage includes the description of how the "real world" operates, and it presents a detailed model of the business function and processes being implemented and of the data that is required to perform these functions. Activities in this stage may be iterative, as each function is refined and more is known about the required data [COUG 74]. It is important that the data defined during this stage be consistent at each iteration.

2.3.1 Requirements Definition: Describe Functions and Data

Application requirements definitions describe business or operational goals in user-oriented terms. Requirements definitions answer such questions as:

1. What needs to be done to achieve the stated goals?

2. What kinds of reports or products are needed?
3. What activities produce these reports?
4. Where does the source of information come from?

Thus to define requirements, it is necessary to describe functions in terms of the business activities of an enterprise, and the way in which these functions use the data. In fact, the description of the business functions is the focal point of problem definition in subsequent database design stages. The way these business functions use the data is described with respect to the data input and the data output of these functions.

It should be recognized that the requirements definition and analysis phase is an iteration, at a greater level of detail, of the systems planning procedure. Whereas the initial planning phase dealt at a conceptual level and was confined to high-level business functions and data clusters, this phase deals with more specific system processes and activities and detailed data elements (see Figure 2.4). Requirements are defined in terms of the data elements which belong to data clusters that describe entities in the real world.

A data cluster is a named collection of data items where data items are the most elementary unit of data in a user database. Usually a data

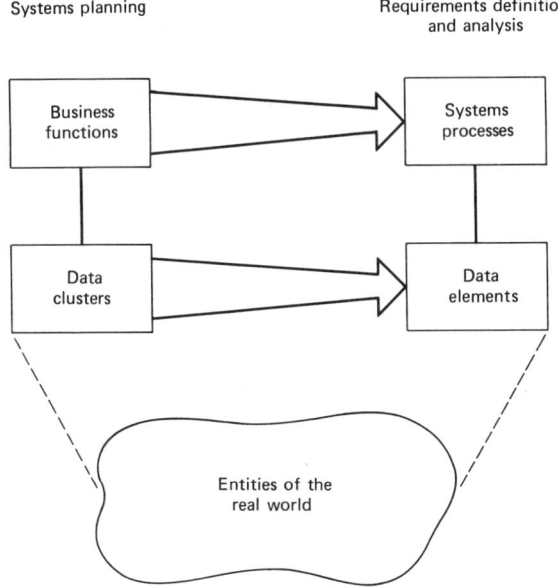

Figure 2.4 Requirements definition and analysis: a refinement upon system planning.

cluster takes the form of a data file record. For example, the entity named *region* might be described by six data items:

1. Region code.
2. Name of region.
3. Street address of region.
4. City of region.
5. State of region.
6. Zip code of region.

Additional data items of region information might include names of key managerial personnel, telephone area code and number, and so forth.

These entities, their attributes, and the relationships between these entities can be used to create a model of the real world in terms of data. This model is a more detailed iteration of the previously defined global Conceptual Data Model. We now refer to it as a *Detailed Conceptual Model* (see Fig. 2.5).

Figures 2.5a through 2.5d describe a method for creating and documenting a Detailed Conceptual Model using one of the currently available proprietary methodologies.* This model is useful for several reasons.

1. *As a system planning tool:* The model depicts "where we are" in the spectrum of business information automation. The model — not being encumbered by data application (or use), physical form, and structure — shows the data which supports the information needs of the company in its purest form. By the use of specially designated colors (or any other effective technique), those kinds of information which are presently automated may be distinguished from those that are not (and potentially might be), thus pictorially describing possible future areas for automation. It illustrates areas that have the greatest potential benefit from automation.
2. *As a means of understanding the effect of one system upon other systems:* The model is central to making system design decisions regarding: a) the integration of a new system with existing systems; b) the abolishment of an existing system which is potentially integrated with other systems; and c) the potential effects of a significant change in the data element make-up of a specific data aggregate (record).
3. *As a general communications tool:* The Detailed Conceptual Model can serve as a common reference point in written or oral communi-

---

*This material is used by permission of Peat, Marwick, Mitchell & Co.

cation regarding a wide variety of systems and/or data related topics. It becomes the primary mechanism to bridge the gap between the user community and the system staff.

4. *As a database design aid:* The Conceptual Models will also be used in the structuring of an optimal database design by providing a guide for the detailed study of the various access paths to the data, the frequency of use of those access paths, and whether individual paths are followed (used) in a real-time mode versus batch mode, or seldom traversed.

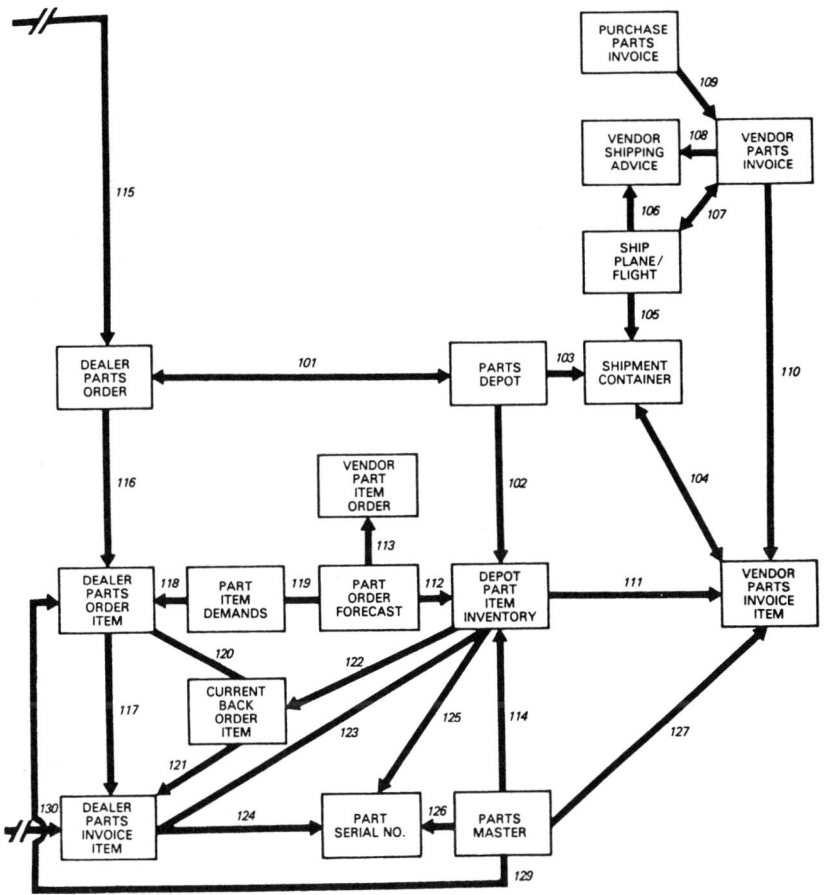

PARTIAL CONCEPTUAL INFORMATION MODEL

Figure 2.5 Sample Detailed Conceptual Model. Used by permission of Peat, Marwick, Mitchell & Co. (Continued on the following page.)

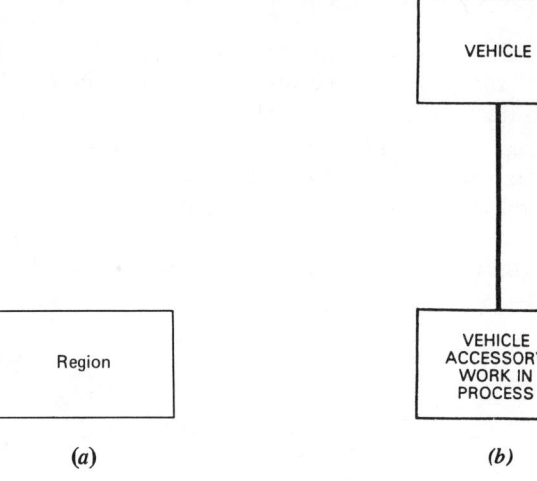

Data Clusters are depicted as rectangular boxes.

Figure 2.5a A Data Cluster.

For one vehicle, there is only one accessory work-in-process record containing all accessories which are to be installed. They are related by vehicle identification number.

Figure 2.5b One-to-one relationship.

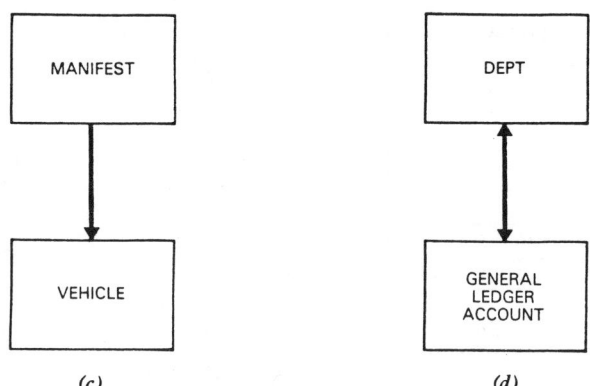

For one manifest number, there are many vehicles and those vehicles relate to only one manifest. They are related by vehicle identification number.

Figure 2.5c One-to-many relationship.

For one department, there may be many G/L account numbers used; and, any one G/L account may be used by many departments. The data aggregates are related by department number.

Figure 2.5d Many-to-many relationship.

All material used by permission of Peat, Marwick, Mitchell & Co.

DD/DS: A TOOL FOR REQUIREMENTS DEFINITION AND ANALYSIS

The examples shown in Figures 2.6a, 2.6b, and 2.6c show the various parts of the model which can be documented in the DD/DS at the detail level.

The DD/DS can be used in helping document an information requirements model independent of implementation considerations, that is, a Detailed Conceptual Model for the application. The Detailed Con-

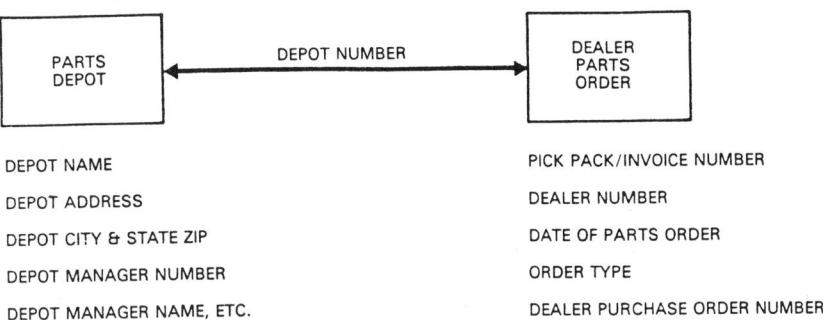

(a)

Figure 2.6a Documenting a data relationship (many-to-many). Used by permission of Peat, Marwick, Mitchell & Co.

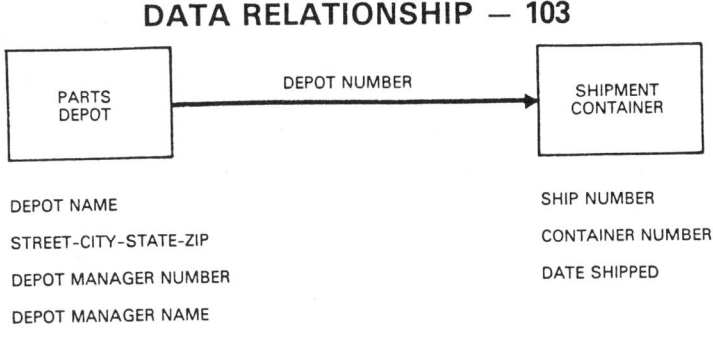

(b)

Figure 2.6b Documenting a data relationship (one-to-many). Used by permission of Peat, Marwick, Mitchell & Co.

EXAMPLE OF DATA ELEMENT DESCRIPTIONS

ASSET/PROPERTY ITEM   Data about an item acquired which is classified as a fixed asset, or an item of property which is of sufficient value to be controlled. Essential data items included are asset/item, date of acquisition, general ledger account code (to which item is associated) cost of acquisition, current depreciated value, method of depreciation, etc.

FLAT RATE OP CODE   Data about a specific warranty labor operation. Essential data items included are flat rate code and description of the labor operation (e.g. replace clutch).

GENERAL LEDGER ACCOUNT   Data about the basic unit of accounting measurement used. An occurrence of this data is conveniently equated to the ledger card of a manually operated general ledger file (or tray). Essential data items included are the general ledger account code, (which is defined to include area, region, department number, and account number - see below), year-to-date account dollar balance, beginning of year account dollar balance, beginning of year account dollar balance (when applicable), account type code, and individual monthend balances for the twelve months of the fiscal year.

GENERAL LEDGER ACCOUNT CODE

AREA	REGION	DEPT	ACCOUNT
XX	XX	XXX	XXXXXXX

PART TYPE   Data which describes a broad categorization of parts. Each part item is associated with one part type. Essential data includes the part type code and description of the part type. At present, there are only three occurrences of this data:

     2 = Regular Part
     6 = Accessory
(anything else) = Other

PARTS DEPOT   Data about the individual parts depot facility. Essential data items include the depot's assigned number (e.g. 10 = Master Parts Depot, 14 = Los Angeles Parts Deport, 11 = Sacramento Parts Depot, 15 = Dallas Parts Depot, etc.), name (e.g. Jacksonville Parts Depot), address, city, state, zip code, phone number, name of Depot Manager, etc.

Presently kept manually and as a bogus Dealer Master File record. There are twelve parts depots.

PARTS DISTRICT   Data about a subdivision of a region based upon a list of dealerships which are served by the same district parts manager. Essential data items inlcuded are parts district number, name of district parts manager, sales point numbers of the dealerships which comprise the service district, and date of last district alignment.

(c)

Figure 2.6c Documenting data elements for the Detailed Conceptual Design. Used by permission of Peat, Marwick, Mitchell & Co.

ceptual Model is a model of the real world operation of an application. It requires detailed documentation of the entities, their characteristics, and their relationship to each other. The DD/DS provides a mechanism for the descriptions of the Detailed Conceptual Model. Having used a DD/DS in the planning phase, documenting the Detailed Conceptual Model requires adding only the additional details.

2.3.2 Requirements Analysis: Manipulate Functions and Detailed Conceptual Model

Analysis of requirements can be a tedious process that requires manipulation of the business functions and of the Detailed Conceptual Model. It is important to have a detailed inventory of all the data elements in the enterprise relevant to this application, and to understand all the relationships among these metadata entities.

An important part of this analysis is to determine how the functions or processes use the data, an example of how this can be used is illustrated with Figure 2.7, in the "data versus business process" matrix. In this matrix, the relevant business functions in the enterprise are listed on one axis. This matrix defines the relationship between Data Clusters and business processes, and illustrates which business processes share which data elements.

Further information used in the analysis is collected and recorded in the transaction matrix (see Figure 2.8). The *transaction matrix* is used to describe individual functions. In this matrix, the function code is defined, with a function name, the source of the transaction, estimated complexity of processing (including its estimated volumes), and the processing mode.

Systematic and thorough definition of the data elements and business processes of the application area is necessary to create a Detailed Conceptual Model that represents the user's application realistically. Having this as the framework, new requirements for information by the user can be defined in the context of the Detailed Conceptual Model and supporting matrices. The detailed Conceptual Model and business processes are manipulated and analyzed to produce the database and system design for the new system.

2.3.3 DD/DS Supports Requirements Definition and Analysis Activities

The DD/DS is used in requirements definition and analysis to document the requirements as these are defined, and to support their analysis.

2.3.3.1 Documentation Aid

The DD/DS records description of business processes, including information about the operation of the business process, its potential uses,

EXAMPLE OF SUPPORTING MATRIX FOR INFORMATION MODEL

DATA USAGE SUMMARY

		PROGRAM ADMIN				SALES PROPOSALS				AFFILIATE RELATIONS					SALES ADMIN			ACCTNG. SERV.			ON AIR OPS		ADV	NET SVS	PGM FLM	
DATA GROUP		1	2	3	4	14	15	17	25	9	10	11	12	5	16	18	20	21	23	24	6	8	19	22	7	13
SALES	1	X	X		X	X	X	X	X		X	X					X									
	2	X	X		X	X	X	X	X		X	X			X	X	X									
	3	X	X	X	X	X	X							X	X	X										
	4	X	X	X		X								X							X					
	5	X	X	X	X	X	X						X	X	X							X	X			
	6	X	X	X		X						X	X	X	X							X	X			
OPERA- TIONS	7	X	X	X															X							
	8	X	X															X	X	X						
	9	X	X																							
	10									X																
	11										X							X			X	X				
	12										X															
AMOL	13	X	X		X					X	X	X	X						X		X	X			X	X
	14										X															X	X
	15										X	X	X					X		X						X	X

X—Implies both updating and reading of each data group

Figure 2.7 Data versus business process matrix. Used by permission of Peat, Marwick, Mitchell & Co.

EXAMPLE OF SUPPORTING MATRIX FOR INFORMATION MODEL

COMPLEXITY/MAGNITUDE/FREQUENCY BY FUNCTIONS

	FUNC #	FUNCTION NAME	COMPLEXITY (1-5)		PROCESSING MAGNITUDE (1-5)		FREQ
			OL	BATCH	OL	BATCH	
Sales Admin	1	Prepare Proposal	2.5	2.0	3.5	2.5	D
	2	Prepare Contracts	2.5	2.0	2.5	2.0	D
	3	Prepare Product Schedules	4.0	3.0	2.5	2.0	D
Oper Acctng	4	Announce & Format Programs	3.0	3.0	2.5	2.0	D
	5	Prepare Commercial Insertion Schedule	4.0	3.5	4.5	3.0	D
	6	Prepare Log	5.0	3.0	5.0	3.0	D
	7	Bill Client/Agency	3.0	3.0	2.5	4.0	D
	8	Affiliate Compensation	4.0	3.5	2.5	4.5	D,M
	9	Maintain Material Inventory	3.0	2.5	3.0	3.0	D
Affil Del	10	Profile Maintenance	2.0	N/A	2.0	N/A	D
	11	Station Clearance	3.5	3.0	4.0	3.0	D
	12	One Time Only Preparation	3.5	3.0	3.0	3.5	D
	13	Cut-In, Coop, Local Sale Processing	4.0	3.0	2.0	4.5	D
	14	Management Clearance Reporting	2.5	2.0	3.0	4.0	D,W
	15	Station Performance	2.5	3.0	2.5	4.0	D,W,M

Figure 2.8 Example of transaction matrix. Used by permission of Peat, Marwick, Mitchell & Co.

the data elements that are required to produce the desired results, their attributes, and their relationships to other processes, that is, those processes that will be affected by this process. The DD/DS is the repository of the documentation for the data elements and entities comprising the Detailed Conceptual Model, the model of the user's application data needs without implementation constraints.

2.3.3.2 Analytical Aid

After the data requirements are defined, it is important to determine how much of that required data is already available by reviewing the current data resource inventory, so that unnecessary redundancy is not introduced. Another step in the analysis is to determine if the requirements can be satisfied by modifying existing data. The assistance of a DD/DS is invaluable at this stage, especially if the DD/DS already has a complete inventory of the enterprise data. This is further supported when the data defined in the DD/DS has common definitions, which can facilitate the analysis process.

The DD/DS can support analysis by generating and manipulating the data versus business process matrix, and the transaction matrix. In many cases, using these matrices, the DD/DS can produce summary reports with either relationship or usage information.

Many procedures and methodologies have evolved to help in defining and analyzing requirements [LEON 80]. Most of these procedures and methodologies have recognized the need for a DD/DS to assist in the process [GANE 79; TEIC 77; SIBL 74]. By using a DD/DS, greater control can be maintained over the development of a system, since it provides the means for determining the status of the development effort. Data element and business process descriptions, representative of the way a business application operates in real life, serve to control subsystem and program development by injecting real-life delimiters to the specifications being developed. Furthermore, these descriptions are based upon the data cluster and business function descriptions generated in the planning phase at a level of detail upon which control can be effectively exercised.

The DD/DS is a source for identification and documentation of system and data components; of the characteristics and relationships of these components, that is, the descriptions of the detailed conceptual model. This in turn can be used in defining database structures, which fits into the domain of database design.

2.3.4 What the Last National Bank Did

Continuing with the banking example described in the case study, we focus on the use of the DD/DS in defining and analyzing information requirements for the Demand Deposit Account Application.

LNB was required to use the DD/DS in performing its requirements definition and analysis activities. These activities were included in LNB's second SDLC stage, systems requirements. The product of this stage for LNB is a set of functional specifications — a milestone or checkpoint which LNB's Systems Assurance Committee (SAC) must approve before the development team is allowed to continue.

In the DDA pilot conversion project, the development team had to define the functions of the current DDA system and its relationship to other application systems. Documentation of the existing system was placed in the DD/DS. Simultaneously, user requirements were obtained. The analysts captured information on all aspects of users' needs, including data requirements (e.g., volume, access rate, response time), processing requirements, security, restart, and recovery considerations. The DD/DS was used in documenting all the data, processing, security, and other requirements. With the aid of the DD/DS and the information obtained in the preceding steps, the analyst was able to determine what data is available, how it is being used, how it can be accessed, who has primary responsibility for its definition and upkeep, and most important, whether there is conflict in using this data, that is, what impact it will have on other application systems.

The analyst needed to determine the kinds of reports, charts, and tables required for this application; what these reports should contain, and what they should look like, including the reports that must be sent to the customers; the accounting information needed to operate the bank on a daily basis, as well as the kinds of reports demanded by upper management for decision-making purposes. This analysis is designed to determine both the data that is required to meet the reporting needs, and whether the required data is available.

The analyst developed a list of all the data elements associated with the entities defined in the planning phase, based upon the business processes required to support the Demand Deposit Account System. Using the DD/DS, detailed business processes and data element descriptions were developed making sure no duplications were introduced and making appropriate authorized use of existing data elements in the DD/DS (see list of data elements in Appendix).

Next, LNB's analyst developed a data versus business process matrix and a transaction matrix. Using these, the analyst produced a detailed conceptual model. These efforts resulted in a coordinated and controlled definition of the functional requirements specifications for the pilot DDA system. These specifications were submitted to SAC for approval.

If no DD/DS were available, the bank might have designed the DDA pilot as another application under the DBMS without regard to other data availability, such as what customer data may exist in other systems already. For example, the name of a customer may be defined in the savings account application as last name, first initial, and middle initial; while in the DDA system, the name of the customer may be defined as last name, first name, and middle initial. In one case, the length of the data element, "customer-name," may be 18 characters, while in the other it may be 32 characters. This results in files of uncoordinated, independent, and redundant data, due to the same data being defined differently in the different files. This brief example points to the need for coordination and consistency.

Actually, LNB did use the DD/DS to define and analyze its requirements. However, the DD/DS was not used previously in documenting the system planning effort, thus, control and traceability in subsequent efforts was lessened. The merits of using the DD/DS at that early stage of the system development effort were not made evident in that it could have provided accountability to the planning effort, and a means for insuring that consistency and coordination were maintained throughout the requirements and analysis phase.

2.4 DD/DS: A TOOL FOR DESIGN, IMPLEMENTATION, TESTING, OPERATION AND MAINTENANCE

In the previous section, the DD/DS was shown to be an important tool in defining and analyzing information requirements. Likewise, the DD/DS plays an important role in the remaining development activities.

To illustrate the extent to which these activities use the DD/DS, this section discusses some of the remaining development processes, in particular, design, programming, reorganization, and conversion.

2.4.1 The Design Phase

System design objectives differ from requirements objectives in that design activities are intended to find a "how-to" solution. In the previous two phases business functions and system processes, described what must be done; the design phase describes how these functions and processes can be accomplished with data processing support. These same functions and processes are specified in terms of systems components, program components, program modules, and individual routines. Design specifications require extensive use of metadata. Recording these metadata in the DD/DS is very useful because the DD/DS can provide a means for maintaining control over the system design specifications and can aid in insuring that requirements stated earlier are consistent with the implementation [ATRE 80]. This can be accomplished at the common denominator between the "what" and the "how", which is the data element.

The design phase, whether logical or physical, requires the use of the DD/DS for storing the descriptions of the systems components, such as subsystems, program modules, data structures, data access techniques, and data flow. Specifications during the design phase include functional characteristics of a system, their interactions with each other, and the data that the components require to operate. Generally, the design phase is logically divided into two closely related aspects: system design and database design.

Systems design specifies the characteristics of the program modules, control structures, program logic, implementation requirements, and data usage, that is, what data come into the program, what happens to it internally, and what comes out. Implementation constraints and performance characteristics are also described. Data usage characteristics are also included, such as size, volume, and frequency.

Database design involves describing the data required by the programs, beginning with previously developed definitions of the data elements, records, and descriptions of storage structures and access strategies. These are used to generate a desired data structure or schema for the database. Also from these descriptions, the program's view of the data, or subschema can be generated.

The DD/DS should be used in documenting the logical and physical database design. Further, the DD/DS should be used actively to assist in the design by generating the DBMS control blocks from the metadata. The DD/DS can also assist in application program designs, by providing the means for documenting transactions, programs, reports, and traditional files. Requirements from users gathered in the previous stage can be translated into technical terms and entered into the DD/DS. Metadata stored in the DD/DS can then be used in generating COBOL FDs for the application programs; program logic description can be used in preparing a preliminary user's manual—just to name a few DD/DS benefits.

Metadata is important in the remaining activities of the system development life cycle, such as programming, DBMS usage, database reorganization, testing and validation, data security, and conversion.

2.4.2 Programming Phase

Metadata about the program and about the data can be retrieved from the DD/DS to help in programming tasks. Pertinent metadata retrieved from the DD/DS can be incorporated directly into the programs being coded as the data definition block. For COBOL application programs, data division descriptions are defined and generated into the COBOL copy using the metadata generation capability of the DD/DS. Edit and validation parameters are part of the program's metadata, and when invoked from the DD/DS, these can serve as edit checks against incoming data.

If a DBMS is used, the DD/DS can provide the metadata that the DBMS's require. With centralized data definitions in the DD/DS, the latter can provide the schema and the subschema for the DBMS. This ensures integrity and consistency in the data used.

If there is need for reorganization or restructuring of the database, changes can be made at the metadata level to insure a smooth transition between the old and the new database. Moreover, the use of a DD/DS will help in assessing the impact on systems, related programs, and other databases from the changes made in database structures, regardless of whether these changes are at the logical or physical level of design [SOCK 79].

Use of metadata can be extended to testing and validation. Once the characteristics of the database are recorded, it would be easier and possibly more reliable to generate test data using metadata recorded in the DD/DS. Metadata is also an important element in conversion, especially in generating source and target formats from the metadatabase using the DD/DS.

2.4.3 DD/DS Supports All SDLC Activities

In short, the DD/DS can be used to support activities throughout the system development process including the maintenance and operation phases. It should be made mandatory for persons involved in systems development and operation to rely on the DD/DS as the single authoritative source for the metadata. Systems designers and analysts should use the DD/DS during requirements definition and analysis, and during the system design stages. Programmers should use the DD/DS to assist them in writing the program, by incorporating the metadata from the DD/DS (e.g., the COBOL data division), incorporating edit and validation parameters, and generating test data. Database designers should use the DD/DS to generate the schema and subschema for the DBMS.

2.4.4 What the Last National Bank Did

To summarize events already described in previous sections, LNB is undertaking a massive conversion effort to a more modern technology. The DDA system is its pilot DBMS application, for which the bank currently has a conventional file application system that handles the DDA activities. The bank must convert from the existing file system to one utilizing DBMS. Information about the existing application system is already described in the DD/DS.

The bank's database administrator (DBA) plays an important role during this entire process. The DBA must determine whether, in creating the new DBMS application, there are any new requirements not already met by the existing version, such as a change in tasks to be performed, a sudden change in processing volume, or increased usage, and so forth. Most important of all, the DBA must determine the relationships and differences between the system under modification and the systems in the operational environment. Since the DBA has primary responsibility for the content and operation of the DD/DS, the DBA in fact has much of the required information available already, for example, information that describes the current system's inputs and outputs, source and destination of those I/O's, personnel responsible for the data, organizational units that interface with the system, programs used by the system, and so forth. Thus, the DBA has the information about the current system on hand, and the information about the target system derives from thorough conceptual, requirements, and design stages. With this information, the bank DBA described both the old and the new structures to the DD/DS, and was then able to convert the old files into the new database input. The DD/DS contained documented formats for both the old system and the new, and thus was able to generate a schema for the DBMS. The DD/DS also aided in the population of the new database. Since edit and validation rules were already stored in the DD/DS, the DBA only had to invoke these to achieve controlled edit and validation with minimal amount of "cleanup" required. Moreover, the DBA was able to generate reliable test data to test the new system.

Without the DD/DS, LNB would have had a much more difficult task in its development and conversion effort. Without DD/DS assistance in conversion, it would have required a great amount of effort in populating the database. All the data would have had to be manually translated, or at best, specialized data translation software would have been required. A great amount of data validation would have been required to account for an added margin of error due to manual translation; and extensive cleanup would have been necessary.

The DD/DS in effect improved staff communication; reduced data redundancies; increased control over the development of the pilot system with automated metadata generation; created more reliable documentation; and facilitated promulgation of standards.

2.5 DD/DS: A TOOL FOR DOCUMENTATION AND STANDARDS

An early recognized benefit of a DD/DS is its ability to produce consistent and complete documentation about databases, programs, and systems. Traditionally, documentation has been the last task to be completed. It is often not begun until the system is just ready for delivery, since it is mistakenly thought to be nonessential for completing the system. In effect, as the saying goes, "the system works without it!" That is one reason why documentation is usually poor, outdated, inaccurate, incomplete, and often nonexistent. The other reason is that, to most system professionals, development activities are the most exciting, because they are considered creative tasks, while writing about a system — documenting — is dull and routine, and not at all as creative.

Documentation is a very crucial element in systems development. Software technologists recognize this and have discussed and written about it, yet it does not make it any easier or more palatable to do.

That is why automated means should be used in producing systems and database documentation.

The DD/DS is one tool which can be used to overcome these difficulties by automatically producing documentation about the database and the system. In this light, the DD/DS should be used routinely to augment current documentation efforts, and to supplant a large percentage (60% to 70%) of existing systems and data documentation requirements. When used in the normal course of development, the DD/DS can lessen the monotony and repetitiveness of the task of documenting, and it can assist in completing the system development effort on time, delivering an end product which is well documented. This would work most effectively if the DD/DS were employed so that the system wouldn't work without it.

2.5.1 Application Systems Documentation

Application systems can be documented using a DD/DS. Each of its components would be identified as a meta system *entity,* and each entity described in detail, with information that is descriptive and necessary to enable a system analyst, designer, or DBA to be able to utilize the meta system entity.

For example, a system/subsystem could be described with the following attributes: *identifier* and *description, responsibility* and *relationship.* The identifier is the name of the system and the description is narrative support; responsibility should have recorded information about the person or the department that has primary responsibility for maintaining the system; and relationship provides the information about what other systems or system components the current system is dependent on, uses, or affects.

Within the application system, the transactions are described in detail, that is, what data actually represents events which take place in the system. First, all possible transactions within the system can be enumerated, with their names, their nature, the data required, and so forth. Outputs from the application system can also be enumerated, with their format and the types of outputs produced, each described in detail. Finally, to complete the picture, the source documents can be described as to its originating department, the author, the person or department responsible for the source document, its disposition, and so forth.

2.5.2 Program Documentation

Program documentation is more detailed. It includes identification of the program and description of its functions, its inputs, outputs, the language it was written in, storage requirements, the person responsible for maintaining and operating it, scheduling information, operating requirements, and the relationship to other programs, files, systems, and so forth.

2.5.3 Data Documentation

Documentation of the metadata should be described in as many levels as is necessary to define the Conceptual Models. Most often, the documentation of the metadata involves the enterprise's data elements, the records, the files, and the databases.

The most basic level of metadata, the data element, is the most detailed. Metadata which can be used to document the data element are: name or identification; characteristics, such as length and value range; ownership; relationship to other elements, to other records, files, databases, and programs. Next higher in level of detail is the record. Types of metadata similar to those which describe the data element can be used to describe the record entity. And so each data entity type is documented in turn, until a complete inventory of the data resource is entered into the DD/DS.

2.5.4 Standards

A well documented system is necessary to establish communication between the system and the user. The documentation tells the user the characteristics and capabilities of the system, and it makes the system easier to use. Moreover, good documentation helps in data resource sharing. Standards can help to promote sharing of resources in a controlled environment. In the computing field, especially, the same terminology is often used to mean different things in different contexts. Thus, in some cases, standards are necessary so that everyone uses the same data name to mean the same thing.

While it is not within the scope of this chapter to discuss all possible data elements or the standardization of the content of the data, it is appropriate to consider the data-related standards that can be supported using the DD/DS. There are two types of data-related standards: *Data definitions standards,* at the "type" level; and *Data format conformance,* at the "occurrence" level.

Data definition refers to a standard way of describing data. One example is the naming of the data. The naming standard may be in the form of rigid rules or established conventions for assigning names to data entities. All user areas within the enterprise will know that, for instance, when the data element, "customer-name," is used in files, program, and reports, this data element means the same throughout the enterprise. In some cases, a *keyword rule* is incorporated in the description of the data elements. Keyword rules are used as an indexing mechanism.

Data format conformance is content related. It means that a data element, in addition to having the same name throughout the enterprise it also must conform to a common set of format rules for the data element to retain the same meaning. Moreover, these must be accepted throughout the enterprise. For example, all data elements involving "Date" should have the same format throughout the enterprise – and only that format should be assigned. Similarly, if codes are to be used throughout the enterprise, these must be uniform. If an acceptable code for a state is a two-letter code, that must be the universally accepted code in the enterprise, and no other code, either three-letter or four-letter should be used.

The DD/DS can facilitate the introduction and enforcement of such standards, via a set of editing rules to be included in the DD/DS. These editing rules can, in effect, edit and validate acceptable codes, so that nonconforming codes are not acceptable. The DD/DS can be used as both the promulgator and the enforcer for data standards. It can be used to promulgate because the DD/DS can be made to record only acceptable standard data definition. Databases or application systems requesting data entities will only be able to retrieve standard descriptions of data entities and will only have standard data names.

The DD/DS can be used to monitor and to enforce standard data definitions because through its edit and validation facilities, the DD/DS can screen out nonstandard, or nonconforming data elements. If and when nonconformance is detected, the DBA can take appropriate action.

2.5.5 What the Last National Bank Did

LNB was fully cognizant of the importance of documentation and standards in system development. In fact, one of its major departments, which is under the Assistant Vice President (AVP) for Data Administration, is the Department of Standards and Documentation. Its responsibilities includes the development of database standards and guidelines, maintenance of the DD/DS, and review of new systems to insure conformance with LNB standards. In particular, this department is responsible for:

1. Developing and administering procedures for data collection and documentation.
2. Developing procedures for utilizing the DD/DS as a data collection and documentation tool.
3. Developing procedures to ensure security and integrity of databases.
4. Maintaining and disseminating the database Standard Manual.

Many of the bank's important data standards were implemented and enforced using the DD/DS. For example, there were already common standards for customer numbers and common codes for savings plans. These standard names were used throughout the bank.

The bank has plans to document its entire EDP environment using the DD/DS, after the pilot application is successfully completed. The system characteristics will be described to the DD/DS, including its various components, interfaces, and other pertinent information. Individual programs, auxiliary programs, and utility routines will all be described to the DD/DS — including such details as programming language used, control structures required, responsible person, relationships to other programs or modules, and functions performed. Data for the system will also be described, beginning with the most detailed description of individual data elements, their characteristics and usages, relationships and ownership, all the way up the data hierarchy through records, files, and data bases.

This will insure the LNB's systems documentation generated by the DD/DS will reflect invariably the actual implemented system. Thus, the bank will avoid the problematical situation in which documentation does not agree with the system. If the DD/DS generates the metadata for the system, the documentation will be accurate, up to date, and complete, especially if LNB implements an active DD/DS.

Without a DD/DS, the bank may need to allot many more resources, in terms of personnel, time, and money to document the system, and to insure that standard names for data entities are being used consistently throughout the bank. Development time could increase significantly if all the documentation were done manually, and the probability that the documentation reflected the actual system may not be very high. To insure that only standard data names are used in all application systems in the bank would be a very tedious and potentially error-filled task. In short, the bank would have to increase the size of its DP staff, and the cost for maintaining the system could be considerably higher.

2.6 DD/DS: A TOOL FOR OPERATIONAL CONTROL THROUGH METADATA GENERATION AND METADATA AUDIT TRAIL

If the enterprise's data is already described to the DD/DS, then this tool can be used to generate metadata for the operational programs. In so doing, a certain degree of control is gained over the metadata that these programs use, and thus, over the programs themselves. Metadata generated by the DD/DS is certain to conform with the enterprise standard, and to have the most current and complete information about the data. Changes made to the metadata are controlled and propagated to all affected components. Further, by invoking the appropriate security and control restrictions, the DD/DS will only permit authorized persons or systems to access the metadatabase, thereby controlling access to the source of all data definitions. Only those programs or persons having the appropriate access permit would be allowed to extract and manipulate metadata from the DD/DS. This security control over the metadata, ultimately helps to insure the integrity of the data.

2.6.1 Operational Control

As an operational control tool, the DD/DS has unlimited potential; for example, it can aid in the operational control of application programs, the DBMS, and report generation interfaces. The DD/DS can control the operation of application program in several ways. By generating the metadata for each application system, the DD/DS ensures that:

1. The data definitions used in application programs conform to enterprise standards.
2. The data definition is current, consistent, and complete.
3. No unnecessary data redundancy is introduced into the application system.
4. If changes are made to metadata in one part of application system, it is flagged for changes throughout the system.
5. Edit/validation criteria defined in DD/DS are invoked to ensure format and content conformance; potential conflicts in usage are flagged.
6. The application system is documented concurrent with development.

Moreover, when the DD/DS is active, application programs can be locked from being executed if metadata changes have been made that could affect the application or its data in production mode. The DD/DS's metadata generation capability is discussed in greater detail in Chapter 6.

As a control tool for the DBMS, the DD/DS can provide the sole source of data definition; thus, changes made to any data definition would be propagated to all affected areas within the DBMS. In essence, the DD/DS is in proprietary control over the schema and subschema necessary for the DBMS to operate. In an environment with an active DD/DS, DBMS data definitions functions could not be invoked without first passing through the control of the DD/DS.

The DD/DS can also serve as a control tool on the report generation interface, when the latter requires that all report generation requirements for metadata be satisfied through the DD/DS. This strategy

DD/DS: A TOOL FOR OPERATIONAL CONTROL 55

would insure that only properly authorized persons are permitted access to the database. Thus, the DD/DS serves as an access control mechanism to the report generation interface based upon metadata requirements. Likewise, actual reports could be validated for reasonableness through the DD/DS. (See Section 2.8 on end-user support.)

2.6.2 Audit Trail Aid

The DD/DS contains valuable audit trail information about the data. For example, it could describe in detail where and how the data is used, and it identifies what program uses the data, where it appears in the program, what it is used for, what its relationships are to other programs, and whether any transformations were performed on the data.

The DD/DS contains information about the users of the data, who they are, what they do with the data, how they use it, and so forth. It describes the physical devices that process the data, and documents the software that use it, such as a DBMS. In addition, the DD/DS also contains information about the kind of data that is used by the programs, the users, the physical device, the DBMS – these are all entities described in the DD/DS.

All this information is important when tracing incorrect data entry or unauthorized access into the data processing environment. Evaluating this information can help identify the extent of an error; and it may be possible to identify the person responsible for perpetrating the error, or illegally accessing the data base. (See Section 5.4.3 for characteristics of DD/DS output.) These output facilities can enhance the user's ability to use the DD/DS as an audit trail aid.

Audit trail information is important in maintaining operational control over the database environment, in evaluating performance characteristics, and in assisting the EDP Auditor in the conduct of an audit. Chapter 11 addresses the subject of DD/DS and the auditor.

2.6.3 What the Last National Bank Did

In our case study, the bank has not yet achieved a high degree of operational control using the DD/DS. To do so, LNB would have had to use the DD/DS as the only access mechanism into the entire data resource pool, and to use the DD/DS as an absolute control tool. This concept is too revolutionary and does not reflect reality yet for LNB. While the benefits of the DD/DS are accepted and understood, it must also be recognized that humans in an enterprise are not yet willing to relinquish such great control to a software tool. Thus the bank expects to evolve into an environment where greater operational control can be exercised using the DD/DS in the future.

2.7 DD/DS: A TOOL TO SUPPORT THE DISTRIBUTED DATABASE ENVIRONMENT

The concept of a distributed database is defined as the logical integration of data resources that are physically distributed over geographically dispersed processing systems. Our definition of a distributed database includes the supposition that the user process accessing a distributed database is not aware of geographic dispersion. Distributed databases can take many forms. The common kinds of distribution alternatives for databases are: replication, partitioning, partial replication, or partial partitioning. Regardless of how the databases are distributed, a DD/DS is required to support the development and operation of distributed databases. In the previous sections, the importance of a DD/DS in a centralized database environment was discussed. In a distributed database environment, a DD/DS plays a critical role in insuring the consistency, the integrity, and the currency of the data. Chapter 10 discusses in greater detail the role of the DD/DS in the distributed environment.

The user of a DD/DS in a distributed database environment enhances cross-nodal communication among the physically dispersed databases, by providing the metadata about the location of the data over the nodes in the network, metadata about the logical relationships of the data between nodes, and metadata on a global level describing the entire data resource. Thus, the DD/DS serves as a critical logical link in this environment.

The DD/DS is a required tool in supporting logical and physical database design in the distributed database environment. Through the DD/DS, database designers can obtain a complete picture of the data resources available to the enterprise, whether locally or on a physically distant node. Using the DD/DS will insure standard usage and standard definition of global data, and it will also insure that unwanted redundancies are kept to a minimum. In the case of replicated databases, the DD/DS serves to account for and to coordinate desirable redundancies, and where possible, to enforce the standard to be followed in defining these data and the format to which the data must conform.

Operationally, the DD/DS is important in describing the data available in sufficient detail to allow data mappings between local nodes. But, perhaps most importantly, the DD/DS is used as the primary mechanism for locating data over the network.

This *network data directory* function of a DD/DS exists in currently implemented prototype distributed database systems, albeit not always identified as a DD/DS function. This facility may be found as a complicated algorithm that performs many of the DD/DS's functions, but on a limited scale.

Current technology has not yet achieved widespread distribution of databases as we have defined the term. However, many enterprises have found it advantageous to distribute their processing loads to geographically dispersed locations, while linking these processing systems and databases into a network. While this is not a case of distributed database, it is a case of data dispersion using distributed processing. Thus, a DD/DS in a previously centralized environment can evolve into supporting a distributed processing environment with dispersion of data. The DD/DS is particularly important in aiding the newly distributed environment in maintaining data independence from the potentially varied operating environments at the various nodes, and from potentially different DBMSs residing at different nodes, while evolving into distributed databases as the technology develops.

The established capability for metadata generation in the centralized environment should extend to the distributed environment. The DD/DS should, in fact, become the focal point of access in distributed databases. The metadata generation capability in a DD/DS would assist in the orderly development of the distributed environment. It would insure that data defined for the dispersed databases are consistent with those of the previously centralized environment; it would be the repository for any information about local anomalies in the data used; and it would ultimately help in generating the most current and complete information about the entire enterprise's data resources.

It should be noted at this point that distributed environments may evolve from the linkage of a number of currently centralized sites. There is no way of assuring that these central sites, which may become nodes on the new network, will have homogenous data or DBMSs. The DD/DS will be required to assist in the coordination and control over these heterogeneous environments. Furthermore, the DD/DS may play an important role in supporting the data translation process necessary to support data and process mapping across heterogeneous nodes. In this light, it should be recognized that an independent DD/DS which is highly active in nature may be necessary to support these requirements.

2.8 DD/DS: A TOOL FOR END-USER SUPPORT

An end-user is defined as the ultimate consumer of information produced from data. End-users interface into a database environment through a variety of mechanisms, which may include:

1. Report Generators.
2. Query Languages.
3. Preformatted interface supported by application programs.

End-users normally make use of information provided through these interfaces based upon a priori knowledge of the context and meaning of the information supplied. When end-users are not fully aware of the information environment at their disposal, support mechanisms are required which can describe:

1. Available information.
2. Meaning of information.
3. Constraints on usage.

These types of support involve the use of metadata to support the end-user. Ad hoc or predetermined queries can be supported directly, or upon request, with the background necessary to make effective use of the query response and means of available information.

An example from the LNB environment helps illustrate the value of this support. A bank manager involved in evaluating a customer for a potential liability limit on a line of credit queries the newly implemented DDA database for information regarding the average daily balance of the subject customer's account. To properly evaluate the response provided, it would be necessary to know exactly how the average daily balance is calculated. This information, as well as other customer information menus, could be made available (at the terminal) to the bank manager, by utilizing the DD/DS in a support role to the end-user interface facility.

End-user interface mechanisms which utilize the DD/DS to supply metadata to end-users could significantly enhance the utility of information to the end user.

2.9 SUMMARY

This chapter discussed the usages of the DD/DS in various aspects of data processing and management. A hypothetical case study, the Last National Bank, was used to illustrate the benefits of using a DD/DS, by contrasting the effects of using and not using this tool in each situation.

The DD/DS is beneficial when used throughout the systems development life cycle (SDLC) of a system. The possibilities include:

1. Systems planning.
2. Requirements definition and analysis.
3. Design.
4. Implementation, programming, testing, and conversion.
5. Documentation and standards.
6. Operational control and audit trail.
7. End-user support.

REFERENCES

In addition, the DD/DS is found to be an indispensable component of the distributed database environment.

Understanding how a DD/DS can be used is a prerequisite to approaching the issue of designing and implementing a DD/DS. Chapters 3 to 7 explore the design and implementation issues for a DD/DS.

REFERENCES

[ATRE 80] Atre, S., *Data Base: Structured Techniques for Design, Performance, and Management,* Wiley, New York, 1980.

[BCS 77] British Computer Society, Data Dictionary System Working Party, "The British Computer Society Data Dictionary Systems Working Party Report," Appeared in *Data Base,* Vol. 9, No. 2, Fall 1977 and *Sigmod Record,* Vol. 9, No. 4, December 1977.

[COUG 74] J. D. Couger, and R. W. Knapp, Eds., *Systems Analysis Techniques,* Wiley, New York, 1974.

[FIPS 76] "Guidelines on Documentation for Computer Programs and Automated Data Systems," National Bureau of Standards Federal Information Processing Standards Publication 38, Washington D.C., 1976.

[GANE 79] Gane, C. and T. Sarson, *Structured Systems Analysis: Tools and Techniques.* Prentice-Hall, Englewood Cliffs, NJ, 1979.

[LEON 80] Leong-Hong, B. and R. Merwin, "Software Requirements Definition and Analysis: Concepts, Tools, and Example," Proceedings of the International Computer Symposium 1980, Taipei, Republic of China, December 16-18, 1980.

[SIBL 74] Sibley, E. H. and Hasan Sayani, "Data Element Dictionaries for the Information Interface," in Hazel McEwen, Ed., *Proceedings of the First National Symposium on the Management of Data Elements in Information Processing,* January 1974, pp. 285-304.

[SOCK 79] Sockut, G. and R. Goldberg, "Database Reorganization – Principles and Practice," *ACM Computing Surveys,* Vol. 11, No. 4, December, 1979.

[TEIC 77] Teichroew, D. and E. A. Hershey, III, "PSL/PSA: A Computer-Aided Technique for Structured Documentation and Analysis of Information Processing Systems," *IEEE Trans. Software Eng.,* Vol. SE-3, No. 1, January 1977.

[TSIC 77] Tsichritzis D. and A. Klug, Eds., *The ANSI/X3/SPARC DBMS Framework Report of the Study Group on Database Management Systems,* AFIPS Press, NJ, 1977.

3

Foundations for Design of the Data Dictionary/Directory System

The Data Dictionary/Directory System is an information system about the enterprise's data. Its underlying design philosophy is to enable the sharing of the metadata among all segments of the enterprise's users, both data processing and non-data processing personnel. In this respect, the design of a DD/DS should be based on the *database approach,* and therefore it should follow the same methods and procedures as in the design of any database-supported application system.

This design philosophy is introduced here to provide a theoretical foundation for designing a DD/DS. As with the design of information systems intended for the end-user, there are two aspects in the design of the DD/DS: the system or functional aspect, and the database aspect. Both of these are driven by requirements for information about the enterprise's data resources.

Because the design of the DD/DS is based on the database approach, emphasis will be placed on the design of the DD/DS's database, the metadatabase. The discussion of the conceptual design of the metadatabase begins with the identification and detailed description of the metadata entities that must be addressed, followed by a description of the relationships, and the metadata structures that can be used to implement the metadatabase design.

In designing the metadatabase, it is important to bear in mind that it will be shared among many types of users, each contributing metadata to the DD/DS, each having different needs for the same metadata, and each having a different logical view of the metadata [ASTR 72]. The design of the software that processes the metadatabase will be explored in subsequent chapters, from the viewpoint of functional requirements.

3.1 DD/DS DESIGN PHILOSOPHY

It was established in earlier chapters that there are many similarities between user data and metadata administration and control. By extension, there are many similarities between the objectives and functions of the systems that administer and control these two types of data. For example, they are both designed to enable data sharing among various user groups, to maintain data independence, and to assure the integrity of the data with which they must deal.

The fact that the DD/DS will serve the metadata needs for a wide variety of users in the enterprise is an important factor in establishing a design philosophy for the DD/DS. The DD/DS will provide metadata for the data administrator (DA), database administrator (DBA), systems analysts, programmers, and end-users (see Figure 3.1). Many of these users of the DD/DS will require diverse and different logical views of the metadata. The ability to provide coordinated and consistent metadata throughout the enterprise while maintaining flexibility and responsiveness for metadata users, will depend upon the ability to utilize the database approach in designing and building the DD/DS.

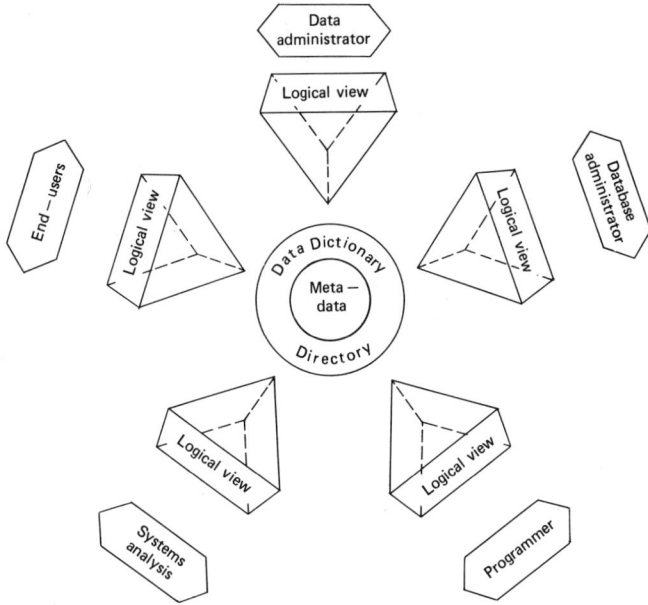

Figure 3.1 DD/DS users.

DD/DS DESIGN PHILOSOPHY

An example of two different logical views will help illustrate the need for the database approach in designing the DD/DS. Consider the need for metadata about data element usage in programs. The database administrator requires a logical view of the metadata which satisfies the request, "List all the programs which utilize a data element zipcode." This request is issued when the DBA (who has enterprise-wide responsibility for data) needs to determine the extent of the impact that any contemplated changes to the data element "zipcode" will have on all the programs in the enterprise. The programmer, on the other hand, is concerned primarily with the particulars of a specific program. The programmer's logical view is designed to satisfy a different request — which may be the opposite of the DBA's — such as the metadata for the data element "zipcode," used in the program "cust-account."

3.1.1 Use of the Database Approach

The necessity to support such diverse logical views of metadata among a large community of users requiring up-to-date, consistent, and reliable information about the enterprise's data resources requires the database approach in the design of DD/DS.

Database-supported information system design, as discussed in Chapter 2, is based upon the requisite understanding of the "business functions" that will be supported by the contemplated system. Thus, it is necessary to understand and model the "real-world" business function. This is accomplished by describing its operational flow, especially for those functions involving the use of information; decomposing these functions into discrete operations; and describing both the information that goes into the function and the expected products. This characterization of the functions to be performed in translated into data-processing terminology as the objectives of the system, or the functional requirements for the system, and the data flow, the required input, and the expected products are the information requirements for the system.

Likewise, the design of the DD/DS (intended to support the metadata needs of an enterprise) should be based on the requisite understanding of business functions that will be supported by the contemplated DD/DS. These business functions are the activities of the information services and data-processing staffs of the enterprise. Typically, these business functions include:

1. Development of new application systems.
2. Maintenance of existing application systems.
3. Operation of the data processing facility.

The need for metadata in performing these functions is the basis for the design of the DD/DS, inasmuch as these needs define the intended use of the DD/DS. Chapter 2 described the various potential uses of a DD/DS; a particular design of a DD/DS would be based upon some subset of this list of possible uses.

After choosing the specific activities (or uses of metadata) which the DD/DS will support, these activities should be decomposed into a sufficient level of detail to identify the specific requirements for metadata in each activity. The sum of all the metadata requirements across all the activities represents the statement of metadata requirements for DD/DS.

3.1.2 Foundation for Metadatabase Design

Metadata requirements are then translated into a conceptual metadatabase design for the DD/DS. This is accomplished in exactly the same way that a conceptual database design is generated for a user database. The basic procedure is as follows:

1. Identify the objects or entities which require description in order to perform the activities.
2. Describe these entities in sufficient detail to avoid ambiguity.
3. Identify and describe the relationships between these entities.

The process of conceptual database design for the metadatabase follows these same steps (see Figure 3.2). However, the activities in Step 1 are data-processing staff activities instead of end-user activities; the entities described in Step 2 of the process are entities in the data-processing environment, instead of entities in the end-user's environment; and the relationships of Step 3 are relationships between data-processing entities instead of end-user entities.

Consistent with the terminology using the prefix *meta,* we distinguish between the entities of the data-processing environment and the end-user's world by adding the meta prefix for data-processing environment entities. Thus, the procedure for designing the conceptual representation of metadatabase for a DD/DS would be as follows:

1. Identify the meta-entities.
2. Define the meta-entities.
3. Identify and describe the meta-entity relationships.

The conceptual metadatabase design represents the foundation of DD/DS design process. Functional use of the DD/DS is now described in terms of the metadatabase design. Input procedures, output specifications, and metadata generation requirements are all fully dependent upon and described in terms of the conceptual metadatabase design.

CONCEPTUAL DESIGN OF THE METADATABASE

As with the conceptual database design for any information system, the metadatabase conceptual design provides the flexible, but nevertheless firm foundation for subsequent design specification.

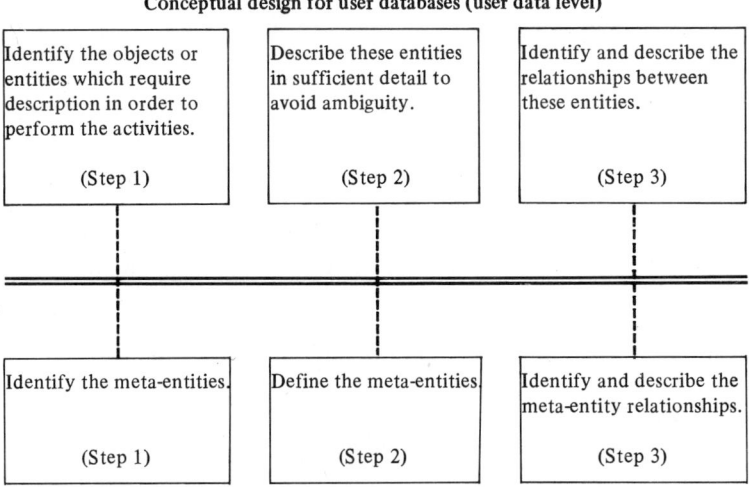

Figure 3.2 Conceptual design for user databases and metadatabases.

3.1.3 Input/Output and Generation Facilities Design

The design of the entire Data Dictionary/Directory System is driven by the design of the metadatabase. It is not surprising, therefore that the input/output (I/O) facilities design, and the metadata generation capabilities are functionally dependent on the design of the metadatabase. In fact, the features of the I/O facilities may vary from very simplistic to very sophisticated. A new feature can be added as needed, depending on the characteristics of the metadatabase; and conversely, the contents of the metadatabase can limit the features that are functionally feasible to implement. For example, if the meta entity structure for the metadatabase includes data communications aspects, then DD/DS functions, such as I/O facilities and metadata generation features should be able to support the data communications environment.

3.2 CONCEPTUAL DESIGN OF THE METADATABASE

There are three steps in creating the conceptual design of the metadatabase (see Figure 3.2):

Identification of the meta-entities.
Definition of the meta-entities.
Identification and description of the meta-entity relationships.

Meta-entities represent objects that exist in the data processing or the database environment. Examples of meta-entities are data element, file, program, user, and terminal.

There are three basic categories of meta-entities: Metadata entities, metasystem entities, and meta-environment entities.* Meta-entities which represent data objects, such as data element, record, file, transaction, database, and report, are referred to as *metadata entities*. Meta entities which represent processes and components which exist as part of the data processing environment, such as system, program, module, and function, are called *metasystem entities*. Meta entities which represent objects or entities connected with the physical environment, such as terminal, user, hardware, and node, are called *meta-environment entities*. Each of these classes of meta-entities is discussed in greater detail in Chapter 4. For the purpose of brevity and convenience, we shall drop the prefix "meta" and refer simply to data, system, and environment entities, unless the context requires specific use of the prefix "meta."

3.2.1 Metadata Entities

Metadata entities represent data objects in the data processing environment which require description in order to perform a specific data processing function. Figure 3.3 illustrates the five most common metadata entities which often appear in physical representation and require description in order to carry out data processing activities. Other data entities used to describe logical views include, but are not limited to: transaction, report, form, screen, and subschema. For example, to be able to design and code a program one must define data elements, groups, records, and files. The fact that data elements are contained in groups, groups are contained in records, and records are contained in files is represented by using the data structure diagramming technique of using an arrow (→) to denote a one-to-many (1:n) relationship (see Chapter 2, section 2.3). For example, the fact that a group may contain more than one data element is represented by an arrow (→) which connects the record and the data element in Figure 3.3.

Which data processing function requires the description of the data

---

*Note: Another approach to categorizing entity types allows only two categories of meta entities: data and system. Under this classification, the only entities that qualify as data entities are those which are in some way related to a database. Everything else falls in the metasystem category. In this book, we use the three-category approach.

CONCEPTUAL DESIGN OF THE METADATABASE

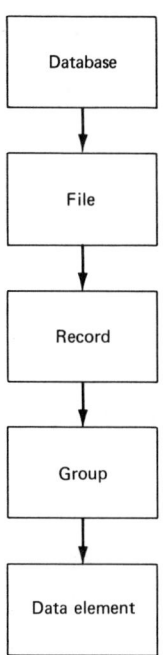

Figure 3.3 Hierarchical entity structure diagram for metadata entities (no data independence).

entity "database"? If there are no databases in the data processing environment, then one would suppose that this data entity would not be required. If the enterprise is involved in building or using databases then this data entity is extremely important. Later in this section, we will see other aspects of conceptual metadatabase design which are unique to the database environment. For the moment, we recognize that even without the use of databases there are important requirements for metadata entities and a supporting DD/DS.

Currently, we recognize the need to describe data objects. However, this does not provide a complete picture or model of the data processing environment (with or without databases). In order to describe sufficiently how data is used, it is necessary to identify and describe system entities.

3.2.2 Metasystem Entities

Metasystem entities represent objects in the data processing environment. These objects are usually the components that make up the structure, "system". Example of system entities are program, module, subroutine, and system.

One of the most important system entities is program. The description of this entity is necessary in order to support systems development and maintenance activities. Information about who wrote the program, the language it is written in, and the number of changes applied to it are some of the metadata that can be collected about this entity.

System entities cannot exist in a vacuum. In order to be meaningful, they must be described in terms of the environment under which they operate. These are part of the environment entities.

3.2.3 Meta-Environment Entities

This type of meta-entity represents objects that make up the data processing or database environment. Examples of environment entities are user, communication lines, terminal, hardware components, office, and organization.

Environment entities are particularly useful when describing information flow through the enterprise, or when modeling a business function. For this latter application, it is very important to be able to describe the entity "user" that performs a given "function." Such attributes as responsibility, authority, originator, and recipient are examples of information that might be collected about the environment entity "user." Each of these objects can be described. The issue is, however, whether each one of these objects requires description in order to perform data processing activities. In recent years, designers and surveyors of commercial Data Dictionary/Directory Systems (DD/DSs) have recognized that providing the functional capability to describe more objects by supplying more system and environment entities in the metadatabase allows DD/DS users greater flexibility and greater support for modeling the data processing environment using the DD/DS. When the metadatabase design contains relatively few system entities it can be difficult to do more than just concentrate on the description of data entities. This deficiency can be somewhat mitigated by including in the description of the data entities, references to the identity of the system entity of importance.

For example, suppose that our DD/DS cannot describe programs. However, the data entity record can be described by listing names of the programs which use the record in question. Then by searching the DD/DS for a specific program name and "inverting" the list, one could obtain a list of all records used by a given program. This will provide a description of a program from the point of view of the records that the program accesses, rather than providing metadata about the program itself.

3.2.4 Representing Physical/Logical Views

A particularly challenging aspect of metadatabase design is the requirement to represent in the DD/DS multiple logical views of the same physical representation.

CONCEPTUAL DESIGN OF THE METADATABASE

Creating and maintaining many diverse logical views serviced by a single physical representation is the essence of the database approach [DATE 81]. This concept, separating the usage of data (the logical view) from its physical representation (the physical view) is the basic idea of data independence. In its report, the ANSI/SPARC/Database Study Group on Database Management Systems referred to these views as the "internal" (i.e., physical), and "conceptual" (i.e., the composite logical) schema [TSIC 77]. We have chosen not to follow the ANSI/SPARC terminology.

When the DD/DS is used to describe a database with data independence characteristics it is necessary to have more than one description of each data entity. Each data entity has several logical views and one physical view. For example, a record may take logical and physical characteristics. A record's logical characteristics may, in fact, differ from its physical counterpart. Such difference might include the sequence of data elements within the record, the existence of blank fields, the presence of an edit mask, and physical format representation (e.g., binary versus packed decimal) might differ at the data element level.

The need to support physical/logical aspects of data entities in order to support data independence characteristics is accomplished by utilizing the relationships between the metadata entities. These are discussed in the following section.

3.2.5 Meta-Entity Data Structure

The final step in the procedure to create a conceptual metadatabase design is to identify the meta-entity relationships and thereby construct a meta-entity structure diagram for the metadatabase [BCS 77]. The relationships between meta entities determine the meta entity structure of the metadatabase. First, we discuss the relationships between data entities; then we will expand the discussion to include relationships between data entities, system entities, and environment entities.

Figure 3.3 illustrated a hierarchical meta-entity structure which represents the following relationships:

Databases contain *files*.
Files contain *records*.
Records contain *groups*.
Groups contain *data elements*.

The hierarchical representation of relationships between metadata entities precludes the ability to describe more than one logical view of the data entity. Furthermore, the logical view described must be precisely equal to the physical representation. Thus the hierarchy shown in

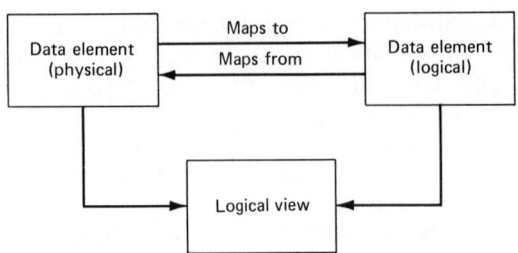

Figure 3.4 Basic network relationship required for describing data-independent metadatabases (data element level).

Figure 3.3 is useful only in an environment where there is no data independence.

With the introduction of data independence comes the requirement to describe many different logical views, to map these logical views to *and* from a single representation. This requires the use of many-to-many (m:n) relationships and introduces the use of the network data structure into the meta entity structure.

Consider the simplest data entity, the data element (see Figure 3.4). A data element in its logical view may be derived (mapped) from many data elements. For example, the data element "average daily balance" is derived by applying an algorithm which uses the values of many other data elements (daily balances). On the other hand, the physical representation of most data elements in the database would be used to realize or generate (map to) specific data element logical views. For example, the physical representation of "average daily balance" might be used to realize data elements in many different logical views used to generate customer statements, calculate interest charges, or simply satisfy inquiries.

Similarly, the same many-to-many relationship exists between logical records and physical records (see Figure 3.5).

It is important to recognize that the logical and physical metadata entities are connected in the real world by a logical view (see Figures 3.4 and 3.5). A specific occurrence of a logical record and a physical

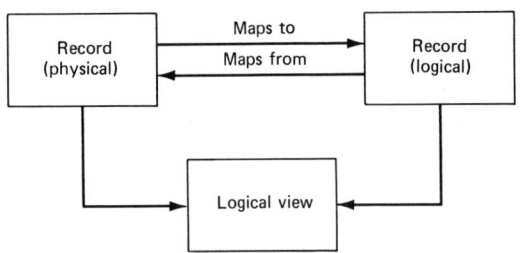

Figure 3.5 Basic network relationship required for describing data-independent metadatabases (record level).

CONCEPTUAL DESIGN OF THE METADATABASE

record are "connected" because the two are "contained in" the same logical view. Figure 3.6 illustrates how the physical records stored on a customer database are connected to the logical records in the DBMS system buffers, because they are required to produce a logical view for the program buffer of an application program.

This specific example holds true for all logical to physical mapping relationships. The same holds true for transactions, reports, screens and so forth. Furthermore, it clearly illustrates the need to utilize network structures in representing the metadata entity structures for a database environment with a significant level of data independence.

The meta-entity structure diagram must be expanded to include the system entities identified as being required because they represent objects which require description in the data processing environment. Typically, relationships among system entities and between data and system entities require network structure for their representation. That is to say, they also involve m:n relationships.

Among the most common of these relationships is the m:n relationship between program and data element. A program may utilize many data elements; whereas, a data element may be used in many different programs. This many-to-many relationship is necessary to perform basic data processing activities. Thus, it must be included in the meta-entity structure diagram.

Another common relationship in meta entity structure diagrams is the recursive relationship. This type of relationship is drawn in Figure

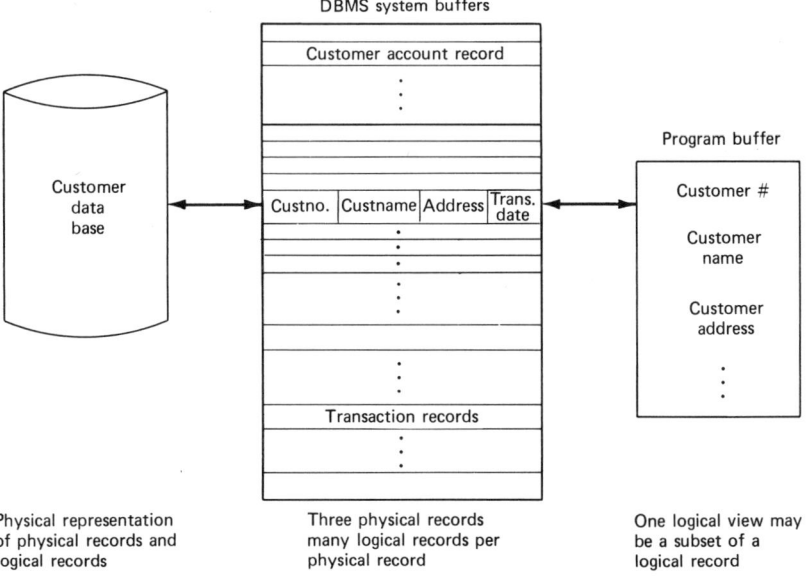

Figure 3.6 A logical view connects logical/physical records.

72   FOUNDATIONS FOR DESIGN OF THE DATA DICTIONARY/DIRECTORY SYSTEM

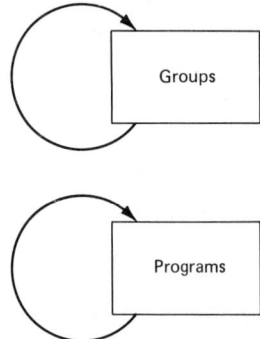

Figure 3.7   Recursive entity structure for metadata.

3.7 for the group data entity and the program system entity. The recursive relationship is necessary when the meta entity can be comprised of itself, or participates in a relationship with itself. For example, groups can contain other groups. Programs can contain other programs. When this type of relationship is important in the architecture of systems, then it should be included in the metadatabase design. Most commercial DD/DSs provide this capability for at least one data entity and one system entity in the meta-entity structure for their respective metadatabases.

The overall perspective provided by the ability to use meta-entity relationships to model a data processing environment cannot be overestimated. Relationships are an important concept for the DD/DS user. For example, they enable the DBA to implement such functions as "change/effect" analysis, in which the DD/DS is asked to determine what would be the impact on the entire environment, if an entity or its attributes were changed. The basic DBA goal of broad-based coordination and control is provided by this ability to model the data processing environment of the real world.

In Figure 3.8, a sample meta-entity structure is shown, which represents a network meta-entity data structure diagram. This diagram represents the conceptual metadatabase design of DATAMANAGER, a product of MSP, Inc. The entities represented in this data structure diagram are of two types: data and system entities. The recursive entity, system, is made up of other systems and programs. This in turn is made of modules and files.

Files are collections of groups (which may in itself be composed of other groups) and items. Databases are made up of files and other databases. A group is a recursive entity which is a collection of items, and can contain other groups, and finally, the data items which is the smallest definable unit. Taken together, this meta-entity structure represents the DD/DS metadatabase at the conceptual level.

Note that the entity database in the DATAMANAGER meta-entity structure is recursive and is connected to files with a dashed line. This

SUMMARY

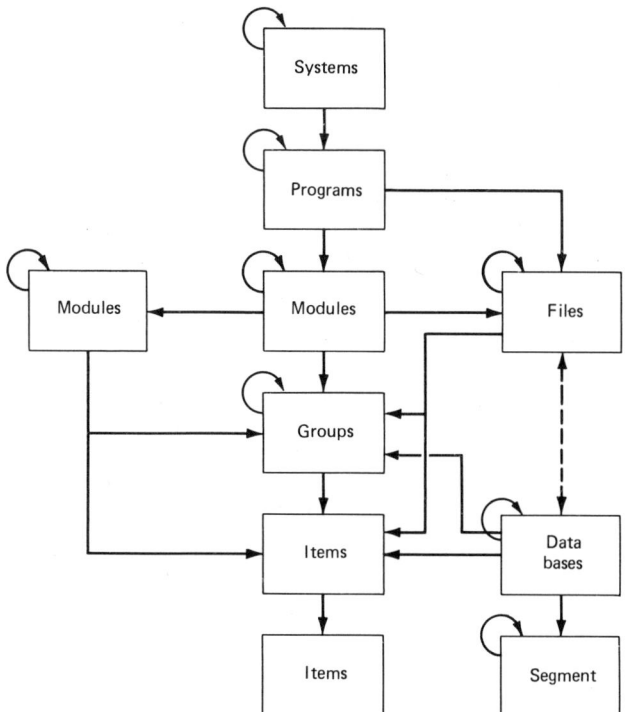

Figure 3.8 Sample meta-entity structure diagram (DATAMANAGER) [MSP 78]. Used by permission of MSP, Inc.

connotes the use of the recursive relationship, in its most general form, to establish DBMS specific metadata entity structures. This is then connected onto the conventional meta-entity structure through the file entity, which is the physical common denominator between DBMSs and conventional file systems.

3.3 SUMMARY

This chapter has shown that the design philosophy for a DD/DS should be based on the database approach. The DD/DS is an information system about the organization's metadata, and the objectives of the DD/DS design are to provide a logically integrated metadatabase which can be shared among various levels of user groups.

In designing a DD/DS it is necessary to consider the metadata, the metasystem and meta-environment entities. The design process for the DD/DS should follow the same methods and procedures as other database-supported application systems, starting with a conceptual model.

In this chapter, the design philosophy and the conceptual metadatabase design for the DD/DS were discussed, as a foundation for Chapters 4 and 5, which will deal with more specific aspects of a DD/DS design.

REFERENCES

[ASTR 72] Astrahan, M. M., E. B. Altman, P. L. Fehder, and M. E. Senko, "Concepts of a Data Independent Accessing Model," in *Proc. 1972 ACM SIGFIDET Workshop,* September 1972, pp. 349-362.

[BCS 77] "The British Computer Society Data Dictionary Systems Working Party Report," in *Data Base,* Vol. 9, No. 2, Fall 1977, and *Sigmod Record,* Vol. 9, No. 4, December 1977.

[DATE 81] Date, C. J. *An Introduction to Database Systems,* 3rd ed., Addison-Wesley, Reading MA, 1981.

[MSP 78] MSP, Inc., *DATAMANAGER Fact Book,* Management Systems and Programming Limited, Lexington, MA, 1978.

[TSIC 77] Tsichritzis, D. and A. Klug, Eds., *The ANSI/X3/SPARC DMBS Framework Report of the Study Group on Database Management Systems,* AFIPS Press, NJ, 1977.

4

Meta-Entities and Attributes

The most important aspect in the design of a Data Dictionary/Directory System is the design of the metadatabase. In the preceding chapters, it was established that the design of a metadatabase drives the design of the entire DD/DS. An important aspect of the metadatabase design is to determine and analyze the needs of the DD/DS users. These were extensively discussed in Chapter 2. At first, the formulation of these needs may be conceptual in nature. As they are refined, they are expressed in a "common" language, using appropriate building blocks: meta-entities, and their attributes.

Chapter 3 discussed the concept of metadatabase design and the notion of meta-entities. This chapter provides additional insight into meta-entities and attributes, the essential components in the design of an information structure. Each meta-entity describes a component of the information structure in the data environment, therefore, it is critical to establish a "common" frame of reference.

Unfortunately, at present, there is no uniformity in the nomenclature used for these building blocks. Indeed, this confusing situation is exacerbated by using the same words in referring to different concepts. For example, the term *record* has different meanings in different situations, and for different DD/DS packages. Even more common are the cases when different terms are used to refer to the same concept.

In this chapter, a set of generic terminologies are defined for the meta-entities and their attributes. This is done so that commonality can be established for future discussions, not to suggest that the generic terminology introduced should be universally accepted. Where possible we have chosen the most common nomenclature in use.

4.1 META-ENTITY

A *meta-entity* represents objects that exist in the data processing and/or data base environment, for example, file, program, and user. Meta-entities are the basic building blocks of the metadatabase design (see Figure 4.1). This section discusses the various types of meta-entities, especially those found in commercial DD/DSs.

4.1.1 Nonstandard Nomenclature

Nomenclature among commercial DD/DSs is varied and causes confusion. This problem extends even into the use of the term *meta-entity* to describe the "building block" concept of the DD/DS metadatabase. Of the commercial DD/DS packages, only DATA CATALOGUE 2, Cullinane's Integrated Data Dictionary (IDD), and INTEL's Integrated Data Dictionary utilize the term *entity*. Other terms used to refer to the concept of a meta-entity in commercially available DD/DS packages are listed below:

Commercial Package	Term for Meta-Entity
DATAMANAGER	Member type
DB/DC Data Dictionary	Subject category
LEXICON	Item
ADABAS Dictionary	Entry
UCC-10	Element
Data Control System	Category

From this partial list alone, one can see the difficulty arising from diverse terminology. Notice, for example, that two DD/DSs (LEXICON and UCC-10) have opted for terms (Item and Element, respectively) which are typically used to refer to specific metadata entities.

As can be expected, the choice of meta-entities differs from one DD/DS to another. Some differ superficially, that is, only in name, others differ in the depth and breadth of the information structure they provide. The set of meta-entities varies from DD/DS package to package, according to the structure, the scope, and the intent of each vendor and each DD/DS. Some have more entities than others. Most DD/DS packages have adequate meta-entities for describing the data objects of the processing environment. Much of the variance among the vendor-supplied software is in the meta-entities used to describe system objects and physical aspects of the environment. Another important difference is the ability to use a set of meta-entities for conventional metadata descriptions, as well as for DBMS-oriented metadata descriptions.

Commercial Systems Meta-Entities	ADABAS Data Dictionary (Software ag)	DATA CATALOGUE 2 (TSI)	DATACOM/DATA DICTIONARY (ADR)	Data Control System (CINCOM)	Data Control System (Haverly)	Data Dictionary System (ICL)	DATAMANAGER (MSP)	DB/DC Data Dictionary System (IBM)	EDICT (INFODATA)	Integrated Data Dictionary (Cullinane)	Integrated Data Dictionary (INTEL)	LEXICON (Arthur Andersen & Co.)	PRIDE/Logik (M. Bryce Assoc.)	Self-Generating Data Dictionary (Haverly)	TIS (CINCOM)	UCC-10 (UCC)	UNIVAC Data Dictionary (UNIVAC)
Elements	Fields	Elements, items	Elements, fields	Elements	Data item, field	Item	Items	Data items, fields, group I	Elements	Elements	Items	Element	Element	Standard elements, Local elements, fields	External field, physical field	Element, field	Data item
Groups	Group fields	Groups		Elements		Group	Group			Elements	Structure	Group, subgroup			Physical field	Dataset, group	Group
Records		Record, set, segment	Record	Element	Record	Record, record group	Segment	Records, segments		Record	File record, subschema record, schema record	Segment	Record	Standard record, local record	Internal Record, Logical view	Segment	Record
File	File	File, area, dataset	File	File	Areas, file	File, vfile	File			File	File	File	File	Standard file, local file	File		Area/file
Database	Database	Database, Schema	Database	Database	Schema	Schema, subschema	Database	DL/I database, Non-DL/I database	Databases	schema, subschema, DMCL	Databases	Databases, sensitivity			Schema	Database	Schema/database
Module	Module	Module	Module		Module	Module	Module	Modules		Modules	Subprogram		Module		Module	Module	Module
Program	Program	Task	Program	Program	Program	Program, extract program	Program	Program		Program	Program	Program, validator	Procedure/ Program (operation)	Program	Procedure (program)	Program	Run-unit
System	System	System	System, job	System	System/ subsystem	System	System	Application system		System	Work unit	System	System/ subsystem			Application	Runstream
Report	Report	Report	Report	Report, source document	Report	Report program				Report	Report		Output	Report	Procedure		
Transaction		Task		Transaction				Transactions		Transactions	Process, transactions	Entry				Transaction, queue	
Physical devices										Physical terminal, line						Logicality	
Users	Users/ owners	User	Person	User		User, end-user end-user view	Users owners	Dictionary users	Elements	Users	Users		Entity			User	DBA analyst application

Figure 4.2 Meta-entities.

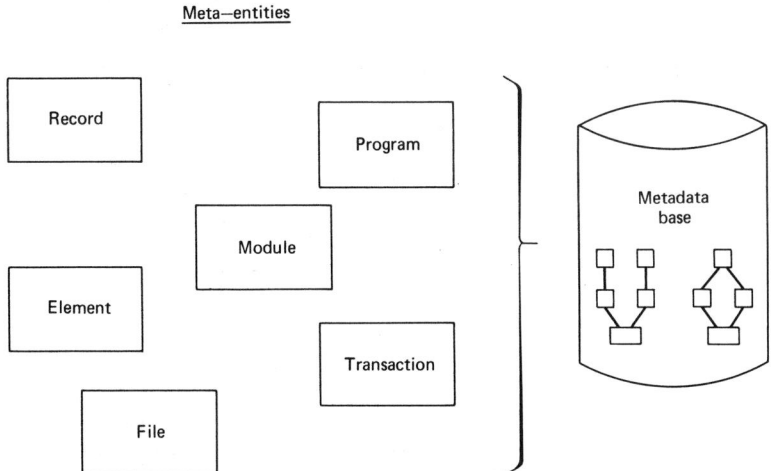

Figure 4.1 Meta-entities are the building blocks for metadatabase design.

Nevertheless, there is at least one entity that recurs in each system: the element, albeit not always with the same name.

Because of the diversity in the names used for these meta-entities, Figure 4.2 presents a matrix of representative meta-entities. This matrix can serve as a useful reference guide when looking at the nomenclature used by the various commercial systems. Figure 4.2 does not present a comprehensive list of meta-entities supported by each of the commercial DD/DS packages, just a comparison of nomenclature for those meta-entities discussed in this chapter.

4.1.2 Classification of Meta Entities

As discussed in Chapter 3, meta-entities can be generally classified into three groups: data entities, system or processing entities, and environment entities (see Figure 4.3).

Data entities are used to describe or represent objects or entities which are units or aggregates of data, for example, data elements, records, databases, files, and reports.

System or processing entities are used to describe or represent objects or entities that are processes, systems, or components thereof, such as programs, modules, and systems.

Environment entities are used to describe or represent objects or entities which are connected with the physical environment, for example, terminals, nodes, and users.

Data Entities	System/Processing Entities	Environment Entities
Element	System	Physical devices
Record	Subsystem	Computer system
Group	Program	Terminal
File	Module	Line
Database	Transaction	Users
Screen		Node
Report		Function
Subschema		Organization

Figure 4.3 Three groups of meta-entities.

At this point, it is useful to note that if a DD/DS is predominantly concerned with large numbers of system and environment meta-entities, it evolves into a system-wide dictionary. Conversely, when a DD/DS is only concerned with data entities, and specifically with data elements, it becomes a Data Element Dictionary (DED).

The following paragraphs describe some of the more commonly found meta-entities.

4.1.2.1 Data Entities

Element is the most basic and elementary discrete unit of data that can be identified and described in the DD/DS. This entity cannot be further subdivided. But it can be recursive. It can be used also for aggregation to form other entities such as group, or record. For example, "social security number" is a data element.

Group is an aggregate metadata entity, composed of data elements and/or other groups. When group contains other groups, the recursive feature is required. An example of a group is "address," which is made up of these elements: "street address," "city," "state," and "postal code."

Record is an aggregation of one or more related data elements or groups that is treated as a unit. As an illustration of the varying use of terms, where IMS is concerned the term segment is used in place of record, but the two concepts are very similar. An example of a record is "employee record," consisting of an aggregate of these data elements: employee name, SSN, employee age, and employee address.

File is a set of related occurrences of data elements, groups, and records, which is treated as a unit. A file may contain occurrences of different types of records, and it may contain many occurrences of records of the same type depending upon the specific DD/DS implementation. A file may be a component of a conventional data processing system or a physical component of a DBMS storage structure. For example, "employee file" could consist of "employee personnel record", "employee work record".

Database is a collection of DBMS files, records, groups and elements. The description of a database varies from one DD/DS to another depending on the constituent basic units. Databases are usually described when the use of a DBMS, or relationship to a DBMS, is possible. Usually, the database entity includes the schema of the DBMS.

Report is a formatted presentation of information — usually output from a module, a program, a system, or a DBMS. It should be noted that a variation of the report entity could be used to represent "soft" output, that is screens. Example: employee history report. Report is an example of a logical view entity.

4.1.2.2 Processing Entities

Module is a subset of statements of a computer program which are internal or external to the program, and which performs a discrete task within a program. When modules can be nested to several levels, a recursive structure is required. An example of a module is the "ascending sort" module.

Program is a set of statements that specify action(s) in a programming language. It may be an aggregation of one or more modules that performs one or more functions. For example, a "print salary" program may consist of three modules: "sort", "print salary", and "heading format" modules.

System is a collection of related programs, and/or modules, and/or other systems which collectively perform a set of functions in its entirety. System is at the highest level of the processing entity types. It can be described in terms of processes, programs, modules, databases, files, records, and elements; for example, the Demand Deposit Account System.

Transaction is a discrete event-oriented activity that can be accomplished with or without the aid of the computer. This entity can be used to indicate a manual task, or an online transaction.

4.1.2.3 Environment Entities

Physical device is an entity with sufficient generality that it can be used to describe such facilities as a CRT terminal, a teletype device, a printer, or an intelligent terminal.

User is an entity which represents a person, a department, or a functional group that is involved with an information system, and can be identified to the DD/DS. Users can be identified in terms of the functions they perform, their responsibility with respect to a given system, and their authority; for example, the DBA, the system analyst. Some DD/DS's use this entity as part of the access control mechanism.

4.1.2.4 Expansibility Entities

In addition to the three broad categories of meta-entities – data, system or process and environment – some DD/DSs have added a fourth category of entity, *the ad-hoc expansibility entity,* can be thought of as a *user-defined* entity that allows DD/DS users (DBAs) to define entities other than those provided by the particular DD/DS package. This class of entity will be discussed at greater length in a later section, in connection with the expansibility capability.

4.1.2.5 Other Entities

Some of the entities that are not discussed here, but appear in some of the DD/DSs mentioned are: form, keys, fields, schema, subschema, job, source and destination, queue, datasets, tuples, areas, etc. In each case, these entities are explained in the respective reference manual for the individual system.

Thus, the meta-entities defined in this section are not exhaustive, but they do represent the more commonly used ones. As can be seen, the names used for the same concept may vary from system to system. Furthermore, each system has a number of other entities which are peculiar to the individual system, in order to accommodate a specific feature or a certain DBMS data structure.

An interesting point arises with the schema/subschema meta-entities. While no doubt these are data objects in the database environment, by declaring them as meta-entities, another level of abstraction is established. This is because, unlike other meta-entities (e.g., data element), the schema/subschema contain metadata in their real world occurrences.

4.2 ATTRIBUTES

The next crucial building block in the design of a metadatabase is the *attribute*. Attributes are used in describing characteristics and "properties" of the meta entities (See Figure 4.4). In this respect, attributes are to meta-entities as adjectives are to nouns.

Like the meta-entities, there are various kinds of attributes. Some should be common to all types of entities, for example, name, and ID, (which can be used as alternate access keys in the DD/DS, and should not be confused with entities). Some are inherent to only one of the

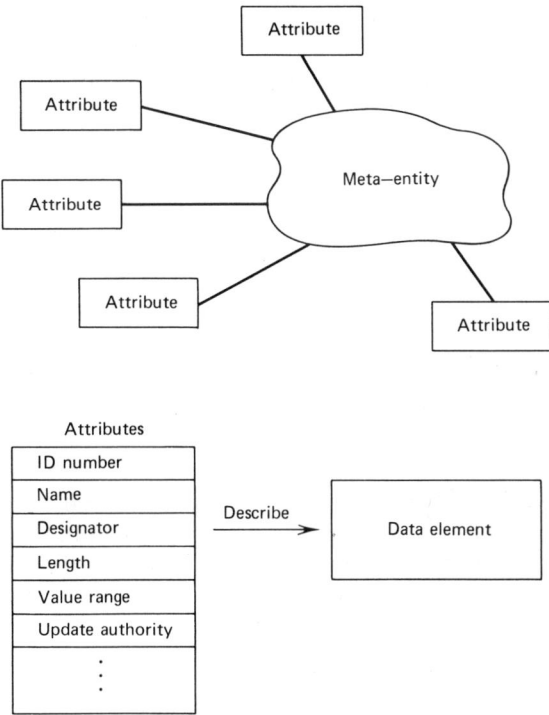

Figure 4.4 Attributes describe meta-entities.

meta-entity types. For example, *programming language* is applicable only to the system entity *program*. Attributes can be generically grouped into the following categories:

1. Identification
2. Representation
3. Relationship
4. Statistical
5. Control
6. Physical
7. User-defined

Each category of attributes provides a particular kind of information about a meta-entity. In the following paragraphs, each category of attributes will be described with specific examples, followed by a selection of attributes for data entities, system entities, and physical entities.

4.2.1 Identification Attributes

These are used to name, designate, describe and/or identify an entity. An entity may be known by more than one identifier or name at different times, places, and under different circumstances. The identification attributes include:

Name is the unique name of the entity, as it is known in the DD/DS.

Synonym is an identifier, a code, or another name that can be used to substitute for the DD/DS entity name. This can be the name by which other entities know the entity. Typically, synonyms refer to user oriented substitute names.

Alias is an identifier, a code, or other name that can be substituted. Typically an ALIAS is used for system oriented alternate names. Alias is used when all other characteristics of an entity are the same.

Programming Language Name is the name for an entity as it is used in a program. Often, language syntax restricts the number of characters permissible in a name, which makes it necessary to have different names for the same data element when the data element is used in different programs. An example of this is COBOL Name and FORTRAN Name.

Description is the attribute used to describe carefully and succinctly the entity, using natural language text. Usually in free form, the description may be used to tell what the entity is, why it needs to be described, special characteristics, and restrictions on its use not described elsewhere in the DD/DS.

4.2.2 Representation Attributes

These are used to describe the characteristics of an entity as they are implemented in the environment. For example, a data element is represented in terms of the following characteristics:

Character type describes the type of characters used in representing the content of the data element, such as alphanumeric.

Source describes the source of the element, such as computed element from program x.

Length describes the size of the element.

The way a program is implemented can be described with the following attributes:

Programming Language indicates the programming language in which the program being described is written.

ATTRIBUTES

Program Size describes the size of the program in terms of lines of code.

Processing Type indicates whether it is batch program or online.

Parameters describes the number and types of parameters required.

4.2.3 Relationship Attributes

These are used to denote connections or links between two meta-entientities, as in the case of usage of one entity by another. Examples of relationship attributes are:

Keyword indicates that two or more meta-entities possess a descriptive word which can be identified as a keyword for analysis and reporting purposes.

Link is used to describe a linkage path between one meta-entity occurrence and another in terms of system architecture.

Usage explains how one entity is used by another entity.

Calls refers to the subroutines or utilities the program or system calls.

Access Path describes the allowable retrieval path for data structure between meta-entities.

Set describes relationship between two types of records (in CODASYL terms).

Mappings indicates the relationship between a data entity and a processing entity.

It is very important to recognize that this category of attributes can be used to describe the concept of meta-entity structure. The reader is referred to the discussion in Chapter 3 on metadatabase design and meta-entity structure diagrams.

There are two approaches to metadatabase design regarding relationships. One approach states that relationships can have attributes, and therefore can be treated as an entity class. The second approach subscribes to the idea that relationship is just another category of attributes. This book adopts the latter approach. The rationale being that, should the need arise for a particular relationship to have attribute, then an entity type can be created (bearing the name of the relationship), using the expansibility facility.

4.2.4 Statistical Attributes

Statistical attributes indicate how the meta-entity is used in the overall system or environment, including frequency of usage.

Frequency indicates the average frequency that the entity is accessed, such as daily, weekly, and/or annually.

Response refers to the response time of the processing entity — this is primarily pertinent to System/Processing entity.

Log Information shows statistics on when an entity is accessed, by whom, and the activity that is performed.

Usage Statistics records summary of usage. This information may be obtained from an operating system or a performance monitor.

Performance Statistics records information about the performance of a processing entity. Information may be obtained from the operating system or a performance monitor.

Estimated Life indicates the volatility of an entity, such as how stable the entity is, and whether it will be changing dynamically.

Statistical attributes are particularly well suited for implementing the concept of a dynamically updated DD/DS. Statistical attributes could be updated in the future by the system's performance monitor and immediately reflect changes in usage patterns and response time (see 12.2.3).

4.2.5 Control Attributes

These attributes include information about the "flow" of the entity (for data entities), ownership information, security information, access control information, entity status information, and user-related information. Among these are:

Authority is used to describe the level of authority of a user to the DD/DS, for example, update is restricted to the data administrator.

Password records the password code associated with the level of authority of a user.

Owned By describes ownership of entity, indicating restrictive use of that entity to owner.

Status describes the operational status of the entity, such as test, operational, or archival status. The status attribute could be implemented in a sophisticated manner. For example, each of the associated statuses has a restrictive clause which indicates the types of allowable processing to various levels of authority: a *test* status indicates that the entity can be updated or detailed subject to the appropriate level of authority; an *operational* status indicates that the entity can be modified only with approval and knowledge of certain levels (usually higher than for test status) of authority; and an *archival* status indicates it is a "read-only" entity. In addition, status might have user-defined characteristics.

ATTRIBUTES

Version is a variation of the concept of status. For example, a program running at version 2 may have been changed twice, and if necessary it can be traced back to the original version.

Security Level indicates the level of security at the entity level. For example, an element may be defined as having a security level of *classified* which is intended inhibit usage of any user with authority level below that of, say, a data administrator.

Data Flow describes the point of origin and the point of destination of a data entity. For example, the data element *employee name* originates from Form SF-171, and will flow to the *employee information* database.

Edit and Validation Criteria are used to specify the restrictions and constraints in terms of allowable values that an entity can take on at the occurrence level. This attribute is implemented most commonly at the data element level and includes such items as range, uniqueness checking, permissible values, and the like.

4.2.6 Physical Attributes

These are used to describe physical characteristics of the entities or requirements for the entities. They are particularly applicable to system and environment entities, though not exclusively so. These include:

Storage Media records information about the storage media for the Data and System/Processing entities, for example, DISK.

Storage Size describes the computer space requirements for the Data and System/Processing entity, for example, 64 K-bytes.

CPU describes the central processing unit name and size required to operate the processing entity, for example UNIVAC 1108.

Terminals describe the kind of terminals the processing entity requires, for example, CRT, IBM-3270.

Operating System describes the version and level of the operating system necessary to support the processing entities, for example UNIX.

4.2.7 User-Defined Attributes

User-defined attributes allow the users to add new attributes that are not provided by the DD/DS package, in order to expand the description of a meta-entity. In this respect, this attribute goes hand-in-hand with the user-defined expansibility entity, since they both serve to extend the capabilities provided by the system.

Also in the user-defined category of attributes is the free-form attribute. This attribute is intentionally left blank, or undefined by the vendors, in the definition of its format to allow the user to define how this blank space should be used.

4.2.8 Using Attributes Across Entities

Of course, within each category, attributes are different for data, system, or environment entities, since individual entity types have different characteristics and properties. Further, individual packages tailor their attributes to fit their own descriptive needs, especially in the cases involving DBMS support. Nevertheless, in most cases, the vendor-tailored attributes will fit into one of the above seven categories.

There are some attributes that are common to all entity types, for example, ID, name, keyword, description, version, and status. It is very important not to confuse the commonality of these attributes across entities with the concept of the entity itself. Some authors [ROSS 81] have classified these attributes as entities and established relationships to all other entities. This approach reflects confusion with two ideas: one of usage, that is, the idea of access key to the metadatabase; with the idea of description, that is, the concept of an entity being described in the metadatabase.

Figure 4.5 shows a sample of attribute commonality and variance within each category of attributes. A representative of each of the three meta-entity categories is shown in the matrix, with the seven categories of attributes.

4.3 THE EXPANSIBILITY CONCEPT FOR THE METADATABASE

Expansibility, also known as *extensibility,* is the capability that allows a user to *expand* the vendor-standard meta-entity structure, to suit specific enterprise needs. When fully implemented, this powerful capability allows the user to add new meta-entities and new attributes to the dictionary structure. These new meta-entities and attributes are in addition to that which the vendor provides as conventional facilities. Sections 4.1.2.4 and 4.2.7 briefly discussed entity expansibility and attribute expansibility, respectively.

The expansibility capability enhances the power and the flexibility of a DD/DS as an effective tool for managing metadata. If a DD/DS has this facility, it could potentially provide a three-dimensional enhancement to the dictionary, because the user can add new meta-entities, enhance the description of an existing (or new) entity with new attributes, and establish new relationships between the new entity and existing entities, between existing entities, or between new entities. An example of this is Cullinane's IDDs User-Defined Entity Type, User-Defined Relationship, User-Defined Comments, Class, and Attributes.

	Entities		
Category of Attributes	(Data) Element	(Process or System) Program	(Environment) User
Identification	Name ID Description Synonym COBOL-Name Alias	Name ID Description	Name ID Description of position
Representation	Character type Source type Length Picture clause Format Justification Content type Initial type	Programming language Number of parameters Segmentation Type of code	Function code
Statistical	Freq. of access Access type Volatility Volatility	Performance status Log information Access type Processing type Overlay indicator	Usage code (read only, update, etc.)
Relationship	Keywords Occurs in Indexed Used in Appears in Relationship	Keywords Calls subroutine	Creator User Modifier Maintainer Related person
Control	Password Encryption Version Status Origin Destination Value range	Password Encryption Version Status	Responsibility code Level of security Authority
Physical	Storage media	Storage location Storage media Storage size Compiler Expected CPU time CPU Procedure Required peripherals	Department Contact-phone Mail address
User-defined	User-defined	User-defined	User-defined

Figure 4.5 Sample entities/attributes matrix.

Some DD/DSs have provided a specific meta-entity for their entity expansibility feature, while other DD/DSs have implemented a "generic" mechanism, or function, to allow the user to add new entities and attributes. Among the DD/DSs that have special entities for expansibility are DATA CATALOGUE 2 with its expansibility meta-entities dictionary, entity, category, and field; which allow the user to create a "custom dictionary"; ICL's Data Dictionary system has the expansibility meta-entities element, property, and construct, which allow the user to define his own dictionary schema, which includes syntax and semantics; Cullinane's IDD has User-Defined Entity Type.

Among those systems that have implemented generic capability are INTEL's IDD, through its XDD; and ADR's Datacom/DD through its User Defined Facility.

The expansibility capability must also include the necessary function to "recognize" the expanded dictionary structure, and to allow processing — that is, adding, deleting, changing, accessing, reporting, and controlling — the new entities and attributes. Without these processing facilities, the entities and attributes added through the expansibility facility would be meaningless.

4.3.1 Adding Entities and Attributes

In the case of existing entities, it is possible to add attributes either by adding free-form attributes, or by establishing new attributes for a given set of entities. This is known as Attribute Type Expansibility. For example, for the entity *report*, it is possible to add a free-form attribute *disposition*, which may be a narrative attribute to explain what to do with a specific *report*; or it may be desirable to add an attribute security code that applies to all data entities, including the report entity.

The DD/DS user may create a new entity to describe a data, a system, or an environment meta-entity hitherto not provided by the system. This is known as Entity Type Expansibility. To create the new entity, one must:

1. Define the meta-entity.
2. Define its relationships to other meta-entities in the metadatabase.
3. Create new attributes that can be used to describe the new entity, or use existing attributes for this purpose.

4.3.2 Guidelines for Using Expansibility

Creating a new meta-entity and adding the consequent attributes is not the same as giving license to invent a whole new set of entities and attributes that bear no resemblance to existing entities and attributes. On the contrary, the new set of entities and attributes should be based

THE EXPANSIBILITY CONCEPT FOR THE METABASE

on the existing ones. For example, a user can create a new processing entity, *source document*, to describe the organization's information flow. Source document may be similar in many respects to the DD/DS-provided meta-entity, *form,* so the attributes created should be patterned after the attributes of the meta-entity form. Continuing this example, the user-defined entity *source document* and the existing one for *form* may have the following attributes:

SOURCE DOCUMENT	FORM
Name	Name
Number	Number
Description	Description
Date	Date
Subject	Subject
Purpose	Purpose
Responsibility	Responsibility
Originator	
Destination	
Used-in	
Disposition	
Security Code	

The expansibility capability is important because it enables the user to describe the processing environment more accurately by being able to add entities not provided by the conventional system facilities. A DD/DS user is therefore not constrained by the idiosyncracies or conventional capabilities of a given system. In effect, this is like giving the user a designer's ability to expand the capabilities of the DD/DS tool. However, this capability should only be used with careful planning and consideration.

In general, there are three basic, common-sense rules that apply to the design of a metadatabase and, therefore, to using the expansibility concept (see Figure 4.6):

> Maintain consistency in the design of the metadatabase.
>
> Maintain a balance in the definition of entities and attributes.
>
> Use clearly defined, unambiguous attributes.

Figure 4.6 Guidelines for entity/attribute design.

1. Maintain consistency in the design of the metadatabase. That is to say, do not use the same attributes to mean different things for different entities, because this leads to confusion, and in the end creates descriptive ambiguity. It is important that the two basic building blocks in the design of the metadatabase (entities and attributes) be consistent and uniform to all extent possible.
2. Maintain a balance in the definition of entities and attributes. Too many entities and not enough details in the description of these entities could be as bad as too few entities and too many attributes for the few that there are.
3. Use clearly defined and unambiguous attributes, thus contributing to the derivation of precise definitions for the metadatabase. In the end this contributes to ease of use.

4.4 SUMMARY

In this chapter, a set of consistent generic terminology has been defined, the various classes of meta entities have been described, and the types or attributes are identified and described. Meta entities and attributes are the two critical, essential components for the design of a metadatabase. A special concept, the *expansibility* concept is described which serves to extend the usefulness of a system by allowing the user to define new meta-entities and consequent attributes, and to add new attributes to existing entities. This is a very important feature, and one that provides added power and flexibility to a DD/DS package.

REFERENCES

[ADDS 78] *ADABAS Data Dictionary System Overview,* Software ag of North America, Inc., Reston, VA, ca. 1978.

[DC2 77] *DATA CATALOGUE 2 Reference Manual,* Synergetics Corp., Bedford, MA, 1977.

[DCS 81] *Data Control System Technical Overview,* CINCOM Systems, Inc., Cincinnati, OH, May 1981.

[DCS 78] *DATA CONTROL SYSTEM 1100 Level 7.0,* Haverly Systems, Inc., Denville, NJ, Oct. 1978.

[DDD 78] *DATACOM/DD Data Dictionary and Directory System Concepts and Facilities* (Release 2), Applied Data Research, Inc., Dallas, TX, Sept. 1978.

[DATA 81] *DATAMANAGER Users Manual,* (Release 4.0) MSP, Inc., Lexington, MA, May 1981.

[DBDC 78] *DB/DC Data Dictionary* (Release 3.0) *General Information Manual,* GH20-9104-1, 3rd Edition, IBM Corp., San Jose, CA, Oct. 1978.

[EDIC 77] *INQUIRE/EDICT: A Manual for Users,* INFODATA Systems, Inc., Falls Church, VA, Aug. 1977.

REFERENCES

[IDDS 78] *ICL Data Dictionary System Reference Manual,* International Computers Limited, Putney, London, Oct. 1978.

[IIDD 80] *Intel's Integrated Data Dictionary Overview,* Intel Systems Corp., Austin, TX, 1980.

[IDDS 79] *Integrated Data Dictionary System* (Release 2.0) *User's Guide,* Cullinane Database Systems, Inc., Westwood, MA, Oct. 1979.

[LEXI 76] *LEXICON User's Manual,* Arthur Andersen & Co., Chicago, IL, 1976.

[LOGI 78] *PRIDE/Logik Data Management Manual,* M. Bryce and Assoc., Inc., Cincinnati, OH, 1978.

[ROSS 81] Ross, R. *Data Dictionary Systems and Data Administration* AMACOM, New York, 1981.

[SGD 79]   *SGD Overview,* Haverly Systems, Inc., Denville, NJ, ca. 1979.

[TIS 79]   *TIS – A Technical Overview,* Publication Number P16-0210-00, CINCOM Systems, Inc., Cincinnati, OH, 1979.

[UCC 77]   *UCC-10,* (Version 2.0) *User's Guide,* University Computing Co., Dallas, TX, Dec. 1977.

5

Input and Output Facilities

The Data Dictionary/Directory System requires means for entering, manipulating, and delivering information regarding its contents. The preceding chapter dealt with the design of the content of the DD/DS, that is, the metadatabase. In this chapter, the input and the output facilities of the DD/DS are discussed.

The input facility is the vehicle for entering metadata into the DD/DS. The components of this facility are: a language that can be used to define the metadata and the means for getting these definitions into the DD/DS. The language used in defining the metadata is generally known as the Data Definition Language (DDL) for the DD/DS. This chapter describes the characteristics of this language, including usability requirements and implementation approaches (e.g., keyword-oriented and preformatted). Tools for populating the DD/DS, that is, for getting the metadata into the system, are explored. Specifically, tools for batch bulk-loading and online individual updates are discussed. Special input features, such as machine-readable input used to facilitate the definition and the population of the metadatabase are also discussed (see Figure 5.1).

A critical point for applying integrity controls on the metadata is the time that the metadata is being entered into the system. This chapter will also address the integrity functions that should be incorporated in the input aspects of the DD/DS, such as edit and validation of DD/DS input, and access control features for the DD/DS.

The value of the DD/DS depends upon the information that can be obtained from it. The second half of this chapter discusses the output facilities of a DD/DS. Every available DD/DS package provides a set of output facilities, and one of the ways in which the power of a DD/DS can be measured is by the robustness and the versatility of its output capabilities. Perhaps one of the most important issues in this regard is

INPUT AND OUTPUT FACILITIES

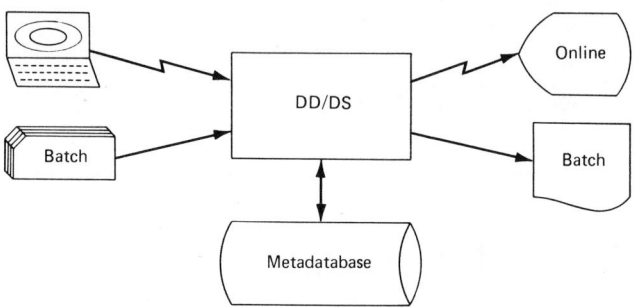

Figure 5.1 Input/output capabilities of the DD/DS.

the one concerning online versus batch output, and the flexibility of the products that can be obtained in each instance. Another aspect of this same issue is the facility for formulating ad-hoc queries in an on-line environment, versus generating preformatted, commonly used reports. The capability to generate user-defined reports is a valuable aid for automating documentation for specific requirements.

5.1 INPUT FACILITIES FOR THE DD/DS

There are two aspects to the input facilities for the DD/DS: the language used in defining the contents of the DD/DS, and the software used in processing the language and in accepting the metadata input. This subsection will concentrate on the language aspects of the DD/DS.

5.1.1 The Language for Defining Metadata

The language used for describing the metadata and for defining its structure is known as the *DD/DS Data Definition Language (DDL)*. A DDL is a critical component of a data management system. Without it, the system cannot define its data structures, and the data contained therein cannot be interpreted or assigned any meanings. All DDLs must have both syntax and semantics. That is, the language must have a grammar that prescribes a basic format for its statements. Each statement consists of *primitives,* or lexical units arranged according to a set of syntactical rules. Further, each syntactical rule has an associated semantic rule that assigns meaning to the syntax. The dictionary DDLs of current systems vary significantly in scope and implementation. Some of the developers have implemented the dictionary DDL strictly as a definition language. Others have implemented the DD/DS DDL with augmented commands that allow for adding, deleting, and updating entries in the metadatabase. That is, it is implemented as a command language. Implementation methods aside, there are basically two aspects

INPUT FACILITIES FOR THE DD/DS

to this language: definition and manipulation. In this section of the chapter, we are primarily interested in both aspects of the language, and will use the term *data definition language* or DDL to mean these aspects of the language, however it might be implemented.

The syntax of the DDL is described as being "complete" when the language is capable of establishing "all" the entity types for the system, and it can describe "all" the attributes for those entities. *Complete* here does not mean that is can be mathematically or formally proven.

A typical DDL statement has a *verb* that specifies the action to be taken, such as add or delete; it has an *entity type* declaration that specifies the type of entity that will be defined, for example, element or file; it has an *object* which selects the entity occurrence that is to be acted upon, such as *savings-account-number* or *savings-transaction file*; and it may have a number of clauses that qualify or restrict the definition statement. The DDL syntax also requires separators — punctuation marks that serve as terminators or delimiters. For example:

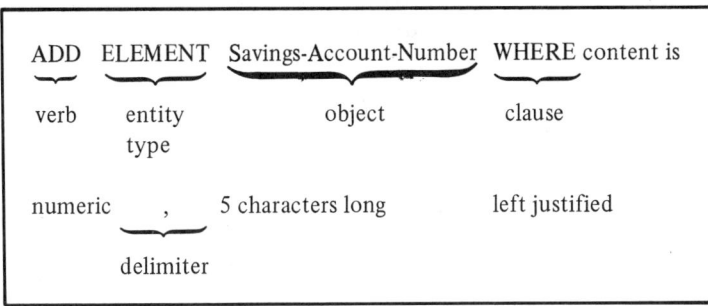

This type of syntactical form for DDL statements lends itself to transaction orientation. That is, individual DDL statements can be processed independent of all others.

Users, analysts, and designers use the DD/DS DDL to define the meta-entities to the system. Thus, the DDL should be flexible and easy to use to enhance its usability to a diverse audience (see Figure 5.2).

Ease-of-use means that the user does not have to follow complex procedures to define an entity or its attributes. Ease-of-use must also insure that users know exactly what they are defining; this helps insure trustworthiness in the metadatabase. An easy to use DDL is also generally *user-friendly*. That is, it provides the users with features that allow them to use the system without prior intensive training, for example, *menu selection*, which lists the individual components of the commands, with the proper syntax, allowing the user to "fill in the blanks" with appropriate entries; it has a *command glossary*, which lists all the com-

Desirable Characteristics of DDL for Metadata
1. Easy to use
2. User friendly
3. Menu selection
4. Command glossary
5. Abbreviated commands
6. No sequence constraints

Figure 5.2 Desirable characteristics of DD/DS DDLs.

mands allowed in the DDL, with brief explanations of what each means, what each does, and what the allowable options are; and *help commands*, allowing users to request help in proceeding with the next step. (See example in Figure 5.3, of a DB/DC Data Dictionary Screen.)

In addition, a user-friendly *command language* allows one to use abbreviated commands. Depending on the expertise level of the definer, a user-friendly DDL permits the user to choose the *concise mode* if the user is familiar with all the commands but wants to invoke the help features as a reminder, or one may invoke the *verbose mode*, if more guidance is required, including a more detailed explanation of the commands.

In defining the metadata, it is important to follow the user's natural course of definition, rather than forcing a particular sequence for definition. It is equally important to avoid artificial constraints. Thus, it is not advisable to force the use of either bottom-up or top-down sequence for defining files, records, and fields by dictum. Instead, it is much better to follow a natural structure. It is quite acceptable, initially, to define *hanging* or *interim entities* if there is insufficient information to complete a full sequence of structured definitions. However, it is important, to replace these interim entities with permanent ones, as soon as it is possible, to insure integrity in the DD/DS.

5.1.2 Types of DDL Format

The previous section addressed the usability issue of a DDL for metadata. The design of the DD/DS DDL format has direct impact on this issue, and is therefore examined here in greater detail.

Basically, there are two approaches: *keyword-oriented* and *preformatted*. Each of these is aimed at a different audience, and is discussed in the following paragraphs.

The keyword approach requires that a keyword or set of keywords, such as command identifiers or element type identifiers, be present in a

INPUT FACILITIES FOR THE DD/DS

```
FIELD      NAME:
           CODE:              OCC:          STAT:
DATE:                BYTES:                 TYPE:

DESC:

(COBOL & ASSEMBLER DATA) —
   USAGE:        SIGN:        BLANK:        JUST:         SYNCH:
   PICTURE:
   OCCURS:

   VALUE:

(PL/I DATA) —
PLIFMT:         SCALE/OPT:          MODE:
ALIGNED:        PRECLEN:     PRECSCL:
DIM1: (     :     ) DIM2: (     :     ) DIM3: (     :     )
   PLIPIC:
INITIAL:

Action Specifications for
EDIT Mode:
=================================================================
ACT:  1—PROC  2—REGEN  3—DESC  4—ALIAS  5—SEGS  7—PL/I  10—HDR  11—EXPLAIN
      6—USERDATA—NO:___  8—RELATED—FIELDS:___  9—REUSE
                    ( system response line)
```

```
Action Specifications for
DISPLAY mode:
=================================================================
ACT:   2—REGEN  3—DESC  4—ALIAS  5—SEGS  7—PL/I  9—REUSE  10—HDR  11—EXPLAIN
                                                        13—INQATTR
                    (system response line)
```

Figure 5.3 Typical DD/DS input screen. From DB/DC Data Dictionary General Information Manual, Release 3.0, Doc. #GH20-9104-2.

given DDL statement (see Figure 5.4). Such keywords are a specially reserved set of words that cannot assume any other meaning than the special meaning the DD/DS assigns to these reserved words. Examples of keyword-oriented DDLs are found in MSP's DATAMANAGER, Synergetic's DATA CATALOGUE 2, and Cullinane's IDD. Some keyword-oriented systems have a strict set of syntax rules that dictate the placement of each component of the language statements. Others are more lenient and allow an essentially free-form English-like statement, so long as the pertinent keyword is present in the appropriate relative position.

The keyword approach is relatively flexible, because there are few restrictions placed on the coding of the DDL statement. Generally, these statements require the presence of one or more keywords and appropriate verbs and delimeters. These keywords may be abbreviated, and there may be a number of optional clauses. Because of this flexibility, experienced data-processing professionals prefer this approach. The

```
*
*      DATA CATALOGUE 2 - FREE FORM TRANSACTIONS
*
****
*
ADD ELE=INVOICE-DATE
*
****
DES
 1 THIS IS THE DATE ON WHICH WE PREPARED AN INVOICE FOR GOODS
 5 SOLD OR FOR A DEBIT MEMO. THE INVOICE DATE IS USED FOR
15 COMPUTING THE AGE OF AN ACCOUNT.  IT MUST BE A VALID DATE
20 AND SHOULD BE SUBJECTED TO EDIT SO THAT ITEMS WITH A DATE NOT
25 EQUAL TO TODAYS DATE ARE SUBJECTED TO INQUIRY.
NAM
 1 DATANAME=INVOICE-DATE,SYMBOL=INVDAT
ATT
 1 LENGTH=6,FORMAT=N,NATURE=DATE,PICTURE=9(6)
****
*
ADD ELE=INVOICE-NO
*
****
DES
 1 INVOICE NUMBER IS THE UNIQUE NUMBER WE ASSIGN TO EACH BILL.WE
 5 PREPARE FOR GOODS SOLD OR SERVICES RENDERED.  IT MAY BE
 8 ASSIGNED BY THE BILLING SYSTEM   WHICH ASSIGNS NUMBERS IN ASCENDING
10 SEQUENCE. THE VALUE ROLLS OVER EVERY 10 MILLION INVOICES.
15 DEBIT MEMOS ARE GIVEN INVOICE NUMBERS BY THE BILLING DEPT.   THESE
25 ARE THEN TRANSMITTED TO EDP TO ADJUST THE AUTOMATIC NUMBERING
****
*
ADD ELE=INV-AMOUNT
*
****
DES
 1 THIS IS THE AMOUNT OF AN INVOICE.    IT IS THE AMOUNT
 2 COMPUTED BY THE BILLING PROGRAM AS THE TOTAL DUE THE CO.
 3 FOR THE MERCHANDISE SOLD, INCLUDING ALL TAXES AND EXTRA
 4 CHARGES AND LESS ANY MERCHANDISE DISCOUNTS.
```

Figure 5.4 Keyword approach. From the DATA CATALOGUE 2 System Overview Manual.

keyword approach may be more error prone, however, precisely because of the lack of rigidity in the coding conventions. Under these circumstances, it is very easy to commit errors of omission, such as leaving out an entire clause. Using this approach can lead to ambiguity, especially in those situations in which the keywords are context driven.

The DDL using a preformatted approach is much more rigid than its keyword counterpart; the rigidity is in the format of the DDL statements. In preformatted DDL statements, there is only freedom in choosing the appropriate statements, and in filling in pertinent variable names; all other parts of the statement are predefined. Preformatted DDL statements are generally less error prone, especially in cases of omission.

In some cases, DDL statements are sequentially numbered so that omission errors can be easily discovered. In many cases, these statements are fill-in-the-blank or multiple-choice statements, with self-explanatory prompting messages. Preformatted DDL formats are well suited for use on a CRT screen terminal, with menu selection capability, and lend themselves to being used in conjunction with the help facility. Preformatted DDL statements can be user-friendly, and are ideal for use by the inexperienced user. An example of a preformatted DDL can be found in DB/DC Data Dictionary (see Figure 5.3).

The preceding paragraphs addressed the issue of the advantages and disadvantages that can be obtained from using DDLs, from two aspects: usability and flexibility. To summarize (see Figure 5.5), the keyword-oriented DDL is much more flexible to use for the experienced data-processing professional, who is familiar with procedural languages; this form of language may be too complex and cumbersome for the non-data-processing user who is more comfortable with more structure and more automated assistance.

DDL Format	Advantages	Disadvantages
Keyword format	Flexible For experienced DP personnel	Ambiguity Errors of omission
Preformatted	Less ambiguity For inexperienced users	Less flexibility Cumbersome

Figure 5.5 Keyword versus preformatted DDL.

The preformatted DDL is more appealing to the end-user who may have no data-processing experience. This user feels more secure in being able to summon help from the system with the typing of a help command, or some such automated assistance feature. An experienced data-processing person, however, such as a database designer or a DBA would find the various assistance features too cumbersome and the prescribed formats too confining and inflexible.

To serve the widest spectrum of users, then, it may be necessary to provide multiple forms of definition facilities. Some commercial systems provide more than two DDL facilities, for example, DATA CATALOGUE 2 provides five: free-form, tutorial, free-form with prompting, batch-tailored, and batch-bulk.

One approach, common in "homegrown" DD/DSs, is to design the DDL as keyword-oriented first, then convert it to preformatted. The flexibility of the keyword-oriented approach lends itself to this strategy. The converse is not true, because converting from a preformatted approach to the keyword approach is much more difficult.

DD/DSs that are implemented using DBMS facilities may have data definition facilities that are closely related to the host DBMS's DDL facility. These are generally procedural and more keyword-oriented. Such DDLs often are not "complete" with respect to defining traditional non-DBMS files.

5.1.3 Standards for DD/DSs

With the diversity of data definition languages among commercial DD/DS packages, there is no industry-wide common approach to the definition of data. This gives rise to great confusion for the user. The arguments for a standard data definition language for the DD/DS resemble and parallel the arguments for a standard DDL for a DBMS (see Figure 5.6). Most commonly, it is argued that a standard DD/DS DDL may provide a common approach to defining data. This implies that the standard DDL would be able to recognize a predefined set of meta-entity structures, and that the command syntax would be uniformly defined. The most obvious benefit of a standard DDL is that it might contribute to reducing personnel training cost. Once the standard DDL is learned, the analyst/programmer would no longer need to learn a different language each time a different DD/DS is used. A standard DDL would be as useful as the commonality of COBOL among programmers today.

Advantages	Disadvantages
Reduced personnal training cost	Vendor resistance
Reduced conversion cost	User resistance
Increased data sharing	DBMS-DDL compatability

Figure 5.6 Advantages and disadvantages of a standard for DD/DS DDL.

Another often touted benefit is that a standard DDL may help reduce conversion cost. If the DD/DS is capable of recognizing uniform meta-entity structures, conversions may be effected by simply feeding the data descriptions from the source system (call it System A) to the target system (call it System B), since the DDL processor in System B would recognize meta-entity language defined by the DDL in System A. A standard DDL may reduce conversion cost, because it is no longer necessary to translate the data definitions from one system to another.

Finally, an additional advantage of a standard DDL is that it may increase data sharing, because all the data would be defined using as their basis the same language, rules, and syntax. Different segments of the enterprise would use the standard DDL to define the data in a uniform manner even if more than one DD/DS package is used in the enterprise.

The realities of our complex society are that standardization may not be a favored course of action for vendors preferring to retain the unique features of their products, rather than to make sacrifices for a common approach. Most vendors have a preferred way of implementing a DDL for their DD/DSs. The unique features of the vendor's DD/DSs are chosen to provide a unique capability that other vendors may not have. Another reason is that the DD/DS may be an adjunct product to an already established software product, such as a DBMS. Thus, adherence to a standard DDL that may force a vendor to relinquish a competitive edge in the marketplace is generally not a welcomed strategy.

On the user's side, there is also resistance. It is very difficult to force diverse kinds of users to give up their favored mode of operation for a standard, common approach. Problems arise with ownerships, ego, and old habits.

There are currently two ongoing efforts to standardize the DD/DS. The National Bureau of Standards has an effort to develop a Federal Information Processing Standard (FIPS) Data Dictionary System standard intended for Federal agencies' use [NBS 80]. The second effort is an American National Standards Institute (ANSI) effort. ANSI established a Technical Committee, X3H4, to develop a national voluntary standard for an Information Resource Dictionary System (IRDS) [WINK 81]. The ANSI effort started in July of 1980. Both efforts are scheduled for development by 1983 or 1984. Both the ANSI effort and the NBS effort are aimed at developing software specifications for the entire Data Dictionary/Directory System. An important part of their programs of work must necessarily address the issue of languages, and specifically, the definition language.

Standardization efforts for DBMS DDLs have been underway for several years. The Conference on Data System Languages, Data Description Language Committee (CODASYL-DDLC) developed the DDL specifications which the American National Standards Institute (ANSI) Data Definition Language Technical Committee, ANSI/X3H2 (DDL) subsequently adopted as the starting point for its program of work. There have been suggestions that since the purpose of a DD/DS DDL is similar to that of the DBMS DDL, the DD/DS standardization effort should coordinate with the DBMS's DDL effort. This, indeed, is an issue that should be addressed by the various standards development bodies.

5.2 INPUTTING OF METADATA

Once the metadata is defined using the DDL, the next important operation is to enter it into the DD/DS. This can be accomplished differently depending on specific requirements. For example, the initial loading of data into the DD/DS may be in bulk fashion (in batch mode); automated tools can be invoked as well, while individual updates may be in an online interactive fashion. The approach chosen is influenced by availability of facilities, operation, and time constraints (see Figure 5.7).

Input Method	Prevailing Circumstance
Batch-bulk loading	Initial loading
	Large quantity of metadata entries are expected
Online input/update	Unpredictable time frame and quantity of updates
	Used in conjunction with teleprocessing
	Coordinated with online programming
Input from machine-readable sources	Initial population of DD/DS with load/unload mechanism
	Converting existing metadata from other sources
Input by reference definition	Facilitate new entity and attribute definitions
	Use with expansibility concept

Figure 5.7 Guide for use of metadata input methods.

5.2.1 Batch Versus Online Input

When a large number of individually generated metadata updates are anticipated, and both the time frame and the quantities are unpredictable, then the online update method is preferred. In some cases, online programming is coordinated to accommodate the online entry of metadata updates. Use of the online input facilities in this manner creates a requirement that is related to the authorization issue. In this case, the status attribute becomes very important. The issue is related to the integrity of the metadata, which will be discussed at greater length in another subsection.

When there is a large quantity of metadata to be loaded into the DD/DS, it becomes necessary to use batch facilities. (This is the only sensible way of doing it!) Entering bulk amount of data definitions in the DD/DS in an online mode can be very tedious, cumbersome, time consuming, and error prone. Thus, using the online approach for bulk loading can be very inefficient.

The current trend is towards use of online update, which is generally supported in conjunction with an existing teleprocessing system. This enables the DD/DS to have interactive capability, as well. The fact that a teleprocessing capability enables the DD/DS to provide greater availability, and thus cause some risk of exposure is explored further in the next subsection. DD/DSs should provide both the batch-bulk loading

INPUTTING OF METADATA 103

capability and an online update capability, so that a user has the flexibility to choose the best method depending on the operation that needs to be performed.

Another feature of online capability, in most commercial DD/DSs, is the use of online screens, which are displayed on a terminal. The screen and the session design are very important. They must be designed to be user-friendly in order to provide maximum advantage of the visual aid that the terminal will give the metadata. A well designed session guides the user in defining the correct information. Some screens are designed using a fill-in-the-blanks format, and others are designed for menu selection of commands and keywords. Examples of systems that provide this facility are DB/DC Data Dictionary and UCC-10.

5.2.2 Special Input Features

The previous sections addressed the data definition language and the input or data entry capabilities of the DD/DS. In this subsection, other special input features of the DD/DS will be described. Specifically, this section addresses three kinds of special input features: input from machine-readable sources, input by reference definition, and rejection of incomplete entries.

Machine-readable input may be used during initial loading of the metadatabase, to facilitate the population of the DD/DS. Generally, a load/unload mechanism is used for this purpose. This type of input can also be used when converting metadata that already exists from other machine readable sources. A special case of this is the *application program code scanner,* which picks up data definitions from existing (e.g., COBOL) programs' data division or file definition. Along the same lines, a *Database Definition* (schema and subschema) *scanner* can be used to extract data definitions from the schema of a DBMS.

These features are necessary conveniences, especially to facilitate the use of a DD/DS for populating a metadatabase initially. This is typically a tedious and time consuming task, without the support of automated tools. However, the use of these facilities can be easily abused, especially if it is used routinely, as a crutch, or as a shortcut to a boring task. The overuse of these features in an uncontrolled manner can threaten active DD/DS control. This happens when the scanner facility is used to pick up the definitions after they have been placed in the application programs on a regular basis. In this situation, the DD/DS is no longer the place where the most current data definitions are maintained. The DD/DS, although automated, is passive with respect to the application program. The metadata is not integrated into the DD/DS until after the definitions are found in the application program (and the DBMS, as the case may be), and the DD/DS is updated using the scanner facilities.

The *reference definition* feature is used to facilitate the meticulous and tedious job of defining new entities and attributes of metadata for the DD/DS. This feature is one of the mechanisms by which the expansibility concept can be implemented. Reference definition is based on the premise that many metadata descriptions have common characteristics, and one can therefore employ a shortcut method of defining the meta-entity by invoking this facility. In principle, this is definition by exception; for example, "the definition of entity A is like entity B, except . . ." Having this capability contributes greatly towards a DD/DS's ease of use. This ease of use is particularly noteworthy in the expansibility concept, where its use enhances the utility of the Data Dictionary/ Directory System in its ability to define new, but not necessarily entirely different, entity occurrences.

Although it may be unrealistic to require complete metadata decription, there are some metadata attributes that the DBA may designate as being mandatory. These attributes are usually related to identification, and edit and validation attributes. The DD/DS can provide an automated mechanism to control completeness. The DBA would define the completeness criteria. This concept is also related to the metadata integrity issue, and will be discussed in the next section. Among the mechanisms that the DBA must implement to meet the completeness criteria are: the *reject function* that will cause an incomplete entry to be rejected from the system; *partially complete* entries that are "accepted but flagged" to indicate that these require further attention. The DBA would have the discretion to determine which attributes are required, and which are not.

5.3 METADATA INTEGRITY

The value of the DD/DS as a tool for coordination and control is directly related to the completeness, accuracy, and the currency of the metadatabase. To insure that the DD/DS is correct and up-to-date is to insure metadata integrity.

The lack of metadatabase integrity may be due to many different reasons, including: technical malfunctioning of the software (or hardware) used to update the metadatabase; erroneous, incomplete, or incorrect metadata due to unintentional error, carelessness, or ignorance; and criminal sabotage of the metadatabase. Our interest in this section, however, is confined to integrity problems caused by erroneous, incomplete, or incorrect metadata. There are three aspects of interest in metadata integrity which address these problems:

1. Quality of metadata.
2. Security and control of metadata.
3. Backup and recovery.

METADATA INTEGRITY

The following sections discuss each of these aspects.

5.3.1 Quality of Metadata

The quality of the metadata, that is, its consistency, correctness, and currency, should be monitored by the DBA by defining and inserting integrity checks, such as edit rules, validation checks, and control checks. The DBA has the responsibility for correcting and controlling the errors detected by these procedures.

It is important to recognize that integrity criteria must be carefully considered so that integrity checks and rules can be incorporated into the overall DD/DS implementation. This is usually accomplished in the DDL processor and in the DD/DS software that updates the metadatabase. Some of the integrity checks along with specific checking rules are listed below.

1. *Completeness:*
   Edit check to discover and reject incomplete entity entries.
   Edit check to detect incorrectly defined metadata entity and attribute types.
   Cross-check metadata at input time to insure complete meta entity structures.
2. *Consistency:*
   Edit check for redundant or inconsistent definition.
   Edit check for reasonableness of metadata attribute values, i.e., testing for value range for extremes and for threshold.
   Edit check for logical relationships among meta-entities.
3. *Accuracy/validity:*
   Edit check for correctness of metadata values.
   Procedures for checking of updates by DD/DS users.
   Implementation of an active DD/DS.
4. *Currency:*
   Procedures to ensure that errors are corrected when found.
   Procedures to ensure that metadata changes are entered on a timely basis.
   Implementation of an active DD/DS.

Along with these integrity criteria and the mechanisms to implement them, there must also be mechanisms for controlling the proliferation of errors that are detected. There should be procedures to insure that once the edit and validation facilities have found errors, that these errors are rejected, and that the erroneous metadata is corrected before it reenters the system.

In most enterprises, it would be the DBA's responsibility to identify and incorporate the integrity criteria, to set up audit procedures, to define the procedures, and design the mechanisms for editing, and to provide for error correction.

5.3.2 Security and Control of Metadata

Another important aspect of metadatabase integrity is security and access control. Access control mechanisms should be built into the DD/DS. These features should be invoked to preserve the integrity of the metadatabase.

Inadequate control of metadata, from the security aspects, can hinder greatly the effectiveness of the metadata as an important resource. Inadequate assignment of security levels may result in unauthorized entry into the metadatabase and resulting unauthorized modification to the metadatabase. Even putting aside the issue of criminal sabotage, this lack of control can result in a serious compromise to the metadata integrity. Thus, it is very important to assure that the proper levels of security are assigned to the metadatabase and its users. Security codes may be assigned at the entity level, the attribute level, the user level, and at the metadatabase level.

Some systems allow access to the DD/DS to be restricted through *status-level* security [DATA 81, GAJN 80, LEXI 76, THOM 79]. Where available, this is implemented through the status facility. Status is an attribute that describes whether the entity is in test status, operation status, or historical status. As expected, a test-data entity would be freely modified because it does not affect the operational metadatabase; the operational data entity would only be modified under restricted circumstances, and only by a qualified person or process; and historical data entities would only be read. In some cases, the user can specify a large number of status values.

When necessary, security codes can be assigned to individual system and/or metadata entities, or to part or all of the metadatabase. These codes may be associated with a password, and may be used to restrict access to specific meta entities or to the entire metadatabase. This type of security is implemented directly via a *password* facility, an *authority* facility, and possibly an *ownership* facility. The *password* facility requires that users identify themselves with a password code and/or a user-identification code. The *authority* facility declares to the DD/DS the level of access the user is permitted, that is, to write, to read, to browse, to delete, to update, or more than one of the above. This information, in effect, would restrict the user's ability to perform operations for which there is no permission. For example, a user having read-only privileges will be rejected when attempts are made to update the metadatabase. *Ownership* information further amplifies for the DD/DS the *authority* information. *Ownership* information provides the association of a *user* defined as a meta-entity, with certain *authority* with specific entity types and/or occurrences.

The *authority* facility serves as an effective screening mechanism for controlling access to the metadatabase. For example, by only allowing retrieval access to those users who have the appropriate authority level, metadata will be restricted to only authorized users. Access could also be limited to an approved class of entity or attributes. In the case of update (i.e., change, delete, add), the same restrictions could apply. Only those users with the permission to add, change, or delete would be allowed to do so. An authority code would be matched with a *password* code at the entity/attribute type or occurrence level to ensure that this is carried out. These measures serve to protect the security of the metadatabase against unauthorized modifications, addition, or deletion.

These types of access control are dependent upon password control and user-identification codes. The user ID may or may not be based upon the user being known as a defined entity to the DD/DS. In any case, passwords must be carefully assigned, maintained and controlled.

In some systems, there may be a complex hierarchical structure of password assignments. For example, a DBA may have the highest level of security, allowing access to all the data in the metadatabase, and with the authority to do all the functions permissible by the DD/DS. The DBA may then delegate some of this responsibility to a DB designer who has the authority to add and read data entities, but is not allowed to change or delete. The DBA can subordinate or subset his password, so that the DD/DS recognizes this.

When the DD/DS is dependent on a DBMS for managing the metadatabase, the security of the metadata may be protected by the DBMS security mechanism. In many enterprises the DBA has the ultimate responsibility for the DD/DS security. It is within the scope of the DBA function to define the use of password, authority, and ownership facilities.

5.3.3 Backup and Recovery

A third aspect in safeguarding the integrity of the metadatabase is the capability for backup and recovery in case of a failure in the DD/DS that results in loss of metadata. Generally, this capability is provided as a DD/DS utility, or as a function of a DBMS utility.

5.4 OUTPUT FACILITIES

The value of a DD/DS can be judged by the kind of information it can produce, and by the way it is presented. The output facilities of a DD/DS is the one aspect of the system that touches most users, and thus the adequacy and usefulness of the output is often the metric used to determine the relative usefulness of the DD/DS as a system for the management of data as a resource. Thus, it is extremely important to design and choose these facilities so that the output produced meets the needs of diverse groups of DD/DS users.

Output facilities must be addressed from at least two dimensions: functions and languages. Behind the reports produced or the queries answered, there has to be implemented the capability to manipulate the stored metadata, in order to produce the desired output in the desired format. Language is the mechanism whereby requests for reports or for queries are submitted to the DD/DS. These two aspects of the output facilities will be explored further.

5.4.1 Output Requirements

Requirements for output include: consistency, currency, and accuracy of the information extracted, and understandability and clarity of the reports. This set of qualities has to do with the fact that the output of the metadata information system is generally what systems analysts, DBAs and end-users use in their decision making. Therefore, information contained in the output must be consistent, accurate, and timely, to be meaningful. And the formats and presentations of the reports must be easy to understand and easy to use. Thus, these qualities are important when designing the outputs from the DD/DS.

5.4.2 Batch Versus Online Output

An important issue that requires early consideration is the one regarding online versus batch output (see Figure 5.8). Online output is required when:

1. Users need to look at the same data in many different ways (i.e., there is a need for diverse logical views);
2. the metadatabase is very large, but the data needed for retrieval represents a small amount; and/or
3. the metadata changes frequently, that is, the metadatabase is volatile.

In these situations, an online output facility would make available to the user the most up-to-date and accurate metadata. Online output can also be more versatile, because users have the capability to customize output to suit their immediate needs. An example of an online output is a change effect report, which may be invoked just after an update to the metadatabase.

Batch output (also known as off-line) is needed when: The metadata-

OUTPUT FACILITIES

Method of Output	Prevailing Circumstance
Online output:	Needs diverse logical views
Query facility	Large metadatabase, but small segment needed for retrieval
Preformatted screens	
	Volatile metadatabase
	Answer ad-hoc requests
Batch output:	Metadatabase is static
Reports (preformatted)	Large amount of metadata output
User-Defined reports	
	Routine reports

Figure 5.8 Guideline for use of metadata output method.

base is static — that is, it does not change very much; and/or the amount of metadata involved in the output is very large.

When output volume is great, often the most expedient solution is to schedule the output generation to a later time, when the processing load is not too heavy. An example of a batch output is the Comprehensive Data Dictionary Report (i.e., a formatted dump of the metadatabase).

In practice, both types of outputs are needed. The online output is needed to answer queries that are not routine; and the batch output option is needed to satisfy the high volume routine processing needs. The current trend is to provide dual capabilities. One option is to provide online output facility when there is an existing teleprocessing system. Another option, when true online output has not been designed, is to provide online access of batch-oriented output. This latter approach, however, is only an interim solution, and is often not an adequate solution for the requirement.

5.4.3 Characteristics of DD/DS Output

As indicated earlier, one of the major objectives of the design of output facilities is usability, clarity, and understandability in the outputs produced. There are basically two forms of output: *screens*, which are oriented to a display terminal, and *reports*, which can be produced online or batch. Regardless of which form of output is chosen, it is very important to design these carefully, with ease of use as one of its major criteria. In general, if an output is too cumbersome or difficult to use, it will not be used, and the objectives of a metadata information system will fail. A screen or report output that has ease of use as its major design objective is a major contributor to the success of a meta-

Integrated Data Dictionary
Standard Reports

Detail reports
  Class report
  Attribute report
  System report
  User report
  Program report
  Module report
  File report
  Record report
  Element report
  Inactive element report
  Task report
  Queue report
  Destination report
  Logical terminal report
  Physical terminal report
  Line report
  Panel report
  Map report

Key reports
  Attribute/record report – key
  Attribute/element report – key
  Class report – key
  Attribute report – key
  System report – key
  User report – key
  Program report – key
  Module report – key
  File report – key
  Record report – key
  Element report – key
  Task report – key
  Queue report – key
  Destination report – key
  Logical terminal report – key
  Physical terminal report – key
  Line report – key
  Panel report – key
  Map report – key

Summary reports
  System report – summary
  User report – summary
  Program report – summary
  Module report – summary
  File report – summary
  Record report – summary
  Element report – summary
  Task report – summary
  Queue report – summary
  Destination report – summary
  Logical terminal report – summary
  Physical terminal report – summary
  Line report – summary
  Panel report – summary
  Map report – summary

Cross-reference reports
  File/record report
  File synonym xref report
  Record synonym xref report
  Element synonym xref report
  Element description report
  Element designator report
  File activity report
  IDMS set activity report
  IDMS record activity report
  IDMS area activity report
  Element/program xref report

Special-purpose reports
  Level number report
  Module text to card utility
  Module text to output file
    utility

Figure 5.9a Sample listing of standard reports provided by Cullinane's IDD. *Source:* Slide shown at a presentation given at ANSI/X3H4 meeting in Dallas, TX, May 1981.

OUTPUT FACILITIES

data information system, and it is a major factor in the replacement of existing documentation requirements.

Security requirements are greater for environments using DD/DSs with online access and retrieval facilities than for those restricted to the batch use. As indicated earlier, the security issue also has a bearing in designing the output facilities. The concern at output time is to insure that unauthorized persons *do not* gain access to information in the metadatabase.

Data Dictionary/Directory Systems generally provide the capability to produce standard or preformatted output reports (or screens) (see Figure 5.9*a*). These are desirable particularly for often used reports. There are four groups of reports that fall into this category (see Figure 5.9*b*). These are: Catalog reports, glossary reports, entity structure reports, and control reports. Each of these groups is described briefly below.

Report Category	Major Use
Catalog reports	Inventory
Glossary reports	Analysis
Entity structure reports	Analysis
Control reports	Metadata management

Figure 5.9*b* DD/DS report categories.

1. *Catalog reports* (or screens) provide descriptions of all the attribute values for a specific entity. It may be a catalog for a specific entity or an inventory of all the entities in the metadatabase. In some organizations, a periodic dump or catalog of its metadata inventory is printed and bound for distribution throughout the enterprise.
2. *Glossary reports* (or screens) are attribute oriented. They provide all the values for one or more attributes (but not all) over a specified set of entities, that are usually of the same type. The glossary reports are essential for cross reference listing and analysis.
3. *Entity structure reports* (or screens) provide information on the relationship between entities. These reports can be used in describing an information structure, and as such are essential for database design analysis and cross reference analysis.
4. *Control reports* (or screens) are used to record changes occurring in the metadatabase, and can serve as an audit trail of DD/DS transactions. Control reports also provide security related information to the DBA. These reports are essential support tools for the Data Base Administrator.

5.4.4 Ad Hoc Output

In addition to these standard or predefined report facilities, two other output facilities should be considered: the query facility, and the report generation facility. Both of these output forms have one thing in common: they are intended to support needs that cannot be anticipated.

The *query facility* is generally associated with an online and interactive capability and is usually designed with ease of use as one of its primary objectives. A query facility is oriented to a short response format. It generally has a browsing facility, for example, for searching keywords and handling special requests. A query facility often has associated with it a keyword-oriented language, and it allows the users to formulate their own requests.

A *report generation facility* allows users to customize format and content of reports to meet needs that are unique to an enterprise. As such, this facility provides the flexibility not included in standard reports, and can be used to fill ad hoc requests from users. Report generation can be made to fit specific documentation requirements, including record layouts for design and analysis, and report layouts for management. It is also important in making effective use of the expansibility feature of DD/DSs.

5.5 SUMMARY

This chapter has addressed three very important aspects of a DD/DS design: *input facilities, metadata integrity,* and *output facilities.* In discussing the input facilities, several important aspects were discussed:

1. The design of the DDL, and the importance of the usability issue in this aspect of the DD/DS design.
2. The standards issue.
3. The input mechanisms used to populate a DD/DS, including special input features.

In discussing design of integrity functions for the DD/DS, two major ingredients for metadata integrity were recognized: the quality of the metadata, and the security and control of the metadata.

Finally, in discussing design of the output facilities, the issue of online versus batch output was addressed, followed by a discussion on predefined output, as opposed to query facility and a report generation facility. Another form of output will be discussed in the next chapter: the metadata generation capability. Because this concept is so important to the active DD/DS, it is addressed in a separate chapter.

REFERENCES

[DATA 81] *DATAMANAGER User's Guide,* MSP, Inc., Lexington, MA, 1981.

[DBDC 78] *DB/DC Data Dictionary (Release 3.0) General Information Manual* GH 20-9104-1, 3rd ed. IBM Corp., San Jose, CA, October 1978.

[DC-2 77] *DATA CATALOGUE 2 Reference Manual,* Synergetics Corp., Bedford, MA, 1977.

[GAJN 80] Gajnak, G., "The Requirements for Staging/Review/Approval Mechanism in the IRDS Standards," Working Paper ANSI/X3H4-80-17, August 1980.

[LEXI 76] *LEXICON User's Manual,* Arthur Andersen & Co., Chicago, IL, 1976.

[NBS 80] National Bureau of Standards, "Prospectus for Data Dictionary System Standard." NBSIR 80-2115, Washington, DC, September 1980.

[THOM 79] Thomas, D., "Security Aspects of a New Data Dictionary System (DDS)," Working Paper ANSI/X3/SPARC/DBS-SG/DDS-TG-79-23, August 1979.

[SCHN 80] Schneiderman, B. *Software Psychology: Human Factors in Computers and Information Systems,* Winthrop Publishers, Cambridge, MA, 1980.

[WINK 81] Winkler, A., "Introduction to X3H4," ANSI/X3H4 Administrative Document A81-34, June 1981.

6

Automated Interfaces for Metadata Generation

In Chapter 1, the concept of an active DD/DS was introduced, based on the relative dependence of another program or process on the DD/DS as its source of metadata. The more programs or processes there are that rely on the DD/DS as the only source of metadata, the more active the DD/DS is said to be.

The active DD/DS requires both the software capability to produce the metadata that is required by other software systems, and an enforcement mechanism to insure that all requests for metadata must go through the DD/DS. The second ingredient is usually an organization-dependent requirement that is implemented using administrative procedures.

In this chapter, we address the first requirement, the software capability to generate metadata for other software components and the DD/DS-implemented enforcement mechanisms. In most commercial systems, this software capability is implemented as an automated interface between the DD/DS and the affected software component. An *interface,* in this sense, is an automated link between two software components which may perform one or more functions such as translation and formatting.

Enforcement of the usage of the interface is dependent on administrative procedures. Wherever in this chapter it is stated that the active use of the DD/DS provides for control because it is the only source for metadata generation, the existence of adequate supportive administrative procedures and organization structure is assumed.

In order to describe the kind of service that the DD/DS can perform for a dependent program or process, each of them will be briefly introduced, explaining their purpose and function, the metadata that they require, and how the DD/DS can insure metadata consistency, timeliness, and integrity for these tools through its metadata generation capability. It is not within scope of this book to explain each tool in detail, nor to discuss motivation for their use.

Specifically, subsequent sections in this chapter address the metadata generation capability of the DD/DS for the following:

Application programs: The generation of Data Division or File Descriptions for COBOL programs, and Data Descriptions for PL/1 programs, from stored definitions in the DD/DS's metadatabase.

End-user facilities: Examples of metadata generated for end-user facilities include formatted input forms, screen formats, edit masks, synonym resolutions, and derived data and mapping functions.

Integrity functions: Examples are the edit and validation tables, and security profiles for meta-entities.

Database Management System (DBMS's): Examples are the DBDs and PSBs generated for IMS, and the schema and subschemas generated for IDMS.

Special-purpose utilities: These include, but are not limited to database design aids, test data generators, conversion software, database performance simulators, requirements analyzers, and operating systems job control.

General purpose: For unanticipated or special purpose applications.

6.1 METADATA GENERATION AND THE ACTIVE DD/DS

Metadata generation is the ability to produce data descriptions for use by other processing components, based on stored definitions maintained by the DD/DS in a metadatabase. For example, the metadata generation capability for a DBMS is the generation of the schema and the subschema. The metadata generation capability for an application program is the generation of the data division for COBOL programs, or the data descriptions section for PL/1 programs. In utilizing the DD/DS in this manner, the processing component issues commands and their associated parameters that cause a specifically designed interface to produce metadata for the processing components in the desired target form.

The automated metadata generation capability is the basic mechanism for implementing the active DD/DS. An active relationship with any or all components of the processing environment is established and maintained by generating the metadata for the components on an exclusive basis. Thus, an active DD/DS is more than just a repository of metadata as a form of documentation. It controls processing programs by controlling their use of metadata.

A COBOL program cannot execute without its data descriptions. If a COBOL program can only get its data descriptions—the file description of the Data Division which describes the data for that COBOL program—from the metadata stored in the DD/DS, then the DD/DS is said to be active with respect to the application program. Similarly, if the DBMS can only get its metadata (e.g., schema) from the DD/DS metadatabase, then the DD/DS is said to be active with respect to the DBMS. The *scope of activity* of a DD/DS is dependent on the number of processing components that rely on the automated metadata generation capability. It should be noted that the processing component must go through the DD/DS for its metadata. If the component can obtain its metadata from any other source, then this processing component is said to be passive, but with potential to become active.

6.1.1 Spectrum of DD/DS Activity

There is a full spectrum of activity for DD/DS's [PLAG 78], ranging from the purely active to the purely passive DD/DS, with gradations in between. These may be categorized as:

Purely Active DD/DS: A DD/DS which generates metadata such that using components of the environment depend exclusively on the metadatabase for their metadata.

Potentially Active DD/DS: A DD/DS which generates metadata but the using components of the environment do not depend exclusively on the metadatabase for their metadata.

Passive DD/DS: A DD/DS which does not generate metadata and does not have control over where and how a user (human or processing component) obtains the required metadata.

The current generation of DD/DSs have features that make them potentially active, such as the schema generation facility, the edit and validation capability, and security and access control features. In this context, the DD/DS provides the users with the capabilities that can be invoked as options, but are not necessarily enforced.

6.1.2 Active DD/DSs and "Binding"

This spectrum of activity is dependent on several factors:

The *scope* of an active DD/DS, which is measured in terms of the number of processing components which depend solely upon the DD/DS for their metadata.

The *directionality* of the interface between the DD/DS and the other processing components.

The *degree* of relative activity, which addresses the operational control that the DD/DS exerts on the other processing components measures the level of control realized as a result of separating the data description (i.e., the metadata) from the procedural code. The basic issue is when the data description, once separated, is bound again to the procedural code. This is referred to as the *binding time*.

Binding time affects the level of control because, once data descriptions are bound to a program the program is no longer dependent on the DD/DS for metadata. Thus, the longer binding time can be delayed, the greater the level of control. The earlier the binding is accomplished, the less control is achieved.

There are basically two categories of binding time with respect to the metadata and a using component. Note that the two categories have gradations within them, as well. The two categories follow.

Binding to the program (compile time): A program is a coded set of instructions, an instance of which executes as a process. (A program is to a process as a record type is to a record occurrence.) If the metadata is bound to the program this is accomplished in and/or around the point in time when the program is compiled.

Binding to the process (execution time): A process is an executing instance of a program. (In CODASYL terms, a process is roughly equivalent to a "run unit.") If the metadata is bound to a process it is accomplished in and/or around the point in time when the process is executing.

Thus, the *degree of activity* of a DD/DS is said to be greater if its binding is accomplished to the processes which depend upon it for metadata; the *degree of activity* is said to be lower if binding is accomplished to the programs which depend upon it for metadata.

6.1.3 Benefits of an Active DD/DS

As the only source of data descriptions, the active DD/DS has direct control over metadata and over the programs and/or processes using metadata. The active DD/DS can be used in this way as an important mechanism for controlling data security and data integrity. It can help ensure that metadata used in the data processing environment for implementing access control and data checking is current, valid, and consistent, and that data is defined according to predefined rules, conforming to the enterprise's standards. The active DD/DS may help by serving as an "enforcer" with respect to metadata generation, access control, and data validation.

There are a number of specific benefits which can be realized when the using components are dependent on the DD/DS as their sole source of metadata. The active DD/DS has the following advantages:

1. *Elimination of redundant metadata definition.* By obviating the necessity to redefine the data separately for each using component, the DD/DS reduces tedious data definition work.
2. *Insured consistency in the metadata.* Since the metadata can only be obtained from the DD/DS, all the using components and the DD/DS will have consistent metadata, assuming, of course, that the DD/DS content is itself consistent.
3. *Establishment of control over metadata usage.* Since the using components are dependent on the DD/DS for their metadata, the usages of the metadata are controlled. Using components not authorized to execute can be blocked by withholding metadata.
4. *Establishment of control of metadata changes.* By centralizing the source of metadata, all changes to existing data descriptions can be reflected throughout the environment in an orderly and consistent fashion. Unauthorized changes can be controlled.
5. *Implementation of data independence.* By separating the physical from the logical view and automatically generating the logical view greater data independence is achieved [STON 74].

It should be noted here that the drawback of a highly active DD/DS is the overhead it introduces when binding time is accomplished during execution. Furthermore, some maintain that a central repository for metadata upon which processing components are dependent is cumbersome and causes bottlenecks.

The following sections in this chapter discuss the preceding concepts of an active DD/DS with respect to specific metadata dependent components of a data processing environment. These include

Application programs
End-User facilities
Integrity programs/processes
DBMSs
Utilities and special-purpose programs

For each of these cases, we introduce the using component from a functional standpoint, describe its needs for metadata, discuss the alternatives regarding degree of activity, illustrate, using a specific example, and finally enumerate the potential benefits of using this strategy.

The example we use in this chapter for metadata generation is drawn

```
           PRINT OF EMPLOYING-COMPANY
00100      ITEM
00200      ENTERED-AS CHARACTER 30
00300      HELD-AS CHARACTER 30
00400      REPORTED-AS PICTURE "X(30)"
07000      ALIAS LOW-LEVEL 'EMPEMP'
08000      CATALOG 'EMPLOYEE','DESCRIPTION'
09000      DESCRIPTION
09100      'NAME OF OUTSIDE COMPANY OR INTERNAL DEPARTMENT OF THIS ORGANISATION'
           END OF PRINT


           PRINT OF EXPERIENCE
00100      GROUP
00150      HELD-AS
00200      CONTAINS EMPLOYING-COMPANY,
00300               EXPERIENCE-CODE,
00400               EXPERIENCE-YRS
07000      ALIAS LOW-LEVEL 'EMPEXP'
09000      DESCRIPTION
09100      'EXPERIENCE GAINED (INCLUDING EXPERIENCE GAINED WITHIN THIS ORGANISATION)'
10000      NOTE
10100      'ACCURACY'
10200      '   REFERENCES OBTAINED FROM LAST TWO'
10300      '   EMPLOYING ORGANISATIONS'
           END OF PRINT


           PRINT OF EXPERIENCE-CODE
00100      ITEM
00200      HELD-AS NUMERIC 2 CONTENTS RANGE 01 TO 99
00300      ENTERED-AS NUMERIC-CHARACTER 2
00400      REPORTED-AS PICTURE "99"
07000      ALIAS LOW-LEVEL 'EMPPOST'
08000      CATALOG 'EMPLOYEE','CODE'
09000      DESCRIPTION
09100      'EXPERIENCE CODE TAKEN FROM STANDARD CODING BOOK'
           END OF PRINT


           PRINT OF EXPERIENCE-YRS
00100      ITEM
00200      HELD-AS NUMERIC 2 CONTENTS
00300              RANGE 01 TO 10
00400              ELSE RANGE 01 TO 15
00500                 IF EMPLOYEE-DEPARTMENT EQ 180
00600      ENTERED-AS NUMERIC-CHARACTER 2
00700      REPORTED-AS PICTURE "99"
07000      ALIAS LOW-LEVEL 'EMPYRS'
08000      CATALOG 'EMPLOYEE','NUMERIC'
09000      DESCRIPTION
09100      'NUMBER OF YEARS EXPERIENCE'
           END OF PRINT


           PRINT OF QUALIFICATIONS
00100      ITEM
00200      HELD-AS CHARACTER 10
00300      ENTERED-AS CHARACTER 10
00400      REPORTED-AS PICTURE "X(10)"
07000      ALIAS LOW-LEVEL 'EMPQUA'
08000      CATALOG 'EMPLOYEE','DESCRIPTION'
09000      DESCRIPTION
09100      'QUALIFICATION OBTAINED AND DATE OF CERTIFICATE (SHOWN AS MM/YY)'
           END OF PRINT


           PRINT OF SOCIAL-SECURITY-CODE
00100      ITEM
00200      ENTERED-AS 1 ALPHANUMERIC 15
00300      ENTERED-AS 2 CHARACTER 15
00400      HELD-AS ALPHANUMERIC 15
00500      REPORTED-AS PICTURE "XXXBX(5)B999BXXXX"
07000      ALIAS LOW-LEVEL 'EMPSSC'
08000      CATALOG 'SALARY','CODE'
09000      DESCRIPTION
09100      'CURRENT EMPLOYEE SOCIAL SECURITY CODE'
           END OF PRINT


           PRINT OF TAX-CODE
00100      ITEM
00200      HELD-AS NUMERIC 4 CONTENTS IS 538
00300              ELSE IS 670
00400              ELSE RANGE 1000 TO 6000
00500      ENTERED-AS NUMERIC-CHARACTER 4
00600      REPORTED-AS PICTURE "9999"
07000      ALIAS LOW-LEVEL 'EMPTAX'
08000      CATALOG 'SALARY','CODE'
09000      DESCRIPTION
09100      'EMPLOYEE TAX CODE SENT BY TAX OFFICE'
10000      NOTE
10100      'ACCURACY'
```

Figure 6.1 Sample Metadata of an Employee Record. From DATAMANAGER Example Book.

from MSP's DATAMANAGER. The basic metadata for the example is shown in Figure 6.1.

6.2 METADATA GENERATION FOR APPLICATION PROGRAMS

Most business enterprises today use their computers for application program processing. This section addresses the use of the DD/DS in facilitating application program development, and increasing the quality and control of application programs through the DD/DS's metadata generation facility.

Broadly, *application* means the application of computer technology to a business function such as personnel management, savings account processing, and inventory control. Specifically, an application program is a computer program that automates one or more functions within such an area, for example, "compute daily balance." An application program is usually implemented in a high-level language, such as COBOL, FORTRAN, or PL/1. It is generally implemented according to an algorithm, or logical, procedural solution to a problem. The application program usually consists of three components: input, processing, and output.

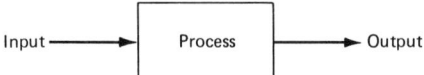

6.2.1 Metadata Needs

The input and output components must be described in the program. That is, it is necessary to describe to the program what, and in what format, to expect the incoming data. This description is metadata. In COBOL, this description is found in the data division's file definition section. In PL/1 this metadata is called data division.

Regardless of the programming language used, an application program needs data descriptions, or metadata. This also includes the program's subschema and its working storage description. The program's subschema is the way the program "sees" the data, or the program's logical view. One program's logical view may differ from another program's logical view. However, both programs may utilize the same physical data, which is part of the overall schema.

6.2.2 DD/DS Provides Consistent Metadata

To ascertain that all application programs get consistent metadata, the DD/DS must be able to provide more than one logical view to the application programs. In the database environment, these programs

```
        00187   PRODUCE RECORD-LAYOUTS FROM P1U02MEMP           Produce record layouts from the master
        00188   PRINT GIVING DESCRIPTIONS.                      file P1U02MEMP. Record layouts are
                                                                generated dynamically by DATAMANAGER
****************************************************************************************************
*                                                                                                  *
*  DESCRIPTION OF EMPLOYEE-MASTER-RECORD                                                           *
*                                                                                                  *
****************************************************************************************************
* *DEC  *HEX  *                               *                            *                      *
* *OFFSET*OFFSET* LEVEL & NAME                *LENGTH* TYPE  ALIGN*  REMARKS                       *
****************************************************************************************************
*   0 *   0 * 1 * EMPLOYEE-MASTER-RECORD      * 205 * GROUP  *  EMPLOYEE MASTER FILE RECORD        *
*---------------------------------------------------------------------------------------------------*
*   0 *   0 * 2 * EMPLOYEE-CODE               *   4 * NUM    *  4 DIGITS                           *
*                                             *                *  STANDARD EMPLOYEE CODE           *
*---------------------------------------------------------------------------------------------------*
*   4 *   4 * 2 * EMPLOYEE-IDENTIFICATION     * 100 * GROUP  *  NAME, ADDRESS AND TELEPHONE NUMBER OF AN
*                                             *                *  EMPLOYEE                         *
*---------------------------------------------------------------------------------------------------*
*   4 *   4 * 3 * EMPLOYEE-NAME               *  30 * CHAR   *  EMPLOYEE SURNAME, FIRST NAME AND MIDDLE NAME
*---------------------------------------------------------------------------------------------------*
*  34 *  22 * 3 * EMPLOYEE-STREET             *  40 * CHAR   *  EMPLOYEE STREET NAME INCLUDING ANY APARTMENT
*                                             *                *  NUMBER                           *
*---------------------------------------------------------------------------------------------------*
*  74 *  4A * 3 * EMPLOYEE-TOWN               *  20 * CHAR   *  EMPLOYEE HOME TOWN NAME AND POST CODE
*---------------------------------------------------------------------------------------------------*
*  94 *  5E * 3 * EMPLOYEE-TELEPHONE          *  10 * NUM    *  10 DIGITS                          *
*                                             *                *  EMPLOYEE TELEPHONE NUMBER INCLUDING CODE
*---------------------------------------------------------------------------------------------------*
* 104 *  68 * 2 * EMPLOYEE-DEPARTMENT         *   3 * NUM    *  3 DIGITS                           *
*                                             *                *  EMPLOYEE DEPARTMENT CODE         *
*---------------------------------------------------------------------------------------------------*
* 107 *  6B * 2 * EMPLOYEE-SALARY             *   5 * NUM    *  5 DIGITS                           *
*                                             *                *  YEARLY SALARY. INCLUDES GEOGRAPHICAL
*                                             *                *  ALLOWANCES                       *
*---------------------------------------------------------------------------------------------------*
* 112 *  70 * 2 * EDUCATION                   *  40 * GROUP  *  EDUCATION RECEIVED BY EMPLOYEE INCLUDING
*                                             *                *  PROFESSIONAL TRAINING            *
*---------------------------------------------------------------------------------------------------*
* 112 *  70 * 3 * COLLEGE-NAME                *  30 * CHAR   *  NAME OF COLLEGE/FACULTY            *
*---------------------------------------------------------------------------------------------------*
* 142 *  8E * 3 * QUALIFICATIONS              *  10 * CHAR   *  QUALIFICATION OBTAINED AND DATE OF *
*                                             *                *  CERTIFICATE (SHOWN AS MM/YY)     *
*---------------------------------------------------------------------------------------------------*
* 152 *  98 * 2 * EXPERIENCE                  *  34 * GROUP  *  EXPERIENCE GAINED (INCLUDING EXPERIENCE
*                                             *                *  GAINED WITHIN THIS ORGANISATION) *
*---------------------------------------------------------------------------------------------------*
* 152 *  98 * 3 * EMPLOYING-COMPANY           *  30 * CHAR   *  NAME OF OUTSIDE COMPANY OR INTERNAL*
*                                             *                *  DEPARTMENT OF THIS ORGANISATION  *
*---------------------------------------------------------------------------------------------------*
* 182 *  B6 * 3 * EXPERIENCE-CODE             *   2 * NUM    *  2 DIGITS                           *
*                                             *                *  EXPERIENCE CODE TAKEN FROM STANDARD CODING
*                                             *                *  BOOK                             *
*---------------------------------------------------------------------------------------------------*
* 184 *  B8 * 3 * EXPERIENCE-YRS              *   2 * NUM    *  2 DIGITS                           *
*                                             *                *  NUMBER OF YEARS EXPERIENCE       *
*---------------------------------------------------------------------------------------------------*
* 186 *  BA * 2 * TAX-CODE                    *   4 * NUM    *  4 DIGITS                           *
*                                             *                *  EMPLOYEE TAX CODE SENT BY TAX OFFICE
*---------------------------------------------------------------------------------------------------*
* 190 *  BE * 2 * SOCIAL-SECURITY-CODE        *  15 * ALNUM  *  CURRENT EMPLOYEE SOCIAL SECURITY CODE
****************************************************************************************************
```

(a)

Figure 6.2a Record layout generated by DATAMANAGER. Additional metadata for the last seven entries are shown in Figure 6.1. From DATAMANAGER Example Book.

must go through the DD/DS for their subschema definition. The DD/DS, through an interface to the various programming languages can generate data descriptions for COBOL, PL/1, or BAL. Figures 6.2a, b, c, and d illustrate, in turn, a record layout, and the source code data definition for COBOL, PL/1 and BAL as they might be generated by DATAMANAGER.

Certain programming languages allow the definition of working storages or temporary storages. Working storage is used for data that has temporary value to a given program, and it is useful for tracing the activity of a program during execution. Descriptions of the working storage may also be stored in the DD/DS, since the application program also needs this kind of metadata. Some systems, such as ADABAS DD and INTEL'S IDD, recognize the importance of these, and have provided such capabilities.

METADATA GENERATION FOR APPLICATION PROGRAMS

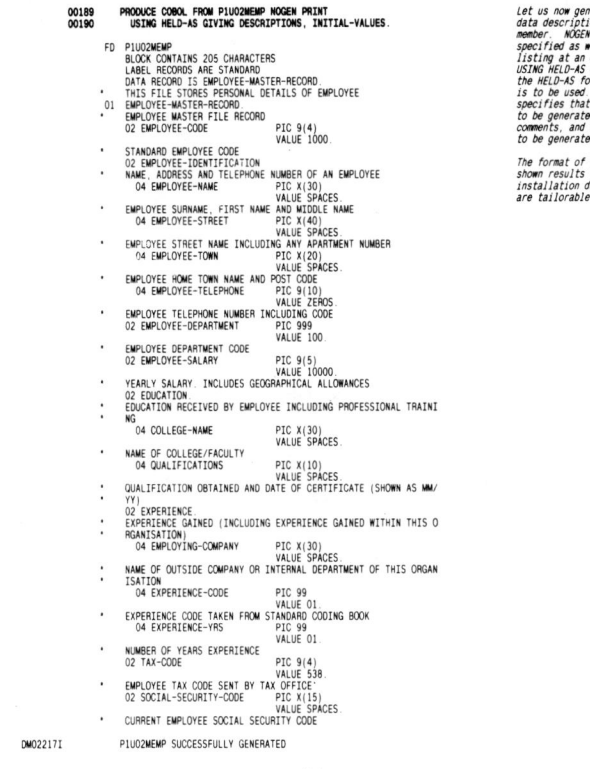

(b)

Figure 6.2b Generated source code data definition for COBOL. From DATA-MANAGER Example Book.

The examples presented in Figure 6.2a–d show how application program metadata are extracted from actual metadata actually stored in the DD/DS. It is also interesting to compare how the same metadata is generated for different languages, as shown in Figure 6.3.

6.2.3 Degree of Activity with Respect to Application Programs

The metadata generation facility can be provided as an option to the application program, or it can be provided as a requirement. When it is presented as an optional facility, the DD/DS is not active, but only potentially active. When it is a required path for the application program, then the DD/DS is said to be active. In this latter role, the application program can only get its metadata through the DD/DS. Possible architectural placements of the DD/DS are illustrated in Figure 6.4,

```
00191     PRODUCE PL/1 FROM EMPLOYEE-MASTER-RECORD PRINT
00192     NOGEN USING HELD-AS REPLACING 'EMPLOYEE' WITH 'EMP'
00193     GIVING DESCRIPTIONS.
  DCL
  1 EMP_MASTER_RECORD
                                    /*EMPLOYEE MASTER FILE RECOR*/
                                    /*D                          */,
    3 EMP_CODE                      PIC '(4)9'
                                    /*STANDARD EMPLOYEE CODE     */,
    3 EMP_IDENTIFICATION UNAL
                                    /*NAME, ADDRESS AND TELEPHON*/
                                    /*E NUMBER OF AN EMPLOYEE    */,
      5 EMP_NAME                    CHAR (30)
                                    /*EMPLOYEE SURNAME, FIRST NA*/
                                    /*ME AND MIDDLE NAME         */,
      5 EMP_STREET                  CHAR (40)
                                    /*EMPLOYEE STREET NAME INCLU*/
                                    /*DING ANY APARTMENT NUMBER  */,
      5 EMP_TOWN                    CHAR (20)
                                    /*EMPLOYEE HOME TOWN NAME AN*/
                                    /*D POST CODE                */,
      5 EMP_TELEPHONE               PIC '(10)9'
                                    /*EMPLOYEE TELEPHONE NUMBER  */
                                    /*INCLUDING CODE             */,
    3 EMP_DEPARTMENT                PIC '(3)9'
                                    /*EMPLOYEE DEPARTMENT CODE   */,
    3 EMP_SALARY                    PIC '(5)9'
                                    /*YEARLY SALARY. INCLUDES GE*/
                                    /*OGRAPHICAL ALLOWANCES      */,
    3 EDUCATION UNAL
                                    /*EDUCATION RECEIVED BY EMPL*/
                                    /*OYEE INCLUDING PROFESSIONA*/
                                    /*L TRAINING                 */,
      5 COLLEGE_NAME                CHAR (30)
                                    /*NAME OF COLLEGE/FACULTY    */,
      5 QUALIFICATIONS              CHAR (10)
                                    /*QUALIFICATION OBTAINED AND*/
                                    /* DATE OF CERTIFICATE (SHOW*/
                                    /*N AS MM/YY)                */,
    3 EXPERIENCE UNAL
                                    /*EXPERIENCE GAINED (INCLUDI*/
                                    /*NG EXPERIENCE GAINED WITHI*/
                                    /*N THIS ORGANISATION)       */,
      5 EMPLOYING_COMPANY           CHAR (30)
                                    /*NAME OF OUTSIDE COMPANY OR*/
                                    /* INTERNAL DEPARTMENT OF TH*/
                                    /*IS ORGANISATION            */,
      5 EXPERIENCE_CODE             PIC '99'
                                    /*EXPERIENCE CODE TAKEN FROM*/
                                    /* STANDARD CODING BOOK      */,
      5 EXPERIENCE_YRS              PIC '99'
                                    /*NUMBER OF YEARS EXPERIENCE*/,
    3 TAX_CODE                      PIC '(4)9'
                                    /*EMPLOYEE TAX CODE SENT BY */
                                    /*TAX OFFICE                 */,
    3 SOCIAL_SECURITY_CODE          CHAR (15)
                                    /*CURRENT EMPLOYEE SOCIAL SE*/
                                    /*CURITY CODE                */;
  DM02217I    EMPLOYEE-MASTER-RECORD SUCCESSFULLY GENERATED
```

We now produce PL/I data descriptions from EMPLOYEE-MASTER-RECORD, and, as for COBOL we specify PRINT, NOGEN and USING the HELD-AS form. Source language comments are generated from DESCRIPTION clauses. In addition we use a REPLACING clause to generate 'EMP-' instead of 'EMPLOYEE-'

As with source language genartion of COBOL, output formats are tailorable

(c)

Figure 6.2c Generated source code data definition for PL/1. From DATAMANAGER Example Book.

```
X250          00194   PRODUCE BAL FROM EMPLOYEE-MASTER-RECORD NOGEN PRINT
              00195   USING HELD-AS ALIAS LOW-LEVEL GIVING DESCRIPTIONS.

              EMPMASRC  DS   OCL205     EMPLOYEE MASTER FILE RECORD
              EMPCODE   DS   ZL4        STANDARD EMPLOYEE CODE
              EMPIDEN   DS   OCL100     NAME, ADDRESS AND TELEPHONE NUM
        *                                BER OF AN EMPLOYEE
              EMPNAME   DS   CL30       EMPLOYEE SURNAME, FIRST NAME AN
        *                                D MIDDLE NAME
              EMPSTR    DS   CL40       EMPLOYEE STREET NAME INCLUDING
        *                                ANY APARTMENT NUMBER
              EMPTOWN   DS   CL20       EMPLOYEE HOME TOWN NAME AND POS
        *                                T CODE
              EMPTELNO  DS   ZL10       EMPLOYEE TELEPHONE NUMBER INCLU
        *                                DING CODE
                             END OF GROUP EMPIDEN
              EMPDEPT   DS   ZL3        EMPLOYEE DEPARTMENT CODE
              EMPSAL    DS   ZL5        YEARLY SALARY. INCLUDES GEOGRAP
        *                                HICAL ALLOWANCES
              EMPEDU    DS   OCL40      EDUCATION RECEIVED BY EMPLOYEE
        *                                INCLUDING PROFESSIONAL TRAINING
              EMPCOL    DS   CL30       NAME OF COLLEGE/FACULTY
              EMPQUA    DS   CL10       QUALIFICATION OBTAINED AND DATE
        *                                OF CERTIFICATE (SHOWN AS MM/YY
        *                                )
                             END OF GROUP EMPEDU
              EMPEXP    DS   OCL34      EXPERIENCE GAINED (INCLUDING EX
        *                                PERIENCE GAINED WITHIN THIS ORG
        *                                ANISATION)
              EMPEMP    DS   CL30       NAME OF OUTSIDE COMPANY OR INTE
        *                                RNAL DEPARTMENT OF THIS ORGANIS
        *                                ATION
              EMPPOST   DS   ZL2        EXPERIENCE CODE TAKEN FROM STAN
        *                                DARD CODING BOOK
              EMPYRS    DS   ZL2        NUMBER OF YEARS EXPERIENCE
                             END OF GROUP EMPEXP
              EMPTAX    DS   ZL4        EMPLOYEE TAX CODE SENT BY TAX O
        *                                FFICE
              EMPSSC    DS   CL15       CURRENT EMPLOYEE SOCIAL SECURIT
        *                                Y CODE
                             END OF GROUP EMPMASRC
  DM02217I       EMPLOYEE-MASTER-RECORD SUCCESSFULLY GENERATED
```

The generation of Assembler descriptions are now shown from EMPLOYEE-MASTER-RECORD. Again we specify PRINT NOGEN and USING the HELD-AS form. Source language comments are generated from DESCRIPTION clauses. In addition, LOW-LEVEL aliases are generated in place of member names.

(d)

Figure 6.2d Generated source code data definition for BAL. From DATAMANAGER Example Book.

METADATA GENERATION FOR APPLICATION PROGRAMS

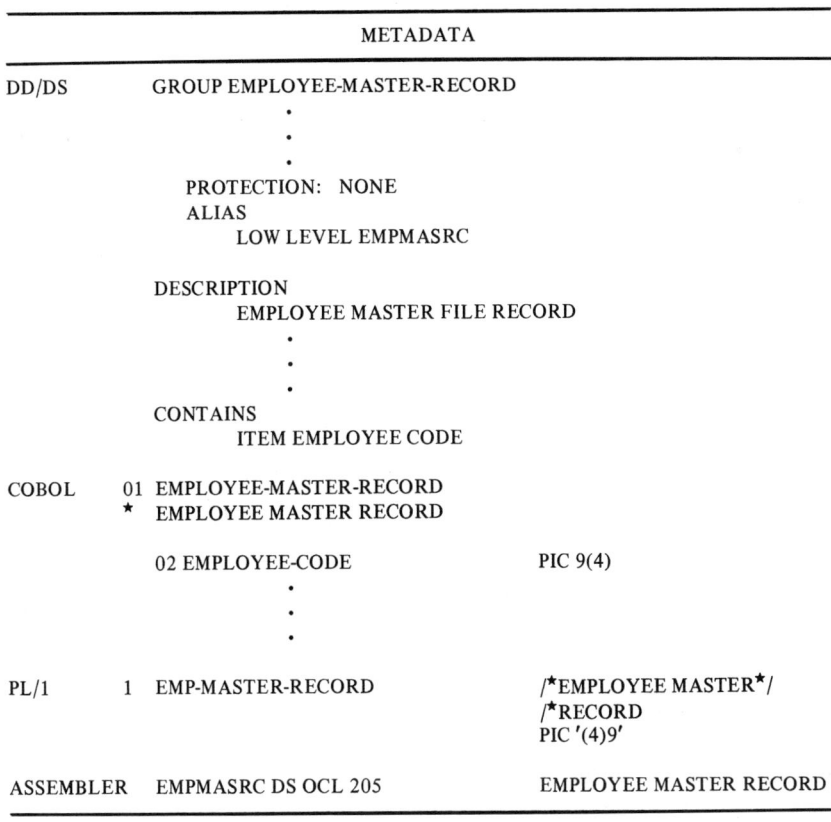

Figure 6.3 Generated metadata. From DATAMANAGER Example Book.

which shows the interactions of an active DD/DS with respect to application program processing.

As described in Section 6.1.2, the degree of activity of the DD/DS, with respect to the host language determines the level of control over the metadata. The notion of binding time was introduced as a key in determining how active the DD/DS is with respect to another processing component. The later the binding between the metadata and the procedural code occurs, the more active is the DD/DS. For example, a program that was successfully compiled, and has the metadata bound to the process already, will find that if a data element in the DD/DS changes between the time the program was compiled (the metadata was bound to the process) and the time it is executed, that the program being executed will not contain the most current or the most correct metadata. The integrity of the metadata in this case may suffer significantly.

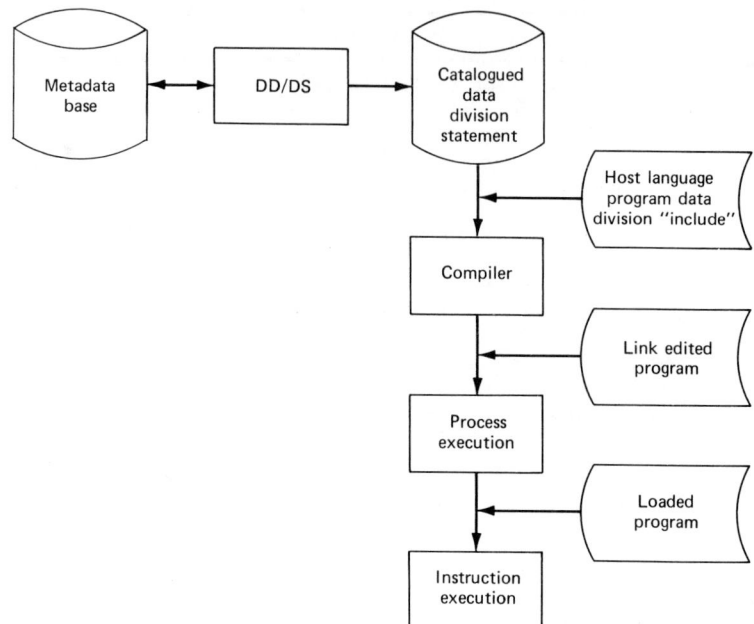

Figure 6.4 DD/DS application program interface.

A possible solution to this problem may be a procedure for version-checking as close as is practical to process execution start-up. This may be done by comparing names and time-date-stamps among the executing process and the executing DBMS process, which would presumably have the most recent version of the metadata. It should be noted that the program control checking at instruction execution time would likely require special hardware.

Thus, if the DD/DS metadata is bound to the program at compile time, the DD/DS does not attain a high level of control over the process, and is not as active as if the binding occurred at linking/loading time. And this is less active than if binding occurred at process execution time.

The reader is referred to Presser and White [PRES 72] for a more detailed and in depth discussion of the trade-offs in binding time options that are available. It should be noted that even though the highest degree of control is attainable with this latter scenario, as a practical matter, binding with DD/DS metadata is normally accomplished in and/or around compile time (see Figure 6.5).

6.2.4 Copy Library

A useful facility that supports programming development is the copy library. A *copy library* contains stored data descriptions, or segments of code, that are often used and have been successfully compiled. Users'

METADATA GENERATION FOR APPLICATION PROGRAMS

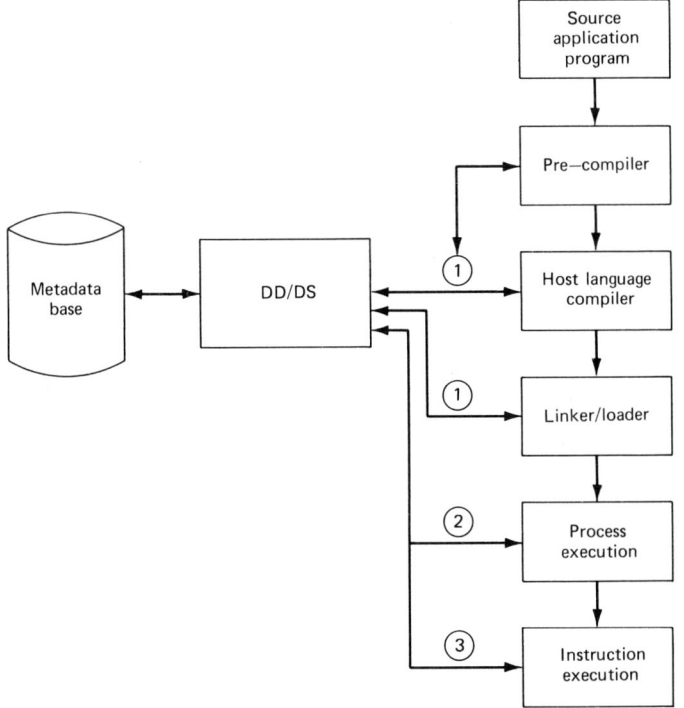

Figure 6.5 Degree of DD/DS activity with respect to application programs. Options are: (1) Compile time binding; (2) Process time binding; (3) Instruction execution time binding.

programs "include" record or data descriptions (or codes) from the copy library (or COPYLIB) each time a statement such as one of the following is specified:

COBOL: 01 dataname COPY segment-identifier (COPY-NAME)
BAL: COPY segment-identifier (COPY NAME identifier)
PL/1: % INCLUDE segment-identifier

The record or data descriptions — metadata — can be generated from the DD/DS for inclusion in the COPYLIB. LEXICON is one of the DD/DSs that provides such a facility.

6.2.5 Source Program Library

Often used programs, pieces of programs, and utilities are sometimes stored in source-image form in source-program libraries, instead of copy libraries. Likewise, often used metadata may also be stored in the source libraries. Examples of such systems in use today are ADR's

LIBRARIAN, and Pansophic's PANVALET. Some dictionaries interface to these source libraries, and provide these with needed metadata, notably, DATACOM/DD, and LEXICON interface with LIBRARIAN.

For example, to use LEXICON's "Source Library Interface," the user specifies the desired source library interface module, such as LX LIBRN; and calls the necessary LEXICON program, such as LEX140 or LEX163.

Since the DD/DS contains the most current and accurate metadata, this would insure that the catalogued programs are current.

6.2.6 Benefits of Using an Active DD/DS

There are many advantages to using an active DD/DS with respect to application programs. Among these are:

1. *Reduced coding:* If most of the metadata required by the application program already exist in the DD/DS, it would be highly efficient to use the source-language generation functions available in the DD/DS to provide the application programs with the required metadata, thereby reducing required coding.
2. *Consistency of documentation:* The DD/DS data descriptions are generally well documented, since each entity is described thoroughly following DD/DS rules and conventions. Therefore, the DD/DS can generate documentation, including in-line documentation in an application program. This is highly desirable, because documentation thus produced is highly consistent.
3. *Establishes control over metadata:* An active DD/DS supports control through the "binding" of the metadata or processes. Design implementation and operation considerations will determine when the binding will occur, and therefore, the level of control desired. If changes are made to the metadata only in the DD/DS, this will insure that all changes are permeated to all components requiring metadata, since that is the only source of metadata for the application programs. This requires version checking at load or execution time.

Technical advantages can also be translated into other less tangible benefits. These will be addressed in a later section.

6.3 METADATA GENERATION FOR END-USER FACILITIES

End-user generally refers to a person or group of people who are the consumers of information and who have little or no experience with data processing technology, but have need for data processing services,

METADATA GENERATION FOR END-USER FACILITIES

for example, a bank teller or an airline reservation agent. End-user facilities refer to those tools, or capabilities that are designed to assist this group of users in using data processing resources. The main requirement for end-user facilities is that these tools or facilities *must be easy to use*. This means that the end-user does not need to learn a complex programming language or procedure to use these facilities. End-user facilities are generally interfaces, or front-end processors, to other more complex systems. Thus, a banking activity system may have a front-end processor that allows a teller (an end-user) to type in a question concerning a client's balance, using terminology that the teller is familiar with, rather than data processing abbreviations or other data processing terminologies. The end-user need have no knowledge of how the banking activity system works, being interested only in the client's balance.

There are a wide variety of end-user facilities. For the purpose of this discussion, this section will only address two types of end-user facilities: report (and screen) generators and query language processors.

6.3.1 Report Generators and Screen Generators

Report generators are special-purpose host-language application programs, or specialized software packages, such as CINCOM's SOCRATES, LEXICON's Report Writer or Software ag's NATURAL, which allow end-users to format their own reports. Report generators allow the end-user to "get at" the information stored in the information system. Generally, a report generator requires that the user describe the desired report, including the type of data that is to be selected for the report (i.e., the logical view), and the conditions that determine the kind of data to be selected for manipulation into a report.

Two other types of descriptions are required from the users in addition to the above: description about the data that is stored, including mapping specifications and, most important, description of the report layout.

Thus, a report description must include the following elements (see Figures 6.6*a, b*):

1. Description of data to be used, referencing an identifier (i.e., a unique name).
2. Selection criteria for data to be included on the report.
3. Sequence of report.
4. Heading, title, and other "housekeeping" information.
5. Details of what elements to go on what lines.
6. Calculations to be performed on the elements.
7. Totals to be printed.

```
REPORT NO.      LX145030              REPORT WRITER COURSE                                PAGE        1
PAGE-THIS ITEM         1               REPORT RWAA001                                     DATE 06/18/80
                                        SPECIFICATIONS

 SEQUENCE NUMBER                                  REPORT SYNTAX
 ---------------      ----------------------------------------------------------------------

  RWAA0010020         $$********************************************************************
  RWAA0010030         $$  REPORT IDENTIFICATION                                              *
  RWAA0010040         $$********************************************************************
  RWAA0010050         DESIGNATOR 'BASIC REPORT'
  RWAA0010060         TEXT 'MONTHLY REPORT LISTING ALL CUSTOMER NUMBERS, PLUS GENERAL CUSTO
  RWAA0010070         MER INFORMATION AND THE NUMBER OF ACCOUNTS WITHIN EACH STATE'
  RWAA0010080         FREQUENCY RECURRING
  RWAA0010090         $$********************************************************************
  RWAA0010100         $$  SELECTION = ALL CUSTOMERS                                          *
  RWAA0010110         $$********************************************************************
  RWAA0010120         INFO-SET ENTRY-ID ENAA001
  RWAA0010130         SELECT ALL
  RWAA0010140         $$********************************************************************
  RWAA0010150         $$  SEQUENCE = STATE           - ELAA009                               *
  RWAA0010160         $$             CUSTOMER NAME   - ELAA003                               *
  RWAA0010170         $$             CUSTOMER NUMBER - ELAA001                               *
  RWAA0010180         $$********************************************************************
  RWAA0010190         SEQUENCE ELAA009
  RWAA0010200                  ELAA003
  RWAA0010210                  ELAA001
  RWAA0010220         $$********************************************************************
  RWAA0010230         $$  TITLE AND HEADING INFORMATION                                      *
  RWAA0010240         $$********************************************************************
  RWAA0010250         TITLE-LINE STANDARD
  RWAA0010260         HEAD-LINE STANDARD
  RWAA0010270         $$********************************************************************
  RWAA0010280         $$  DATA-LINE FOR EACH CUSTOMER                                        *
  RWAA0010290         $$********************************************************************
  RWAA0010300         DATA-LINE
  RWAA0010310                SPACE 2 BEFORE
  RWAA0010330             ITEM ELAA001
  RWAA0010340             ITEM ELAA003
  RWAA0010350             ITEM ELAA005
  RWAA0010360             ITEM ELAA006
  RWAA0010370             ITEM ELAA007
  RWAA0010380             ITEM ELAA008
  RWAA0010390             ITEM ELAA009
  RWAA0010400             ITEM ELAA010
  RWAA0010410             ITEM ELAA011
  RWAA0010420             ITEM ELAA012
  RWAA0010430         $$********************************************************************
  RWAA0010440         $$  TOTAL-LINE BY STATE                                                *
  RWAA0010450         $$********************************************************************
  RWAA0010460         TOTAL-LINE
  RWAA0010470                ON CHANGE IN ELAA009
  RWAA0010480                SPACE 4 BEFORE
  RWAA0010490                TOP-OF-PAGE AFTER
  RWAA0010500             ITEM '** TOTAL FOR STATE'                 LOC   2
  RWAA0010510             ITEM ELAA009                              LOC  22 DECODED
  RWAA0010520             ITEM '-- NUMBER OF CUSTOMERS :'           LOC  42
  RWAA0010530             ITEM COUNT1                               LOC  68
  RWAA0010540                COUNT-OF ELAA003
  RWAA0010550                TEMP-EDIT LENGTH 6 RULE 01
  RWAA0010570             ITEM '-- NUMBER OF ACCOUNTS :'            LOC  93
  RWAA0010580             ITEM SUM1                                 LOC 118
  RWAA0010590                SUM-OF ELAA011
  RWAA0010600                TEMP-EDIT LENGTH 4 RULE 03
  RWAA0010620             ITEM SUM2                                 LOC 125
  RWAA0010630                SUM-OF ELAA012
  RWAA0010640                TEMP-EDIT LENGTH 4 RULE 03
  RWAA0010660         $$********************************************************************
  RWAA0010670         $$  GRAND TOTAL                                                        *
  RWAA0010680         $$********************************************************************
```

(a)

Figure 6.6*a* An example of Report Description. Reprinted by permission of Arthur Andersen & Co.

```
RHAA001690      TOTAL-LINE CHANGE IN REPORT
RHAA001700         SPACE 3 BEFORE
RHAA001710         ITEM T-COUNT AND TOTAL FOR'                          LOC    2
RHAA001720                                                                    24
RHAA001730            SUM=D-COUNT LENGTH 7 RULE 01
RHAA001740         ITEM 'NUMBER OF CHECKING ACCOUNTS :'                 LOC   32
RHAA001750                                                              LOC   74
RHAA001760            SUM=C-SUM1
RHAA001770         ITEM 'NUMBER OF SAVINGS ACCOUNTS :'                  LOC   84
RHAA001780                                                              LOC  115
RHAA001790            SUM=S-SUM2
RHAA001800         ITEM * EDIT LENGTH 7 RULE 01
RHAA001810   $$************************************************************
RHAA001820   $$ END OF REPORT RHA001                                       **
RHAA001900   $$************************************************************
```

(b)

Figure 6.6b An example of Report Description. Reprinted by permission of Arthur Andersen & Co.

REPORT NO. LX145030
PAGE-THIS ITEM 1

REPORT WRITER COURSE
REPORT PWAA001
CROSS REFERENCE

PAGE 2
DATE 06/18/80

IDENTIFIER	DESIGNATOR	REFERENCE	USAGE	REFERENCE	USAGE	REFERENCE	USAGE
COUNT1	RESULT FIELD	RWAA0010530	TOTAL-LINE	RWAA0010740	SUM-OF		
ELAA001	CUSTOMER NUMBER	RWAA0010210	SEQUENCE	RWAA0010330	DATA-LINE		
ELAA003	CUSTOMER NAME	RWAA0010200	SEQUENCE	RWAA0010340	DATA-LINE	RWAA0010540	COUNT-OF
ELAA005	STREET NUMBER	RWAA0010350	DATA-LINE				
ELAA006	STREET NAME	RWAA0010360	DATA-LINE				
ELAA007	STREET SUFFIX	RWAA0010370	DATA-LINE				
ELAA008	CITY	RWAA0010380	DATA-LINE				
ELAA009	STATE	RWAA0010190	SEQUENCE	RWAA0010390	DATA-LINE	RWAA0010470	CHANGE
		RWAA0010510	TOTAL-LINE				
ELAA010	ZIP CODE	RWAA0010400	DATA-LINE				
ELAA011	CHECKING ACCOUNT	RWAA0010410	DATA-LINE	RWAA0010590	SUM-OF		
ELAA012	SAVINGS ACCOUNT	RWAA0010420	DATA-LINE	RWAA0010630	SUM-OF		
ENAA001	CUSTOMER ACCOUNT ENTRY	RWAA0010120	ENTRY-ID				
REPORT	RESULT FIELD	RWAA0010700	CHANGE				
SUM1	RESULT FIELD	RWAA0010580	TOTAL-LINE	RWAA0010800	SUM-OF		
SUM2	RESULT FIELD	RWAA0010620	TOTAL-LINE	RWAA0010850	SUM-OF		
T-COUNT1	RESULT FIELD	RWAA0010730	TOTAL-LINE				
T-SUM1	RESULT FIELD	RWAA0010790	TOTAL-LINE				
T-SUM2	RESULT FIELD	RWAA0010840	TOTAL-LINE				
'** TOTAL FOR STATE'		RWAA0010500	TOTAL-LINE				
'**** GRAND TOTAL FOR'		RWAA0010720	TOTAL-LINE				
'-- NUMBER OF ACCOUNTS :'		RWAA0010570	TOTAL-LINE				
'-- NUMBER OF CUSTOMERS :'		RWAA0010520	TOTAL-LINE				
'CUSTOMERS'		RWAA0010770	TOTAL-LINE				
'NUMBER OF CHECKING ACCOUNTS :'		RWAA0010780	TOTAL-LINE				
'NUMBER OF SAVINGS ACCOUNTS :'		RWAA0010830	TOTAL-LINE				

(c)

Figure 6.6*c* An example of a report produced using Report Description. Reprinted by permission of Arthur Andersen & Co.

```
REPORT IDENTIFIER RWAA001    ****************************************    PREPARATION DATE 06/17/80
                                         BASIC REPORT                          AS OF DATE 06/17/80
                             ****************************************
                                          TITLE PAGE

              DESIGNATOR     BASIC REPORT

              TEXT           MONTHLY REPORT LISTING ALL CUSTOMER NUMBERS, PLUS GENERAL CUSTOMER
                             INFORMATION AND THE NUMBER OF ACCOUNTS WITHIN EACH STATE

              FREQUENCY      RECURRING

              REQUESTER      N/A

              DISTRIBUTION   N/A

              INFO-SET       ENTRY-ID ENAA001

              VERSION        N/A

              PAPER          N/A

              OUTPUT NO.     9
```

(d)

Figure 6.6d An example of a report produced using Report Description. Reprinted by permission of Arthur Andersen & Co.

```
RHAA001                                  BASIC REPORT                                    06/17/80  PAGE   1

CUSTOMER    CUSTOMER              STREET    STREET           STREET                                  CHECK  SAVE
NUMBER      NAME                  NUMBER    NAME             SUFFIX     CITY           STATE  ZIP    ACCT   ACCT

00003744536 MARGARET L. ANDERSEN  00021     FLEEDWOOD STREET APT S-1    SAUSALITO      CA     90068    1     0

** TOTAL FOR STATE CALIFORNIA    -- NUMBER OF CUSTOMERS :   1                -- NUMBER OF ACCOUNTS :    1     0
```

```
RHAA001                                  BASIC REPORT                                    06/17/80  PAGE   2

CUSTOMER    CUSTOMER              STREET    STREET           STREET                                  CHECK  SAVE
NUMBER      NAME                  NUMBER    NAME             SUFFIX     CITY           STATE  ZIP    ACCT   ACCT

00502070392 ARTHUR ANDERSEN       69        W. WASHINGTON STREET        CHICAGO        IL     60602    1     0
00000237244 BARBARA M. MUELLER    00370     VENETIAN WAY                CHICAGO        IL     60611    3     2
00003290031 CHARLES E. ABRAHAMS   01165     STERLING AVENUE  APT 15B    NORTHFIELD     IL     60093    2     1
00008974523 HARRY J. SMITH        00069     WILMETTE AVE                MT PROSPECT    IL     60626    1     0
00305678901 JAMES THOMPSON        1325      NOYES AVENUE                CARRBORO       IL     60065    1     1
00102970203 JANE BYRNE            745       ASHLAND STREET   APT 532    GLENVIEW       IL     60025    0     2
00002970203 KATHLEEN M. CLARK     01150     PONTIAC ROAD     APT 12A    PALATINE       IL     60015    0     1
00001798302 LEXICON DATA ADMINISTRATOR 00607 WESLEY AVE      PO BOX 7   LINCOLNSHIRE   IL     60632    1     1
00002070392 PETER W. DONOVAN      16600     N. WILLIAMS AVE  APT 307    CHICAGO        IL     60525    1     0
00009234702 STEPHEN B. JONES      18110     W. HILLSIDE AVE  PO BOX 6   EVANSTON       IL     60195    1     1
00007983021 WALTER S. JAGGER      00940     S 14TH STREET    APT R-1    OAK BROOK      IL     60611    1     1
00005678901 WILLIAM L. NILSON     00363     NORTH OAKPARK AV APT 2G     WAUKEGAN       IL     60085    1     1

** TOTAL FOR STATE ILLINOIS      -- NUMBER OF CUSTOMERS :  12               -- NUMBER OF ACCOUNTS :   13    12
```

(e)

Figure 6.6e Examples of reports produced using Report Description. Reprinted by permission of Arthur Andersen & Co.

```
RMAA001                              BASIC REPORT                              06/17/80  PAGE  3

CUSTOMER   CUSTOMER         STREET   STREET    STREET                                    CHECK  SAVE
NUMBER     NAME             NUMBER   NAME      SUFFIX   CITY           STATE  ZIP        ACCT   ACCT

00003202121 JOHN R. SMITH   01240    W. WASHINGTON STREET              CHATTANOOGA  TN   37415    2     1

** TOTAL FOR STATE TENNESSEE    -- NUMBER OF CUSTOMERS :    1           -- NUMBER OF ACCOUNTS :    2     1


RMAA001                              BASIC REPORT                              06/17/80  PAGE  4

CUSTOMER   CUSTOMER         STREET   STREET    STREET                                    CHECK  SAVE
NUMBER     NAME             NUMBER   NAME      SUFFIX   CITY           STATE  ZIP        ACCT   ACCT

**** GRAND TOTAL FOR    14  CUSTOMERS  NUMBER OF CHECKING ACCOUNTS :   16   NUMBER OF SAVINGS ACCOUNTS :   13
```

Figure 6.6f Examples of reports produced using Report Description. Reprinted by permission of Arthur Andersen & Co.

This description is metadata. When the report descriptions are often used, these may be catalogued, or stored, just as the data definitions are stored, and a report generator can "call" these for inclusion prior to execution of the specific request. This metadata can be stored in the DD/DS. Thus, if the report generator gets its metadata from the DD/DS, it would ensure that the end-user gets the information required without having to learn the complexities of specifying all required metadata. Figures 6.6c–f show reports produced based on the specifications in Figure 6.6a and b.

As with report generators, screen generators are also an end-user facility. The screen generator is very similar to the report generators, except that its output form is a screen, usually on a CRT terminal instead of a hardcopy report. In addition to all the required metadata that must be provided for a report generator, a screen generator requires a description of the screen.

The metadata generation facility for the report and the screen generator can be provided either as an option, or as a requirement. When this facility is provided as an option to the report generator (or screen generator), the DD/DS is not active, but only potentially active. When metadata is provided as a requirement, the report (or screen) generator can only get its metadata through the DD/DS. The interface is active. Figure 6.7 shows the interaction of an active DD/DS with respect to a report generator.

6.3.2 Query Language Processors

Query language processors (QLP) are different from host language programs in that QLPs are problem oriented, and request a specific result. In this section, we are not addressing the internal DD/DS query facility, but an external software package that end-users need to assist them in retrieving user data that would otherwise be very difficult to obtain. A query language is the means by which an end-user communicates with the information system. The working of the information system can be (and usually is) transparent to the end-user, who is a non-data processing person. The QLP satisfies the end-user's needs for ad hoc, quick responses from the information system, via simple, English-like questions or commands. With the QLP, the end-user does not need to learn complicated programming languages and procedures, nor to depend on a technician or programmer to implement an information request. Examples of query processors are "Query-By-Example" (QBE) and ADR's DATACOM/DATAQUERY.

Generally, a QLP requires minimal descriptions and instructions to carry out a command. The QLP may require from the user:

1. a description or selection clauses of the data that is to be included in the answer to the query (i.e., establish the search criteria);

METADATA GENERATION FOR END-USER FACILITIES

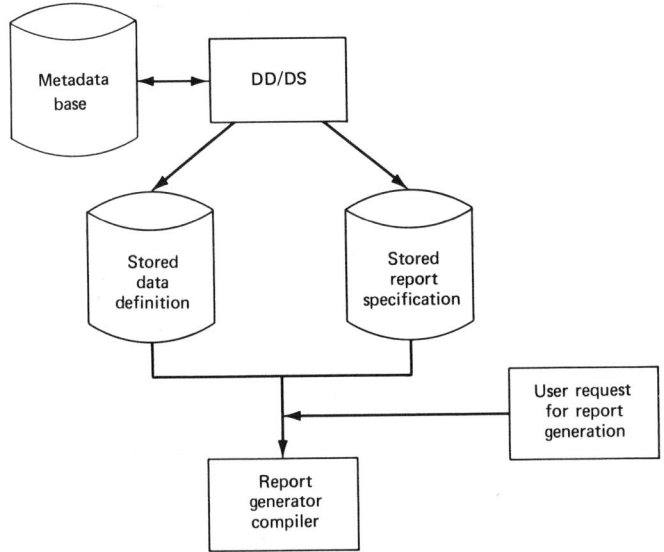

Figure 6.7   DD/DS report generation interface.

2. organization of the data to be retrieved; and
3. a description of a report or screen format so that the processor can display the information to the requesting user.

The information that the QLP requires is metadata. The information that the user requests concerning availability of data entities and legal forms or names are also metadata. This metadata may be stored in the DD/DS. If the QLP gets its metadata directly from the DD/DS, then the end-user would not have to define it redundantly, and it would insure that the end-user gets the information he needs without danger of feeding the wrong information into the process, and without being required to use unfamiliar language.

The metadata generation facility for the QLP may be used either as an option or as a requirement. When the metadata generation facility is provided as an option to the QLP, the DD/DS is not active but only potentially active, because the QLP can get the metadata elsewhere. However, when it is a required path that the QLP must take, then the DD/DS is active with respect to the QLP. In this case, the QLP can only get its metadata from the DD/DS, and cannot accept or change the metadata through any other means. Figure 6.8 shows the interaction of an active DD/DS with a QLP.

A user request through a query processor generally requires knowledge concerning data availability, data validity, and relationships/mapping. In an active situation, the data availability request can be integrated with the QLP and the DD/DS. This data availability function

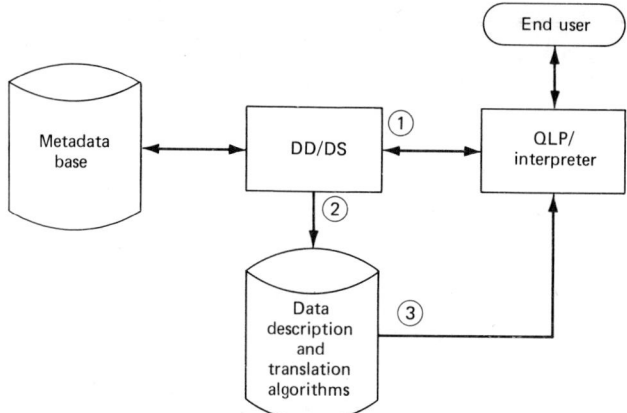

Figure 6.8 DD/DS–QLP interface. ① The Query Language Processor references the DD/DS to ascertain the availability of data to satisfy an end-user request. ② DD/DS generates metadata describing data to be processed and necessary translation algorithms. ③ The QLP uses metadata to generate required response.

would be a front-end function to the QLP. Requests coming from the users would be processed through the DD/DS by the QLP. Having ascertained its availability, it would again use the DD/DS which would generate the necessary metadata in the form of descriptions, and then feed to the QLP/Interpreter for processing.

6.3.3 Benefits

The metadata generated for the report generation and for the query language processors are:

1. screen formats which the end-user facilities use to produce the layout of the requested reports or forms of the answers to the queries;
2. edit masks which the RPG and QLP use to manipulate the data so that it can be displayed as required;
3. synonyms resolution;
4. derived data and mapping functions.

Foremost among the advantages of using an active DD/DS with respect to end-user facilities is that it makes an end-user facility easier to use by obviating the necessity to redefine metadata. Often used reports can be catalogued and retrieved, without redefinition, with easy commands. Specifically, these advantages include:

1. Redundant coding effort is reduced by generating required metadata from the DD/DS.

2. Documentation of end-user data usage is more accurate, current, and consistent.
3. Less user technical knowledge is required. This is particularly important for end-user facilities, because the objective of such facilities is to make the information system as easy to use as possible for a non-data processing user. In this way, data descriptions can be transparent to end-users.
4. The active DD/DS establishes control over metadata changes and disseminates these changes to the requesting end-user facility so that all end-users have the most current and accurate definitions.

6.4 METADATA GENERATION FOR INTEGRITY FUNCTIONS

6.4.1 Edit and Validation

Integrity functions are used to insure the currency and validity of the data processed in application programs. In this context, integrity functions are special kinds of host-language programs. They are often embedded in application programs as, for example, edit checks. Or, they may also appear as separate edit and validation programs. Regardless of where these functions are physically located, they require metadata in the form of edit and validation rules (EVR) and criteria to be used on processed data with application language programs. Examples of the metadata required by these integrity functions are:

1. Range limits: used to determine if data is within specified value ranges, as defined.
2. Constants: to determine if the constants conform to definition, such as checking for alphanumeric characters.
3. Lists of parameters: to determine if all parameters as defined are present, or if some are absent.
4. Conditional parameters: may require computation; checks for branching if certain conditions occur, or presence and absence of a parameter if certain conditions take place.
5. Summary or balance specification: checks that balance is within range (in calculation) or that appropriate parameters are incorporated in summary checks.

In the cases where these edit and validation rules are embedded in the application program, the metadata required by these integrity functions are also embedded in the program. Instead of having these in the application programs, this kind of metadata could also reside in the DD/DS.

When edit and validation rules are implemented as separate routines,

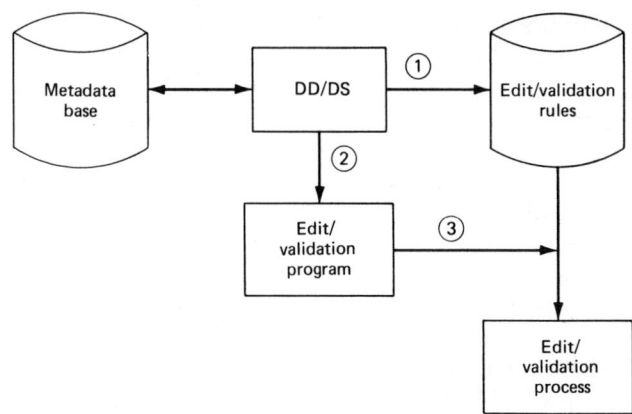

Figure 6.9 DD/DS edit and validation program interface. ① DD/DS generates tables or parameter lists of EVR's. ② DD/DS generates generalized edit/validation programs. ③ Edit/validation program references EVR and is loaded and executed as a process.

these usually are more general purpose in nature, and can be driven by a series of metadata parameters which can then be used to generate the rules. An important consideration in this regard is that edit and validation rules can be specified in declarative language and stored in the DD/DS. In turn, the DD/DS can then generate the tables that drive generalized programs/processes. Extending this concept, it is possible to generate fairly simple generalized programs for edit and validation based on the metadata contained in the DD/DS.

When the DD/DS is used to generate the metadata for the integrity functions, this creates the possibility for an active DD/DS with respect to the integrity function. When the DD/DS is the only source for metadata for the edit and validation routines, then, the DD/DS is said to be active with respect to the integrity function (see Figure 6.9).

6.4.2 Access Control

Another aspect of the integrity function is *access control*, which addresses the protection of data resources from unauthorized access. In most cases, there are generalized access control routines in an information system that protect against unauthorized access to the data resources. Most often, these routines are implemented, based on a security profile which specifies the authority required to gain access to specified types of information. This security profile is often tied to passwords. The security profile and password are metadata, because they describe the security requirements of the data, and they contain authorization information about users, tied to the passwords defined. Although we are suggesting that the security profile and related passwords should be stored in the DD/DS, many data security officers often recommend that these metadata be stored separately, and under more stringent access control.

Passwords are generally a sequence of alphanumeric characters that individual users enter to be identified to the system. Based on these passwords, permission may or may not be granted for accessing the data requested.

The security profile contains information about the level of sensitivity assigned to each entity, and associated permission for access levels. Reconciled to this is the security profile of a user, which also includes sensitivity level and permission of access level.

A DD/DS can generate the necessary parameters to drive the data access control functions, if its metadatabase contains the security profile information and password information. It must be remembered that the access control functions described in this section are not internal DD/DS functions protecting the metadata, but external software.

Like its edit and validation counterpart, security metadata can be stored using a declarative language. Using the metadata already in the DD/DS, the latter may generate actual generalized programs that serve to control access to particular data resources.

If the only way that the access control function can get its metadata is through the DD/DS, then the DD/DS is said to be active with respect to the access control function. If the security metadata is contained in the metadatabase, but the capability for generating this metadata is left as an option to the using function, then the DD/DS is said to be potentially active. Figure 6.10 shows a DD/DS–data access control program interface.

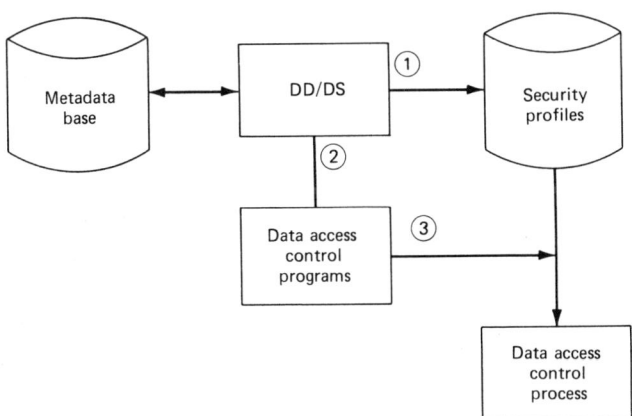

Figure 6.10 DD/DS data access control program interface. ① DD/DS generates security profiles. ② DD/DS generates generalized access control program. ③ Generalized access control program references security profiles and is loaded and executed as an access control process.

6.4.3 Benefits

The advantages of using an active DD/DS with respect to the integrity functions are:

1. An active DD/DS will supply the edit and validation rules and security profiles to the application programs.
2. Improved documentation.
3. Changes to EVR and security profiles can be made in one place, and propagated to the using functions.
4. The active DD/DS establishes control over the metadata and over EVR and security profile changes, since only authorized people are allowed to make the changes, and changes must be made according to established DD/DS integrity constraints.
5. The active DD/DS commits definition to a declarative form instead of a procedural form. This may allow the DD/DS to generate integrity (EVR) tables and security profiles that drive generated generalized programs, as is the case with LEXICON's Input Processor facility.

6.5 METADATA GENERATION FOR DATABASE MANAGEMENT SOFTWARE

6.5.1 DBMS

Database Management Systems (DBMSs) are generalized software tools that provide an integrated source of data for multiple users, while allowing each of these users to obtain a different view of the data in a format which is appropriate to their requirements [CODA 71; SIBL 76]. The DBMS provides a single, flexible facility for accommodating different files and operations. It features easy access to the data, and provides facilities for storage and maintenance of large volumes of data. Most importantly, it provides the capability for sharing the data resources among different types of users. The contents of a database managed by a DBMS is user-data (or operational data), rather than metadata.

There should be a very closely coordinated relationship between the DBMS metadata needs and the DD/DS; this is true whether the DD/DS depends on (or is implemented using) a DBMS, or not. Historically, the earliest versions of the DD/DS were developed to provide assistance to the DBMS in maintaining control over the latter's metadata. This is still true, although the DD/DS is no longer solely dedicated to that purpose.

The DBMS requires metadata in the form of descriptions of user-data that the DBMS stores in its database. Generally, the stored data has a data structure (which is described in a schema) which serves as a template for the data occurrences that constitute the database. The definition of the schema is accomplished using a data definition language (DDL). The DBMS also requires metadata in the form of a subschema, or that portion of the overall schema in which the user is interested. Both the schema and the subschema are necessary for the DBMS to organize, manipulate, access, and control the database. The schema and the subschema are both metadata, and therefore, can be organized as part of the metadatabase.

A DD/DS that is active with respect to the DBMS can serially generate source DDL for the DBMS, or it can share the metadatabase in parallel with the DBMS. In both cases, the DBMS DDL would be superseded by the DD/DS DDL. It should be noted that since metadata required by the DBMS is already stored in the DD/DS, with an active link to a DBMS, it would be natural to share the metadatabase (see Figures 6.11a, b). This issue of serially generating metadata versus parallel sharing metadata is discussed in Chapter 7 in greater depth.

Because many DBMSs have different methods for representing data structures, a DD/DS must have a different interface for each DBMS.

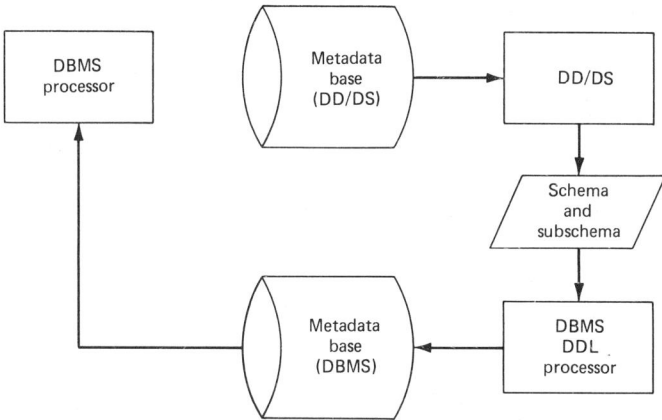

Figure 6.11a DD/DS generated metadata for the DBMS.

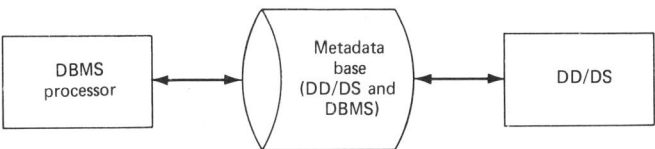

Figure 6.11b DD/DS shares metadata with the DBMS.

144 AUTOMATED INTERFACES FOR METADATA GENERATION

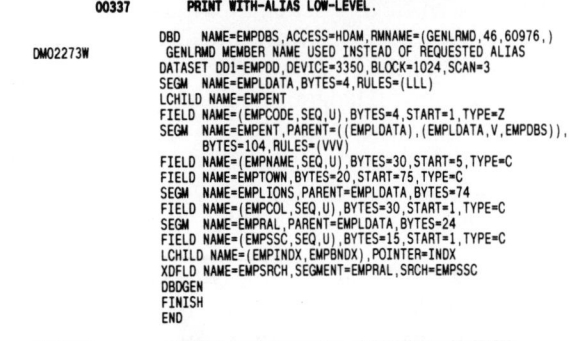

Figure 6.12 Example of IMS DBDGEN using DATAMANAGER.

Although all the DBMSs require similar metadata that is stored in the DD/DS, the way that the metadata is presented to each DBMS differs. Thus, one DD/DS automated interface will only produce the metadata suitable for one target DBMS. For example, IMS requires DBDs and PSBs for its metadata; IDMS requires CODASYL SCHEMA and SUBSCHEMAs, and DMCLs; and ADABAS requires FDs, and Format Buffers. Figure 6.12 demonstrates an IMS DBD generated by DATAMANAGER.

6.5.2 Benefits

An active DD/DS that automatically generates metadata for use by the DBMS can be highly beneficial through:

1. Reducing required coding of metadata; since it is already present in the DD/DS, there is no need to code it again for the DBMS.
2. More accurate documentation of the database, because metadata are automatically generated from the DD/DS.
3. Providing a degree of DBMS and DD/DS consistency.
4. The establishment of control over metadata changes at the schema level and subschema level, and the locking of programs affected by change.

6.6 METADATA GENERATION FOR SPECIAL-PURPOSE UTILITIES

Special purpose utilities are computer programs that are designed to assist a human or a computer process to perform a design or development activity by facilitating specific aspects of the activity. The spectrum of software tools is very large, and detailed discussion of all of them is outside the scope of this section [FRY 78, HARD 77]. However, a number of these will be briefly described to illustrate that special-purpose utilities require metadata in the form of data descriptions for input and outputs. This will show that the assistance of a DD/DS in automatically generating metadata would make these special-purpose tools more reliable to use, since the metadata used by the utilities would be consistent with stored definitions. Specifically, we will address database design aids, database performance simulators, test data generators, audit software, conversion software, and operating system job control.

6.6.1 Database Design Aid

The increasing demand for timely and accurate data has made it imperative to design the database structure in such a way that it would permit multiple users to obtain the data each needs without compromising the needs of the rest of the users, and to produce the required data in a timely fashion. To this end, a number of database design aids have emerged, ranging from highly theoretical tools that seek to solve problems for a class of database structures, to highly specific utilities that perform just one or two specific tasks of the overall database design problem for specific DBMSs [FRY 78]. This class of tools has one thing in common—they all need metadata in the form of input data descriptions and output descriptions. Typically, a database design aid requires input data descriptions which would include:

1. *User data requirements:* These are the descriptions of what data the different users in the enterprise need, including the different entities and their associated relationships and attributes, data that needs to be collected, and the expected results, such as the reporting requirements.
2. *System requirements:* These describe the processing needs of the enterprise against the database, and to the extent possible, define these processes or application systems, including the kind of data required, and frequency of operation.
3. *Operating environment:* Going into the database design aid is also a description of the processing environment, that is, a description of the hardware and software that will be used to process all the above.

The output products of the database design aid would include various database structures, including: the application's logical views or the way that user applications see the data, that is, the subschema; the global view of the database, or the overall information structure for the database, the schema; the physical view of the database—its storage structure (see Figure 6.13a).

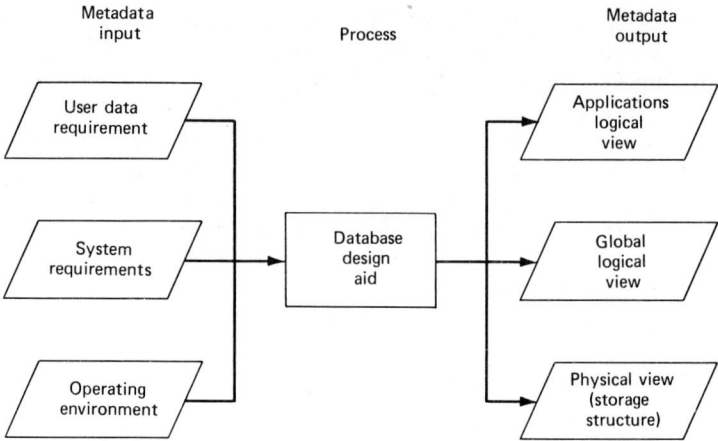

Figure 6.13a Metadata input/output of database design aids.

Much of the information required and produced by a database design aid is found in the DD/DS. Through the automated metadata generation capability, the DD/DS can produce for these database design aids the metadata required for input and receive the output of these specialized utilities (see Figure 6.13b).

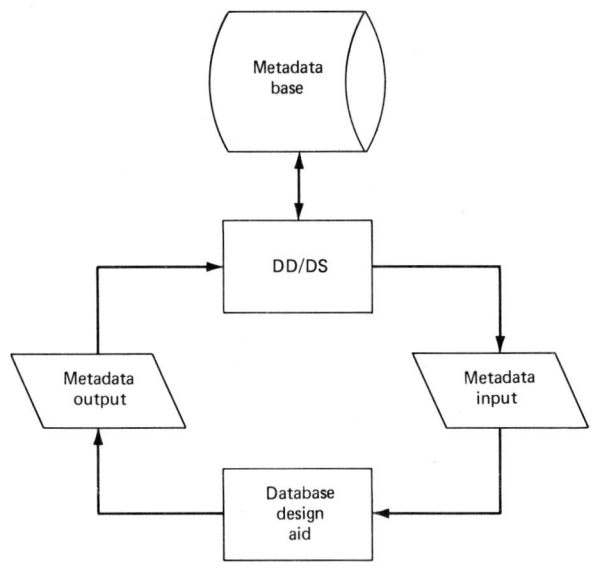

Figure 6.13b DD/DS generates/receives metadata for/from database design aid.

6.6.2 Database Performance Simulators

When databases are operational, there are many problems that arise that the database administrator must attend to. A primary objective of the DBA in an operational environment is to insure that there are a minimum of degradation problems, that there are no bottlenecks, and that existing database structures continue to serve the user population, even with changing demands (DEUT 79). The DBA will require feedback on the performance of the database, and based on these, decisions will be made regarding changes in scheduling, restructuring, or reorganizing the database [SOCK 79]. To do so, the DBA would collect statistics on the performance of the database, such as:

frequency of database access by program,
database access and response time,
database growth, and growth patterns, and
database storage statistics.

These statistics could be collected and fed into database performance simulators to assist the DBA in identifying problem areas in the database. Such a database performance simulator models the behavior of existing systems, based on a set of parameters. Modeling is conducted for various reasons, such as to determine effect of changing equipment or adding applications, and to determine optimal storage structure or access paths.

Performance simulators require metadata in the form of input parameters which describe existing conditions in the database. A DD/DS that is capable of automatically generating the descriptions of these parameters for the performance simulator is said to be active with respect to this tool.

6.6.3 Test Data Generator

Test data generators are special-purpose utilities that are usually invoked to support the testing of software or debugging of software. When linked with a Data Dictionary/Directory System, this enables one to generate test data from the metadata of the DD/DS using the test data generator software. The interface between the test data generator and the DD/DS requires definition of testing operands and values as entities or attributes within the dictionary. Test values can then be generated based on given conditions of other fields, or based on computations of values which are stored or generated. An active DD/DS can automatically generate this metadata from stored data descriptions.

6.6.4 Audit Software

Audit software assists the auditor in monitoring an application system for compliance with accounting rules and practices, in reviewing the efficiency and economy in the use of resources, and in determining whether desired results were achieved. Audit software requires metadata in the form of description of layout and contents of the data file. Much of the metadata required by audit software is contained in the DD/DS.

An active DD/DS, one that would automatically generate the metadata that the audit software requires, is an extremely useful asset for the auditor, because it could provide the basic information required to understand the system being audited and also help prepare the input for the audit software. Examples of metadata that the DD/DS can provide for the auditor include a comprehensive description of the inputs and outputs of the system, description of the processes, the security requirements that should be enforced, and the edit criteria and tests required for the system. File descriptions would be generated directly for the audit software. This is discussed further in Chapter 11.

6.6.5 Conversion Software

Conversion software is a class of tools that is used to transform or translate program or data from one form to another. This is a very complex area, and one which has received a great amount of attention since 1971, both in research and in practical studies [SU 76, GOGU 77, SWAR 77]. There are a number of prototype conversion software packages which may become available. IBM, the University of Michigan, and the University of Florida have been researching this field as evidenced by CONVERT and EXPRESS systems from IBM; Data Translator/Restructurer from the University of Michigan; and "A Methodology of Application Program Analysis and Conversion based on Database Semantics" from the University of Florida. These address primarily logical reorganization, and are intended for use during database conversion, from one DBMS's definition to another DBMS's. Generally, these software tools require metadata in the form of the logical and physical description of the old (source) database, and the logical and physical description of the new (target) database. A third type of metadata that the conversion software requires is the transformation (translation) rules that map the old database into the new database. All of these are metadata. They can be stored in a DD/DS.

An active DD/DS would contribute greatly to obtaining a consistent description of the data by automatically generating the metadata for this type of software.

6.6.6 Operating System–JCL

An active DD/DS can be highly beneficial to the operating system job control function by generating metadata for that process in the form of job control language descriptions.

6.6.7 Benefits

In each of the above cases, the active DD/DS can be highly advantageous to the special-purpose software utility, because it reduces the amount of duplicative coding that would otherwise be required. It provides accurate documentation for the utility, and in effect it establishes better control over these activities. This latter point will hold true only in the active DD/DS situation when the only place that the utilities can obtain its metadata is through the DD/DS. No other means would then be available to input the metadata for these tools. Metadata obtained this way would be consistent and up-to-date.

6.7 GENERALIZED (MULTI-PURPOSE) METADATA GENERATION INTERFACE

In some commercial DD/DSs there are general-purpose metadata generation interfaces that allow retrieval and machine-readable formatting of metadata. These support generally unanticipated needs for metadata, and would be used for special purposes. Generally, this facility requires special syntax. This type of interface is common in many of the currently available DD/DSs and can be used to interface with other commercial software. Some of the independent DD/DSs which have this feature, for example, are DATAMANAGER and Data Catalogue 2.

Systems that have this capability have provided users with the means of extending the metadata generation power of the DD/DS beyond its original scope. In DATAMANAGER, this capability is provided by the User Defined Syntax facility. This concept is also implemented in DBMS dependent systems such as IBM's DB/DC Data Dictionary, through its Program Access Facility.

The generalized metadata generation interface would be useful for filling a gap in unanticipated needs, and it can expand the scope of the active DD/DS.

6.8 SUMMARY

Technically, there are many advantages to having an active DD/DS, such as reduced coding, better documentation, and increased control over changes to the metadata. In each of the previous sections, specific examples were shown on how an active DD/DS can contribute to achieving these benefits. There are, however, some constraints. It is not always possible to have an active DD/DS, even if the capabilities exist. There are organizational or administrative policies that are needed to enforce the use of the DD/DS as the only source of metadata for the organization, (or at least for a particular system component such as a DBMS). An example of such a policy is to require that any data used in the organization must first be defined through the DD/DS, and furthermore, that design of application systems must go through the DD/DS to obtain its data definitions.

The current trend in commercial DD/DSs is to provide the capabilities for making the DD/DS an active system, but to give the user the option to invoke one or more active capabilities via optional interfaces. This approach makes the system more cost effective and flexible for users who may not want or need such a powerful control mechanism.

These and other considerations will be discussed in the next chapters on implementation strategies and selection criteria.

REFERENCES

[CODA 71] *CODASYL DBTG Report 1971,* Association of Computing Machinery, New York, 1971.

[DATA 80] *DATAMANAGER User's Manual,* MSP, Inc., Lexington, MA, 1980.

[DBDC 80] *DB/DC Data Dictionary General Information Manual,* Document Number GH20-9104-1, IBM, San Jose, CA, 1980.

[DEUT 79] Deutsch, D., "Modeling and Measurement Techniques for Evaluation of Design Alternatives in the Implementation of Database Management Software," NBS Special Publication 500-49, 1979.

[FRY 78] Fry, J. P., "Survey of State-of-the-Art Database Administration Tools: Survey Results and Evaluation," University of Michigan Technical Report DSRG78, DE 14.2, 1978.

[HARD] Hardy, T., B. Leong-Hong, and D. Fife, "Software Tools: A Building Block Approach," NBS Special Publication 500-14, 1977.

[LEXI 76] *LEXICON User's Manual,* Arthur Andersen & Co., Chicago, 1976.

[PLAG 78] Plagman, B., and C. Moss, "Alternative Architecture for Active Data Dictionary/ Directory Systems," in *Auerbach Database Management Series,* Portfolio 22-04-02, 1978.

[PRES 72] Presser, L. and J. R. White, "Linkers and Loaders," in *ACM Comput. Surv.,* Vol. 4, No. 3, September 1972, pp. 149-167.

[SIBL 76] Sibley, E. H., Ed., "Special Issue: Database Management Systems," *ACM Comput. Surv.,* Vol. 8, No. 1, March 1976.

[SOCK 79] Sockut, G. and R. P. Goldberg, "Database Reorganization, Principles and Practice," *ACM Comput. Surv.,* Vol. 11, No. 4, December 1979.

[STON 74] Stonebreaker, M., "A Functional View of Data Independence," in *Proc. 1974 SIGMOD Conf.,* ACM, New York, 1974, pp. 63-81.

REFERENCES

[SU 76]   Su, S. Y. W. and D. H. Lo, "A Multi-level Semantic Data Model," CAASM Project, Technical Report No. 9, Electrical Engineering Dept., University of Florida, June 1976, pp. 1-29.

[GOGU 77]   Goguen, N. H., and M. M. Kaplen, "An Approach to Generalized Data Translation: The ADAPT System," Bell Telephone Laboratories Internal Report, Oct. 5, 1977.

[SWAR 77]   Swartwout, D. E., G. Wolfe, and C. Burpee, "Translation Definition Language Reference Manual for Version IIa. Translator, Release 3," Working Paper 77 DT 5.3, Data Translation Project, the University of Michigan, Ann Arbor, MI, 1977.

7
Strategies for Building a DD/DS

In preceding chapters, we dealt with the elements necessary for designing a DD/DS: the underlying philosophy of the DD/DS design; the design of the metadatabase; the discrete building blocks – entities and attributes; the input and output facilities; and the automated interfaces required for metadata generation. We now use these fundamentals to address the issues and concerns facing developers of DD/DSs. In this chapter, we will explore strategies for constructing a DD/DS. Underlying the alternative implementation strategies are three major concerns:

1. *Metadata sharing:* There are two strategies to accomplish this major objective – *parallel sharing* and *serial transfer.* Each strategy has its advantages and disadvantages; further, each strategy requires that certain technical decisions be made early in the design of the metadatabase.
2. *A DBMS for the metadatabase:* The complexity of the metadata structures requires sophisticated software to manage – i.e., access, organize, and control – the metadatabase. Whether these management functions are performed by DD/DS software, or by DBMS software (or any other type of generalized system software), determines whether the DD/DS is implemented as a DBMS-dependent or DBMS-independent system.
3. *User facilities:* The relative usefulness of the metadatabase is highly dependent on the type of user facilities that are available in the DD/DS. One of the earliest design decisions that is made concerning the objectives of a DD/DS deals with who its users will be and what its purpose will be. These decisions are then translated into specific criteria for determining what user interfaces to include in the DD/DS. The strategies for implementing these user facilities are examined in this chapter.

In addressing these three areas of concern, this chapter serves to:

1. Identify and analyze specific implementation options for the benefit of designers and implementors of DD/DS software;
2. Assist potential DD/DS users in selecting a "best" commercially available system;
3. Guide users in implementing a "homegrown" DD/DS.

Implementation strategies may vary to suit a particular set of requirements, such as technical and economic feasibility and usability constraints. Developers often "customize" an implementation to accommodate specific requirements. Thus, each implementation approach reflects the choice of a particular set of design decisions made based on a given set of requirements.

DD/DS implementation strategies can be considered from at least two perspectives: the user's and the developer's. Each perspective has different requirements and concerns, although sometimes one person may play both roles. Developers need to be concerned with efficiency issues, performance issues and technical feasibility (not necessarily in that order). Users, on the other hand, are concerned with ease of use, control over use, flexibility of use, and economic feasibility (also not necessarily in that order). In this chapter, focus is placed on the developer's viewpoint; in a later chapter, the user's views will be considered in greather depth.

7.1 STRATEGIES FOR IMPLEMENTING METADATABASE SHARING

Metadatabase sharing is one of the fundamental principles of a Data Dictionary/Directory System, as was discussed in Chapter 3. Metadatabase sharing implies that more than one user — human users and software components — use the same metadata. It implies also that the metadatabase is so structured that there is only one physical representation of the metadata, and there may be multiple logical views of that metadata which may serve multiple users. Metadata sharing may be implemented differently for each DD/DS, depending on who shares the metadata, what metadata is shared, and how the metadata is shared. Figure 7.1 shows the two major types of sharing:

Among users of the DD/DS (e.g., the DBA, the DA, the system developer, the database analyst, and the end users);

Among software components for which metadata is being generated and/or extracted.

STRATEGIES FOR IMPLEMENTING METADATABASE SHARING

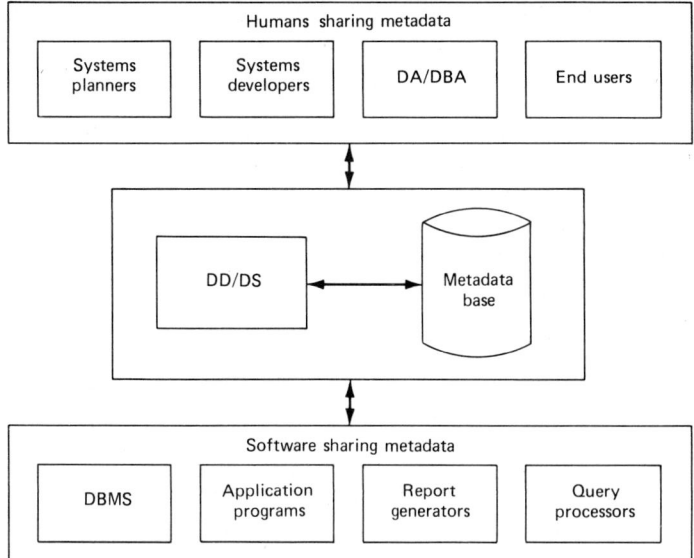

Figure 7.1 Two categories of DD/DS users sharing metadata.

In the first case, each of the human users shares the metadatabase for different reasons:

1. *The DBA/DA* uses the metadatabase to control the data resource for the entire organization, by insuring the currency and accuracy of the metadata; by insuring that only standard definitions are used throughout the enterprise, and by requiring that all access to the metadata is through the DD/DS.
2. *System Designers/Developers* share the metadata to facilitate system design and system implementation activities. The metadatabase contains descriptions about currently existing and planned systems and data. The DD/DS provides these descriptions to the system developer, to insure consistency and adherence to current standards and procedures.
3. *End-users* access the metadatabase to obtain information about existing data and system resources in the enterprise, to assist them during information retrieval in support of decision making and other business functions.

Metadatabase sharing among human users is accomplished through coordination and control, and through DBA-established standards and procedures. Administrative procedures insure this process. The degree of sharing is dependent on the effectiveness of the coordination and control functions, and on the effectiveness of standards and procedures.

Metadatabase sharing among software components such as DBMS, report generators, and query processors is accomplished through interfaces that automatically generate metadata for the software, as explained in detail in Chapter 6.

The objectives of metadata sharing for software components are:

to facilitate metadata definition for the target software component;
to maintain metadata consistency, currency and accuracy; and
to establish control over metadata usage.

Thus, report generators, DBMSs, query processors, application programs, and other software components can use the same metadata that is stored centrally in the metadatabase. The interface that is responsible for generating the metadata for the target component produces the metadata in the form that is appropriate for use by the individual components. For example, DBMSs require metadata that can be used to generate a schema and a subschema, or to produce data definition language statements used in defining the DBMS schema and subschema. The interface responsible for generating the metadata for the DBMS must be able to select the required metadata from the metadatabase and be able to convert this metadata into the appropriate form.

The implementation of metadata sharing among software components is accomplished by metadata generation. This metadata generation can be accomplished either via *parallel* access to a common metadatabase, or via metadata generation on *serial* usage basis.

7.1.1 Parallel Sharing

Parallel sharing of metadata represents the "database approach" to metadata sharing. As discussed in Chapter 3, this implies that this method allows all segments of the enterprise to share the metadata by creating and maintaining *various logical views* that are supported *by one single physical representation*. This means that there is only one collection of metadata and that, from the user's perspective, it is stored only once in the metadatabase, and that each software component gets the metadata it needs directly by sharing this one common source. Further, the software components might not have their own independent sources of metadata. Metadata is provided by the DD/DS. Since the metadata exists only in the DD/DS metadatabase, the different logical views, that is, the metadata requirements of the individual software components, must be generated from the single physical metadatabase.

An example of parallel metadata sharing can be found in the Cullinane product line. Cullinane's DBMS is IDMS and its DD/DS is IDD. Figure 7.2a shows IDMS as sharing metadata in parallel with the IDD. Neither the IDMS nor the IDD have (nor need) a separate source of

STRATEGIES FOR IMPLEMENTING METADATABASE SHARING

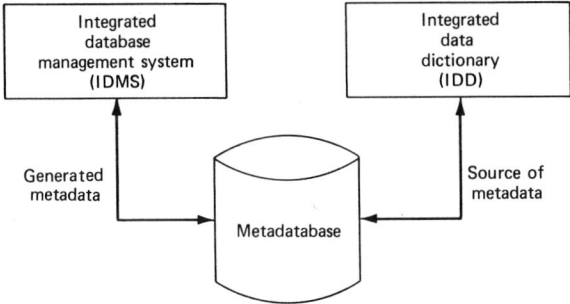

Figure 7.2a Parallel sharing of the metadatabase between a DBMS and a DD/DS.

metadata. Instead, it appears as if IDMS uses the same metadatabase and shares it with IDD for the schema and subschema that IDMS requires. However, note that even in the case where IDMS and IDD share the same metadatabase, at run time execution, the IDMS nucleus actually uses a load library which contains metadata that is physically separate from the metadatabase. Strictly speaking then, at run time, IDMS is using a separate metadatabase. Figure 7.2b shows the details of how metadata is handled in the Cullinane database product line.

Likewise, if a report generator shares metadata in parallel with the DD/DS, the report generator need not have its own separate source of metadata. The common metadatabase would contain the metadata that the report generator required, including parameters that specify a report, such as report descriptors and format specifications.

Parallel sharing of metadata is particularly applicable with a highly active DD/DS. Software components using an active DD/DS, by definition, can only obtain metadata through the active DD/DS. Thus, for example, application programs written in a high-level programming language such as COBOL, would require that the program obtain the metadata from the active DD/DS. If the compiler for the high-level language could access the metadatabase directly, then the sharing would be in parallel with the active DD/DS.

Parallel sharing can be more efficient, both in terms of storage and retrieval. Metadata is stored only once, and it is mutually accessible to the DD/DS and to all sharing components (see Figure 7.3). This facilitates update, since the affected metadata would be changed only once. Parallel sharing insures that the metadata is current, contributing to the level of integrity of the metadatabase, which is thus easier to maintain. (This, however, would not necessarily imply that the metadata is consistent with actual usage, if runtime execution is from a separate metadatabase).

Parallel sharing of a metadatabase can be implemented effectively only when both the DD/DS and the sharing software component (e.g., the DBMS) are implemented on an integrated basis, presumably by the

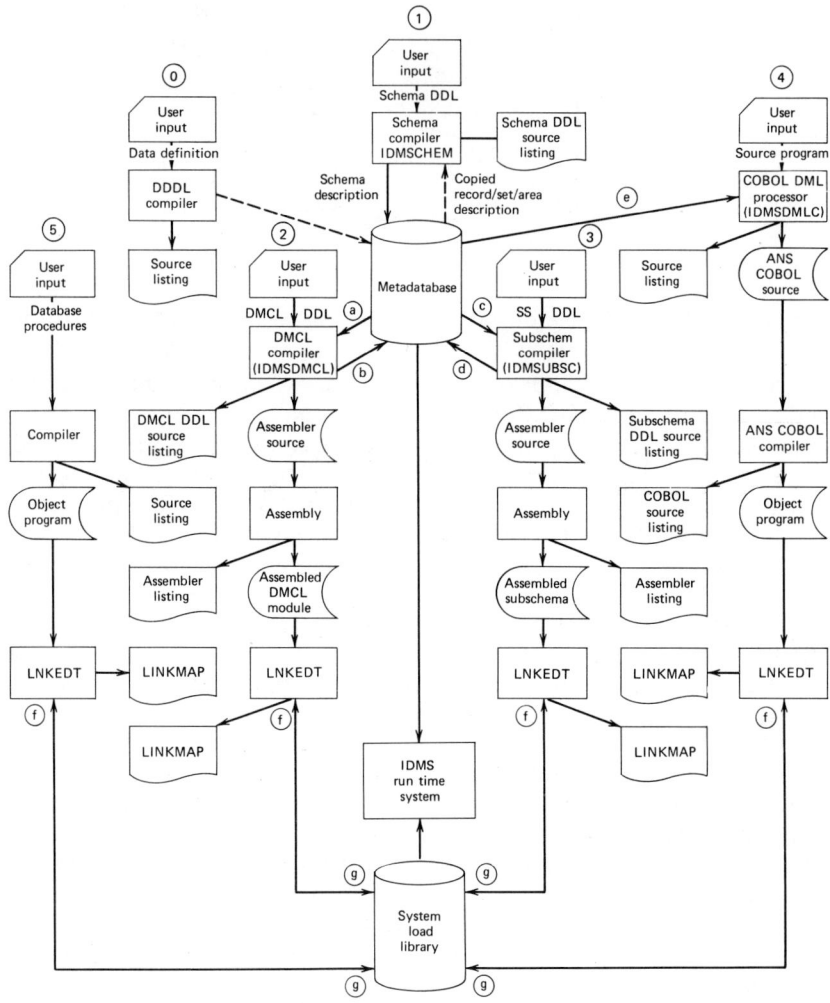

Figure 7.2b Runtime implementation of metadata for an IDD/IDMS environment. Courtesy of H. Roos, C. Kocks, KK&C, Holland.

DATA FLOWS

a) Area/file/journal information
b) Device-media descriptions
c) Record/set/area information
d) Subschema descriptions
e) Protocol/non-IDMS structure information
f) Standard operating system information

INPUTS

0) Data Descriptions Prepared for IDD
1) SCHEMA DDL
2) DMCL Code
3) SUBSCHEMA DDL
4) COBOL Source Code
5) DB PROCEDURE source code

STRATEGIES FOR IMPLEMENTING METADATABASE SHARING

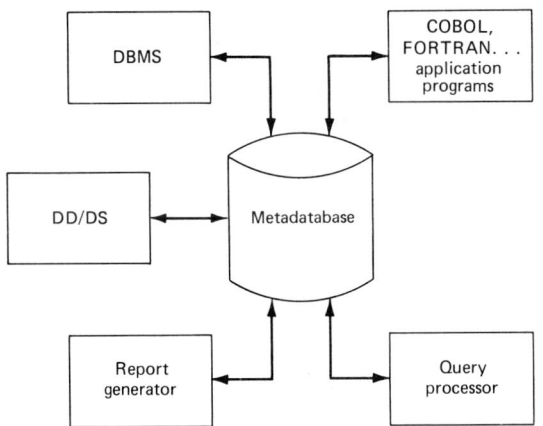

Figure 7.3 Parallel sharing of metadata among software components.

same vendor. This is necessary because there are software adjustments that must be made in the sharing software components to accommodate parallel sharing. For example, the data definition tables or blocks of the DBMS would be replaced by the directory portion of the common metadatabase. As previously mentioned, an example of this strategy is found partially in Cullinane's IDMS and IDD. Cullinane's IDD, as a product, evolved from customers' database experience. IDD was originally designed to enable sharing its metadatabase with IDMS. IDMS in turn was modified so that this sharing could be possible.

7.1.2 Serial Sharing

Serial sharing of metadata by the DD/DS from a metadatabase is a more flexible, and therefore more common, approach. Under this strategy, each software component usually has its own independent mechanism for entry of metadata. In addition, the sharing component may also obtain its metadata from the DD/DS through a metadata-generation mechanism for convenience and for accuracy. In this type of sharing, there could be a lesser degree of reliance on the control over the currency and accuracy of the metadata, since each sharing component could have the metadata updated, independent of the DD/DS. There are four important issues that distinguish serial sharing from parallel sharing:

1. Metadata sharing occurs at the process level — that is, between the processing components (see Figure 7.4)
2. Each processing component has its own entry mechanism for metadata, such as a DDL processor.

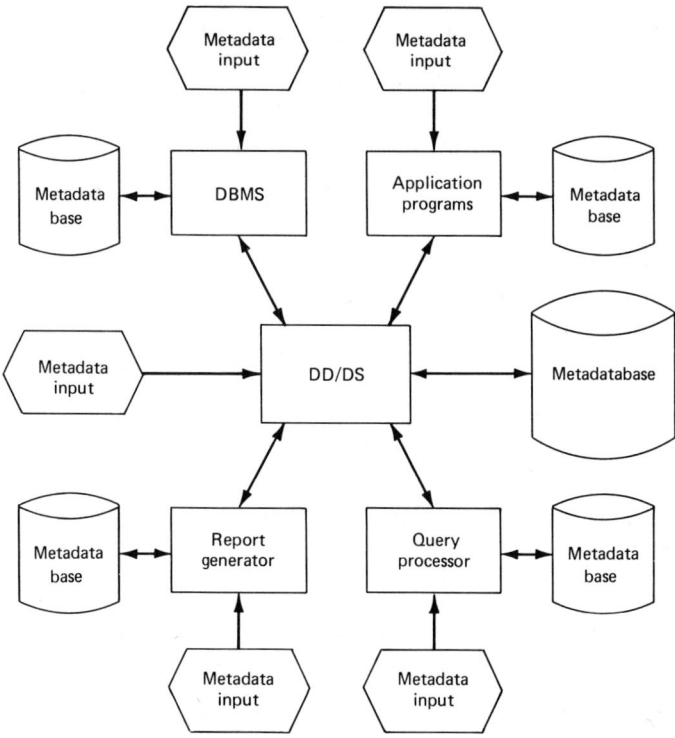

Figure 7.4 Serial sharing of metadata among software components.

3. Reliance on the controls for currency and accuracy of the metadata is more strongly dependent on other factors, such as administrative procedures.
4. Updates of the metadata must be performed both in the DD/DS metadatabase and in the software component's metadatabase.

Most commercial DD/DSs are based on serial metadata generation. This is the most expedient way of implementing metadata sharing, since this method does not require the sharing software component to be modified significantly. Sharing occurs between the software components and each of the components, that is, the DD/DS and the DBMS (see Figure 7.5), or the DD/DS and the RPG processor, have its own source of metadata. In this fashion, for example, UCC-Ten shares its metadatabase serially with IMS. UCC-Ten contains the metadata that is required to generate the DBDs, PSBs, and STAGE-1 SYSGENs for IMS. Upon request, UCC-Ten can "pass" metadata to IMS via an interface between UCC-Ten and IMS. By using this strategy, there was no need for the vendor to modify IMS.

STRATEGIES FOR IMPLEMENTING METADATABASE SHARING

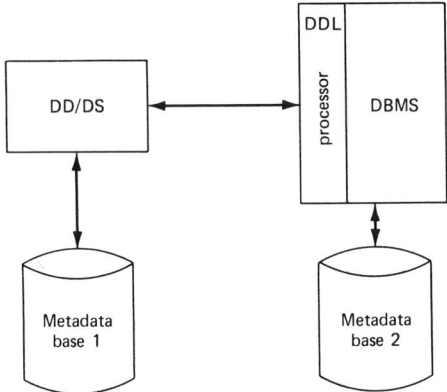

Figure 7.5 Serial sharing of metadatabase between a DD/DS and a DBMS.

DATAMANAGER is another DD/DS that shares its metadata serially with other software components, such as IMS, Mark IV, and application programs. DATAMANAGER, in fact, can share its metadata with several DBMS, including ADABAS, IDMS, SYSTEM 2000, and TOTAL. Via its automated interfaces, DATAMANAGER is capable of generating metadata for these DBMSs without having had to modify the target DBMSs software.

This approach is by no means confined to independent DD/DS software vendors that have no DBMS products of their own. Even DBMS vendor-supplied DD/DSs are built this way. For example, IBM's DB/DC Data Dictionary is built to share its metadata serially with IMS, and Software a.g.'s ADABAS Dictionary is likewise built to share its metadata serially with ADABAS. These vendors' strategy can be explained as follows: Parallel sharing requires substantial modification to the software that will be sharing the metadatabase with the DD/DS. A well established DBMS product, with an established clientele, discourages any significant modification to the DBMS product which may adversely affect existing business, unless the modification to the DBMS can be engineered in a manner which is transparent to the user.

In summary, the most expedient way of implementing metadata sharing is through serial usage, via automated interfaces that enable the DD/DS to generate metadata for the using component, such as the DBMS, without having to modify the DBMS.

Serial generation also encourages increased metadata sharing by the DD/DS user. This type of sharing is flexible because users can access the metadatabase directly. Users can create "new" generation facilities by implementing additional interfaces that provide communications between the DD/DS and a "new" software component.

There are advantages to both strategies of metadata sharing (see

Strategy for Sharing Metadata	Advantages	Disadvantages
Serial	Ease of implementation	Alternate metadata sources
	Flexibility	Less coordination and control
		Requires more metadata updates
Parallel	Single source of metadata	More difficult to implement
	Greater coordination and control	Requires adjustments to "target" component

Figure 7.6 Parallel versus serial sharing of metadata.

Figure 7.6). Perhaps the best strategy is to develop a hybrid implementation of metadata sharing for the DD/DS, so that parallel sharing can be used when coordination and control of the metadatabase are required. Serial usage can then be implemented when ease of implementation and flexibility of use are needed.

7.2 SOFTWARE MANAGEMENT OF THE METADATABASE

The design of a metadatabase revolves around the database concept. This design strategy allows sharing among many types of users, each contributing metadata through the DD/DS, and each using metadata for different needs, that is, each requiring a different logical view of the metadata. The resulting complex metadata structure suggests that database management software is required to manage the metadatabase.

7.2.1 Database Management Requirements of the Metadatabase

As discussed at length in Chapter 3, the conceptual data structure of a typical metadatabase is a complex network structure, supporting many to many (m:n) relationships (see Figure 7.7). This structure is necessary to support effectively the representation of metadata based upon the concepts of data independence — by describing diverse logical views and the mappings of these views from a single representation. The conceptual data structure also contains *recursive relationships* — which can be used to accommodate the situation where a meta-entity can be comprised of itself, as is the case with most of the entities in Figure 7.7. Also, the conceptual data structure can include multiple levels of hierarchy as illustrated in the following relationships (also shown in Figure 7.7):

SOFTWARE MANAGEMENT OF THE METADATABASE

programs contain *modules*
files contain *records*
records contain *elements*

Using the database approach for the design of the metadatabase implicitly requires that the DD/DS create and maintain many diverse logical views of the metadata itself that may be serviced by a single physical representation of the metadata. One way to satisfy this requirement is to support the previously mentioned relationships between the meta-entities. The various logical views of metadata are generally simple, but nevertheless diverse. They may include relationships of the type one-to-many (1:m), and the more complex many-to-many (m:n) relationships that may span many meta-entities. For example, the data

INTEGRATED DATA DICTIONARY STRUCTURE

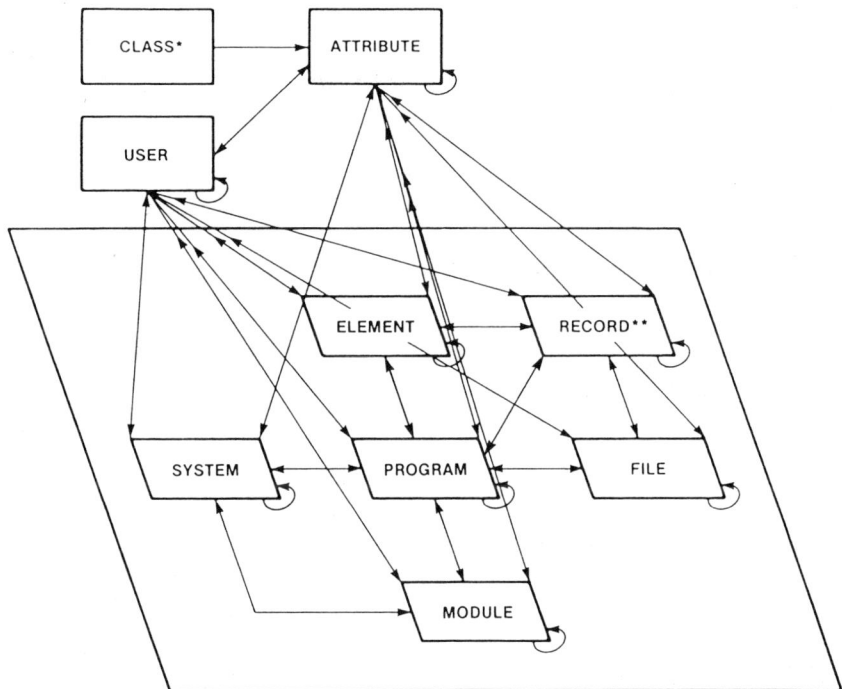

*User Defined Entity Types
**RECORD, REPORT or TRANSACTIONS

Figure 7.7 Sample meta-entity structure diagram (IDD, Cullinane). Courtesy of Cullinane Database Systems, Inc.

element "available credit" is a derived element, which is obtained by applying an algorithm that uses the data elements, "credit limit," "amount of loan," and "finance charge." Thus, the physical representation of "credit limit" may be used to realize data elements in many different logical views, which in turn are used to satisfy diverse requests.

The requirements for logical views of metadata imply that there is a high degree of metadata sharing. Thus, there must be a mechanism, that is, software capability, that enables the data structures to support mapping from logical to physical, and to manage metadata sharing.

Another requirement, the need for accessing the metadatabase, is also very complex. To begin with, multiple entry points are necessary to permit access at any point in the data structure, whether it is at the top or at the bottom of the structure. For example, access must be allowed at the data element level, at the record level, at the database level, or at the system level. Another type of access is that of conditional retrieval based upon the values of selected attributes, so that data elements for example meeting a number of attribute requirements, can then be selected for retrieval.

Relatively speaking, the volume of accesses for a metadatabase are low, especially when compared with the volume of access for a user database. Likewise, the size of the metadatabase is much smaller than a typical user database. Thus, given that one of the access requirements may be the need for the metadatabase to be online for both retrieval and update, considering the relative small size of the metadatabase, this may be a practical course of action.

7.2.2 Database Management Services for the Metadatabase

The foregoing design requirements of the metadatabase indicate the need for complex database management software to manage the metadatabase. This type of management software is required to provide for organization of the metadatabase, so that the logical data structure can be implemented to support the complex meta-entity structure that is the basis for the metadatabase. It must also be able to implement a storage structure that would enable the physical representation of the meta-entity structure.

In addition, database management techniques are necessary to support the access patterns of users of the metadatabase. Access in this sense means both retrieval and update. The access pattern of a metadatabase is highly skewed towards update when an entry is new; however, as the entry stabilizes, almost all the accesses are retrievals. Furthermore, access software is necessary to enable the metadata to be manipulated so that a variety of different types of conditional retrievals can be performed. These requirements point to a need for both direct and inverted index access methods, or some combination thereof. The

SOFTWARE MANAGEMENT OF THE METADATABASE

DBMS software capability is also required to provide various aspects of metadata control. These include security, recovery and correctness.

1. *Security control* for metadata requires software capabilities to manage and determine whether a user is authorized to access the DD/DS; the type of access the user is authorized for, such as whether the user is allowed to read and/or write metadata; the relative sensitivity of specific meta-entity types and occurrences (e.g., descriptions of employee records may be more sensitive than similar information regarding product data); and the identification of individual users and their passwords.
2. Metadata *recovery* techniques must be used to back up the DD/DS to prevent errors or loss of data in case of a system crash, or in the event of an erroneous update applied to the metadatabase. The software that restores the metadata from the back-up source is the recovery software. The back-up source may be a copy of the entire metadatabase, and/or before and after images of updates.
3. Metadata control also encompasses insuring the *correctness* and completeness of the metadata via such facilities as edit and validation and error control procedures.

All of the above services (see Figure 7.8) require complex software to manage the metadata. The current generation of commercial DD/DSs has utilized two strategies for implementing software management of the metadatabase [LEON 77, PLAG 77]:

Dependent DD/DS, which use a database management system facilities for the DD/DS;
Independent DD/DS, which use software facilities that are built into the DD/DS.

The following sections describe these two strategies.

Metadata Organization	Metadata Access	Metadata Control
Complex network data structures	Retrieval and update support	Security
Recursive structures	Conditional retrieval	Backup and recovery
Logical/physical mapping	Sophisticated access methods	Edit/validation

Figure 7.8 DBMS services for the metadatabase.

7.3 DEPENDENT DD/DSs

When the management of the metadatabase is performed using DBMS facilities, the DD/DS is said to be *dependent* on that DBMS. In this situation, the DD/DS actually takes advantage of the features of a particular DBMS to implement the structure and organization of the metadatabase, as well as all of its support functions.

The dependent DD/DS is usually implemented as an application under the DBMS, and thus often adopts the application-oriented structure and organization strategies of the DBMS. This includes using the access facilities of the DBMS and the security and control features provided by the DBMS. Under these circumstances, the implementation of the DD/DS is much easier than if these facilities are not already available. This helps explain why DBMS vendors and other developers choose to create DD/DS products as dependent systems. Another equally important reason is that they can create a "family" of products that are interdependent with one another. Some examples of these are: IBM's DB/DC Data Dictionary and IMS; INTEL's SYSTEM 2000 and IDD; Cullinane's IDMS and IDD; CINCOM's TOTAL and Data Control System; and Infodata's INQUIRE and EDICT.

To summarize, implementors prefer this approach because:

1. *The development effort for the DD/DS is much easier.* Many of the facilities that are necessary to manage the metadatabase are already provided by the DBMS, and little additional effort for developing these functions is required.
2. *The selling effort to current DBMS users is easier.* From the vendor's point of view, a dependent DD/DS is a good implementation strategy, because users of the DBMS are already a captive market, and "selling" the DD/DS facility becomes a relatively easier task. These users already have considerable resources invested in their DBMS, and therefore are more likely to also obtain the associated DD/DS. It should be noted that independent vendors of DD/DSs may choose this approach, also, by "piggy-backing" on a popular DBMS, such as UCC-Ten on IMS.
3. *Technical software coordination issues between a dependent DD/DS and a DBMS are minimized.* With a single coordinated organization working on the DBMS and the DD/DS software, implementation is much easier. This, however, is only true when the DBMS vendor is also the developer of the DD/DS, as is the case of IDMS and IDD, IBM's IMS and DB/DC DDS, and INTEL's SYSTEM 2000 and IDD.

From an acquisition perspective, a dependent DD/DS creates a stronger commitment to the associated DBMS, within the user organization. This is true because the DD/DS relies on the DBMS to perform all of its basic database management functions. Without these DBMS facilities, the DD/DS would not be able to function at all. Since the DBMS must be present, the likelihood of the user organization's continued use of the DBMS is greater.

In some cases, a DBMS vendor can make a dependent DD/DS operational without actually requiring users to pay the purchase price of the DBMS. This would be desirable when the user needs only the DD/DS and not the DBMS. In this case, the DD/DS supplier provides the required DBMS functions embedded with the DD/DS modules. This is a halfway situation for the vendors and the users. It is to the vendor's advantage to sell the entire family of products offered, rather than an individual piece of software of the database environment; and it is to the user's advantage to have the facilities of both the DD/DS and the DBMS so that application development can be coordinated.

An additional user-oriented advantage of dependent DD/DSs deals with active DD/DSs. Active DD/DSs have built-in facilities for control of the metadatabase, specifically through the metadata generation facilities. A dependent DD/DS and its associated DBMS provide a consistent framework for user recording of metadata, since a more uniform and consistent set of rules, conventions, and teminologies will be used in implementing common DBMS and active DD/DS facilities.

A disadvantage of the dependent DD/DS is that it is difficult to implement in a multi-DBMS environment, since the functions, the structures, and the conventions of the DD/DS are oriented towards one specific DBMS. Interfaces to other DBMSs from the dependent DD/DS are not a desirable consideration from the vendor's view, nor are they feasible to implement without vendor assistance.

7.4 INDEPENDENT DD/DSs

When the management activities — the organization, access, and control function — of the metadatabase are performed by software built into the DD/DS, the DD/DS is said to be *"independent"* of any DMBS, or "free-standing." Independent DD/DSs are self-contained systems, and do not require the facilities of any other general purpose DBMS to operate. The independent DD/DS is organized as a metadata information system, with the data structures, access methods, manipulation, and control functions built in as an integral part of the DD/DS package. Examples of independent DD/DSs are DATAMANAGER, DATA CATALOGUE 2, and LEXICON.

The chief advantage of the independent DD/DS is that it is not tied to a specific database management system. From the independent DD/DS vendor's point of view, this is a strong selling point, since they can promote the flexibility of an independent DD/DS. The independent DD/DS's flexibility derives from its ability to support a multi-DBMS environment, which is facilitated by metadata generation interfaces (using the serial method) to more than one DBMS. These interfaces permit the DD/DS and the DBMS to communicate with each other via the automated metadata generation facility, thus making it possible for the DD/DS to be an active control mechanism.

The independent DD/DS provides more flexibility to the user because it has the capability to support more than one DBMS. However, the independent DD/DS is more difficult for the vendor to implement and maintain, because the implementor cannot take advantage of facilities from a DBMS to implement the DBMS functions required by the DD/DS, and instead, must build all these basic functions into the DD/DS itself.

In a multiple DBMS environment, the user must choose carefully to insure that the DD/DS is capable of supporting all the DBMSs in that installation. For example, if a user organization had SYSTEM 2000, ADABAS, IMS and IDMS, an independent DD/DS that supports these DBMSs would be recommended.

Another situation in which the independent DD/DS might be suggested is where the user organization is just going database, and the recommended course of action is to implement the DD/DS first, followed by the implementation of the DBMS. In this circumstance, an independent DD/DS may be preferable, because the DD/DS;

1. Will minimally constrain the selection of the DBMS.
2. Can be operational without dependence on or prior installation of DBMS facilities.
3. Will be functional by the time the DBMS is in place and will in fact facilitate the design and implementation of application databases using the DBMS.
4. Will assist in defining the metadata for non-DBMS files.

Independent DD/DSs generally have interface capabilities to a number of DBMSs. These are usually provided as options of the DD/DS package and may require special considerations for support of metadata generation of schemas and subschemas. In the past, vendors have only "promised" these capabilities. Users are encouraged to insure that an interface is actually available. Further, users must devote efforts to establish the rules and conventions to insure that the interface is used properly.

7.5 THE SUBSUMED DD/DS IMPLEMENTATION APPROACH

There is yet another approach for implementing the DD/DS: the *subsumed* approach. This approach is a variation of the dependent DD/DS. There is no new architectural component for realizing the functions of the DD/DS. The subsumed approach implements the metadatabase as just another user database, using all existing facilities of the database environment, without creating an architecturally independent component in the hardware/software structure. This approach is generally popular among developers of self-contained, small computer systems, such as the IBM System 38 or TANDEM's product line. In this approach, the "system" performs the DD/DS functions.

When the DD/DS is subsumed, all the functions of a DD/DS are supported; however, they are subsumed under the DBMS or other system functions (see Figure 7.9). For example, the data definition function exists, but it is performed by the DBMS. The data structure support for the metadata is provided also by the DBMS or the system. Likewise, data manipulation functions and retrieval functions for the metadata are performed by the DBMS or the system. In all respects, the DBMS treats the metadatabase as another application database. In this manner, users actually perform DD/DS related activities, but they do not perceive the existence of a DD/DS function, and in some cases, may not be aware that they are performing DD/DS functions. In the subsumed case, users do not have to make any decisions concerning the

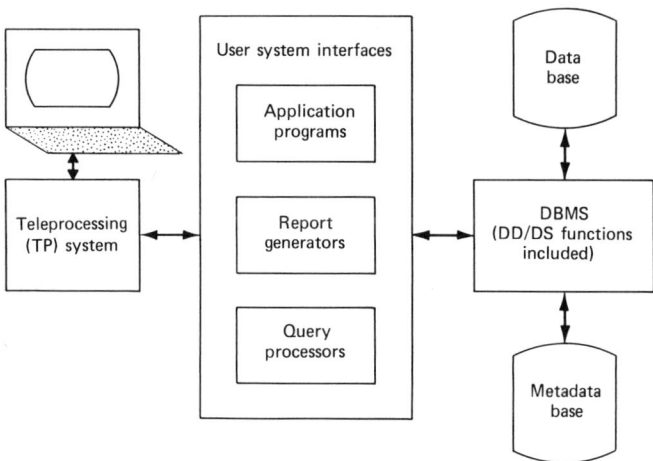

Figure 7.9 Subsumed DD/DS architecture.

selection of a DD/DS, nor do they have specially designed features or facilities that are considered as pertaining only to the DD/DS domain.

There are advantages to this approach, such as being able to provide the complete system in one package, which simplifies implementation for vendors and users alike, and being able to provide "transparent" DD/DS functions. Manipulation and retrieval of the metadata can be performed via one system, and users need learn only one set of languages, terminology, conventions, rules, and so forth. Thus, the subsumed architecture is a highly feasible implementation approach for small computer systems such as TANDEM and IBM's System 38. These systems have been built with support for dictionary/directory functions.

However, by following this approach, one of the most important functions of a DD/DS cannot be realized easily: to control the usage of the metadata, sinch the DD/DS is not an architecturally independent component, and one application of a DBMS cannot be expected to control the overall DBMS.

Another shortcoming exists for the multiple DBMS environment. With a subsumed DD/DS, it is not possible to support a multi-DBMS environment, since there are architectural differences among the various DBMSs, and these differences must be satisfactorily resolved before being able to communicate with each other.

7.6 STRATEGIES FOR IMPLEMENTATION OF USER INTERFACES FOR THE DD/DS

User interfaces are the means by which a user communicates with the metadata information system to obtain desired results. In this respect, user interfaces for the DD/DS are similar to those required for any typical information systems. The user requiring metadata information from the DD/DS can obtain it interactively — in a conversational manner, or in a structured formatted report. The most important requirements for these DD/DS user interfaces, regardless of the manner in which they are ultimately implemented, are that the interface must be easy to use, and it must be flexible. Among the many types of DD/DS user interfaces, the most common are those that provide output from the system and those that allow the user to manipulate or update the system. The specific tools include report generation, and query processing, combined with online support for update and retrieval.

7.6.1 Requirements for the User Interface

The *report generation user interface* provides the capability to produce formatted metadata reports using precoded programs. These reports are usually predictable and have standard formats. The general format of the reports does not vary from request to request, unless specifically changed by a modification in the report specifications. An example of these preformatted reports is the "entity catalog" report, which lists all the entities and attributes in the metadatabase. The formatted reports obtained using the report generation user interface is usually a very lengthy report, such as the entity report, which dumps the metadatabase in a formatted manner. Unanticipated, lengthy reports can be prepared also using this facility. An example of this type is a cross-reference report on specific attributes on an entity listing.

Query processing allows the user to retrieve metadata information in a more selective, impromptu manner allowing, for example, keyword searches. This means that the user can select those entries that have a specified keyword value, and either retrieve that entry, or perform further manipulation on the found entry. It is possible also to formulate a query to perform conditional retrievals based upon multiple attributes, such as

*"select all entities which have
version number greater than
2 and access indicator equal to a.*

Possibly the most important feature of query processing is ad hoc browsing — that is, the ability for users to retrieve selectively the contents of the metadatabase without cumbersome, lengthy reports. In addition, query processing is very effective for formulating ad hoc requests that serve to satisfy users' day-to-day metadata information needs — those that only have value based upon being accurate and timely. These functions are generally performed via a query language. This language can be potentially very powerful, depending on the features provided, and its relative ease of use. Generally, the query language is implemented for online and interactive use so that responses to the queries are obtained within a very short time interval.

Update and retrievals can be done online easily if this facility is user-friendly. A user-friendly online update facility is desirable because it facilitates updating the metadatabase, and it encourages the use of this facility to perform the ad hoc update and retrieval. An example of one such application is when the DBA needs to update the password file, or the security profile of the users of the system. Under these conditions, there might be a risk in submitting the update as a batch job, since it would increase the likelihood of unauthorized access to confidential information.

Of course, the availability of online capability should not preclude update and retrieval from being done in batch mode. Batch mode is preferable when there is massive metadata that needs to be updated.

7.6.2 Strategies for the User Interface

It is clear that the user inferfaces for DD/DSs are similar to those for other information systems. Existing facilities for supporting such interfaces can be applied to the metadatabase. DD/DS vendors with separate user interface products at their disposal may take advantage of them in the implementation of the DD/DS. This approach would make it easier to implement the DD/DS, and it makes it easier for DD/DS users to integrate these facilities and to learn them. This is especially true if these user interfaces already exist in the user organization prior to acquisition of the DD/DS. Thus, it should be clear that this concept is simply an extension of the concept of using the DBMS to support the metadatabase in a dependent DD/DS.

This strategy can be illustrated with the case of an existing report writer available for support of report requirements. An interface can be built between the DD/DS and the existing Report Writer in which the metadata for both components can be shared, and in which the DD/DS can utilize the services of the report writer to format and produce the desired metadata reports. CINCOM has done this with its DCS Dictionary and SOCRATES (CINCOM's Report Writer product). Likewise, the DD/DS developer should use existing query processor facilities and existing online support facilities to implement these user interfaces in the DD/DS.

From the user's point of view, this strategy provides an integrated approach to the business of managing and controlling information. The advantage derives from the fact that rules, conventions, terminologies, and languages will be consistent, and users need not be concerned with contradictory concepts or conventions.

This approach makes it easier for developers as well, since vendors with a family of products can effectively create a complete environment, in which the various software products are interrelated. For example, CINCOM has created such an environment with its Total Information System (TIS) by linking the new generation of its products with those that CINCOM already markets (see Figure 7.10).

As one might expect, DD/DS vendor implementations vary in the details of the approach taken. In most cases, vendors who already have an existing product line choose to use their own existing software. This is the case with CINCOM's SOCRATES; Cullinane's use of its report generation facility, CULPRIT, and its On Line Query Processor OLQ; and Arthur Andersen & Co.'s use of its report writer, Report Description Language (RDL), which generates user programs that extract from the user's datasets. Vendors use existing teleprocessing facilities to implement the online features of their DD/DS. For example, DATA-MANAGER can use CICS or TSO.

DD/DS vendors also have incorporated their own unique user interface facilities to provide needed user facilities. For example,

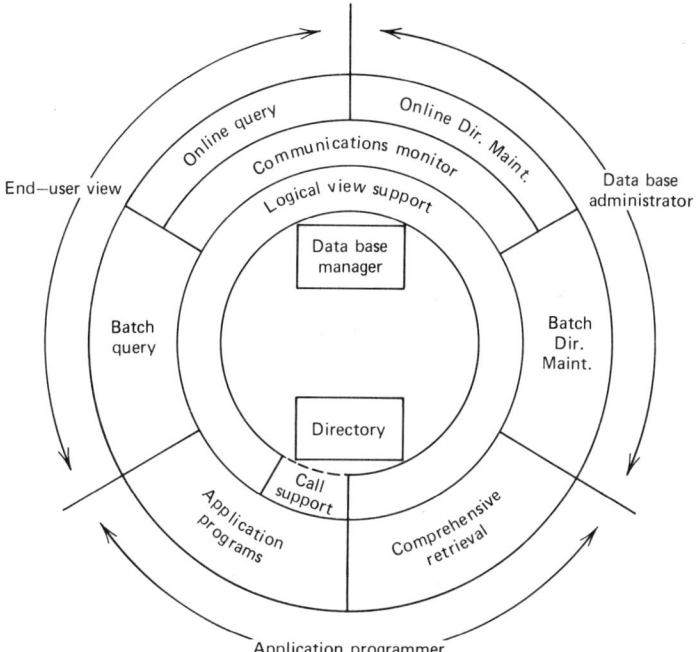

Figure 7.10 User interfaces to TIS. Courtesy of CINCOM Systems.

DATAMANAGER has its own query language facility. IBM's DB/DC Data Dictionary uses special online support capabilities to enhance user-friendliness through screen formatting and prompting.

Developers of DD/DSs, especially those planning to implement an in-house system, should carefully investigate the facilities already available in the enterprise and should consider using the existing user interface facilities. It is counterproductive and inefficient to "reinvent the wheel" in the design of any system. Thus, developers are encouraged to assimilate what already exists and to use these as building blocks. In general, this approach of using available tools and facilities tends to facilitate development of the DD/DS by making its implementation faster and more economical [HARD 77]. This is true because the required components already exist, and no extra time or resources need be spent in designing and implementing that module. This represents savings in time and money and creates a higher degree of consistency among the components of the information environment.

7.7 SUMMARY

This chapter has addressed implementation options for the DD/DS, from the developer's point of view. In building a DD/DS, a designer must be concerned with:

Metadata sharing.
Choice of DD/DS implementation strategy.
User interface facilities.

The objectives of metadata sharing are to:

1. Maintain metadata consistency, currency, and accuracy.
2. Facilitate metadata definition for the target software component.
3. Establish control of metadata usage.

Three types of DD/DS implementation strategies discussed are:

1. *Dependent.* These DD/DSs utilize DBMS facilities to perform their data management functions (organization, access, and control).
2. *Independent.* These DD/DSs perform their own DBMS functions (organization, access, and control) via software built into the DD/DS.
3. *Subsumed.* These DD/DSs are architecturally transparent and are built into the system as a whole.

This chapter also discussed user interface facilities that DD/DSs require to respond effectively to users' needs, such as report generators, query processors, and the online interface. Implementation strategies for these facilities were discussed, recommending the utilization of existing facilities whenever possible.

This chapter serves as a framework for classifying currently available DD/DSs and as an introduction to selection criteria for the DD/DS, which are presented in the next chapter.

REFERENCES

[HARD 77] Hardy, T., B. Leong-Hong, and D. Fife, "Software Tools: A Building Block Approach," NBS Special Publication 500-14, 1977.

[LEON 77] Leong-Hong, B. and B. Marron, "Technical Profile of Seven Data Element Dictionary Directory Systems," NBS Special Publication 500-3, 1977.

[PLAG 77] Plagman, B. K., "Criteria for the Solution of Data Dictionary System," in *Auerbach Database Management Series,* Portfolio 22-04-01, 1977.

8

Classification and Selection Methodology for DD/DSs

The Data Dictionary/Directory System is a valuable software tool requiring significant monetary investment and substantial commitment from an enterprise's management. Therefore, when acquiring a DD/DS, it is very important that careful consideration be given to the selection and evaluation of commercially available packages. Although cost can be an important factor in the selection process, it is often not the deciding factor. Selection of the DD/DS, as is true of other hardware and software, must be based on the needs of the enterprise.

Each DD/DS, whether in-house developed or commercially available, has unique characteristics. In order to assist in the objective evaluation of these systems, this chapter presents a framework for classifying DD/DSs that highlights similarities and differences among the various DD/DS packages. This framework, based upon the material in Chapter 7, also helps in focusing on an appropriate methodology for evaluating DD/DS packages. The methodology of evaluation includes criteria for selection. Analysis of DD/DS packages based upon these criteria and the suggested use of weights can serve to maximize the objectivity of evaluation and selection of DD/DSs.

Systems managers are often faced with the choice of buying versus building a software package. The trade-offs which must be considered in making this decision include economical considerations, resources constraints (e.g., availability of the appropriate level of technical expertise), timing, and technological constraints (e.g., availability of a DD/DS that will run on a specific hardware configuration) [PLAG 77].

This chapter begins with a description of a framework for a taxonomy of the DD/DS, followed by the description of a methodology that can be used in evaluating DD/DS's. Finally, a discussion of the make versus buy issue concludes the chapter.

8.1 CLASSIFICATION OF COMMERCIALLY AVAILABLE DD/DSs

Commercial DD/DS's can be classified along two dimensions based upon functional control capabilities i.e., metadata generation, and implementation strategy for metadata management. Although most DD/DSs are built with many comparable facilities, they differ in the level of functional control and the way each implements these functions. These differences provide the framework for classifying the commercial packages.

8.1.1 The Metadata Generation Characteristic

The first dimension in this classification scheme, metadata generation, determines whether a DD/DS is active or passive, and if active, whether the metadata sharing is in parallel or serial. These concepts were introduced in previous chapters. For ease of reference, they are summarized below:

1. *Passive DD/DS* contains documentation of the database environment; a passive DD/DS does not require that the DBMS (or other processes or system components) depend on the DD/DS for its metadata.
2. *Active DD/DS* is measured by the *scope* and *degree* of control exercised through metadata generation. Thus, a DD/DS is said to be active with respect to a processing component (e.g., a DBMS or an application program) if and only if that component can only obtain its metadata from the DD/DS.
3. *Parallel sharing* of the metadata occurs when the users' perspective metadata is stored only once in a metadatabase, and all processing components obtain their metadata from one common source. Sharing may be concurrent.
4. *Serial sharing* occurs when each processing component has its own source of metadata. The active DD/DS is based upon administrative controls.

8.1.2 The Metadata Management Characteristic

The second dimension, metadata management, determines whether the DD/DS is (a) *dependent* on a DBMS or (b) *independent* of the DBMS. These alternative strategies were discussed in Chapter 7. Summarizing:

1. *A dependent DD/DS* requires DBMS facilities to perform its metadata management functions, and to implement the data structure and access methods of the metadatabase.

CLASSIFICATION OF COMMERCIALLY AVAILABLE DD/DSs

2. *An independent DD/DS* performs all the metadata management functions through software that is built into the DD/DS. The independent DD/DS does not require DBMS software to perform any of its functions.

8.1.3 A Taxonomy for Classification of DD/DSs

Figure 8.1 presents a classification of commercial DD/DS packages using this taxonomy. The distribution of commercial systems shown as entries in this matrix bears out the fact that the most expedient approach to metadata sharing is to use the serial-sharing strategy for both the dependent and independent DD/DSs. Though currently the majority of DBMS vendors with DD/DSs belong in the serial-sharing classification, as more DBMS vendors (and hardware vendors) develop their new DD/DS capabilities, the trend may be towards more parallel sharing in active DD/DSs.

Metadata Management		Metadata Generation	
		Active	
	Passive	Serial Sharing	Parallel Sharing
Dependent	Data Control System (Haverly) EDICT (INFODATA) UNIVAC DD (UNIVAC)	DB/DC Data Dictionary (IBM) Data Control System (CINCOM) Integrated Data Dictionary (INTEL) ADABAS Dictionary (Software ag) UCC-10 (UCC) DATACOM-DD (ADR)	Integrated Data Dictionary (Cullinane) Data Dictionary System (ICL) TIS Directory (CINCOM)
Independent	PRIDE–Logik (M. Bryce) Self Generating Dictionary (Haverly)	LEXICON (Arthur Andersen) DATAMANAGER (MSP) DATA CATALOGUE 2 (TSI)	Not applicable

Figure 8.1 Taxonomy of commercial DD/DS packages. Pride-Logik is active with respect to application programs. LEXICON has been withdrawn from the market.

Another trend which may contribute toward further integration of the DD/DS with other software components is the vendors' effort to produce a complete set of software for an information environment. One example is CINCOM's new product line, TIS. The Directory component of TIS is expected to be active with respect to all the components in the database environment, and will probably share the metadata in parallel.

As expected, the cell, "Independent with Parallel Sharing" shows no entry, and is labeled "not applicable." As explained in the last chapter, there must exist software dependencies between the DD/DS and the DBMS that would make the DD/DS useful to only the target DBMS. This is contrary to the implementation philosophy of a vendor building an independent DD/DS, whose strongest operational benefit is its flexibility to interact and share metadata with more than one DBMS.

All three independent DD/DSs are shown as being active with serial metadata sharing. This is consistent with the implementation philosophy of providing the capabilities for metadata sharing without requiring software modification in the sharing component. This classification scheme sets the stage for defining a selection methodology, which is addressed in the next section.

8.2 AN EVALUATION AND SELECTION METHODOLOGY FOR DD/DS PACKAGE ACQUISITION

The DD/DS can be a valuable tool for the management and control of an enterprise's data resources. Careful attention should therefore be given to the evaluation and selection of a DD/DS to insure that the package that is selected is the most useful, and will best fit the organization's needs. The considerable amount of planning that goes into selecting hardware and software should be applied to the selection of a DD/DS.

8.2.1 Appointing a Selection Team

As is true with selection of hardware and other software, the first task in the selection process is to establish an objective selection team [FIPS 80]. The team members should include representatives from such areas as:

1. *Data (base) administration (chair).* Since the responsibility for the administration and control of the DD/DS is usually in the domain of the DBA, the DBA is normally nominated to lead the team.
2. *Technical services.* Responsible for the technical software issues associated with installing and maintaining a DD/DS.
3. *End-user areas.* Users of the DD/DS during ad hoc query sessions and other times.

4. *Systems design.* Users of the DD/DS during systems development and enhancement.
5. *Operations.* Operation of the DD/DS
6. *Internal auditors.* Users of the DD/DS as a control and audit tool.

8.2.2 Establishing Requirements for Selection

An organization-wide requirements analysis should be conducted to determine the use, management, and control needs for the data resources. Results of this study should be used as input in the planning process which would ordinarily precede the DD/DS selection process. The requirements study should provide information relative to the following issues:

1. *The current operational environment, and planned changes.* This would describe the current software and hardware environment, discuss planned changes in software or hardware, including modifications and enhancements.
2. *The organization's data management and control needs.* These would include:

    Types of data resources — what they are, where they come from, where they are used, and to what extent data is shared in the organization.

    Types of users — analysts, programmer, clerks, managers, and so forth.

    Types of use — online, batch, automated and non-automated.

    Types of controls required — administrative policies, security concerns, and integrity concerns.

    Types of metadata (in terms of meta entities and attributes) required.

    Types of services required of the DD/DS — such as inventory all data elements used in the organization, provide automated documentation for databases, and generate metadata for other software components.

8.2.3 Establish Methodology for Selection

The selection team should establish and publish the methodology it will use. If the organization already has an established software/hardware selection methodology, then that methodology can be adopted and modified according to the specific needs of data administration and control. In the absence of an established selection methodology, the team must develop one. The suggested methodology described in Figure 8.2 is discussed in more detail in the following paragraphs.

Step Number	Description of Step
1	Enumerate required steps
2	Select an evaluation team
3	Establish a briefing and training program
4	Identify and describe selection criteria
5	Identify mandatory and desirable criteria
6	Assign "weights" to criteria
7	Evaluate packages against selection criteria
8	Calculate scores
9	Recommend selection

Figure 8.2 Selection methodology for DD/DS packages.

1. *Enumerate required steps.* Enumerating the steps, or establishing a "critical path" chart with well-defined milestones, required to perform the selection is usually an administrative procedure which is necessary to establish ground rules. This step could be very informal, or very formal, depending on the team and the enterprise. The DBA, generally the chairperson for the team, should assume overall responsibility for this task, soliciting comments and suggestions from prospective team members.
2. *Select an evaluation team.* The evaluation team should be selected to reflect the importance of the DD/DS decision. Representation should be solicited from all parts of the organization that will be impacted by the installation of the DD/DS. Comments made earlier in this chapter about selecting an objective team apply here.
3. *Establish a briefing and training program.* A plan for briefing management must be developed early in the selection process. This is necessary to keep management informed regarding the major considerations involved in the selection process. In addition, a training program must be developed to provide selection team members with information regarding concepts and details of DD/DS features.
4. *Identify and describe selection criteria.* Identifying and describing the selection criteria are probably the most important tasks of the selection and evaluation team. Selection criteria should be based

on organizational needs (as determined by the requirements analysis) and based on state-of-the-art DD/DS capabilities. This step is critical. Each criterion must be described in such a way that there is no room for misinterpretation at the time of evaluation by the various members of the team. For this task, it is necessary to define commonly used terms clearly and concisely, explaining each one such that all the team members have a common understanding of terms, concepts, factors and criteria.

5. *Identify mandatory and desirable criteria.* The selection criteria must be classified into mandatory and desirable categories. The mandatory category contains criteria that each DD/DS *must* meet if it is to be considered further. An example of a mandatory criterion would be the capability to run on hardware of the installation. Excluding the packages which fail to meet mandatory requirements early in the process saves time and effort. Absence of a desirable characteristic will not eliminate a DD/DS from consideration, but its presence will be used in evaluating the various qualifying packages competitively.

6. *Assign weights to criteria.* Each criterion is assigned a weight proportionate to its importance to the organization based upon the requirements established by the selection team during the planning process. The weights are used to compute a score during the evaluation process.

7. *Evaluate packages against selection criteria.* Each DD/DS package that meets the mandatory requirements is evaluated against the set of selection criteria prepared earlier in Steps four (4) and five (5). A rating is given to each package for each evaluation criterion.

8. *Calculate scores.* The scores for all the criteria are computed by multiplying ratings by weights and adding these scores for each DD/DS package. The results can be compared by category with those of other packages to provide insight in the selection process.

9. *Recommend selection.* The score is used as the basis for recommending the final selection, taking into consideration all relevant factors.

This methodology provides a framework for objective evaluation of DD/DS packages. It can also be used to assist in planning the design of an in-house system, or to assess the need for possible enhancement to an existing DD/DS. This is accomplished by using the selection criteria as a "baseline" DD/DS package and then creating an in-house design or evaluating an existing DD/DS against the baseline. The focal point of this selection methodology, as stated earlier, is the selection criteria identified and defined in Step 4.

In the next section, the nine categories of selection criteria shown in

Figure 8.3 are suggested as guidelines in the development of customized selection criteria that would fit individual needs. Defining a set of selection criteria for universal use, applicable to each and every case, would not be effective because selection criteria should be based as much as possible on each individual organization's needs. Likewise, mandatory requirements and desirable features are organization-dependent.

1. Data description facility
2. Data documentation support
3. Metadata generation
4. Security support
5. Integrity support
6. User interface
7. Ease of use
8. Resource utilization
9. Vendor support

Figure 8.3 Categories of evaluation criteria.

As an aid in the overall evaluation, a matrix can be used to record the evaluation scores (see Figure 8.4) for each major category. The two axes of the matrix identify the nine categories of evaluation criteria, and the DD/DS package under evaluation.

The entries in the matrix consist of scores computed in Step 8 for each DD/DS package under each category of evaluation criteria as shown in Figure 8.4. Each of these categories is further subdivided into more descriptive subcategories, each of which is assigned an "evaluation weight" in Step 6, based on specific needs. These weights are used to calculate the scores for the DD/DS packages. Total scores are compared as a basis for making a decision in selection, design, or modification of a DD/DS.

8.3 SELECTION CRITERIA FOR DD/DSs

Each of the nine categories of selection criteria are briefly described in this section, together with their respective subcategories [PLAG 77].

Categories of Evaluation Criteria	DD/DS (Coded)										
	DC 2 (1)	DATA-MANAGER (2)	DCS (CINCOM) (3)	DB/DC (IBM) (4)	IDD (Cullinane) (5)	PRIDE/LOGIK (6)	DCS III (7)	IDD (INTEL) (8)	INQUIRE-EDICT (9)	DDS (ICL) (10)	..... (11)
Data description facilities											
Documentation											
Metadata generation											
Security support											
Integrity support											
User interfaces											
Resource utilization											
Ease of use											
Vendor support											
Total score											

Figure 8.4 Composite evaluation sheet.

8.3.1 Data Description Facility

This category addresses the breadth (meta-entities) and depth (attributes) of metadata which can be described to the DD/DS. In addition, the mechanisms that allow these descriptions to be entered into the DD/DS are evaluated. Under this category, the following factors would be considered:

1. Breadth and depth of entity types and attribute types allowed, that is, how many types of entities, and how many attributes per entity are allowed. The meta-entity structure is evaluated.
2. Does the DD/DS support expansibility; the ability to define new entity and attribute types?
3. Types of data structures that can be described, such as tree, network, and recursive.
4. Host language data structures supported, such as COBOL, FORTRAN, ASSEMBLY, and PL/1.
5. Types of input facilities allowed:

    The data definition language (DDL) provided by the DD/DS should be evaluated in terms of ease of use and flexibility. The DD/DS's DDL may be preformatted and/or keyword-oriented.

    Input and update facilities, such as, does the DD/DS have bulk loading facilities, online update facilities, user screens?

    Does the DD/DS allow machine-readable input that can be used during initial loading of the metadatabase? This feature is especially important for an environment that is heavily oriented towards COBOL file processing. This feature allows for the population of the DD/DS metadatabase from the host language (e.g., COBOL) code.

6. Entity structure definition support: Does the DD/DS provide the skeleton structure for the user to build on when complete entity structures are unknown?
7. Mandatory/optional definition: Does the system support a set of definitions that are considered mandatory (i.e., without which the description of a meta-entity occurrence would be considered unacceptable), such as identification attribute and relationship attributes? Does it support definitions which are optional but desirable, such as "responsibility" attributes?
8. Reference definition facility: Does the system have the ability to define new entity and attribute occurrences based on similar characteristics of other occurrences already defined?

8.3.2 Data Documentation Support

Closely related to the data description facilities category, this evaluation category addresses the ease with which documentation can be obtained from the metadatabase of the DD/DS. The following subcategories may be evaluated:

1. Completeness of attribute descriptions: Does the DD/DS provide the complete range of attributes required for documenting the organization's information environment?
2. Does the DD/DS provide expansibility capability for the attributes which cannot be satisfied under number 1?
3. Status control: Can the DD/DS control the status of descriptions; for example, does it allow "test" and "production"?
4. Edit/validation support: Can the DD/DS adequately document edit and validation criteria for user data?
5. Version control: Does the DD/DS allow the metadatabase to contain more than one version of the same entity type occurrence?
6. Security support: Can the DD/DS adequately describe the security of user databases?
7. Ability to supplement/replace existing forms of documentation; for example, can it provide in-line documentation for COBOL programs and record layouts?
8. Does the DD/DS have the ability to generate data structure diagrams?
9. Can the DD/DS produce keyword-in-context (KWIC) and/or keyword-out-of-context (KWOC) indices?

8.3.3 Metadata Generation

This facility is very important for the organization wishing to have an active DD/DS in the database environment. The following subcategories should be addressed:

1. Scope of Activity: Determined by the number of software components with respect to which the DD/DS is active. For example, does the DD/DS generate metadata for:
   DBMSs?
   Procedural (host) languages?
   Report generator?
   Edit/validation processors?
   Access control processors?
   Test data generation for databases?

2. Mode of sharing metadata: This aspect reflects the implementation strategy used by the DD/DS to control the operating environment in terms of metadata sharing. Does the DD/DS share metadata:
   in parallel?
   serially?
3. Degree of activity: Generation-time requirements determine the degree of activity in terms of metadata binding at the time of:
   compilation of programs,
   loading of programs, and
   execution of programs.

8.3.4 Security Support

To determine the capability to protect the metadatabase from unauthorized access, the following must be evaluated:

1. Is there the capability to protect the metadatabase with password control and functional access control through assignment of security levels to the metadata?
2. Are security features provided by the DD/DS, or by the DBMS?
3. Are security facilities coordinated with the DBMS and transaction processor to insure effective control during online activity?

8.3.5 Integrity Support

This category is closely related to security and is concerned with the integrity and trustworthiness of the metadata. DD/DS packages should be evaluated for features which specifically support metadata integrity:

1. Are edit and validation functions present that allow checking for completeness, consistency, currency, accuracy, and validity of metadata?
2. Are error reporting functions provided?
3. Can the DD/DS recover from destruction of all or part of the metadatabase?
4. Does the DD/DS recognize the "owner" of metadata?
5. Does the DD/DS support multiple metadatabases? How are they controlled?

8.3.6 User Interface/Output

The details of this category will depend on how the DD/DS will be used. The output of the DD/DS is the most tangible proof of usability to users. In any event, this category should be a highly influential factor in selecting a DD/DS. If the user can understand the outputs of the DD/DS, then the DD/DS is a valuable tool. Therefore, it is important to determine how many, and how easy to use these outputs are:

1. Standard reports: How many, and how suitable are these to the organization's needs?
2. Ability to select upon retrieval: How flexible is the DD/DS in allowing users to discriminate output?
3. Online DD/DS capability for both retrieval and update is desirable if there is need for quick responses.
4. Ad hoc query interface is a desirable capability, especially if the organization uses online capabilities for development.
5. How many and how suitable are the administrative and control reports which will be used by the DBA?
6. Does the DD/DS interface with a report writer?
7. Can users customize metadata reports using their own specification?
8. Does the DD/DS allow for automated output? Into what media?
9. Is the DD/DS capable of supporting audit trail requirements?

8.3.7 Ease of Use/Flexibility

Perhaps the most critical factor, as far as a user is concerned, is how easy the DD/DS is to use. The effectiveness of the DD/DS will be impaired if it is difficult to use. Thus, even though ease of use is evaluated implicitly in other categories, it is explicitly addressed from the point of view of how easy it is to learn to use the DD/DS and how easy it is to make the DD/DS do what one wants it to do. Thus, the following should be evaluated:

1. Ease of learning: Evaluate the extent to which training is required.
2. Expertise: Determine the level and type of technical expertise required for various users of the DD/DS, such as whether DP expertise is required, whether or not the DD/DS provides help facilities, such as menu selection, prompters, and help commands, which allow new users to benefit from the system soon after installation.
3. Determine whether the user has the ability to extend the facilities of the system through user exits, or whether the system is fixed, allowing no additions.
4. Determine whether the DD/DS provides the flexibility to allow coordination with existing procedures, standards and practices, or whether everything is installation-dependent in an operational sense.

8.3.8 Resource Utilization

This category addresses the resources needed to operate the DD/DS. These include:

> memory required;
> secondary storage necessary, peripherals required;
> other software required;
> system generation features;
> reorganization requirements for the metadatabase; and
> operating mode — batch, online, or distributed.

8.3.9 Vendor Support

This category evaluates the vendor commitment to support the product and the services that vendors will provide before, during, and after installation. The evaluation should focus on whether it is an advantage or a disadvantage if the DD/DS is produced by a DBMS or an independent vendor. Thus, the following should be analyzed:

1. Commitment to enhancements and long term support to the DD/DS.
2. Responsiveness to users' needs, especially when users request modifications or improvements for specific capabilities.
3. Reliability and integrity of vendor support.
4. Operational support for "bugs," necessary throughout the life of the system.
5. Training provided in terms of: amount of classroom training, training documents, and training format.
6. Documentation: A good DD/DS should include good documentation. DD/DS documentation provided by the vendor must be evaluated on its comprehensiveness and the accuracy with which it describes the system's features and functions.
7. Users' group: Does the vendor support users' group for the DD/DS? The presence of a user group provides a forum for interchange of ideas and is generally beneficial.

The nine evaluation categories can be used as a basis for customizing a specific set of evaluation criteria for an individual organization by adding and/or enhancing criteria and by assigning weights to each criterion according to its relative importance to the organization. The process used in assigning these weights is similar to the process of calculating a weighted average. It insures proper emphasis on appropriate

SELECTION CONSIDERATIONS

aspects of the features of DD/DS packages during the evaluation process.

8.4 SELECTION CONSIDERATIONS

The purpose of presenting the taxonomy of DD/DS packages at the beginning of this chapter was to establish the framework for the DD/DS selection process and the use of the methodology for evaluation. This section discusses how the taxonomy helps to focus attention on the critical selection considerations for DD/DS packages. The discussion focuses on the two dimensions of the taxonomy matrix:

active versus passive DD/DS, and
independent versus dependent DD/DS.

8.4.1 Active Versus Passive DD/DS

The selection team should focus attention on the issue of whether or not the enterprise requires a passive or an active DD/DS. Some non-database environment situations may require only a passive documentation tool to support project administration. Should this be the case, the selection process may be simplified by addressing fewer criteria. In the event that administration and control requirements necessitate an active DD/DS, the selection criteria will no doubt be more extensive. However, the number of DD/DS packages to be considered might be reduced based upon additional mandatory criteria.

8.4.2 Independent Versus Dependent DD/DS

An important consideration is to determine the degree of commitment to a particular DBMS for the foreseeable future within the organization. Such a commitment may indicate the choice of a DD/DS which is dependent on the DBMS in question. For example, a long-term commitment to a DBMS such as ADR's DATACOM DB may indicate the choice of ADR's DD/DS, DATACOM DD. Such a choice may be justified based upon the considerations set forth in Chapter 7.

8.4.3 Special Cases

A particularly difficult situation might arise when the commitment is to a DBMS which is not widely used. With little or no choice of commercial DD/DS packages the organization can do one of two things: a) select an independent DD/DS and build an in-house interface between the DD/DS and the DBMS, or b) develop a DD/DS using the dependent, or the subsumed approach, that is, implementing a metadatabase as an application database under the DBMS, and use all the facilities of the DBMS for management and operation. Both approaches imply considerable in-house developmental efforts.

Commitment to a more widely used DBMS for which there exists more than one commercial DD/DS with interfaces, presents a wider range of choice to the enterprise. For example, an organization that is committed to Cullinane's IDMS has two choices: 1) select an independent DD/DS, such as DATAMANAGER, which has an interface to IDMS; or b) select Cullinane's own IDD. The underlying advantage in choosing IDD is that the metadata for both IDD and IDMS will be the same, and can be shared in parallel. Another advantage is that both the DBMS and the DD/DS are likely to use the same conventions. The advantage of choosing an independent DD/DS is that it provides flexibility for future developments in the event that there were a change of DBMSs, that is, in the event the DBMS commitment is not that strong.

If an organization has long-term commitments to more than one DBMS, it may benefit from selecting a DD/DS which has the flexibility to interface with more than one DBMS, such as an independent DD/DS like DATA CATALOGUE 2 or DATAMANAGER.

A related consideration in determining available DD/DSs are environment constraints. For example, organizations that have IBM equipment have the largest number of DD/DSs to choose from. This is not true of organizations with other hardware systems. Of the current DD/DSs, only the following have implementations for environments with other than IBM equipment:

DATA CATALOGUE 2, TSI – UNIVAC, Honeywell,* DEC†, Burroughs,† CDC†
PRIDE/Logik, MBA, Inc. – UNIVAC, CDC, Burroughs, Hewlett-Packard, Data General, ICL, Honeywell, DEC
DCS, Haverly Systems – UNIVAC
UNIVAC DD – UNIVAC

Several hardware manufacturers have moved to close this gap, and currently have initiated or recently completed development of DD/DSs that will run on their hardware. These include UNIVAC, Honeywell, Burroughs, Texas Instruments Inc. and Digital Equipment Corporation.

A final consideration in the evaluation and selection process is the decision to either build an in-house system or buy one "off the shelf."

*Note: Limited implementations.
†Special user implementations.

8.5 THE MAKE-VERSUS-BUY ISSUE

Making the decision to acquire a DD/DS is based on a combination of factors: hardware, software, and metadata requirements of the organization. The decision to make or buy the system is heavily influenced by technical and economical constraints, and must be based on pragmatics [LEON 77]. Figure 8.5 presents a flowcharted approach to making the decision regarding "building vs. buying" a DD/DS [PLAG 77].

If we assume that a preliminary survey concluded that commercially available DD/DSs exist that meet stated requirements, then the next step is to determine how well these DD/DSs score with respect to weighted evaluation criteria as described in Section 3 of this chapter. If the DD/DS passes mandatory requirements and scores within a desirable range, then the last step is to determine whether that DD/DS falls within an appropriate price range. The decision to buy is made if the DD/DS meets both the technical and the economic constraints.

If, at any point during this decision path there does not exist a commercially available DD/DS that meets either the technical or the economic requirements, then the option to build a DD/DS should be carefully considered.

It should be noted that even if a DD/DS does not exist that meets all the technical requirements, it may be worth the effort to explore whether there is a DD/DS under development. If such a development effort is uncovered, it should be further determined whether it is reasonable to wait for its anticipated results. If the time frame is acceptable, further evaluation should proceed to determine the extent to which the anticipated DD/DS will meet all the evaluation criteria. This may result in a decision to proceed with plans to buy the DD/DS under development. This may be the decision even if the proposed package does not meet all the evaluation criteria, since it may still be possible to arrange for the DD/DS development effort to be modified to suit the organization's needs. An affirmative answer would argue for continuing the purchase path. A negative answer will again force the decision towards building a new DD/DS.

The build-your-own decision path hinges on three main resources: money, technical expertise, and time. If an organization has all three, then it would be possible to build a DD/DS. If any one of the three resource constraints is absent, then the decision to build should be deferred, lest it be doomed to failure from the start. Here it should be noted that some resources (e.g., technical expertise) can be bought.

The commercial availability of an increasing number of DD/DS packages suggests that the buy alternative should be considered carefully. The buy option can be implemented in a relatively short time. The price is very attractive — currently in the range of $15K–$45K plus a

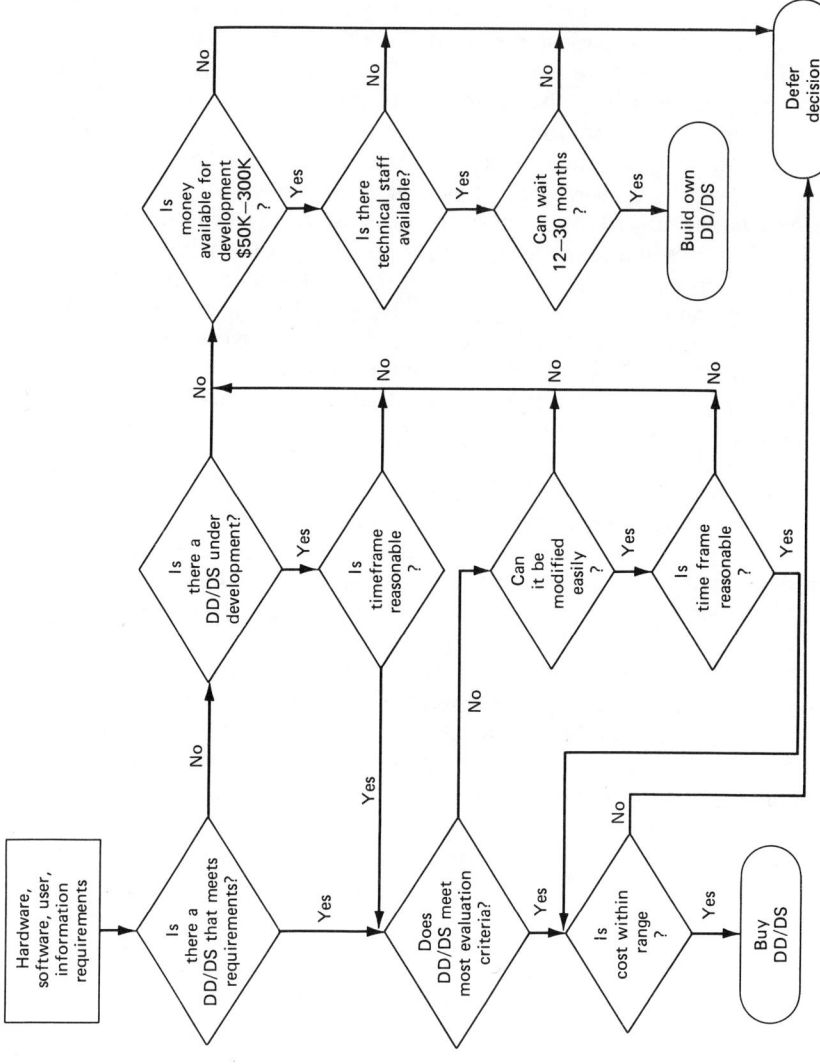

Figure 8.5 Decision path for buying versus building a DD/DS [PLAG 77].

nominal annual maintenance fee — a fraction of what it would take to build a DD/DS. Furthermore, commercial DD/DS packages contain features that are likely to be more comprehensive, including a fairly complete set of entities and attributes; they have ready-to-use input/output facilities; and most provide metadata generation capabilities. Expansibility capability of the DD/DS which allows new entities and attributes to be added, also provides increased flexibility to make the system more compatible with user needs.

Nevertheless, there are some factors inhibiting the purchase of commercial DD/DS packages. Non-IBM mainframes generally have limited choices of DD/DSs, as discussed in Section 4 of this chapter. Organizations with minicomputers and microcomputers have an even more limited selection. A second factor that must be considered is the application environment. For example, a scientific organization which needs to manage its metadata requires a DD/DS that has a very flexible set of entity types and attribute types. This DD/DS needs to be able to describe scientific data, or at least, this DD/DS must have an expansibility facility that would allow the user to describe the scientific data. At present, there are not many DD/DSs (not even DBMSs) that can do the job adequately. A third factor which may hinder purchase of a DD/DS is the software environment in which the DD/DS operates. If no commercial DD/DS exists that will run with existing software (e.g., operating system or compiler), then there may be no other option but to build a DD/DS.

An organization choosing to design its own DD/DS must realize that this option requires a high initial cost in time and money (anywhere from $50K to $300K) and from 12 to 30 months for development time. However, there are several advantages to developing an in-house DD/DS. One such advantage is that in-house knowledge about the DD/DS may contribute to reducing subsequent operational and maintenance cost. Another advantage is that the DD/DS thus built will suit specific user needs much better than a generalized commercial system. The homegrown system is tailored to the specific needs of the organization.

8.6 SUMMARY

This chapter has classified the commercially available DD/DSs into dependent and independent, and then into passive and active categories. This taxonomy serves as a framework for the evaluation and subsequent acquisition decision-making process.

Selection considerations, such as hardware factors and commitment to a single DBMS, were discussed, preceded by a detailed description of a methodology for evaluation and selection of a DD/DS. This description includes a detailed explanation of evaluation criteria. The chapter concludes with a discussion of the trade-offs between making and buying a DD/DS.

REFERENCES

[FIPS 80] "Guidelines for Implementation and Usage of Data Dictionary Systems," National Bureau of Standards Federal Information Processing Standards (FIPS) 76, 1980.

[LEON 77] Leong-Hong, B., and B. Marron, "Technical Profile of Seven Data Element Dictionary/Directory Systems," National Bureau of Standards Special Publication 500-3, 1977.

[PLAG 77] Plagman, B. K., "Criteria for the Selection of Data Dictionary/Directory Systems," in *AUERBACH Data Base Management Series,* Portfolio 22-04-01, 1977.

9

Implementation of the DD/DS in User Organizations

The success of a DD/DS implementation in a given enterprise can be measured in terms of the extent the organization has achieved its original goals with regard to the DD/DS. These include the ability to share data resources across organizational lines and to integrate effectively data usage in the development and operation of information systems. To achieve these goals, implementors of DD/DSs must develop strategies to address two specific problem areas: coordination among users, and technical integration.

After exploring the ramifications of these two problem areas, this chapter presents six specific strategies which can be employed to address the two problem areas. These strategies are:

1. Integration of the DD/DS into the systems development life cycle (SDLC). Indisputably, the DD/DS plays a strong role in SDLC activities. The DD/DS facilitates performance of SDLC activities by establishing common definitions, common rules and procedures, and common data for shared use among application development groups.
2. Defining how the data administrator and/or database administrator will use the DD/DS. The use of the DD/DS in support of data administration (DA) and database administration (DBA) is critical. These two functions, DA and DBA, have the responsibility for the enterprise's entire wealth of data resources. The DD/DS is a major tool in the performance of their duties.
3. Creating data definition standards. Data standardization is perhaps the backbone of the DD/DS. Without it, and without strict rules for enforcing it, the use of the DD/DS would be considerably

weakened. Conversely, the DD/DS facilitates the enforcement of data standardization.
4. Planning the phased population of the DD/DS. Phased population of the DD/DS allows for an orderly assimilation of the organization's data into the DD/DS.
5. Planning for the security of the metadatabase. Preparing for metadatabase security includes determining the sensitivity of the data that will be stored in the metadatabase, and establishing levels of security for accessing the contents of the DD/DS.
6. Planning for software interfaces. If the DD/DS is to be the dominant control tool in the operational environment, it will have to interface with other software components. These interfaces have to be defined, and plans for implementing them must be developed.

Each of these specific strategies is discussed individually after the two problem areas are explored, and the basic planning issues are described. Each strategy is then related back to the two problems in terms of how they are addressed.

9.1 COMMON PROBLEMS USERS FACE IN IMPLEMENTING THE DD/DS *(Everything you thought could go wrong and more!)*

The DD/DS implementation, conceived properly, will have a pervasive impact on the enterprise. This impact will occur on two levels, the user level, and the technical level.

The common problems encountered in DD/DS implementations can be viewed in terms of the impact level, although in reality, problems in one area may be caused by or influenced by problems in the other area. This section discusses many of the things that can go wrong under the general topics of coordination among users, and technical integration.

9.1.1 Coordination Among Users

Recognizing that the DD/DS, if properly utilized, may have an impact on a broad spectrum of the organization, makes it clear that a successful endeavor in implementing the DD/DS requires careful coordination to orchestrate support and goodwill from a large cross-section of the enterprise, both in and outside the EDP community. When coordination among users is lacking, a number of problems will manifest themselves and hinder the realization of the goals set for the DD/DS implementation effort.

A lack of motivation on the part of users of the DD/DSs is the first of many problems caused by a lack of coordination among users. In areas where data usages have already been established, the DD/DS may appear to be a threat, especially to those users who consider themselves exclusive "owners" of data. They will not be inclined to give up the metadata to the custody of a DD/DS. In these situations, getting the users to share data and to use DD/DS facilities is a delicate diplomatic task involving motivation. As a data-diplomat, the DBA must motivate the user to take advantage of the many DD/DS facilities, to participate in DD/DS activities with metadata input, and to contribute in the standardization of the metadata. Users' support can be won by convincing them of the benefits that can be obtained in using a DD/DS, by training them on the correct use of the system, and by insuring that their needs are met. This follows the policy that it is easier to win support from a well informed constituency.

A second problem caused by the lack of coordination among users is the diversity of usage patterns established in using the DD/DS. A lack of standards in the description of data and in the formats for presenting metadata can cause confusion to the point of undermining the original goals of reducing inadvertent data redundancies. Users will not recognize similar data elements without uniform descriptions, causing duplicate instances to be introduced. This lack of standardization arises from poor coordination among users of the DD/DS.

Lack of coordination among DD/DS users also appears when traditional or conventional documentation is not replaced, but continues to be independently generated, either manually or via other software components. This situation is undesirable because the DD/DS may appear to be a burden that is unjustified in terms of supporting the documentation effort. This is caused by neglect to coordinate DD/DS usage among users.

Finally, a fourth problem caused by lack of coordination, occurs when the metadata in the DD/DS does not reflect the actual descriptions of the data contained in the application programs or in the DBMS. This happens when users are generating metadata without making sure that there is consistency in the descriptions.

9.1.2 Technical Integration

It is very important that the DD/DS software is technically integrated into the enterprise. This in turn also helps to insure that user activities are properly coordinated. *Technical integration* means that:

1. The technical staff that supports the implementation and maintenance of the DD/DS must have the required level of expertise to maintain and operate the DD/DS. A lack of depth found in the technical staff in this aspect will severely undermine the DD/DS implementation effort.

2. The DD/DS fits into the operational environment, that is, there are interfaces that allow the DD/DS to communicate with other system components. If the interface mechanisms are cumbersome or nonexistent, then the usefulness of the DD/DS would be potentially limited. The precise extent of required interfaces depends on the expressed needs of the organization — an issue that must be addressed at selection time. Common interfaces that often require attention during implementation are the capabilities to integrate smoothly with such software components as a DBMS, online software (e.g., TSO), and Source Program Library Manager (e.g., LIBRARIAN).

3. The need for DD/DS users to be trained to use the system correctly. Programmers, designers, and the DBA must be taught about the general capabilities of the DD/DS and about the specific facilities of the individual package. Users must also be informed about the rules and conventions for defining, naming, and coding data. User training is a critical aspect of the technical integration of the DD/DS into the enterprise. Lack of it will cause the DD/DS to be both underused and misused.

Subsequent sections in this chapter will discuss six specific strategies which address the problems just presented. Before beginning this discussion, it is important to emphasize the topic of planning the implementation of the DD/DS, an effort which will also help solve the problems arising out of lack of user coordination and technical integration.

9.2 IMPLEMENTATION PLANNING

The decision to implement a DD/DS on an enterprise-wide basis must be coupled with an implementation plan of matching scope. This plan, which should serve as the guideline document for implementing a DD/DS, must be based on the needs and the planned use of the DD/DS. [FIPS 80a] The plan should address at least the following areas:

Authority and responsibility.
Statement of needs/requirements.
Assumptions and constraints.
Implementation strategy.
Schedule and milestones.

While the actual plan may not be organized as above, the document should address these issues. Each of these will be discussed in the following sections.

9.2.1 Authority and Responsibility for Data Resources

Assuming that management commitment has been obtained, and resources budgeted (e.g., manpower, funds, and time) for the acquisition of the DD/DS, the next critical step is to obtain organizational commitment, in terms of user support. Just as if management commitment were withheld, the project would be jeopardized if user commitment were withheld; the entire DD/DS project would fail.

Management support is made evident in the amount of resources that it allocates for the DD/DS efforts, in the policies it establishes, and in the support it gives to ongoing DD/DS-related activities. User support (or lack of it) may not be as clearly demonstrated. If a user organization supports the establishment and use of the DD/DS, the user incorporates DD/DS functions and associated activities into daily operations. Lack of user support, however, can be much more subtle. For example, the user may outwardly agree to utilize the functions of the DD/DS; but operationally, they may be ignored. It is therefore critical that the user organization be included very early in the planning process to help insure involvement and commitment. The plan must reflect user input, and must, to the best extent possible, accommodate user needs. This user input may be obtained in various ways. One suggested approach is to establish a committee, possibly chaired by the DBA, at which user representatives can state their needs, voice their objections, and collectively address common problems. In this fashion, some of the problems that were discussed in Section 9.1 can be solved equitably and objectively.

The function (or person) with the overall responsibility for DD/DS activities may not be the same as the one who has the authority to make the decisions regarding the DD/DS. For example, the DBA may be the person who has the overall responsibility for the DD/DS, but the data administrator may be the one with the authority to make policy decisions. Regardless of who has the authority and the responsibility, a number of organization-wide policies must be established for the use of the DD/DS. These policies must convey clearly the organization's goals for the management and control of the data resources as an objective with very high priority. Rules and procedures must be established to assure compliance with standards, and to resolve conflicts that may arise during the data standardization process.

As part of authority and responsibility, the implementation plan should address budgetary issues. Within the context of each organization is its own fiscal and manpower allocation approach. When the decision is made to obtain a DD/DS, there must be resources provided for the implementation/purchase of the system, and for its long-term operation, including data collection, data entry, data standardization, DD/DS maintenance, and training.

Prior to or concurrent with the implementation of the DD/DS, a data standardization activity must be established. This encompasses all the activities required to ensure consistent definition and usage of the data. These activities include establishing naming conventions, coding conventions, and agreeing on consistent definitions for common data elements to be used by all users. A very common misunderstanding occurs when users think that the DD/DS will establish and enforce data standards. That, of course, is not true. The DD/DS cannot establish standards; standards can only be established by humans. However, the DD/DS can help enforce the established standard. For example, the DD/DS cannot recognize that "SSN" is a synonym or an alias for "social security number," unless the user declares "SSN" and "social security number" to be synonyms in the DD/DS. Once declared, the DD/DS will recognize the use of either term to mean the same data element.

Data standards ensure that common entities are used consistently throughout the whole organization; moreover, data standards allow data collected for one purpose to be used for a different purpose. How the data standardization activity is organized — whether the responsibility is given to a committee, or whether the responsibility is vested on one person — is not relevant to the discussion. What is important is that such responsibility is designated, so that the standardization function can be performed.

Closely related to the responsibility for the data standardization activity is the coordination and control of the contents of the DD/DS. Although the ideal case would be for one group of people to have overall responsibility for the format and content of the DD/DS — that is, for definition, entry, maintenance, and deletion of the meta-data entries — this is not always practical. Sometimes, it is necessary to delegate some responsibility to user organizations. Regardless of who has the responsibility, it is critical that this responsibility for the entry definition, coding, and meaning be carefully defined. In many cases, the DA would be the ultimate authority.

The implementation plan should describe a plan for supporting the DD/DS. As a sophisticated piece of software, it requires training technical personnel to maintain the system, and to assist others in using the system. The technical support staff is responsible for insuring the reliability, security, and integrity of the DD/DS software, and of the metadatabase; for developing special software to meet specific user needs; and for evaluating current capabilities against current demands and projected usage.

To insure that the DD/DS is used correctly and effectively, a training

IMPLEMENTATION PLANNING   201

program must be instituted that addresses the diverse needs of the managers, the users, and the technicians. The responsibility for such tasks should be stated in the training plan.

9.2.2 Requirements Statement

The implementation plan should include the documentation of an in-depth requirements definition study conducted to determine the organization's needs for the DD/DS. This study would also serve to determine the user's requirements, in terms of such general characteristics as ease of use and flexibility, that the system must have. If the effort to acquire a DD/DS has reached thus far, it is likely that the requirements study has indicated a positive need for a DD/DS. A summary or conclusion of such a study should be included with the plan, to justify implementation and selection criteria.

9.2.3 Assumptions and Constraints

A statement of management and technical assumptions should be included in the plan, especially such assumptions and constraints as operating environment and resources — for example, timing, staff availability, hardware/software constraints.

Included in the statement of assumptions and constraints should be limitations on the scope of applicability of the DD/DS, such as, if the DD/DS were intended to support only new development or if the DD/DS were meant for specific application areas, these assumptions should be clearly stated. Additional assumptions and constraints might presuppose, for example, the availability of online software (e.g., TSO) to support interactive access to the metadatabase, or the availability of a DBMS in the case of a dependent DD/DS.

Regardless of the particular nature of the assumptions and constraints involved, this part of the DD/DS implementation plan is intended to establish common acceptance and understanding of the preconditions involved in the DD/DS effort.

9.2.4 Implementation Strategy

The implementation plan, by definition, is a description of the recommended implementation strategy. As such, it should include a discussion of the rationale for choosing a particular approach. (Various approaches are discussed further in the next section.) The choice of an approach should be based on the requirements stated and on the assumptions and constraints found in the implementation plan.

9.2.5 Schedule and Milestones

As a concluding section in the implementation plan, there should be a discussion of the projected schedule, milestones, and critical path elements for the full implementation of the DD/DS in the organization. Implementation may, in effect, be phased. As will be discussed in the section on implementation approaches, this is a cautious but wise approach. Staging allows for an orderly assimilation of the organization's metadata into the DD/DS. This also allows for other processes, such as data standardization, to progress in an orderly fashion.

A statement of schedule and milestones might include PERT/GANTT charts as appropriate, but most importantly this schedule and milestones statement should be integrated into the overall EDP plan of the enterprise. DD/DS installation should be coordinated with other software installation and the population of the metadatabase should be "dovetailed" with plans for application development.

9.3 INTEGRATION OF THE DD/DS INTO THE SYSTEM DEVELOPMENT LIFE CYCLE

The usefulness of the DD/DS in the performance of system development life cycle (SDLC) activities was briefly discussed in Chapter 2. To recapitulate, the SDLC is the collection of activities, usually divided into stages, necessary to develop a system. All systems — hardware, software, application, or other processes — have a system development life cycle. At the end of each stage, a product is "delivered." For example, at the conclusion of the implementation stage, the coded programs are delivered products.

In this chapter, the focus is on the advantages of integrating the usage of the DD/DS into the SDLC for a database environment, as a means of providing solutions for the two problem areas identified: coordination among users and technical integration.

9.3.1 Support of the Database Effort

A DD/DS that is fully integrated into the activities of an enterprise's SDLC helps enforce the shared use of data throughout the enterprise and generally supports the database effort. In fact, a DD/DS integrated into the SDLC may be essential to the success of a database effort, in terms of the same metadata being used consistently throughout the SDLC, and allowing for common goals to be met. Furthermore, the use of a DD/DS throughout the SDLC assists in establishing common methods among application development groups. This will insure that the development groups will have consistent nomenclature, common definitions, and common coding conventions. Development groups can turn to the DD/DS as the reliable source in disputes concerning the correct metadata usage for applications.

Another advantage is that the DD/DS-supported SDLC can be used to integrate data usage among end-users. End-users have in the DD/DS a common frame of reference for their metadata needs and are able to utilize the data resources more effectively without a technician's intervention. The likelihood of winning user support would be much greater in this case, because the end-user would get first-hand experience on the usefulness of the DD/DS. A well-defined system development life cycle may be fundamental to the success of a database effort. A DD/DS-supported SDLC provides further assurance that the goals and objectives of implementing database technology can be effectively realized in the enterprise.

In a database effort, a conventional SDLC may not be suitable to support appropriate levels of sharing data during the development effort. Most of this sharing is at the metadata level. The following section discusses the SDLC for a database environment and highlights requirements for sharing metadata in its various phases.

9.3.2 SDLC for Database Development

When the SDLC activities are oriented primarily towards development of databases and database applications, significant sharing of metadata is necessary in each of the major life cycle phases (see Figure 9.1) [FIPS 80*b*].

During system planning, overall enterprise needs for a system are identified and defined, and metadata is collected for analysis and conceptualization. The advantage of sharing metadata in this stage is that it allows the system planner to rely upon the DD/DS as the definitive source of metadata for use in this first stage in the SDLC.

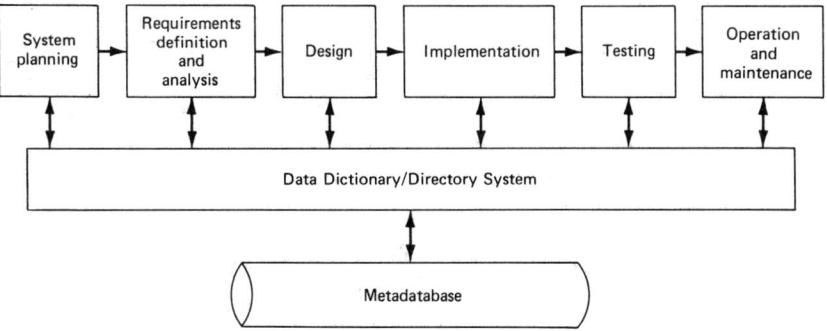

Figure 9.1 Phases of the SDLC and DD/DS support.

Specifically, during the systems planning phase, the DD/DS serves as the repository of information about the organization's metadata. During this phase, information is collected about the organization's needs. Data extracted from this information is described to the DD/DS. To assist in this procedure, the DD/DS's data definition facility is used. Information collected may duplicate entries that already exist in the metadatabase. The DD/DS would assist in this redundancy checking requirement by way of keyword analysis.

During requirements definition and analysis, it is of interest to determine how the systems and databases thus far conceptualized may affect existing systems and applications. The DD/DS assists in determining this impact and relationship via its impact analysis facility and cross-reference capabilities. Another important activity during this stage is the analysis, in terms of both feasibility and cost/benefit, of the system being defined. The DD/DS assists this aspect of the SDLC by providing statistical information about transactions, data occurrences, and usages.

Use of DD/DS during the design phase facilitates modeling of data structures and the process of database design [ATRE 80]. Metadata used in the design process is often a refinement of the metadata already stored in the DD/DS in earlier phases. Such metadata would have been collected during either the system planning phase or the requirements definition and analysis phase. The major concern during design is specifying in detail the functions that must be accomplished and designing the data structures to support these functions. This means that detailed descriptions about system components and program modules will need to be stored in the DD/DS metadatabase. This is beneficial because the DD/DS can provide a means for maintaining control over the specifications of the system modules. Features of the DD/DS such as the "version" facility permit the designer to specify and test alternative strategies using different versions of an entity. The DD/DS segregates and controls the versions, thus insuring integrity during the development process [GAJN 80]. The impact analysis capability in the DD/DS permits designers to determine if the particular design approach under current analysis will have significant adverse impact on a specific program. Another useful feature during this SDLC phase is the change analysis capability. This allows the designer to determine effect on existing data resources of a change in the metadata before the change is actually introduced.

One of the most important features of a DD/DS is its metadata generation capability. During the implementation phase – programming and coding – the DD/DS is most useful when it can generate metadata, such as a data division for a COBOL program, or a schema for a DBMS, or the required metadata for any other software component, such as a report generator. Furthermore, when used in connection with such software tools as a source program library manager, such as **LIBRARIAN**, the DD/DS can assist in "fetching" the desired piece of code for the programs being developed.

Since metadata for data used in the first four phases of the SDLC has been defined, refined, and stored in the DD/DS, it is possible to assist in the generation of test data for use during the testing phase. If a test data generator software package is used, it is possible for the DD/DS to generate the required metadata for the test data generator. The advantage of using a DD/DS in creating the test data is that the test data generator is relying on valid metadata, thus producing data which will be closer to the real world than if metadata were manually coded for generating the test data.

During the operation and maintenance phase, there may be needs for reorganizing or restructuring the database [SOCK 79]. One way of insuring the smooth transition between the old and the new database is by using the DD/DS. The test and production facilities allow the DBA to control changes and to determine the best strategy and structure to choose for the databases. Using a DD/DS during conversion is also beneficial because it assists in the production of both the source and the target structures for the databases.

9.3.3 DD/DS-Supported SDLC Reduces Common Problems

Using the DD/DS as an integral part of the system development life cycle reduces problems associated with coordination among users. Using the DD/DS in the SDLC makes apparent the benefits of using a DD/DS. Motivation for using the DD/DS can be increased. By increasing the coordination and control of metadata usage throughout the SDLC, one of the greatest benefits is that resulting application systems are more effective and more useful for the entire organization, since there is greater consistency in the metadata used to develop the system [WINK 80, ROLL 79].

The DD/DS-supported SDLC also promotes the usage and propagation of common standards throughout the organization. This in turn is conducive to greater exchanges of information and improved communication among the different departments and offices in the enterprise. The DD/DS is a conduit to better communication; the SDLC is the procedure which defines how this conduit should flow.

One of the most palpable benefits of the DD/DS-supported SDLC is the improvement in database and system documentation. The use of the DD/DS in the SDLC enforces this tedious but extremely important aspect of software development. This is possible because SDLC documentation throughout the life cycle is placed directly under the control of the DD/DS. Even the most basic commercial versions of a DD/DS possess this capability to support documentation (at least in a passive mode). By using DD/DS features and reporting capabilities to accept and generate SDLC deliverables and documentation throughout the life cycle, the DD/DS becomes an integral part of the developer's daily routine. Documentation for the SDLC produced by the DD/DS thus becomes a natural byproduct of the development effort, instead of a burden.

Figure 9.2 summarizes the foregoing discussion in terms of six phases of the SDLC, the SDLC functions which can be supported using the DD/DS, and the DD/DS feature which can be applied during the SDLC phase to support a given SDLC function.

SDLC Phase	SDLC Function	DD/DS Feature
Systems planning	Collect information about the organization's data needs	Definition service Cross-referencing Relationship and dependencies Keyword analysis Impact analysis
Requirements definition and analysis	Analyze feasibility, cost/benefit; impact analysis	Impact analysis Cross-referencing Usage Statistical summaries
Design	Specify functions to be accomplished Modelling of structures Design schema	Define detailed characteristics of entities Version control facility Impact analysis report Change analysis
Implementation	Generating schema DDL; COBOL data division Documentation of the database	Metadata generation for DBMS, or COBOL
Test	Produce test data	Support generation of test data
Operation and maintenance	Changes to entities Reorganization/restructuring and conversion	Change analysis and control Test and production facilities

Figure 9.2 The use of a DD/DS in the SDLC.

9.4 THE DATA ADMINISTRATION/ DATABASE ADMINISTRATION FUNCTION

Throughout this book, the *data administrator* (DA) and the *database administrator* (DBA) have been mentioned as key elements in the database environment. In this context, it should be emphasized that the DD/DS is an indispensable tool to the DA/DBA. The DD/DS is, in fact, the DA/DBA's information tool. This section describes the DA/DBA functions. In the next section, the usefulness of the DD/DS to the DA/DBA will be explored emphasizing this approach as a strategy to help mitigate the impact of the two problems of coordination among users and technical integration.

9.4.1 Historical Development of the Function

The DA's and the DBA's responsibilities have evolved. These responsibilities are multi-faceted, variously assuming the roles of manager, arbitrators, enforcers, consultants, technicians, instructors, and diplomats with regard to the enterprise's data resources for which they are responsible.

Data administration and database administration have existed for only a little over a decade. Data administration (DA), when first introduced [CODA 71, GUID 74], was thought of as a purely technical function, with primary responsibility over the well being of databases and database management systems.

As this function was implemented in real world situations, it was discovered that "going database" for these enterprises required more than just appointing a person to be in charge of its databases and its database management systems. These early implementors of the data administration function discovered that in order to provide effective management and control of the data throughout the enterprise there was need for two different types of talents in the person(s) responsible for the enterprise's databases — administrative and technical.

Administrative skill is required to handle managerial and policy affairs, to interact with various groups of concerned and affected people, and to define *what* should be in the organization's databases. This requires skills that include the capability to define, extract, and analyze data and functional requirements that are applicable to the overall database environment from end-user requirements.

In addition, it was recognized that the effort also requires technical skills to determine the implementation issues relevant to the specific databases, and to define *how* the organization's databases will be structured and organized. Technical knowledge is essential for this task, because it is largely related to specific DBMS- or database-related software being used.

This requirement for a duality in skills evolved to the point where specific nomenclature is currently used to differentiate the two types of functions: data administration (DA) for administrative and database administration (DBA) for technical. The establishment of either one or both of these functions is by no means universal, and in fact, the extent to which these functions are implemented varies significantly from organization to organization [CANN 72]. There are extensive reports [GUIDE 74, GUIDE 77] which discuss in detail and attempt to clarify the roles, authority, and responsibilities of both functions. Nonetheless, there is great diversity in implementation from enterprise to enterprise [WELD 81]. In some organizations, both the DA and the DBA functions exist separately, with clearly defined responsibilities and authority. In other organizations, one person or one group of people perform the dual functions of the DA and the DBA.

In organizations where the two functions exist separately, there is opportunity for the demarcation of authority and responsibility among the DA and the DBA to be made more clearly: The data administrator has the overall responsibility for the enterprise's data resources, and is responsible for such nontechnical activities as planning for and defining the conceptual framework for the overall database environment, not just that specifically limited to DBMS usage. Organizationally, the DA would be higher in the management hierarchy, and may in fact have a subordinate database administrator. The DA interacts with end-users, assesses their requirements in terms of overall enterprise needs; therefore, the DA needs to be a diplomat, a public relations person, a judge, and a policeman.

The database administrator, on the other hand, is the enterprise's leading technical expert on database related activities, and has responsibility over the day-to-day operation of all database-related activities. DBAs are involved with the daily decisions and activities that have immediate impact over the enterprise's operational databases. The DBA is involved with the technical design, implementation, maintenance and performance issues inherent in a particular DBMS or other database-related software being used. Figure 9.3 shows one possible organizational structure for a DA/DBA.

The DA/DBA functions are often *not* two distinct organizational units. In fact, the activities may be performed by the same person or group of people. Nonetheless, this person must wear both hats and must perform the dual functions of the DA and the DBA — responsibility for both the technical and the administrative functions of the DA/DBA.

The manner and the degree to which the DA and the DBA functions are actually implemented are decisions which are highly dependent on

THE DATA ADMINISTRATION

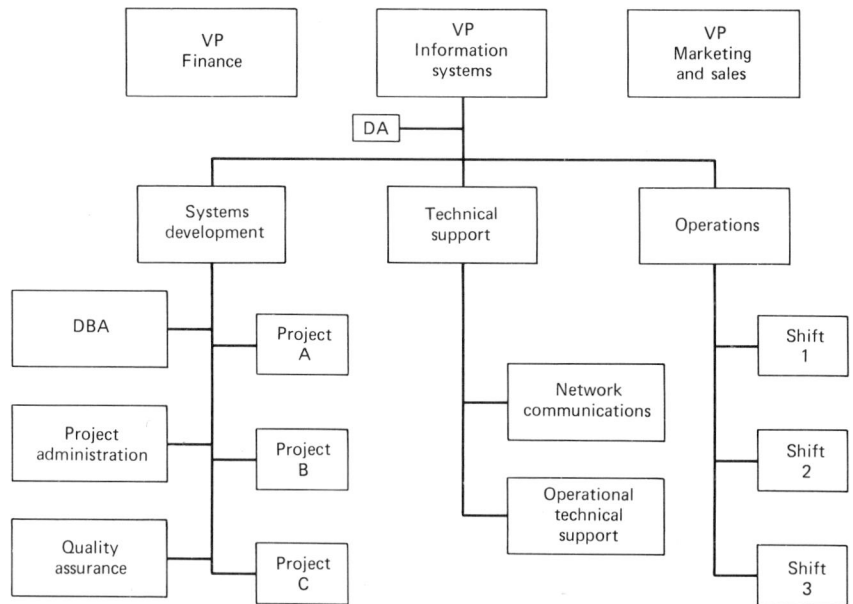

Figure 9.3 Organizational structure showing DA/DBA.

individual organizations. Such decisions must take a number of factors into consideration, such as the degree of commitment to the database environment, scope of applicability, organizational placement, and internal policies [CANN 72, LEON 78, PLAG 80, WELD 81]. Each of these factors influences the effectiveness of the DA/DBA in managing the enterprise's data resources. For example, prominent placement of the DA/DBA function in the organization's hierarchy reflects a management oriented rather than technically based commitment of the enterprise to the database concept. Placed high in the organization's hierarchy, the DA/DBA can induce cooperation from line organizations, and can insure compliance to established database rules and regulations. In general, placement of the DA/DBA function and the accompanying authority for this function can be critical to the success of a data resource management program.

9.4.2 Functions of the DA/DBA

Although there is little agreement regarding the detailed responsibilities, authority, and organizational placement of the DA/DBA function, there is general agreement regarding the areas of functional responsibilities of the DA/DBA [GUIDE 78, LEON 78, LYON 78, PLAG 80, WELD 81]. These areas are listed in Figure 9.4 and are further detailed below, indicating the relative importance or emphasis of the DA versus the DBA function.

Functional Responsibility	DA/DBA
1. Data definition (requirements)	DA
2. Database design and implementation	DA/DBA
3. Access, security, and integrity	DA/DBA
4. Operation, maintenance, and management	DBA
5. Monitoring and evaluation of performance	DBA
6. Development of and compliance with standards	DA/DBA
7. Software procurement and vendor interface	DA/DBA
8. Liaison, consulting, and training	DA/DBA

Figure 9.4   Areas of functional responsibilities for the DA/DBA.

9.4.2.1 Data Definition

From the initial phases of the SDLC, when metadata is first gathered concerning information handling and use, the data administrator has the responsibility for coordinating the activity and devising uniform and consistent descriptions of data. Procedures for defining the specific data entities are part of this responsibility. The definition of the data should be based on clear understanding of each participating user community's requirements, as well as on the enterprise's needs. Beginning from early in the SDLC, this definition responsibility is applicable throughout the system development life cycle, whenever the need arises for defining and/or describing new data entities and relationships.

9.4.2.2 Database Design and Implementation

This set of activities begins with determining end-user data requirements, establishing data availability, developing the data structure and storage structure of the database, both logically and physically, and generating data description language specifications for the DBMS. Activities that are end-user related — those determining end-user data requirements and establishing data availability — are nontechnical activities, and would be within the purview of the data administrator. For example, the DA would be responsible for understanding that users' requirements have both strategic (long-range) and tactical (short-range) implications. The DA must be aware of both corporate long-range plans, and users' long-range needs. Based on such understanding, the DA would develop policies that are intended to insure that the database environment can satisfy the needs of the greatest number of users, and serve the best interest of the enterprise.

It would also be the DA's responsibility to establish data availability, that is, to assist users in satisfying their information and data requirements. This would be accomplished by insuring that the DA's understanding of user needs is transformed into a practical grasp on the part of users on how to extract data from databases on a day-to-day basis.

The DBA's technical expertise is required to define and structure the most effective and efficient database structures and storage structures. The DBA must take into account the needs of diverse users, and the requirements of such technical parameters as the data structure, storage structure, access methods, physical storage media requirements, and alternative search strategies. The DBA is also responsible for maintaining and updating the DD/DS and other support software. Using the DD/DS and other design aids, the DBA generates the data description language, and finally, loads, tests, and implements the database using the DBMS.

9.4.2.3 Database Access, Security, and Integrity

The DA/DBA are both responsible for insuring only authorized access (e.g., reading and writing) to the database. This area of responsibility is intended to provide meaningful control and protection over the database environment, by guarding against unauthorized access to the database, unauthorized copying, unauthorized updating, and destruction of any part of the database. Lack of such controls can result in serious security and integrity problems. Database integrity is related to the DA/DBA's responsibility for the completeness and accuracy of the data.

To strengthen the DA/DBA's control over database access, security, and integrity, there should be a body of *database controls*. It is the purview of the DA/DBA to develop these database controls in conjunction with auditors and designers. Such controls must, of course, reflect usage requirements among the user community. For example, access authorization using passwords and other security procedures are necessary to safeguard the database environment against undesirable illegal usage. But they shouldn't hinder authorized access.

9.4.2.4 Database Operation, Maintenance,
Management, and Documentation

The DBA is responsible for the continued technical well being of the database environment. Therefore, it is a DBA responsibility to insure that the computer operating staff performs its database-related duties properly, by assisting in the establishment of database-related operating procedures, design procedures for the use of special database utilities, and scheduling computer time for database related work. The DBA must take the proper precautions to insure that the database can be restored to its proper state in the event of destruction or damage. To this end, the DBA must develop backup, restart, and recovery measures to provide this capability. The DBA must maintain and update database definitions and database support software. The DBA would also be responsible for reviewing and approving new data definitions and enforcement of data standards.

Among the DA/DBA's purely administrative (and most tedious) tasks, is that of documentation for the database environment. Strictly speaking, documentation ought to be a DA activity. However, on a practical basis it is most often performed by the DBA. This includes the recording of procedures, standards, guidelines, and database descriptions. In this aspect of the DBA's duties, the DD/DS is a welcome tool, for it can be used as the primary source for storage and retrieval of information about the entire database environment.

9.4.2.5 Monitoring and Evaluation of Performance

The DBA continually monitors the database environment to insure an efficient level of performance, while maintaining the integrity of the database. Responsibilities should include reviewing, testing, and evaluating the performance of automated as well as procedural data activities; initiating system improvements assessing the impact of changes; and maintaining state-of-the-art awareness of new tools and techniques that can be used to improve the performance of the database software. The DBA is thus responsible for establishing a program of action to determine and insure stable performance of the database software and hardware configuration. To this end, the DBA must participate with others in devising an organized approach to monitoring the performance of the hardware configuration, the database software configuration (DBMS, DD/DS, and operating system), application systems design, database design, and identifying potential bottlenecks. If the performance evaluation and monitoring activities indicate that there are areas for improvement, either in the database, or in the associated software, the DBA must initiate appropriate actions to correct the problem areas, either through reconfiguration of the hardware/software environment, and/or through reorganization or restructuring of the database in question.

9.4.2.6 Development of and Compliance with Standards

The DBA has overall responsibility to develop and promulgate technical level procedures and guidelines, to insure user compliance with established database rules and procedures, to enforce compliance, if necessary, with established standards and usages. Standard procedures are necessary if there is considerable sharing of data. The DBA must develop standards and procedures for data definition and descriptions. It is of paramount importance that the DA establish enterprise-wide standards and a uniform methodology for data definition; procedures for access and manipulation of the database; and edit and validation rules to insure that the data that is input into the database is of uniformly high quality. With respect to computer operations, the DBA would establish rules and procedures to be used by computer operators that must deal with databases or database software.

It should be noted here that the authority, on a policy level, for standards emanates from the DA. The DBA, using this authority, designs, promulgates, and maintains these standards. In this context, the DA/DBA must have organizational support to enforce the rules, regulations, procedures, and standards that are established. This is necessary in order to share the database, and insure its integrity.

9.4.2.7 *Software Procurement and Vendor Interface*

Since the DA/DBA have the most intimate knowledge of the state-of-the-art in database technology and database-related hardware and software, it is logical to include the responsibility to initiate the evaluation, selection, and procurement of hardware, software, and services required to support the database environment in the performance of DA/DBA functions.

After selection of the hardware, software, service, the DA/DBA is the primary interface between the company and the vendors of database products. This responsibility has as an objective to maintain communication with the vendor company and resolve problems arising from equipment and software failures.

9.4.2.8 *Liaison, Consulting, and Training*

The DA/DBA must maintain working relationships with end-users, systems and application analysts, and with organizational management. The DA/DBA provide consulting services to end-users and others wishing to share data resources; provide information, assistance, and guidance on the use of database facilities; and assist users in solving their problems, and notify users of any changes in policies, rules, and facilities.

The DA/DBA, or their staff, are responsible for the training curriculum of users, staff, and management in order to develop awareness of database concepts and available resources.

9.5 USING THE DD/DS TO SUPPORT THE DA/DBA FUNCTION

The DA/DBA function may be the most important aspect of an enterprise to consider with respect to the DD/DS implementation, because the converse is also true: the DD/DS is important to the DA/DBA [ROSS 81]. In the previous section, the DA/DBA functions and responsibilities were discussed briefly. It was difficult not to mention the DD/DS in that section, because it is an indispensable tool of the DA/DBA.

9.5.1 The DA/DBA's Indispensable Tool

Figure 9.5 shows how the DD/DS can be used as a tool to assist the DA/DBA function in fulfilling the responsibilities discussed in Section 9.4. Each DD/DS feature can be used as a tool to perform a DD/DS function in fulfilling a DBA responsibility.

Specifically, during data definition activities, the DD/DS feature of dictionary and/or directory requests can be used to assist the DA/DBA in establishing data availability for data definition. When the DBA is developing and enforcing standards, the DD/DS edit/validation feature can be used to insure that the data collected conforms to the specified rules and policies.

During database design and implementation, the DD/DS generation feature can be used to facilitate database structuring and organization; to respond to user demand for data, the DD/DS can be used to report on availability of data; and to assist in testing by generating test data from stored definitions.

As an access control mechanism, the DD/DS is an ideal tool. The DA/DBA can define security rules concerning access and manipulation of the enterprise's data resources. These rules can be stored in the DD/DS for establishing access control to the database environment. Validation rules stored in the DD/DS can be used to insure the integrity of the database. All these serve to support the DA/DBA responsibility for controlling database access and security, and maintaining database integrity.

The DA/DBA has responsibilities for maintenance, management, operation, and documentation of the database. The DD/DS can be useful to the DA/DBA for the purpose of documenting the database, since the DD/DS is the central source of information about the entire database environment.

9.5.2 Implementation Sequence of the DD/DS Versus the DA/DBA Function

When an enterprise considers the acquisition of a DD/DS, it is extremely important to consider the scope of the DA/DBA function that the DD/DS is required to support. Deciding on a DD/DS implementation without a prior decision on the DA/DBA functional responsibilities would be much like "putting the cart before the horse."

Inasmuch as the DA/DBA will be the primary user of the DD/DS, the functional responsibilities should be established, and then the DD/DS tools should be acquired to support these responsibilities.

DA/DBA Function	DD/DS Feature	DD/DS Function
Data definition	Dictionary/Directory requests: Searching for specific data	Establish data availability
Database design and implementation	Generation function Test/production facility Report generation	Generate metadata Design storage structures Document databases and other entities
Database access, security, and integrity	Edit/validation features Security features	Control the integrity of the data Control access to the DB environment
Database operation, maintenance, and management	Update procedures Query procedures Reporting facility Cross referencing Failsafe procedures	Back-up-recovery Documentation of DB PROCEDURES Storage and retrieval of information about the organization data resources
Monitoring and evaluation of performance	Test/production facility	Configure new data structures
Development of and compliance with standards	Report generation Security features Edit/validation facilities "STATUS" facility	Document rules and procedures Control access Document standards
Software procurement and vendor interface	—	—
Liaison, training, consulting	—	—

Figure 9.5 The DA/DBA function and the DD/DS.

Within the confines of a real world situation, this is not always practical. In one such situation a quasi-government enterprise acquired the rights to use the LEXICON DD/DS by way of contractual arrangement with the vendor to support an application development project. About eighteen months later it was seriously proposed that LEXICON be adopted as the agency DD/DS, before there was any talk at all of establishing a DA/DBA function for the agency. There was disagreement on technical grounds within the agency and a group of Technical Support persons advocated the acquisition of DATAMANAGER instead of LEXICON. An independent, outside consultant was engaged to resolve the impasse. However, the issue was resolved not by deciding which package was technically more sound, but rather which package could effectively support the agency's plans for its DA/DBA function. A DA/DBA planning project was initiated to help resolve the issue.

Thus, the "proper" sequence of action is planning for implementation of the DA/DBA function, along with a definition of the scope of the database environment, before the implementation of a DD/DS. The net effect will be that as the DA/DBA function evolves, so will the use of the DD/DS.

9.5.3 Administration of the DD/DS

As explained in the previous section, the implementation of the DA/DBA function varies significantly from organization to organization. This function also varies with respect to the administrative responsibilities concerning the DD/DS. The DA/DBA, depending upon the specific organization, may be responsible for one or more of the following DD/DS-related activities:

1. *Metadata entry into the DD/DS:* This means the DA/DBA is not only responsible for approving and/or defining the metadata, but is also responsible for entering the metadata into the DD/DS.
2. *Approval of changes in "status":* This is a critical control activity which is generally the responsibility of the DA/DBA. "Status" usually has integrity and access-control implications for the metadatabase.
3. *Access control to the metadata:* The DA/DBA is responsible for the security and integrity of the database environment, by maintaining control at the metadata level. This topic will be discussed at greater length in section 9.8 of this chapter.
4. *Monitoring adherence to standards:* This is the DA/DBA's responsibility. The DD/DS serves as an excellent tool for this purpose, in both the passive or the active role by highlighting noncompliance via exception reporting.

9.5.4 Using the DD/DS as a DA/DBA TOOL To Mitigate Coordination Problems

Be defining the use of the DD/DS in terms of DA/DBA functions, the implementation strategy is addressing a larger problem: that of effective coordination among users. In this context, the DA/DBA's use of the DD/DS is designed to:

1. Promote common standards among users. Entities that are commonly used throughout an organization should all be defined using the same conventions, and standards for the entire enterprise. This facilitates communication, and promotes the best utilization of the enterprise's data resources.
2. Aid the DA/DBA in producing database documentation using the DD/DS. Since the DD/DS already contains documentation of the database, the use of the DD/DS to assist in this task is only logical.
3. Assist the DA/DBA in facilitating and coordinating the implementation of an active DD/DS; one that will insure accurate representation of actual metadata.

9.6 DATA DESCRIPTION STANDARDS

In Section 9.3, the need for establishing a data standardization program was discussed in the context of DD/DS implementation planning as an organizational activity. Here, we expand on that discussion to address data description standards and procedures.

9.6.1 Standards for the Description Process

Data description standards are essential for shared use of the data. Rules and procedures must be established to control the data description process. This will insure that data described under this controlled environment is understood and usable throughout the enterprise. In this context, the DD/DS serves as the repository of the standard data descriptions and must be adapted to operate within the scope of these standards.

Figure 9.6 describes a sample data element definition procedure, showing how the descriptions are prepared and/or modified.

This procedure is essentially a three-step process:

1. Identify the need for the data element and define the data element.
2. Determine whether the data element already exists, or whether it is a new element. If the element already exists, then it is necessary to determine whether the element descriptions conform to the existing standards. If the descriptions are consistent with existing rules and

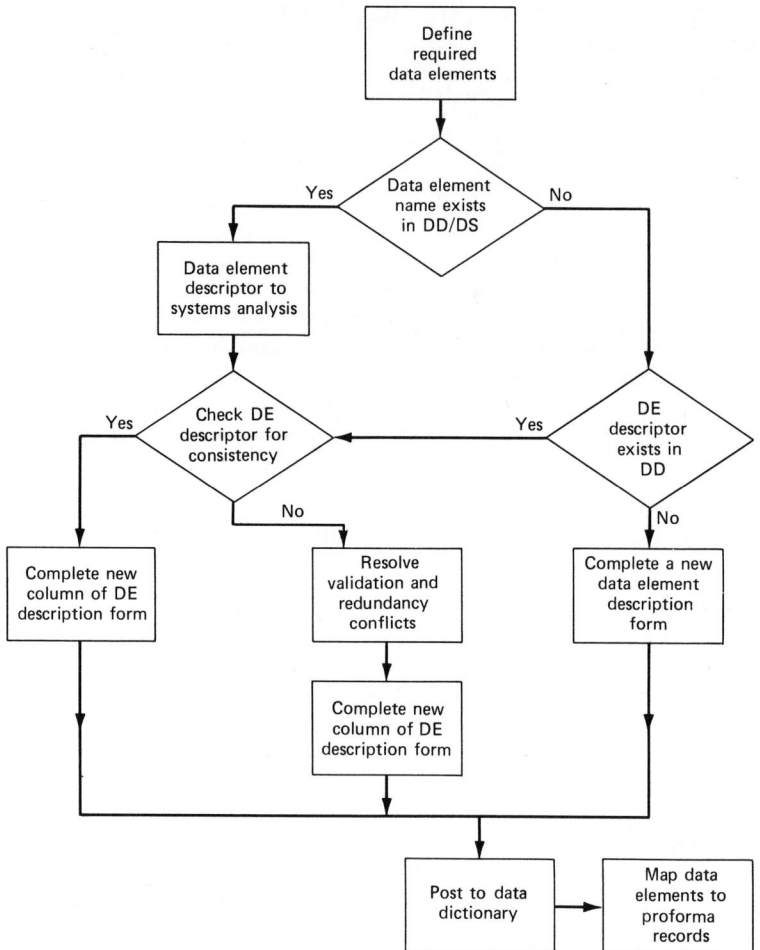

Figure 9.6 Data element definition procedure. DE = data element. Proforma Record = standard record format.

conventions, a new column of a data element description form (or screen) is filled, and the data element is posted to the DD/DS. If at any point, it is discovered that descriptions are inconsistent with existing standards, then the conflict must be resolved prior to posting the element to the DD/DS.

3. Finally, for elements that are new, a new data element description form (or screen) must be filled out, and DBA approval must be sought prior to posting the element in the DD/DS.

9.6.2 Standard Formats for Meta-Entities

Standards are required for the format and content used in defining and describing meta entities of the DD/DS. This means setting standards for the type of information that must be collected for each meta-entity type, and most importantly, the conventions that must be observed in defining these attributes. In effect, this amounts to defining a set of standards for methods of preparing attribute descriptions for the entities for the DD/DS. Of critical importance is the unique identifier of the meta-entity occurrence. This identifier must be defined so that it is unambiguous. Of equal critical importance is the standard for data element descriptions. See Figure 9.7 for a sample standard data element description.

There are a number of general guidelines or cautions for establishing a standard. These cautions are aimed at insuring that the standards are

---

A Data Element must be described in terms of the following attributes:

Data Element	Definition
Identification #:	A seven character unique identifier beginning with ELxxxxx.
	Example: EL00572
Designator:	A short name composed of the keywords of the DESCRIPTION
	Example: CUSTOMER'S LEGAL NAME
Programming name:	An abbreviated form of the DESIGNATOR using only approved abbreviations
	Example: LEGL-CUST-NAME
Description:	A narrative explanation of the data element; the first sentence must identify the real world entity being described. The second sentence may expand on usage characteristics.
	Example: The name of a *customer*, which is the legal name. It may not be the commonly used name. It is usually derived from legal incorporation papers.

Figure 9.7 Sample standard for data element description.

not imposed and subsequently rejected, but accepted and followed. To this end, it is important that those who are defining standards start with a broad base of support. This support base will help considerably, should any controversy arise. One way of obtaining this support is via the concept of *user representation*. As discussed in Section 9.2.1, this mechanism can be established via a user committee organized by the DBA. Such a committee would insure that users' needs are considered in making any decisions that affect them. General participation would be insured in the entire process of standardization and would help considerably in establishing standards and procedures to enforce the standards, thus indirectly enhancing the base of support for DD/DS related activities.

Another means of insuring a path of least resistance for establishing standards is to "float" a standard for approval, with the intent of testing its chances for surviving criticisms and objections. After a standard is floated, the objections and criticisms may be resolved, and approval can be assured.

9.6.3 Data Description Standards
Help Solve User Coordination Problems

Data description standards can be part of an overall strategy to ameliorate a number of problems associated with shared use of data. These include:

1. Promoting wider understanding of definitions. Commonly used data elements, or other entities should have established standard definitions. As these standards are applicable to the entire enterprise, they would be recorded as such, and disseminated to all operating units of the enterprise, with clear, unambiguous, and concise definitions.
2. Standard formats of the entities promote ease of use among end-users in diverse parts of the enterprise.
3. Traditional documentation may, in fact, be replaced by new standard forms, to insure that information is recorded consistently and uniformly.

Although data description standards tend to mitigate problems associated with coordinated usage of data among diverse groups, standards in general are a sensitive subject that most users are not comfortable with. Standards are often viewed as an infringement on users' rights and prerogatives. This is why standards must be treated as a politically sensitive area, and caution must be the vanguard of those who have that responsibility. This is also one of the reasons why early user involvement is essential to the success of the DD/DS-related standardization efforts. This involvement serves three interrelated purposes:

1. To assuage fears that any undesirable standards would be imposed against users' will.
2. To gain users' cooperation by demonstrating for them that they in fact have a strong voice in the making of the standard.
3. To obtain users' inputs — their requirements and their constraints — regarding the standards.

User acceptance of the standardization efforts insures success of this activity. More importantly, the success of standards facilitates the shared use of the enterprise's data resources.

9.7 PLANNING FOR THE POPULATION OF THE DD/DS

The most important single cost-factor for DD/DS implementation is that of collecting and entering metadata into the DD/DS. This process is referred to as *population of the DD/DS*. The population issue must be carefully planned to help reduce its costs and to assist in addressing the problems of user coordination and technical integration.

9.7.1 Cost Factors in DD/DS Population

Four factors contribute to the high cost of populating the DD/DS. These are: collection of metadata, verification of metadata, media conversion/entry, and error correction/recycling.

1. *Collection of metadata.* This is costly because of the need for comprehensiveness in gathering all the required metadata in the enterprise. If there are no existing data description standards, no standard forms, and no standard procedures, the collection task will be considerably more expensive because all collected metadata must be reconciled, metadata may be collected redundantly, and the error rate will be significantly higher. If for no other reason than this purpose alone, the prior existence of standards would reduce the cost considerably.
2. *Verification of metadata.* Established procedures to verify incoming metadata are extremely important for ensuring trustworthy data. This is to insure that the metadata collected is syntactically correct, and conforms to established standards and conventions. Edit and validation routines can be used to verify the syntax of the metadata.

Verification at data entry time promotes higher confidence in the quality of the data, and the cost of using the metadata is reduced.

3. *Metadata conversion/entry.* Very often, data is collected using one recording medium, such as magnetic tape, and processing requirements dictate a different medium, such as disks. Conversion from magnetic tape to disk is then required. If the two media are compatible, there would not be much difficulty. However, if the two media are not compatible, conversion is required, and the cost goes up. The most costly conversion is from manual to machine-readable. However, often machine-readable metadata is embedded and is inaccessible without manual analysis. There are some automated tools available in commercial DD/DS packages for this purpose. Automated Set-Up in DATAMANAGER is one example.

4. *Error correction/recycling.* In massive metadata collection, the error rate is fairly high. Error correction can be very costly, and significantly impacts the confidence of the correctness of the collected metadata. After errors are corrected, it is necessary to *recycle* through the metadata collection procedure. This process can be very costly, and very time consuming.

9.7.2 Alternative Strategies for DD/DS Population

The necessity to devise alternative strategies for populating the DD/DS is great. The following paragraphs present three possible scenarios (see Figure 9.8).

1. *Collect and enter all the metadata in the DD/DS.* This choice, called *total population,* results in a very high cost because it is necessary to collect, define, and describe all the metadata in the entire enterprise. Even assuming that there is an excellent data standardization program in place, this scheme suffers from the fact that it is very difficult to coordinate all the different areas in the enterprise at the same time. This implementation strategy is labor intensive, very tedious, and very error prone.

2. *Limit the DD/DS effort to new development.* This strategy, called *new-only population,* has the advantage that it is low in cost, and the DD/DS is populated as a byproduct of the development process. This has the drawback that by limiting population of the DD/DS to only new applications, the metadata stored in the DD/DS is not representative of the enterprise's data resources. Moreover, coordination is difficult when existing systems contain metadata that is related to, or overlaps metadata in a newly developed system. This creates undesirable redundancy and potential conflicts.

3. *The third alternative is called "selective retrofit".* This limits the DD/DS effort to new development and selectively retrofits related

PLANNING FOR THE POPULATION OF THE DD/DS

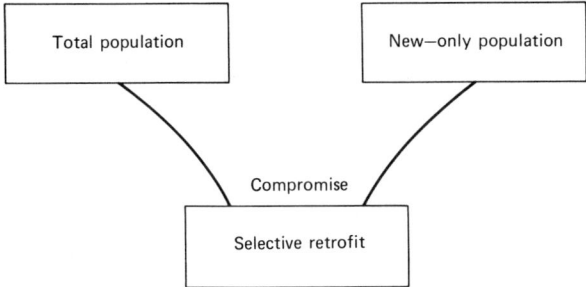

Figure 9.8 Alternative strategies for DD/DS population.

or overlapping areas. In the interest of low cost and facilitating coordination, this method is the most appealing and is a common practice.

9.7.3 Cost Reduction Tools for DD/DS Population

The cost of populating a DD/DS can be reduced by using implemented tools, some of which are available through DD/DS facilities, and by using established procedures. Some commercial DD/DSs offer automated facilities to scan/read machine-readable metadata for inclusion in the DD/DS. This includes processors for COBOL programs and DBMS directories. The advantage of such tools is that it reduces direct labor costs for the DD/DS population effort. However, it offers a major drawback in that these tools can increase the percentage of garbage metadata which the automated input processors cannot discriminate against. Furthermore, there is a temptation to continue to utilize these processors in a manner which will render the DD/DS as a passive tool.

Used in conjunction with error detection and correction procedures, however, these automated scanners/readers can significantly assist in reducing metadata collection costs. These detection and correction procedures are aimed at improving the quality of the incoming metadata. Thus, edit/validation of automated DD/DS input can help assure that metadata entered into the DD/DS is syntactically correct, and conforms with established rules and regulations. Procedures to review and approve entries in a preliminary status prior to entering them as a higher status in the DD/DS would certainly help the quality of the metadata; and finally, procedures to review further the DD/DS content to uncover conflicts and undesirable redundancies, would serve to improve integrity.

9.7.4 Planning for DD/DS Population
Can Help Solve User Coordination Problems

Careful planning for DD/DS population helps address problems that are associated with coordination among users. Wherever possible, planning should be aimed at helping increase motivation among users to share their data, and to coordinate usage by reducing labor intensive tasks; and whenever possible, planning should incorporate the utilization of automated tools, supplemented by standards and procedures to collect metadata, in order to insure the accuracy of the DD/DS content. The net effect is that the DD/DS would be more useful across a wider base of metadata requirements in an effective and manageable program for data resource management.

9.8 PLANNING FOR THE SECURITY OF THE METADATABASE

The implementation of a central repository of metadata with online availability creates new risks and exposures in the enterprise. Availability of the metadata in one central location makes access to the system as a whole easier, thereby increasing the general risk of unauthorized access. This makes the DD/DS a highly vulnerable system.

Protection of the DD/DS and its contents can be made at several levels, depending on the sensitivity of the metadata and of the data itself. An example of this is information about the data resources in intelligence/military applications such as the classification codes of intelligence documents. When security profiles for the metadata entities are stored in the metadatabase, unauthorized access to the metadatabase could be most damaging. This is because presumably one would be able to "crash into" the system using that information.

It is the responsibility of the DA/DBA to analyze critically the sensitivity of the metadata. Specific types of metadata which should be scrutinized for sensitivity include textual descriptions, program-oriented data descriptions, database descriptions (schema), edit/validation rules, and security profiles. The DBA would thus assign security locks or other security measures to each of these areas.

The DBA would choose the appropriate DD/DS options, if available, to implement security requirements. Alternatives which are not mutually exclusive include: establishing levels of security at the metadata entity and attribute type level; establishing levels of security at metadata entity occurrence (attribute value) level; and assigning passwords to users that would allow them to read and write, read only, or update. These three forms of security may be combined into an access control mechanism for the metadatabase, using DD/DS features or DBMS features, or a combination of the two.

Establishing levels of security at the metadata entity and attribute type level means that each entity and attribute type has an associated level of security, and only those users with the proper authorization can actually add, modify, or delete occurrences of the entity and/or values for all attributes of the type in question. An example would be that only authorized personnel would be allowed access to the attribute "PASSWORD."

An example of security at the occurrence level is the status feature with security. The status attribute can be used to control whether the entity in question can be changed or not. That depends on whether it is still being tested, whether it is in operation, or whether it is in archival status. It can thus serve as a security control mechanism. Each entity occurrence given a value for the attribute status, determines whether the entity can be changed or not. For example, a *test* value for status for an entity implies that the entity can be modified; a *production* value for status does not permit alteration of the entity except by authorized personnel; and an *archival* value for status would allow browsing. Combining establishment of essential aspects of security at both levels (type and occurrence) and assigning passwords, are some of the security controls needed to restrict access to unauthorized users.

Each of these alternatives must be examined in view of users' needs. An organization that is highly secure may need to implement all three alternatives, and any other security measures deemed necessary, such as cryptography. An enterprise which may need only ordinary security precautions, such as those against unauthorized access, may need to explore further the individual needs of the users as compared with corporate level needs.

Planning and implementing security for the DD/DS helps solve coordination problems by limiting unauthorized access and update. This access control increases accuracy of the metadatabase because only authorized, well trained people would be able to access and manipulate the metadatabase, thereby eliminating undesirable input.

9.9 PLANNING FOR SUPPORT OF SOFTWARE INTERFACES

Potentially, the DD/DS can satisfy the metadata needs of many data processing components in the computing environment. The active DD/DS is based upon this concept. One way in which the DD/DS can satisfy these metadata requirements is through software interfaces between the DBMS and the DD/DS, which can potentially supply the DBMS with its required metadata, in the form of schema definitions, or DDL streams. Likewise, a software interface between a DD/DS and application programs can provide the application program with applicable data definitions in the appropriate host language.

The DBA must plan the software interfaces in the data processing environment to insure proper integration of the DD/DS. The most basic requirement is to ascertain that the generation capabilities exist in the DD/DS. This is crucial, because if the DD/DS does not have this capability, then the DD/DS would not be able to provide the necessary metadata to the affected software component. The DBA must insure that the formats of the generated metadata are compatible with the requirements of the recipient software component. The DBA must also create provisions to insure against the ability to circumvent the DD/DS. These provisions may be in the form of software locks or procedures which users must follow; this is critical in the case of the active DD/DS.

An often neglected area is training. Planning for support of new DD/DS interfaces requires adequate training, both for the technical staff and for the users. Training provided by the vendor marketing the DD/DS is usually highly technical, and concentrates on the technical details of the system and their interfaces. The DBA could also supply training. Such training may be more user-oriented, emphasizing procedures, and do's and don'ts of using the interfaces. Further training is obtained on the job. This provides the programmers, analysts, and users with real-life examples of how the interfaces work between the DD/DS and the other software components. Users' manuals usually provide adequate and detailed explanation of how the interfaces work, and can be used as references. Finally, there are consulting groups who tailor training courses to fit specific user needs.

In summary, adequate planning at the technical level for the DD/DS software and its interfaces helps mitigate problems caused by lack of technical integration of the DD/DS into the enterprise. This lack of technical integration often occurs because the DD/DS may have been acquired after all the components are in place. In the best of situations, interfaces with other components could only be established after the fact. If interfaces can be established, a semblance of a unified approach to planning the overall environment can be maintained. To complete this picture of technical integration, it is requisite that the knowledge and expertise on the DD/DS be adequate to manipulate all the components, including the DD/DS, as a unified and totally integrated processing environment.

9.10 SUMMARY

In this chapter, the issues concerning implementation of the DD/DS in a user organization were addressed. Technical integration of the DD/DS into the operation of the enterprise is very important. Of equal importance are such factors as organizational and management commitment and user support. An implementation plan was presented as the cornerstone of the DD/DS implementation effort. The plan needs to address such issues as: authority and responsibility for the DD/DS; statement of requirements; assumptions and constraints; implementation strategy, and schedule and milestones.

Next, this chapter explored the need for integrating the usage of the DD/DS into the system development life cycle. By so doing, shared use of data is enforced throughout the enterprise.

The DA/DBA play important roles in the database environment, particularly regarding the DD/DS. To place matters in their proper perspective, it is necessary to understand the roles and functions of the DA/DBA, and then relate the interaction between the DA/DBA and the DD/DS.

Data standards are a critical element of a DD/DS implementation; in fact, they are essential for shared use of data. Rules and procedures must be established to control that process.

The remainder of the chapter addressed such important topics as planning for the population of a DD/DS, which could be the single most costly factor for implementing a DD/DS; planning for the security of the metadatabase; and planning for support of software interfaces.

REFERENCES

[ATRE 80] Atre, S. *Data base: Structured Techniques for Design Performance and Measurement*, Wiley, New York, 1980.

[CANN 72] Richard Canning, Ed., "The Data Administrator Function," *EDP Anal.*, Vol. 10, No. 11, 1972.

[CODA 71] "Feature Analysis of Generalized Data Base Management Systems," CODASYL Systems Committee, May 1971.

[FIPS 80a] "Guideline for Planning and Using a Data Dictionary System," National Bureau of Standards Federal Information Processing Standards Publication (FIPS) 76, August 1980.

[FIPS 80b] "Guideline for Planning and Management of Database Applications," National Bureau of Standards Federal Information Processing Standards Publication (FIPS) 77, September 1980.

[GUID 74] "The Data Administrator: Catalyst of Corporate Change," GUIDE International DA Project Draft Report, 1974.

[GUID 77] "Establishing the Data Base Administrator Function," GUIDE, June 1977.

[GUIDE 78] "Data Administration Methodology," GUIDE Data Administration, Methodology Project, December 1978.

[GAJN 80] Gajnak, G., "The Requirements for Status/Staging/Review/Approval Mechanism in the IRDS Standard," Working Paper ANSI/X3H4-80-17, August 1980.

[LEON 78] Leong-Hong, B. and B. Marron, "Database Administration: Concepts, Tools, Experience, and Problems," National Bureau of Standards Special Publication 500-28, March 1978.

[LYON 78] Lyon, J. K. *The Database Administrator*, Wiley, New York, 1978.

[PLAG 80]   Plagman, B. K. "The Function of Data Base Administration and Control," in *AUERBACH Data Base Management Series,* Portfolio 22-05-01 (REV), 1980.
[ROLL 79]   Rolland, R., "The Role of a Data Dictionary in Application Development," Presented at COMPSAC 79, Chicago, November 1979.
[ROSS 81]   Ross, R. G., *Data Dictionary Systems and Data Administration* AMACOM, 1981.
[WELD 81]   Weldon, J. L., *Data Base Administration,* Plenum, New York, 1981.
[WINK 80]   Winkler, A. J. "Automating System Development," Working Paper ANSI/X3H4-80-18, September 1980.

10

The DD/DS in a Distributed Database Environment

Distributed database management is gaining importance because it provides attractive solutions to some of the complex data processing problems stemming from a geographically distributed organization. Distributed database management enables geographical distribution of data resources and sharing among users by permitting the DBMS to act conceptually as a centralized system, while allowing the databases relevant to an organization to be physically distributed on a network of geographically dispersed computers.

Technological advances in several technical areas have contributed to the emergence of distributed database management systems (DDBMS) as an important area of development. The first of these technical areas is the increasing availability of lower cost computing equipment, which has enabled organizations to install DBMSs in a number of independent computers throughout the organization. The second technical area is the increasing availability of computer communication capabilities which allow interconnection of independent computers in a straightforward, reliable, and cost-predictable manner. These and other factors contributing to this high demand for distributed processing are listed below:

1. The need for faster and easier access to time-critical information to assist in the decision making of enterprises with geographically dispersed organization components, but requiring unified information sharing and processing.
2. Improved communication technology, both in hardware and software, and in computer-to-computer communication.

3. Decreasing cost of computer processing, storage, and other equipments.
4. Increased data communication cost.

As a result of these factors, researchers and developers have been focusing their attention on developing distributed processing and distributed databases technology [ROTH 77]. In particular, the feasibility of applying database technology in a network environment was explored because of these economic and management factors. For example, low-cost local processing can provide fast, interactive services independent of, and sometimes superior to, traditional mainframes for the functions of source data capture, data entry, and editing. Furthermore, distributed management can be reflected in distributed data organization, thus providing responsiveness for local needs and problems along with responsibility for the business functions which the data processing supports.

From a technology standpoint distributed computing power is a prerequisite for distributed processing systems. Such systems can be built with processing, databases, or both being distributed. Distributed processing systems do not necessarily require distributed databases. However, distributed databases can only exist in a distributed processing environment.

The technology supporting distributed databases is actually a hybrid of several technical disciplines, such as networking, communication, database management, and software engineering. This chapter assumes the existence of the underlying technologies, and proceeds to consider the roles of the DD/DSs that are unique to the distribution of the database. It should be recognized that while this assumption may not be currently true, we anticipate the evolution of the technology to the point of its being true in the near future, and thus consider the discussion of DD/DS in the distributed environment and related topics as timely and relevant.

For the purpose of this chapter, the following working definitions are presented:

Network Here intended to mean a computer network, consists of a collection of circuits, data switching elements, and computing systems. The switching devices in the network are called *communication processors*. A network provides a configuration for computer systems and communication facilities within which data can be stored and accessed, and in which DBMSs can operate.

Node Technically, any point in the network at which data is switched can be called a node. Here, a node in a network consists of computer processing facilities, an operating system for executing user and DBMS processes.

THE DD/DS IN A DISTRIBUTED DATABASE ENVIRONMENT

Communication Facilities A collection of processes and physical facilities that interconnect nodes.

Distributed Database Management Those database management functions — organization, access (update and retrieval), and control — that are performed at geographically dispersed locations, and are linked via a computer communication network, such that the user process is unaware of the dispersion.

Distributed DD/DS Those DD/DS functions — collection, maintenance, and dissemination of metadata — that are performed in support of distributed processing and distributed databases.

Distributed Databases The placement of a database or portions of a database in a network environment. Databases can be *partitioned* — that is, the database is broken down into pieces, and the pieces are stored at various nodes of the network or, the database can be *replicated* in nodes across the network (i.e., copies of the databases are placed at various nodes in the network).

From a user's point of view, the facilities offered by a distributed database management system are essentially the same as those offered by a centralized DBMS. While some benefits are directly attributable to the distribution of data, such as increased data availability, there are also some problems that are due primarily to this distribution. One of these problem areas is related to performance issues such as update synchronization and concurrency control; another problem area addresses the critical need for information about the characteristics and the location of the data and the databases in the network. Significant amounts of research work are ongoing in the first problem area [ALSB 76, BERN 77, DEPP 76, STON 79, CHU 76]. The second area of concern is the subject of this chapter.

As with the DBMS, the Data Dictionary/Directory System, when operating on a local node of a distributed processing network, performs the same functions as a regular, centrally located DD/DS, relative to that node. This holds true because each node is a centralized environment in its own right, with respect to itself. But the need to make distribution of data transparent to the user process in a distributed network adds new requirements for the DD/DS. These unique requirements of the DD/DS in a distributed environment are discussed in this chapter in terms of the following:

1. Functional requirements which the DD/DS of the distributed processing environment will have to accommodate.
2. Special features of the DD/DS which would be necessary and/or desirable to meet the demands of the functional requirements
3. User implementation considerations, including distribution strategy for the metadata, and DA/DBA considerations.

10.1 FUNCTIONAL REQUIREMENTS OF A DD/DS IN A DISTRIBUTED DATABASE ENVIRONMENT

Application of database technology to the distributed environment provides rapid and efficient access to data that is distributed across a computer network. While benefits in a distributed database management environment are potentially great, distribution of data also engenders a number of problems not found to be acute in the centralized environment.

Issues which are important in the centralized environment, become critical to the distributed database environment. For example: database consistency, integrity, and reliability become more critical under the distributed environment, if for no other reason than that the data is physically dispersed, and there is need to coordinate all the data. Another concern, the need for uniform management and control of definition and location of data is far more difficult and complex in a distributed database environment. This latter is concerned directly with the functional requirements of a DD/DS.

The DD/DS in a distributed environment must provide all of the services it performs for a centralized environment, these include the use of the DD/DS as a database design aid, as a documentation tool, and as a mechanism for generating metadata. Therefore, it is assumed that the DD/DS will meet the same basic set of functional requirements described in earlier chapters. Distribution of data, however, places added demands on the facilities used to manage and control the data resources in a geographically dispersed environment. The most important demand is the need for transparency of data location with respect to the user process at any given node. This particular demand is met by highlighting three additional functions.

Functions to provide data location in the network.
Functions to support coordination of distributed data.
Functions to support data translation for user processes.

Conceptually, all of these functions are available in all DD/DS's whether in a centralized or a distributed environment. In the distributed environment, these are more critical thus they are highlighted.

10.1.1 The Functional Requirement to Locate Data

The first of these functions, that of providing data location, is the *directory function* of the DD/DS. This function is also known as the *network data directory (NDD)* or the *nodal location directory (NLD)*. Most distributed systems have this function in one form or another, either embedded in other functions or as a separate function [LOOM 81]. Network Data Directory or Nodal Location Directory is a special type of metadata of the DD/DS. The NDD or NLD contains specific information about nodal location of the network.

The DD/DS of a distributed processing environment is more than just a directory function; it includes all the other functionalities of a DD/DS described in previous chapters. While the NDD — the directory function — may only indicate the node within the distributed processing system where the data resides, the distributed DD/DS will also provide information about this data to users of the distributed databases in a computer network. We are most interested in the broader function of coordination that the Data Dictionary/Directory System can serve in the distributed environment.

Thus a discussion of the distributed DD/DS functions must address specific coordination issues, such as coordination of:

Database distribution alternatives.
Distribution alternatives for the metadata.
DD/DS administration in a distributed environment.

These issues are addressed briefly in this section, and at greater length in subsequent sections.

10.1.2 Coordination of Distribution Alternatives for Databases and Metadatabases

Whether the database is distributed by replication or partitioning the distributed DD/DS must be capable of managing information about its physical, logical, and operational characteristics [CHAMP 77, CHU 75, RIES 78]. In the case of *replicated data,* where functionally identical copies of the data are stored at multiple nodes in the network, the distributed DD/DS must have knowledge of the known redundancies throughout the network. Synchronization of updates in this case is critical, because it is imperative that when performing a single update that affects multiple copies of a record occurrence (in a manner transparent to the user), the consistency and integrity of the database must be maintained. The DD/DS as the data locator can function as an aid to a synchronization mechanism used in updating a given record in a replicated database. The DD/DS already contains formats, conventions, and definition for the affected data, and the synchronization program can use this information in updating the database.

A *partitioned database,* where only the applicable portion of the database is located at the user's node, requires that the processing system at the individual node recognize, associate, and process the data at that node. The role of the DD/DS in a partitioned database environment is that of "recognizing" and associating the various pieces or partitions of the "whole" database. It must know the relationships among the pieces, and be able to manage all the parts, such that this physical dispersion of the data is transparent to the user. Distribution alternatives for the databases can and do become much more complex than the two cases cited above. For the purpose of this chapter, however, this description suffices.

The distributed DD/DS also plays an important role in controlling access to the distributed database, especially in restricting access to partitioned and/or replicated data that is classified as sensitive information.

Distribution alternatives for databases depend also on whether the network is implemented with homogeneous or heterogeneous hardware and software across the nodes, that is, what is the relative degree of "sameness" with regard to implementation among the hardware, DBMS, DD/DS, and other components. A homogeneous network is one in which each node has the same hardware and software components. A heterogeneous network has a different implementation of its components at each one of its nodes. For example, a heterogeneous network may have different hardware at the nodes or the same hardware but different DBMSs. Of the two, heterogeneous nodes are obviously more complex.

To a certain extent, the same considerations apply to the distribution of metadata as to the distribution of the database; thus, the coordination issue applies to metadata as well. There are several options in the DD/DS requirements for coordinating metadata across nodes of the network:

1. *A centralized,* or master metadatabase, located at one single location, containing all the required information about the databases and files in the network. Nodes in the network must poll this master metadatabase to find the desired data.
2. *Distributed replicated metadatabases,* the case in which each node in the network has replicated a metadatabase. A copy of all metadata is located at each node, containing information concerning the data in the entire network.
3. *Distributed partitioned metadatabases,* in which each node has its own metadata, i.e., a partition of the entire metadatabase which contains only information about that node. If a request comes in for data not in that node, the user must query all the other local metadatabases in the network until the desired metadata is found.
4. *Hierarchy of metadatabases,* in which there is a "master" and a

"slave" relationship — or centralized and local — which maintains a local metadatabase at each node, in addition to a centralized one, which may or may not be located elsewhere.

Each of these alternatives has advantages and disadvantages in terms of available technology, performance, and cost. In actuality, a choice is made in terms of a hybrid of the four alternatives. Of the four, the fourth one appears to be a viable solution. The various levels of metadata available for locating data in the network provide information at two levels: network-wide, the metadata provides information regarding the node in which the data resides; and locally, within a node, it describes where the data is.

10.1.3 The Functional Requirement for Data Translation

Locating the data in a network is half the problem. Once found, the data may require certain transformations before the requested data gets to the user. This transformation of data from one representation to another, while retaining the same meaning and content, is known as *data translation.* While a certain degree of translation occurs in all network configurations, the most complex and critical translation tasks are required for heterogeneous networks, where processing components at each node are dissimilar.

In the heterogeneous networks, when the system receives a user request for data, first it must determine what data must be accessed and where it is located. The NDD function takes care of that. Once that is determined, the request must be translated in such a way that the target DBMS can understand the request — that is, the request must be translated from one language to another. Upon return, the answer to the request must be translated into a form understood by the original requestor, this is *data translation.* Translation is required from source to target descriptions in terms of data structure, storage structures, and definitional synonyms.

Both the hardware and the software of a heterogeneous network may differ from node to node. An example of this type of network is the ARPANET network. Translation in this case is even more complex, because not only languages need to be translated, but there must be translation between character sets, such as between ASCII and EBCDIC, and between machines with different word lengths, to get the data aligned on proper word boundaries.

These are all physical level translation issues. The problem becomes even more difficult when the network is heterogeneous with respect to DBMSs. In this event, logical translation of data structures will be necessary.

The distributed DD/DS can facilitate these translation processes by providing the metadata mappings to allow the source to be transformed into the target data. This is accomplished by storing in the distributed DD/DS the source and target metadata descriptions to be used by the mapping process. Often, the source and target metadata may be distributed along with the data itself. In other situations it may be stored in the distributed DD/DS. Regardless of the way metadata is distributed, it would be under the control of the distributed DD/DS and it would be managed similarly to generated metadata.

10.2 SPECIAL FEATURES OF A DD/DS FOR DISTRIBUTED ENVIRONMENTS

To support the added demands imposed by the distribution of data over a network, the distributed DD/DS must be able to document information about the characteristics and the location of the data in the network; it must contain data structure, storage structure, access paths and mapping information to allow support of data translation; the network DD/DS must have information about data availability, data accessibility and data usage. In short, the distributed DD/DS can be a central component around which all data management functions revolve in the distributed database environment. This section describes new, unique specific features of the Distributed DD/DS necessary to support these functional requirements.

10.2.1 A New Meta-Entity: Node

The distributed DD/DS must include the ability to support all the meta-entities and attributes found in a centralized DD/DS. In addition, it must feature at least one new meta-entity: the *node*.

Defined upon the node entity is a recursive relationship, which is used to support the description of network topology (see Figure 10.1). The basic attributes necessary to describe the node include:

Identifier. Uniquely identifies and locates a particular node on the network;

Hardware configuration. Describes the hardware environment in terms of components of the node; type and model of the main computer, memory size, peripherals, etc.;

Software configuration. Describes the software environment of the node, including operating system, version, compilers, DBMS software, other pertinent software, access methods, and file structure.

Nodal relationship. Describes the relationship among nodes.

SPECIAL FEATURES OF A DD/DS

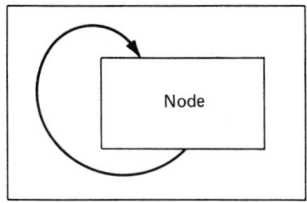

Figure 10.1 The meta-entity *node*.

Communication. Describes the communication hardware and software characteristics, including type of communication equipment, protocol, and transmission links.

Security and access information. Describes the types of authorization required for access, passwords, and other security algorithms.

These and other attributes would allow the distributed DD/DS to assist the user process in locating data in the network. Together with the entities described in Chapter 4 and the new entity, node, the DD/DS could be capable of providing information on data structures, data location, data availability, data accessibility, and data translation maps and access paths.

10.2.2 Metadata Migration Features

Depending on the configuration of the distributed DD/DS in the network [LIEB 77, ABRA 76] — whether it is a distributed replicated master DD/DS, a distributed partitioned master DD/DS, or a hierarchy (master/slave) DD/DS — there must exist features of the DD/DS to allow the propagation and migration of the metadata for the use of the requesting user process.

A dominant node is often found in a **star network** (see Figure 10.2) in which one node acts as the master, or the clearinghouse for all requests from user processes. In a *star network,* there is a master copy

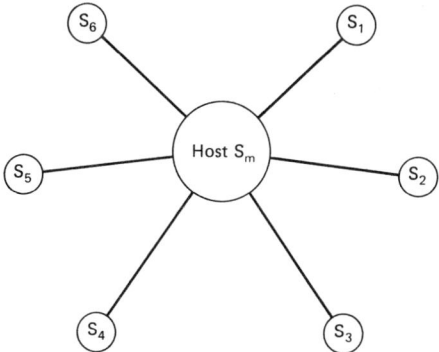

Figure 10.2 Star configuration.

of the database located at a host computer, while copies of selective portions of the database are distributed to individual user nodes. Individual nodes communicate with the base host computer, but not necessarily with each other. In this type of network topology, there is a master DD/DS that is located in the host site. Nodes in the network may have a portion of the master metadatabase replicated, in effect creating a two-level hierarchy of the DD/DS. Each of these locally situated DD/DSs will contain only metadata relating to the data in that particular node. The relationship between the DD/DS at the host site and the node-side is that of a master/slave relationship. A requesting process obtains the necessary metadata by first accessing its local node. If the metadata is not found in the local node, the slave-DD/DS will go to the master DD/DS to get the required metadata. This metadata is replicated, and physically migrated to the requesting node.

A similar situation occurs in the *hierarchical network* (see Figure 10.3). The difference is in the network topology. The hierarchical network supports the master/slave relationship in the database, as well as the DD/DS. This topology consists of a host, or master computer, and a number of dependent, subservient computers at lower levels.

It is possible to have more than one level in a hierarchical network configuration. Like the star configuration, the hierarchical configuration supports a master DD/DS at the host level, and partitioned copies of the DD/DS reside at the slave nodes. If the desired metadata is not found in the local nodes, the master is polled, and the metadata is replicated and migrated to the local node.

In order to support the distributed database management functions in star and hierarchical networks, the distributed DD/DS must be able to metadata as required. The nodes of star and hierarchical networks for recognizing master/slave relationships and for propagating changes to metadata as required. The nodes of star and hierrachical networks

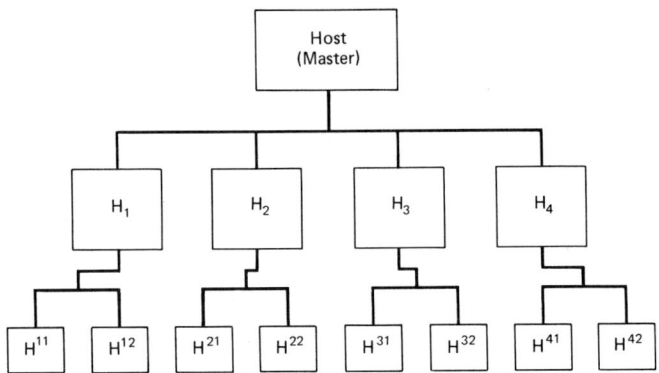

Figure 10.3 Hierarchical configuration.

SPECIAL FEATURES OF A DD/DS

are typically homogeneous in order to facilitate sharing. The *ring network* is more apt to be heterogeneous than the star or the hierarchy. In a ring network configuration (see Figure 10.4), nodes have equal standing with each other, that is, there is no master/slave relationship. Distribution of the database may be fully partitioned, replicated, or some combination thereof. It may consist of autonomous processing systems with nonredundant shared data. A ring network may consist of heterogeneous components; therfore, the need for data translation may be critical. The distributed DD/DS can be located in one of three ways:

1. *Centralized in one node.* It should be noted that for this option, the optimal placement of the DD/DS in the network is critical.
2. *Fully replicated master DD/DSs in all the nodes.* Each should contain information about all the data in the entire network.
3. *Fully partitioned DD/DS.* Each partition contains only that metadata pertinent to the local node.

The first case is an anomaly that forces the ring network to collapse to a star network. The second and third are distinct possibilities in this type of topology. In one respect the fully replicated master is perhaps the most efficient, since all the metadata for the entire network is found in each DD/DS; however, it is not efficient in terms of storage and updating of metadata. The fully partitioned master is perhaps the most effective for the ring structure, when partitioning of data occurs, as well. The greatest danger in this type of network is backup/recovery,

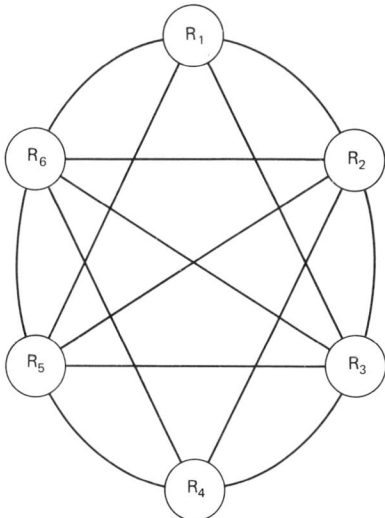

Figure 10.4 Ring configuration.

in case a break occurs in the ring. But, of course, this is true of the data itself, also.

DD/DSs in the ring situation may be heterogeneous. Request for metadata must go through the individual DD/DS, and it may be necessary to poll the entire network to locate the required metadata. Because the DD/DSs are heterogeneous, there is a high likelihood that the DBMSs are also heterogeneous, so that the translation problem is a critical one. Translation and mapping information for various target systems must reside in the DD/DS, or at least it must contain pointers to where these translation rules may be found.

In the ring structure with the fully partitioned DD/DS, as in the other structures, the metadata is propagated by first replicating the required metadata and then migrating to the node with the requesting process. Thus, once again the migrating feature is necessary.

10.2.3 Data Translation Features

Perhaps one of the most important services that a DD/DS can perform, next to providing information about the location of the data, is to provide metadata for the data translation software. In nonhomogeneous configurations, where hardware, software, or both may differ, there must exist common-access mechanisms, for example, language, access methods and, above all, a DD/DS that has the ability to describe source and target representations of data.

The DD/DS in a heterogeneous network can be the repository for a *network schema,* which describes the data stored in the overall network; and each node may have its own node-schema, or *network subschema.* In addition, this network subschema may contain mappings or transformation rules to get to or from the representation found in the network schema.

The DD/DS has the capability of becoming active with respect to network processes through its generative capability, by producing source/target definitions for the network processes which would execute data translation requests. This, of course, suggests an architecturally independent DD/DS component [ALLE 81]. Of course, the DD/DS in a distributed environment, as in the centralized environment, is useful to more than just the databases or the DBMS. In fact, the DD/DS may be a very important tool to support conventional file processing in a distributed environment, for the same reasons that a DD/DS is useful to DBMSs and databases.

10.3 DISTRIBUTION STRATEGIES FOR METADATA

The distribution alternatives available for user databases are also applicable for the metadatabase. While these alternatives have been dis-

DISTRIBUTION STRATEGIES FOR METADATA 241

cussed in a previous section, this section focuses on the trade-offs and circumstances involved for the three basic alternatives (see Figure 10.5): replication, partitioning, and hybrid.

Method of Metadata Distribution	Should Be Chosen If...
Replication	There is a high likelihood that each node will use metadata from all over the network.
	User data is replicated.
	User data is partitioned only at the occurrence level, not at type level.
Partition	Individual nodes do not require frequent access to data in other nodes.
	User data is partitioned at type level.
	There exists a natural partition in metadata source/usage among the nodes.
Hybrid	There exists a master metadatabase along with subservient metadatabases that are full replications of the master metadatabase or partitions of the master metadatabase.

Figure 10.5 Reasons for choosing a method of distribution.

10.3.1 Replication of Metadata

Replication of the metadatabase occurs when copies of the master metadatabase appear at each node. This may occur in conjunction with fully replicated user databases. This strategy may be used in a star network or in a ring network. The advantage of having fully replicated metadatabases in all the nodes is that it makes accessing the data more efficient; the disadvantage is that if the volume of the metadatabase updates is very high, this places undue update overhead requirements on all the nodes.

This strategy should be chosen if:

1. There is a high likelihood that each node will use metadata from all over the network.
2. User data is replicated, because then the metadata will be close to the user data.
3. User data is partitioned only at the occurrence level, and not at the type level, because then the full complement of metadata is needed at each node.

In the case of the hierarchy or the star configuration, a central or master metadatabase is maintained in order to control update over the metadata in the entire network, and to provide global design support for all the nodes. There are other reasons for locating metadata at a node when the data it describes is at another node, and that is to enable development efforts by co-locating the metadata where it is needed. Another reason arises when there are large numbers of query requests using metadata to resolve queries from the nodes.

10.3.2 Partitioning Metadata

Partitioning of the metadatabase occurs when the master metadatabase is distributed so that each node has the metadata pertaining to just that node. There need be no redundancy in this approach. A partitioned metadatabase may be used in conjunction with a fully partitioned user database in a ring network. The advantage of partitioning the metadatabase is that it avoids unnecessary redundancies, and the metadatabase can be dedicated to serving that particular node. Disadvantages include problematical backup/recovery in case of failure in any given node, thereby potentially bringing down the entire network, especially if the required metadata is stored in the "crashed" node. Another problem is the longer access time required for one node to poll all the rest of the nodes, if the desired metadata is not in the local node.

This strategy should be chosen if:

1. There is a high likelihood that the individual nodes do not require frequent access to data in other nodes of the network.
2. User data is partitioned at the type level.
3. There is a natural partition in metadata source/usage among the nodes.

10.3.3 Hybrid Allocation of Metadata

The *hybrid* alternative occurs when both replication and partitioning techniques are used in distributing the metadatabase. This occurs when there exists a master metadatabase along with subservient metadatabases that are either the fully replicated master metadatabase, or partitions of the master. This type of metadatabase distribution approach may be used with a hierarchy of DD/DSs in a hierarchical network or a star network. The advantage of this approach is that it has the flexibility to place an entire copy of the master metadatabase at those nodes which may require the access of data from other nodes in the network; and places partitions at those nodes that only require data from its own node.

The selection of individual alternatives must, of course, take into account other factors such as hardware/software requirements, security and integrity constraints, storage constraints, language constraints, and so forth.

10.4 DA/DBA CONSIDERATIONS

While the DD/DS is a necessity in the distributed environment, it is not the first design consideration. It is a very valuable, perhaps even indispensable, tool that is employed after the distributed system has been designed. First, one must analyze, model, and/or guess what the traffic patterns are going to be. How many database accesses will be restricted to an identifiable subset of the database? How do these accesses divide between query and update? What are the requirements for continued operation in the face of component failure? How current must the database be? If there must be redundancy in the data, what is the requirement for timeliness or consistency?

These and other questions are the purview of the data administrator/database administrator, for they touch upon administrative, policy, and technical design issues of databases. The traditional functions of the DA/DBA must be adjusted to accommodate this new environment. In view of this, the traditional DA/DBA functions are redefined, with small modifications, below:

Data administration is responsible for administration of policies. These include, but are not limited to, issues concerning management of internodal standards and nodal design; administration, coordination and control of data; administration of security requirements across nodes; coordination with legal and privacy requirements; and administration of edit and validation procedures across nodes.

Database administration is responsible for the technical administration of the distributed database. This function must provide, among other things, technical coordination of database design, metadata generation, maintenance of the DD/DS and DBMS software, administration of internodal metadata migration; and for the overall metadata and data security on the network.

One of the critical issues concerning the administration of data across a network is at which node(s) to place the DA/DBA function. In a centralized environment, the question is moot. However, in a distributed environment, with distributed databases, DBMSs, metadata, and DD/DSs, there may be the need for placing a DA/DBA at each node. There is no clear-cut solution to this problem, and it must be examined on a case-by-case situation, taking into consideration all organizational and technical factors.

10.4.1 The DA in a Distributed Environment

The data administrator, in a distributed database environment, establishes policies to be followed in the entire network. The DA may use the DD/DS for assistance. These policies may deal with legal requirements, or with technical requirements established to facilitate interchange of information. On the legal side, the DA may need to establish policies directed at satisfying government-legislated constraints on international transborder data flow, or establishing privacy constraints that affect storage and flow of data.

The DA is responsible for developing and enforcing standards for database contents, data formats, network protocols, access protocols, and distribution at the conceptual level, and for establishing data definition standards that must be followed at all nodes. This is to enable increased sharing of the data resources. The DA can use the DD/DS in this task by enforcing the data definition standard using the DD/DS.

Security and access control is an important responsibility of the DA. These should be defined using the overall security structure for the database, based on individual nodal requirements.

Security refers to the protection of data against deliberate or accidental destruction, unauthorized access or modification of data. In the distributed environment, the opportunities for breaching the security of a system are increased manifold because a greater number of variables are introduced, such as levels of access; for example, a user may be able to access public-use portions of a database that are listed for sharing, but may be denied access to certain other portions of the database. The DA has the responsibility for assigning this kind of access authorization while possibly delegating the definition of multilevel local security restrictions to local DBAs. Security requirements, specifically related to authorization for access, and levels of access may be placed in the DD/DS. The DA also can place in the DD/DS information about delegated authority, such as who to see for access.

The DA has overall responsibility for the integrity and reliability of the network data resources. This would include responsibility to establish edit and validation procedures across all nodes, such as establishing correctness criteria for data and establishing validation rules. The DA can use the DD/DS in this task. Metadata stored in the DD/DS should include these correctness criteria and edit and validation rules, so that individual nodes can access them.

10.4.2 The DBA in a Distributed Environment

The technical administration of network data resources falls in the DBA's hands. These run the gamut of centralized DBA functions, including database design, database creation, database organization, maintenance, and security, but all with distributed overtones. The DBA needs DD/DS assistance in these functions. Using the DD/DS, there can be technical coordination of database designs — this will insure that there will not be too many disparate database structures and organizations, and will ultimately serve to minimize translation problems. The DBA can coordinate and control data definition, and data and storage definitions. The DBA must decide the best strategy to use in distributing data logically, physically, or both.

The DBA must be involved in the logical design of internodal update strategies to minimize synchronization problems. Simulation may be used to help arrive at an optimal solution. The DD/DS can assist the DBA by providing both the metadata required for the database design and related nodal information for simulation purposes.

The DD/DS can be used, also, in generating metadata for distributed database designs for the network DBMS, and for the translation processor. Maintenance of the DD/DS is also the responsibility of the DBA. It is critical that the DD/DS be current in all the nodes, and the DBA must coordinate all the DD/DS updates whenever there are metadata changes or distribution changes. Since the DD/DS is an integral part of the access mechanism to network data, the importance of its currency and correctness cannot be emphasized sufficiently. The DBA must insure that all changes, additions, or deletions are propagated.

Internodal metadata migration may be a necessity, depending on the topology of the network, the DBMSs, and the DD/DSs. This propagation of metadata from one node to another must be controlled, and is also the responsibility of the DBA.

Operational security of the metadata on the network is also in the purview of the DBA. It would be highly undesirable to have unauthorized users access metadata for which they have no authorization. This could jeopardize the integrity of the metadatabase, as well as the associated user database or process.

Database administration in the distributed environment involves coordination of all database activities in that environment, including training, documentation, standards, and data policies. Training and documentation requirements are likely, also, to be extensive because users have to be made familiar with how to obtain data from other hosts.

10.5 SUMMARY

Distributed database is a developing technology. Some of the reasons for distributing data have to do with cost: the cost of data processing and storage are falling much more rapidly than communications costs. Some have to do with increased functionality: low-cost local processing can provide fast interactive services independent of, and often superior to, traditional mainframes for the functions of source data capture, data entry, and editing. And some reasons have to do with management: distributed management can be reflected in distributed data organization, thus providing responsiveness for local needs and problems along with responsibility for the enterprise which the data processing supports.

Distributed databases are most likely to succeed when there is a clear division of data needs either functionally or geographically (or both). The economics are favorable when there is a low probability of internode access for most applications. Successful implementations have been made in businesses where there are natural partitions, such as retail point-of-sale, large banking systems, reservation systems, and manufacturing/distribution systems.

There are some problems associated with distributed databases; some of them have to do with performance issues, others with locating the data in the network. The question of where data is located becomes increasingly complicated when the address space is expanded to include the nodal computers. The question of what data means is exacerbated when the problem of different data types, formats, representations, and precision occurs among heterogeneous hosts in a distributed network. The DD/DS is one tool which addresses many of these problems.

In this chapter, we have discussed some of the special functions and features that a DD/DS requires in a distributed database environment, such as the addition of a new entity type, the node and its attributes, and the ability to provide data location and to support data translation.

Strategies for distributing metadata and the DD/DS were discussed, including a brief description of the most common network topologies: star, hierarchy, and ring.

The DA/DBA functions are critical in the distributed environment, for they become the mechanism for resolving administrative and technical issues arising from distributing data and processing. Their roles in the distributed environment were discussed.

REFERENCES

[ABRA 76]   Abrams, M., R. P. Blanc, and I. W. Cotton, "Network Configuration and Vocabulary," in *Computer Networks: A Tutorial,* IEEE Computer Society, JH3100-5C, June 1976, pp. 2-1 to 2-5.

[ALLE 81]   Allen, F., M. Loomis, and M. Mannino, "The Integrated Dictionary/Directory System," University of Arizona MIS Technical Report 81-163, 1981.

[ALSB 76]   Alsberg, P. A., G. G. Belford, S. R. Bunch, J. D. Day, E. Gropa, D. C. Healy, E. J. McCauley, D. A. Wilcox, "Synchronization and Deadlock," University of Illinois, CAC Document # 185, 1976.

REFERENCES

[ASCH 74] Aschim, Frode, "Data Base Networks – An Overview," in *Management Informatics,* Vol. 3, No. 1, February 1974, pp. 13–28.

[BERN 77] Bernstein, P. A., J. B. Rothnie, D. W. Shipman, and N. Goodman, "The SDD-1 Redundant Update Algorithm (The General Case)," Technical Report CCA-77-09, Computer Corporation of America, August 1, 1977.

[CHAM 77] Champine, G. A., "Six Approaches to Distributed Data Bases," in *Datamation,* May 1977.

[CHU 75] Chu, W., "File Directory Design Considerations for Distributed Databases," in *Proc. First Int. Conf. Very Large Databases,* IEEE, 1975, pp. 543–545.

[CHU 76] Chu, W. "Performance of the File Directory System for Data Bases in Star and Distributed Networks," in *Proc. AFIPS NCC 1976,* AFIPS Press, 1976, pp. 577–587.

[DEPP 76] Deppe, M. E., and J. P. Fry, "Distributed Database: A Summary of Research," *Computer Networks,* Vol. 1, No. 2, North-Holland, Amsterdam, 1976, pp. 130–138.

[LIEB 77] Liebowitz, B. H. and J. H. Carson, *Tutorial on Distributed Processing,* IEEE EH 0127-1, 1977.

[LOOM 81] Loomis, M. E. S. and M. Mannino, "Directories in Distributed Database Management," University of Arizona MIS Technical Report MIS-81-171, 1981.

[RIES 78] Ries, D. and R. Epstein, "Evaluation of Distributed Criteria for Distributed Database Systems," University of California at Berkeley, Memorandum No. UCB/ERL M78/22, May 1978.

[ROTH 77] Rothnie, J. B. and N. Goodman, "A Survey of Research and Development in Distributed Database Management," in *Proc. Third Int. Conf. Very Large Data Bases,* IEEE, 1977.

[STON 79] Stonebreaker, M., "Concurrency Control and Consistency of Multiple Copies of Data in Distributed INGRES" IEEE Transaction on Software Engineering, SE-5, 3, May 1979, pp. 188–194.

11

Control and Auditing Techniques Using the DD/DS

The sharing of data resources across application lines is the single most important development impacting the controllability and auditability of database-supported information systems. The advent of database technology, which introduced the capabilities of data independence on a wide basis, has made achievable the goal of sharing data among multiple and diverse user types. These new information systems must be controlled. Moreover, they must be subjected to the careful scrutiny of both internal and external auditors, who must ascertain that the information system produces results that are consistent with their audit objectives: verification and assurance of the completeness, timeliness, and accuracy of systems processing and output.

A number of concerns face the auditor in dealing with the database-supported information system. These include the following:

1. *Access to data.* Can an unauthorized program gain access to the database? Can an unauthorized program gain access to portions of the database for which it is not authorized?
2. *Update of data.* Once an authorized program has accessed the database, can it be used to update data other than those it is authorized to update? Can the shared use of data among application programs cause cascading errors? How can this risk be reduced and how does one maintain the audit trail of how the errors can and do occur?

3. *Coordination of activity.* How can the need for a consistent level of control across applications be assured? How will users, analysts, and programmers be assured of a common understanding and interpretation of the data and database design?

To some extent, the use of database technology has caused these issues to be of concern to the auditor. Conversely, database technology itself offers the opportunity to mitigate many of these concerns [BCS 77, EVER 77].

The Data Dictionary/Directory System (DD/DS) offers auditors an opportunity to address many of the control and auditability concerns which require their attention [ADAM 76]. This chapter describes how the DD/DS can be used to increase the control and auditability of database supported information systems. Discussion of topics at the end of the chapter is organized to emphasize the issues or control concerns listed above. Specific functions and/or features of DD/DSs are cited first to illustrate how the audit objective can be achieved.

The DD/DS provides specific functions which, while generally intended to serve the data processing professional, for example, the database administrator, also serve to provide important control from an audit perspective and to mitigate certain control concerns in a database environment. There are three categories of DD/DS functions which provide control and audit related functions. These are:

Documentation of data and systems,
Audit trail at the "type" level, and
Control through metadata generation.

The following sections discuss these topics in greater detail.

11.1 CONTROL AND AUDIT-RELATED FUNCTIONS OF THE DD/DS: DOCUMENTATION OF DATA AND SYSTEMS

Data Dictionary/Directory Systems contain a major portion of the documentation of a data processing environment, database-supported or otherwise. Inasmuch as documentation is an important element of the system of internal controls that an auditor is concerned with, and is a major source of information that an auditor uses in becoming familiar with an application system and its underlying databases, the DD/DS in turn becomes a focal point for the auditor.

The auditor insists on comprehensive, accurate, reliable, and current documentation because the written work serves to substantiate and provide physical evidence of the working of the system of internal controls [AICP 78]. Specific documentation regarding the basic components of the system design, including programs and data files, serve as the basis of an auditor's investigation. Many auditors spend an inordinate amount of time interviewing, recording, and formally documenting the systems they are auditing. Some auditors have spent as much as 80% of their audit time simply recording the facts of the system. Besides the basic documentation, the auditor relies on the description of programs and data to provide information regarding the implementation of controls in the system. Specific documentation regarding controls would describe at least the following:

1. *Data integrity and quality.* Documentation would specify for each data element and associated data structure the criteria for correctness, and the rules by which the system ascertains if a given data element or data structure satisfies the criteria for correctness. Such rules would be applied upon loading data and when updating.
2. *Authorization of access.* Descriptions of data would include the sensitivity and privacy requirements for each data element and/or group of data elements. Documentation would describe how security profiles reflected these privacy requirements using the security mechanism of the database environment (e.g., access control using passwords).

For many years the documentation containing this important information was sought by the auditor, but this information was rarely found. As mentioned earlier, many auditors became professional "documentors." Many managers as well as auditors have asked the question, "Why is documentation incomplete, inaccurate, unreliable, out-of-date, or generally unavailable?" Common answers such as "It's boring work!", and "The system works without it . . . Let's get on with it!", are indicative of the problem. The crux of the issue is that, traditionally (see Figure 11.1) . . . "documentation is not part of the system."

The documentation is prepared after the fact, if at all. When the system is maintained, and changes are made, the documentation is always an afterthought. It is no wonder, therefore, that the auditor finds it so difficult to find the documentation required to complete an adequate review and assessment of the system of internal controls.

The DD/DS can provide the vehicle for addressing the basic underlying issue regarding documentation, that is, that documentation is not part of the system. The DD/DS in fact provides a vehicle for documentation which can be an active and integral part of the database environment (see Figure 11.2). There are two aspects to the DD/DS which aid in solving the documentation concerns – both are important!

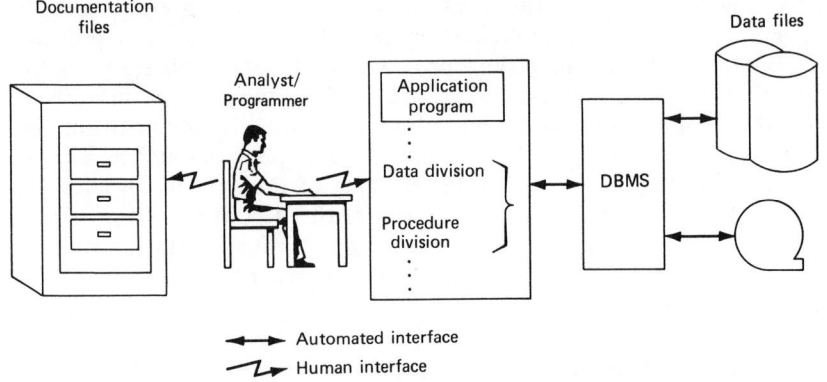

Figure 11.1 Documentation is not an integral part of the system.

11.1.1 Automation of Metadata

The fact that there is an automated centralized repository for data descriptions (including the programs and processes using the data), helps solve the tedious aspect of dealing with volumes of documentation. To some extent, we have applied the technologies of word processing and text editing to documentation.

The ability to update and retrieve data about a system design or database description on an instantaneous basis creates a whole new dimension in documentation. Online availability of metadata is a phenomenon conspicuously unique to the DD/DS.

11.1.2 Active DD/DS

An active DD/DS has been defined as a DD/DS implemented so that components of the data processing environment are dependent upon the DD/DS for their metadata. A DD/DS is said to be active with respect to that component which is dependent upon the DD/DS for metadata.

Let us assume, by way of illustration, that our data processing is organized with all the application programs dependent on the DD/DS for their metadata. That is to say, the DD/DS is active with respect to the application programs. In effect, this means that the data divisions of the COBOL programs would be derived from the content of the metadatabase. There is no other way to generate an FD section than to "include" it or "copy" it from the DD/DS.

Consider the effect of the active DD/DS from an auditor's viewpoint, focusing on the issue of documentation. Whereas in the past the documentation was a passive component of the system (if it was considered

DOCUMENTATION OF DATA AND SYSTEMS

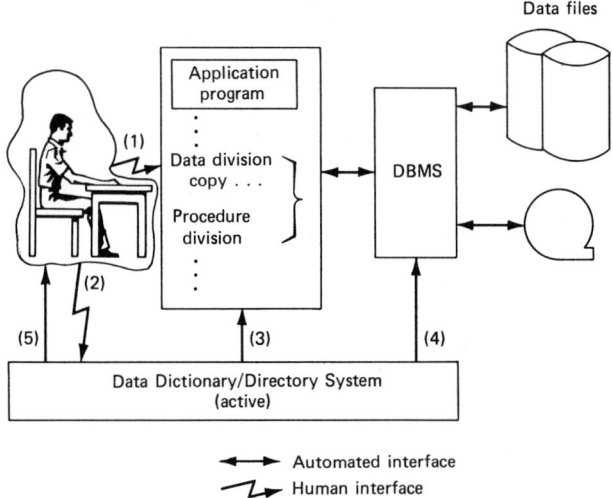

Figure 11.2 Documentation as an integral part of the system: (1) Program code with copy statement for metadata; (2) Metadata for the DD/DS (could be through a DBA) includes all documentation; (3) Metadata generated as a result of copy statement; (4) Metadata generated for the DBMS; (5) Documentation is automatically generated.

part of the system at all), now the documentation when entered into an active DD/DS becomes an integral part of the system actually generating part of the application program code, specifically those portions of the data divisions which depend upon DD/DS metadata. Now, if changes are to be made they must first be reflected in the metadatabase in order to become effective in an application program.

The important point for the auditor from the documentation point of view is that with an active DD/DS the documentation must:

Reflect the real world (complete).
Be accurate.
Be reliable.
Be timely.

It should be noted that the DD/DS is merely a vehicle to solve the problems plaguing documentation. As the old saying goes, you can fill the trough with water; you can bring the horse to the trough; but you can't make the horse drink. A DD/DS must contain metadata, and it must be implemented in a manner such that it can be active. But most important, it must be used as an active DD/DS.

11.2 CONTROL AND AUDIT-RELATED FUNCTIONS OF THE DD/DS: AUDIT TRAIL AT THE TYPE LEVEL

One of the primary control objectives of auditors is the ability to maintain an adequate audit trail during the normal course of processing. Audit trails are then used to recreate, substantiate, and otherwise check on the completeness and veracity of the processing of transactions. Audit trails can be maintained on two levels: the type level and the occurrence level.

The notion of type versus occurrence is closely related to the concept of metadata. Figure 11.3 illustrates the notion of type versus occurrence with respect to the data entities record and data element. Note that all the type level information is metadata, that is, it is information about user data contained in our files.

This concept of type versus occurrence can be extended to include the description of system entities, as well. Figure 11.4 illustrates the notion of type versus occurrence for the system entity program or module. Note that the program as an occurrence is called a *process* (or a run unit in CODASYL terms); thus for example, an application program designed to edit and post incoming orders in an order entry system could be represented as an individual process or run unit for each arriving order, or transaction. If two or more orders arrive such

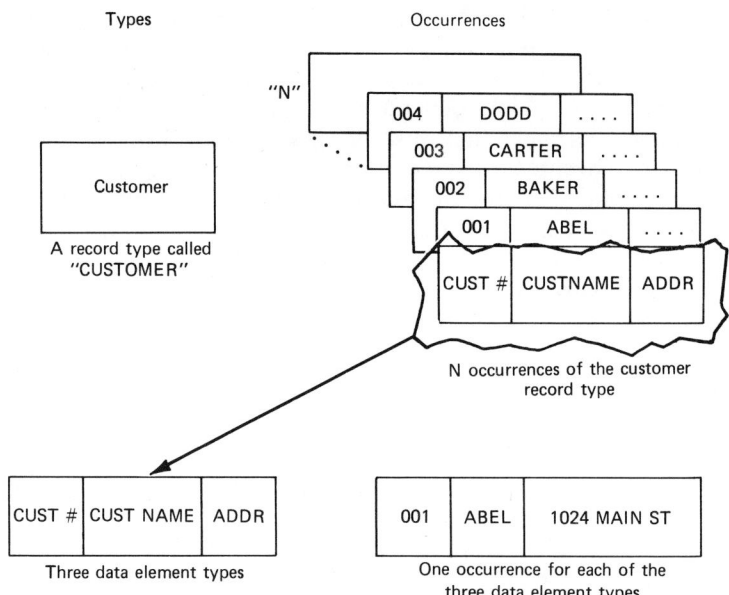

Figure 11.3 The notion of type-versus-occurrence for records and data elements.

AUDIT TRAIL AT THE TYPE LEVEL 255

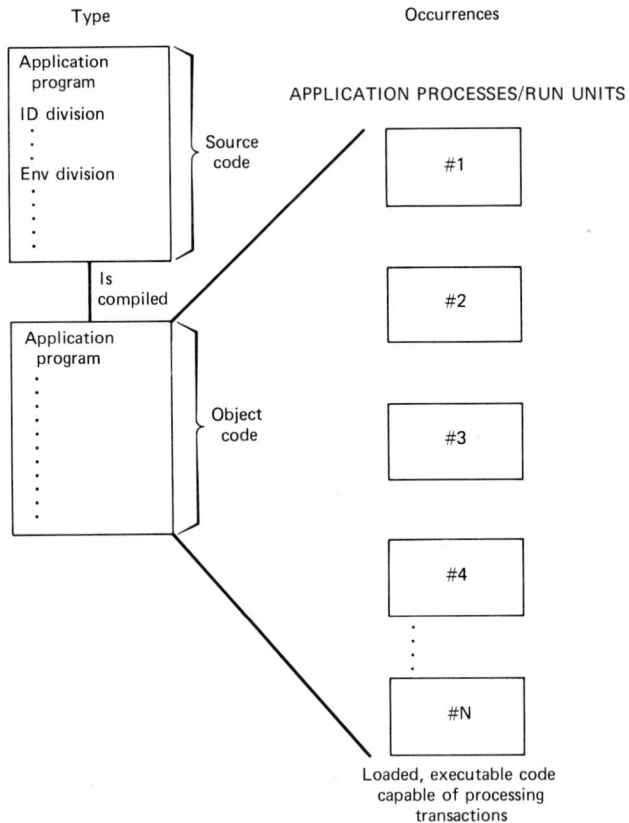

Figure 11.4 The notion of type-versus-occurrence for the program entity.

that the orders are processed concurrently, the single application program would have multiple occurrences, or processes, executing concurrently in the computer. In the case of reentrant code, in a multi-threaded system, a single copy of a program could be executing as multiple processes.

Traditionally, auditors have been concerned with occurrences of data elements, records, and processes, in the course of performing substantive testing procedures. Not a great deal of attention has been afforded to tracing the effect of transactions at the type level. Type level information was important only insofar as it served as documentation. (See discussion above on documentation). In a database environment, the type level information is extremely important, as an audit trail, in the following two situations:

Transaction impact analysis.
Correction of valid, but incorrect, updates.

The following paragraphs discuss these two situations in greater depth.

11.2.1 Transaction Impact Analysis

The American Institute of Certified Public Accountants (AICPA), in its interpretation of accepted accounting practices, Statement on Auditing Standards (SAS 3) [AICP 78], cites the necessity for the auditor to understand the impact of transactions on the system and its outputs. In a shared database environment, this requirement can only be met if the auditor can assess the impact of each transaction on the database itself.

Given the complexity of most database designs, it would be almost impossible to trace the impact of each transaction at the occurrence level. Instead, auditors have come to rely on the type level audit trail to discern the impact of each transaction at the type level. Then, if the audit objectives warrant, substantive testing might include a sampling of some transaction occurrences, and their impact on specific record occurrences would be further scrutinized. With simple sequential database designs, auditors might well rely on the manually prepared documentation to perform Transaction Impact Analysis, however, with the ever increasing complexity of database designs, the DD/DS will be indispensable in its support of Transaction Impact Analysis.

Specifically, the DD/DS will provide complete and accurate information about:

Transaction types,
Record and data element types and data structure, and
The records and data element types which are impacted by each transaction.

Using DD/DS-supplied information, the auditor will be able to understand exactly how each transaction enters the database and how it traverses from one record type to another, and thus be able to assess the degree to which controls may or may not be necessary during transaction processing.

11.2.2 Correction of Valid but Incorrect Updates

It is a well accepted principle (usually referred to as Murphy's Law) that if something can go wrong, it will. The fact that erroneous entries will be made into databases is a foregone conclusion. Furthermore, it must be assumed that such errors will occur in a manner such that there will be no normal transaction to reverse the error. Such errors most commonly occur as a result of valid but nevertheless incorrect values being accepted by edit/validation routines.

The effects of these errors can be devastating. Such errors, by their very nature, are extremely difficult to detect. Often, many cycles of processing may have elapsed before a user realizes that erroneous results are being produced. By the time the error is detected, the error may have cascaded to many unsuspecting user reports, and/or may have caused erosion of the database. *Cascading* errors occur when an output is produced based upon an erroneous value. *Database erosion* occurs when an otherwise correct value in the database is erroneously updated based upon the valid but incorrect entry.

Assuming the error has been detected, the problem is to rectify the situation. Due to the integration and sharing of data among users, this can be difficult in a database environment. The first step in the process is to ascertain the scope of impact on the erroneous entry. This is accomplished by identifying which programs use the erroneous data element, proceeding to the data elements used by that program and along this line until the auditor is satisfied that no erosion has occurred. Thus the scope of an error can be bounded, and only the eroded portion of the database need be affected by subsequent rectification procedures.

The source of this information about which programs use the erroneous data, which programs use the data of those programs, and so on, is the DD/DS. Most commercial DD/DS packages can provide the answers based upon a few simple "where used" queries. Furthermore, as previously mentioned, with an active DD/DS this information is complete, accurate and up-to-date.

However, it should be noted that in order to check on the actual impact of erroneous values, the auditor must consult other sources, such as the recovery log.

11.3 CONTROL THROUGH METADATA GENERATION

The concept of an active DD/DS is based upon the principle that components of the database environment (e.g., application programs, report generators, query languages, and database management systems) must be dependent upon the DD/DS for their metadata. This dependency is implemented through the capability of the DD/DS to generate, or make available, metadata for the dependent components. This ability to generate metadata is also important from a control standpoint. In essence, it is possible to control the development life cycle and execution of all programs in a database environment by using an active DD/DS to generate metadata for these programs.

Every program, by definition, is composed of two parts:

Procedure. The instructions which specify what and/or how the program is supposed to do its work.

Data. The actual data, and descriptions of the data, upon which the program is supposed to do its work.

Both parts of a program are necessary for the program to be able to perform its work. A procedure without data (or data descriptions) is not a program and could never execute. Thus, if the active DD/DS is the sole source of metadata (data descriptions) for a given program, then, in essence, that program is controlled by the DD/DS. It could not be compiled, let alone executed without the metadata generated by the DD/DS.

Control over programs can be achieved from two perspectives:

Development and maintenance, and
execution or production mode.

The following paragraphs discuss how control using an active DD/DS can be achieved from these two perspectives.

11.3.1 Control of Development and Maintenance

When a program is written, the programmer usually conceptually visualizes the program's logical view of the data that the program will process. In a conventional environment, the programmer codes this logical view in the program. Often the logical view is also the physical representation. Thus, in COBOL the programmer codes a Data Division, and in FORTRAN the coder writes FORMAT statements. In a database environment, the subschema is coded to represent the program's logical view, which depending upon implementation alternatives may or may not replace portions of the conventional data descriptions (e.g., the Data Division). With an active DD/DS, all the metadata would be generated by the DD/DS. Without the DD/DS, the program could not even be compiled. Thus, control over the development of new programs can be achieved by using the active DD/DS to control the generation of metadata which is originally entered into the DD/DS.

In a similar fashion, control can be achieved over the maintenance procedures involving changing data descriptions. When data elements are being added or changed, or reorganization or restructuring of the database requires updating of data descriptions, the update is made into the DD/DS. In turn, metadata is generated for the DBMS schema and subschemas, and for the application program. Thus, no change could be made without first entering the change in the DD/DS.

11.3.2 Control of Program Execution

When a change made to a data description (schema) impacts a program, and this program is not updated or recompiled, the active DD/DS could lock out the execution of that application program. This is actually accomplished at run-time execution by comparing the program's "last date compiled" with the subschema's "last date compiled." For DBMSs with subschemas implemented outside the DML of the application program, this technique yields a very effective control through the use of the active DD/DS. For DBMSs with the subschema implemented within the context of the DML (e.g., ADABAS's FORMAT Buffer without the use of ADAMINT), this control technique using the DD/DS tool could not be realized.

The DD/DS has the potential to serve the auditor both as a tool for audit and for control. As an audit tool, it provides the type level audit trail and important documentation; as a control tool, it can be used as a mechanism for controlling program development and change, as well as a control tool over the documentation process. Nevertheless, our analysis would not be complete without looking back to the control concerns of the auditor relative to a database environment and evaluate whether or not these concerns can be mitigated by using an active DD/DS. The following paragraphs address this issue of reducing control concerns in a database environment using a DD/DS.

11.4 CONTROL CONCERNS ADDRESSED BY THE DD/DS

While it is beyond the scope of this effort to enumerate all the control concerns of the auditor relative to the database environment,* we focus on the three primary concerns listed at the beginning of this chapter to highlight the need for new types of audit and control tools and techniques. Figure 11.5 summarizes the manner in which the active DD/DS can be used to address the three control concerns enumerated above.

It should be noted that in order to mitigate control concerns relative to unauthorized access and update, it is necessary to store security profiles in the DD/DS and generate them for the access control program which actually executes. This strategy, in itself, could raise additional control concerns regarding concentration of risk, inasmuch as now the security profiles could be rendered vulnerable in the metadatabase of the DD/DS.

In order to counteract this control concern, most commercial DD/DS packages provide special security mechanisms for the metadatabase of DD/DS. The DBA must provide special considerations in planning and implementing these security mechanisms in order to protect the metadata against unauthorized access or update. This would be especially applicable in an installation where the DD/DS is used in an online mode of operation.

---

*The interested reader is urged to pursue the work of the Joint Research Committee on Auditing Database Systems of the AICPA, CICA and IIA.

	DD/DS Functions		
Control Concerns	Documentation of Data and Systems	Audit Trail at Type Level	Control Through Metadata Generation
Access to data	Security profiles Subschemas	Security profiles Subschemas	Security profiles Subschemas
Update of data	Security profiles Subschemas	Security profiles Subschemas "Where used" list "Uses what" list	Security profiles Subschemas
Coordination of activity	Entity/attribute descriptions Database designs	Does not apply	Edit/validation Schemas Subschemas

Figure 11.5 DD/DS functions which mitigate control concerns.

11.5 SUMMARY

The DD/DS, when used as an active tool for gaining control in a database environment, can be an important contributor towards mitigating the control concerns of the auditor with regard to database implementation. Auditors should therefore become actively involved in advocating the acquisition of DD/DS packages. Implementation of an active DD/DS is fully consistent with the audit and control objectives of the auditor.

REFERENCES

[BCS 77] *Audit and Control of Database Systems,* London, England: The British Computer Society, Auditing by Computer Specialist Group, July, 1977, p. 163.

[EVER 77] Everest, Gordon and R. Weber, "Data Base Support Systems and the Auditing Function," Document No. 22-05-10, *DATA BASE MANAGEMENT* Series, Auerbach Publishers Inc., Pennsauken, NJ 1977, pp. 1–15.

[AICP 78] *Codification of Statements on Auditing Standards – Number 1 to 21,* American Institute of Certified Public Accountants, New York, 1978, p. 561.

[ADAM 76] Adams, D. L., "Systems to Audit Aspects of the Data Dictionary," *EDPACS,* May 1976.

12

The Future of Data Dictionary/Directory Systems

The development of data dictionary/directory systems as an important, and architecturally significant, component of the database environment began in the early 1970s and has proceeded on an evolutionary basis for more than a decade. This evolutionary development has been influenced to a large extent by other factors in database management, and more importantly, in data processing in general. Among these factors are the following:

Recognition of data as a resource.
Widespread use of DBMS packages.
Advent of distributed processing.
Progress in producing automated systems development tools.
Importance of audit and control of information systems.

This chapter examines the trends of development for DD/DSs, and focuses attention on what might be expected in the future. Previous chapters have addressed specific topics impacting future developments. Chapter 10 dealt with the DD/DS in a distributed processing environment; Chapter 11 examined the DD/DS as a tool for audit and control. In a general sense, many preceding chapters contain descriptions of how the DD/DS might function in future years. This concluding chapter gathers together these thoughts and discusses specific features and characteristics of the DD/DSs of the future. This is approached from the point of view of the user. The chapter presents first a scenario of how a DD/DS might be utilized in years to come. The next section discusses functional capabilities which will be necessary in DD/DSs to support these user needs. Technological implementation issues are examined next, followed by brief comments regarding the commercial market for DD/DSs.

12.1 FUTURE USER REQUIREMENTS FOR DD/DSs

Predicting future developments for any generic class of software should be based upon an understanding of a set of assumptions regarding the scenario of the environment in which that class of software would be used. Our assumptions regarding the future information systems environment are presented in this section on two levels: first, in general terms and subsequently in terms of specific user requirements for utilizing DD/DSs.

12.1.1 General Aspects of the Future Environment

The future information systems environment will be characterized by greater demand for easy-to-use facilities, greater need for distributed processing functions, and much more widespread use of database technology (see Figure 12.1). These aspects of the future environment are actually logical extensions of current trends in the industry and are directly related to the availability of smaller and cheaper systems. Following is a discussion of these trends, considered individually.

12.1.1.1 *Easy-to-Use Systems*

The proliferation of user-friendly systems is one clear manifestation of the increasing demand for easy-to-use facilities. More and more, data-processing systems vendors highlight their wares through advertisements directed to the end-users, claiming that useful results can be achieved in a matter of hours and days — not weeks and months. Developers of new systems have also taken note of this trend, recognizing the need for implementing simple, straightforward user interfaces, to insure that their products are, in fact, user friendly.

The characteristics associated with user languages are the most critical for making a system user friendly. The developers of programming languages, report generators, and query languages are all striving to approximate the characteristics of the user languages they design to those of a "natural" language. Indeed, the development of a truly natural language interface for end-users may not be too far off in the future.

Thus, the first general aspect of the future environment is the continuing demand on the part of the end-users, both large and small, for systems that are easy to use.

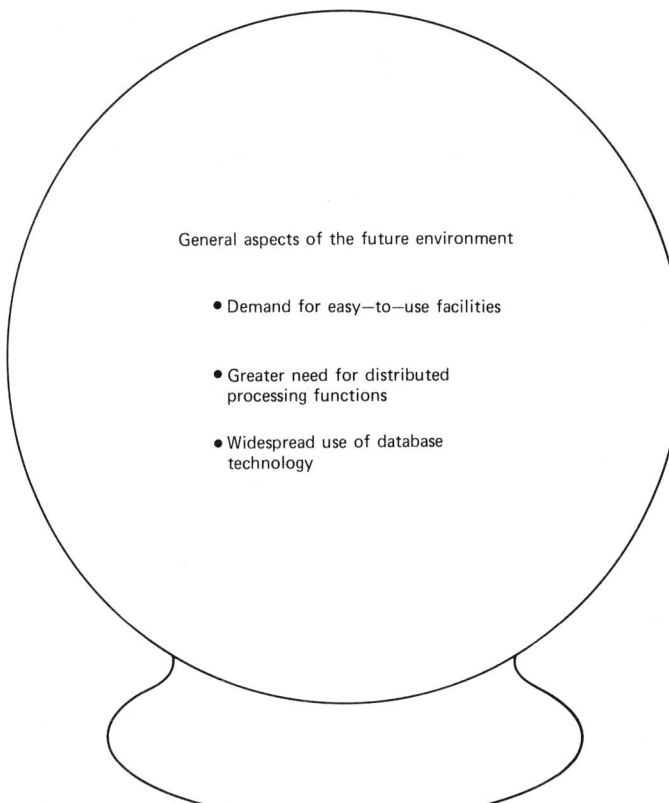

Figure 12.1 Crystal ball of the future environment.

12.1.1.2 Distributed Processing Functions

The current trend to satisfy user requirements for distributed processing functions will continue into the future. As a result of increased availability of necessary technology to satisfy geographical dispersion of data processing functions on an economically feasible basis, users will continue to design and implement systems where data usage is both shared and distributed. Users will require data processing functions in widely dispersed geographical locations. This continuing trend towards distributed processing will be manifested through:

Existing systems evolution.
New applications systems development.

Existing applications systems will be integrated and redeveloped or enhanced to work in unison, to support the user with information where and when it is needed on a reliable basis. New applications will be identified, designed, and built to support business information requirements of the enterprise. The importance of this trend lies in the fact that future distributed processing systems will be comprised of a large number of carryover hardware/software, thus postulating an environment which will be heterogeneous in its hardware and software implementations. Only those systems built and conceived from scratch will have the luxury of being homogeneous.

The second important aspect of the future environment is the continued trend towards distributed processing using heterogeneous hardware/software.

12.1.1.3 Widespread Use of Database Technology

The need to share data resources across organizational and functional lines in an enterprise has been a long recognized business goal. Centralized business management is based upon this philosophy. Nevertheless, data processing systems were not capable of delivering this data sharing characteristic in the form of an information system until the advent of database technology.

The 1970s brought the first wave of widespread use of database technology with the introduction of commercially available generalized database management systems. The first five years of the decade found vendors perfecting the products and establishing the market for the software. The second half of the decade brought the concept of a database environment and data resource management.

The 1980s will bring the truly widespread use of database technology. This was anticipated in the 1960s when DBMSs were first coming out of the research laboratories.

As a direct result of the application of DBMSs to minicomputers and microcomputers, many smaller enterprises will be able to draw upon these technologies to build information systems that share data across organizational and applications lines. Moreover, small user applications in large enterprises will benefit, as well.

The advent of DBMSs for small business information systems may be more significant than applying database technology in large complex enterprises. Many critics of large, complex, integrated, database-supported information systems cite the difficulty to coordinate and manage such a monolithic effort. Integrating small business information systems will not be hampered by the largeness which plagued such efforts in the 1970s.

Database technology will continue to proliferate in organizations where it was introduced in the 1970s. In most cases, database management systems did not penetrate more than 50% of an enterprise's potential data files. The trend towards using DBMSs will continue in the

1980s, so that by the close of the decade, most enterprises with EDP capabilities will have a DBMS and will be using it in more than half the potential areas of its application.

The third important aspect of the future environment is the continued and more widespread use of database technology. This third aspect, in fact, completes the envisioned scenario of the future: Easy-to-use, database-supported, distributed information systems.

The following are three specific requirements for DD/DSs in the future environment:

A tool for data resource management.
Support for the DA/DBA.
A tool for audit and control.

The following paragraphs discuss these issues in greater detail, followed by an examination of specific DD/DS features necessary to support these future requirements.

12.1.2 A Tool for Data Resource Management

The future environment will be characterized by the increasingly accepted trend towards programs designed to support the management of the enterprise's data as an important resource. An increasing number of enterprises will want to use the DD/DS as the tool for managing the inventory of data resources, and for disseminating information about the enterprise's data resources, on an organization-wide basis. The DD/DS may be required to provide metadata to persons working at different levels in the organization, in geographically dispersed locations, and on an ad hoc basis. The need to support a data resource inventory on a company-wide basis may arise out of the recognition of advantages involved in integrating data across functional lines. Or it may become evident as a result of top-down planning efforts. Regardless of the reason(s), pervasive data inventorying will be a commonplace activity in the 1980s and the DD/DS will be needed to support these efforts.

An interesting byproduct of this trend is the fact that this type of need will require a DD/DS regardless of whether a DBMS is installed or not. DBMSs can be used to support data resource management by fostering integration and sharing of data among diverse users. However, it is also true that effective efforts to implement data resource management can be launched and can thrive without the support of a DBMS. The necessary tool for the management of data as a resource is the DD/DS. As the future brings wider acceptance for the concept of data as a resource, the DD/DS will play a more important role in the enterprise.

12.1.3 Support for the DA/DBA Function

Chapter 9 discussed at length the role of the DD/DS in the support of the functions of data administration and database administration. These functions, collectively referred to as DA/DBA functions, have emerged in the 1970s as indispensable for realizing the goals and objectives of the database environment. Closely related to the concept of data resource management, the DA/DBA function of the future environment will continue to rely heavily upon the DD/DS for support.

The DA/DBA function of the future will rely on the active DD/DS to be an integral part of the daily routine of development and operation of systems. Capitalizing on the DD/DS's wide scope of activity (i.e., number of components) and high degree of activity (i.e., the degree of control exerted at binding time), the DA/DBA will use the DD/DS to effectively manage the development and control operations in the future environment.

A key requirement for the future use of DD/DSs is the capability to reflect changes in the database environment on a dynamic basis. Currently, the DA/DBA relies on statistics and other information collected and presented on an independent basis. This, in turn, must be correlated to metadata in the DD/DS and used to analyze performance of operational systems. In the future, the DA/DBA will require that performance data be reflected dynamically in the metadatabase in order to facilitate more timely correlation and analysis of available data.

12.1.4 A Tool for Audit and Control

Recent developments have highlighted the use of a DD/DS as a tool for implementing audit and control techniques. Chapter 11 was devoted to an in-depth discussion of this development. The trend towards making the DD/DS work for the internal and external auditor will continue in the 1980s.

External, as well as internal, auditors will find the DD/DS of the future invaluable as a source of accurate and reliable information about the database (and non-database) environment. A number of specific audit techniques will be based upon using the DD/DS as an audit and control tool. The internal auditor will also find the DD/DS to be useful in supporting the auditor's involvement in various phases of the SDLC, enabling easier review of work at specific milestones.

12.2 DD/DS FEATURES AND CAPABILITIES TO SUPPORT FUTURE REQUIREMENTS

Having examined several scenarios of the 1980s and the user requirements for the DD/DS in that time frame, it is now appropriate to turn

DD/DS FEATURES AND CAPABILITIES TO SUPPORT FUTURE REQUIREMENTS   267

our attention to the specific features and capabilities which will be necessary in future DD/DSs to support these requirements.

Figure 12.2 illustrates a matrix of Future DD/DS Requirements versus desired features and capabilities. The following paragraphs discuss these topics.

12.2.1   Support for SDLC and Project Control Activities

DD/DSs are just beginning to include features designed to support systems development life cycle and project control activities. Special meta-entity types and attributes are needed and specific methodologies for systems and database design must have documentation and analysis aids.

Meta-entities which the DD/DS must include for the future include those which can be used to describe the process of conceptual design. The new entities must describe business functions, data clusters, transactions, and relationships among the new entities and the existing meta-entities. The capability must exist for these high-level design entities to be linked to the detail design level entities so that the SDLC stage of design can be accurately reflected in terms of metadata. For example, it should be possible to map the metadata describing business functions and data clusters, respectively, to system processes and records (see Figure 12.3). Data elements would be the common denominators across levels of design.

With a full complement of data and systems meta-entities, through all levels of design, the DD/DS of the future will have the capability to support database design techniques, structured methods, and other design approaches in the future. Additional entities will be required also to describe adequately the online, telecommunications, and distributed processing aspects of modern-day information systems. Besides the new meta-entity, node, described in chapter 10, there are a host of other new entities and attributes which will be needed to describe the networks, lines, terminals, and other communication characteristics in the distributed environment.

The DD/DS of the future will require new attributes to describe these new entities. It will also require some new attributes for existing entities. For example, the new DD/DS will require special attributes to support the financial aspects of project control. These attributes must reflect actual versus budgeted resources for specific activities related to design functions associated with meta-entities of the environment. Thus, the number of hours budgeted to code a program would be recorded, followed by the actual time spent. With additional entities and attributes, manpower resources could also be controlled in one comprehensive system.

Parallel to the addition of entity types and attribute types to support

User Requirements	Features and Capabilities of Future DD/DSs			
	Facilities to Support SDLC and Project Control	Comprehensive Metadata Generation	Dynamic Collection and Reflection of Metadata	User-Friendly Interfaces
Support for data resource management	More system entities Conceptual design entities	Metadata for system planning tools	Not applicable	Systems planning interfaces
Tool for DA/DBA of the future	Communications and online entities Support for project control DB design support Structured methods support	Complete DBMS metadata Metadata for TP, RPG, query processor, and program generators Metadata for automated systems development Execution time binding	Support performance measurement Support restructuring and reorganization Collect metadata statistics Accesses Response times Device usage	Comprehensive DDL Interactive support – menus, help commands, screens
Tool for audit and control	Documentation for SDLC Documentation for project control	Metadata for generalized audit software	Reliable operational metadata	Query and RPG support

Figure 12.2 DD/DS features and capabilities satisfying user requirements.

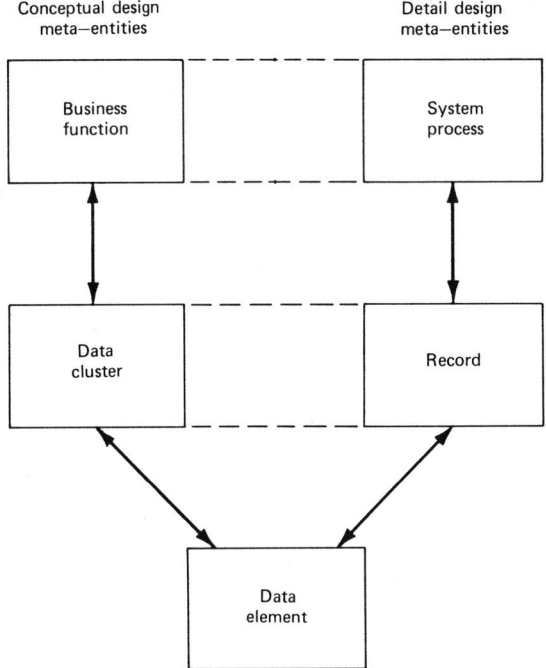

Figure 12.3 Meta-entities at different levels of design.

SDLC functions, the DD/DSs of the future will also enhance the analytical capabilities required to aid in the control of metadata throughout the SDLC of a system, not just during the design stage. It is also expected that the hitherto good documentation that the current DD/DSs provide, will improve in comprehensiveness and flexibility in future generations of the DD/DS. This development will benefit DA/DBAs, software developers and end-users. It will also benefit the auditors, who will be able to use the comprehensive documentation for reviewing and understanding systems being audited.

12.2.2 More Comprehensive Metadata Generation

The active DD/DSs of the 1980s will be delivered using metadata generation facilities. This will include better support in terms of scope and degree of activity of the DD/DS, such as more metadata generation for DBMSs, transaction processors, and other components.

The trend toward providing more comprehensive metadata generation facilities for DBMSs is becoming apparent in the 1980s. Both indepedent and dependent data dictionary/directory system vendors will endeavor to enhance their packages to include such things as SYSGEN support and the ability to generate metadata for database restructuring and reorganization exercises. For vendors with integrated and coordinated product lines, the DD/DS will provide metadata for the majority of the processing components in the environment. Thus, the scope of activity can be expected to increase significantly in the 1980s. Eventually, the DD/DS will be capable of generating metadata on a regular basis for:

Developing online screens.
Managing terminals and lines for data communications.
Edit and validation routines.
Application program generators.

The continuing trend towards automatic program generation will be buttressed by the ability of the DD/DS to support this process with metadata. Whereas in the past, products such as the IBM Automated Design Facility (ADF) for IMS required their own metadata files with the requisite input and maintenance functions, it is our opinion that in the future the IBM DB/DC Data Dictionary will provide the necessary metadata for ADF. Thus, use of this application program generator will become more reliable and coordinated with the overall development effort.

Metadata generation will also be an important factor in insuring that automated systems design and analysis tools gain widespread acceptance. Tools for database design will be closely linked with DD/DSs. This has already happened with IBM's Data Base Design Aid and DB Prototype. The same is true with DATAMANAGER and a newer product called DATA DESIGNER.

More sophisticated design tools will be forthcoming. These may include simulators designed to use metadata from the DD/DS, and dynamic restructuring of the database to "test" changes based upon metadata in the DD/DS.

Further developments may involve the more widespread use of the DD/DS to support test data generation procedures, and to control the test environment in general. Here the DD/DS would control all the metadata for the test system and drive it just as it would the production system. The DD/DS would be used to segregate activities, transactions, and data between test and production environments.

In addition, the extended use of the metadatabase during program execution will yield a higher degree of activity of the DD/DS. This in turn will produce greater control over the executing process. It should

DD/DS FEATURES AND CAPABILITIES TO SUPPORT FUTURE REQUIREMENTS   271

be noted that vendors with integrated product lines and those opting for the subsumed architecture of the DD/DS are most likely to achieve execution-time binding, first for the DBMS, and eventually for all types of programs.

Finally, the DD/DS of the future will be capable of generating metadata for generalized audit software packages used in substantive testing and other phases of the audit.

12.2.3 Dynamic Collection and Reflection of Metadata

Dynamic collection and reflection of metadata is based upon the premise that data regarding the performance and operation of the system is actually metadata that should be organized and managed in much the same manner as all other metadata. The fact is that when performance and operational metadata are used to make decisions, they are used in conjunction with other metadata describing the designed and implemented environment. Thus, by collecting these metadata and maintaining a single metadatabase, the decision-making process that supports performance tuning, reorganization, and restructuring is greatly facilitated.

Furthermore, if and when DD/DS packages achieve the goal of dynamically capturing the performance and operational metadata during or just after execution, the metadatabase can reflect these changes on an immediate basis. This availability can be exploited by utilizing the information to decide heuristically on alternative reorganization and/or restructuring strategies and then issuing the appropriate commands through established DDL commands. This process has been referred to by some researchers as *self-reorganizing DBMS,* or *automatic restructuring.* This capability is closely related to the aforementioned execution-time binding. The ability to achieve this feature will probably come first to those vendors with integrated product lines, or those who have chosen the subsumed architecture for DD/DSs.

The specific types of metadata most likely to be involved in dynamic collection are shown in Figure 12.4. The entity types of static metadata to which they are related are also included.

12.2.4 User-Friendly Interfaces

In response to the requirement for easy-to-use information systems, DD/DSs will emerge in the 1980s with user-friendly interfaces. Specifically, these will include a comprehensive and unified data definition language (DDL), not fragmented by the individual styles and idiosyncrasies of particular DBMSs and/or programming languages. The DDL of the future will be a declarative language which comes "naturally" in

	Meta-Entity Types				
Performance/Operational Metadata	Data Element	Record	Transaction	Physical Device	User
Accesses by key	X	X	X		
Accesses by user	X	X	X		X
Response time			X		X
Access path used	X	X	X	X	X
DB saturation growth		X		X	

Figure 12.4 Performance/operational metadata.

the course of describing the database and/or data processing environment. Most importantly, the user will only have to use one language.

It is more than likely that in the future the report generation and query processors used for the metadatabase will continue to become more friendly to the user. In this case, it can be expected that metadata users will benefit from advances made on behalf of users in general. Interactive support, prompting, and help mechanisms will appear in general, and in the DD/DS as well.

Similarly, the auditor, when finding it necessary to access the metadatabase, will also have an easier job due to the user-friendly features of the interface.

12.3 DD/DS TECHNOLOGY TRENDS

The years to come promise to be exciting with regard to the features and capabilities of the DD/DS which can be expected in the marketplace. The technology is basically in place to facilitate the realization of these trends. Nevertheless, in some areas there are trends which are yet unclear or divergent. These technological trends are all related to implementation issues discussed in Chapter 7. The issues involve:

Architectural placement of the DD/DS in the database environment.
Reliance on the DBMS for support.
External technological trends.

The following paragraphs address these issues, each in turn.

12.3.1 Architectural Placement of the DD/DS

The relative placement of the DD/DS in a database environment was discussed at length in Chapter 7, and to some extent in Chapter 10.

From the perspective of future development, it appears that at least one issue has been well established. It is now widely accepted that the DD/DS is in fact an important independent component of the data processing environment. This acceptance has manifested itself in the commercial marketplace by the existence of more than fifteen commercial DD/DSs. Furthermore, acceptance of the DD/DS as an independent component of the data processing environment will become an established fact because:

The independent DD/DS is necessary to support distributed database management with dissimilar implementations on the nodes of the network.

The independent DD/DS is necessary to support the non-DBMS user.

Nevertheless, it should be clearly noted that the subsumed architecture for DD/DSs, where the system (DBMS, or other) performs all DD/DS functions and there is no visible (to the user) DD/DS component in the environment, is also gaining popularity with the small - to medium-scale systems. There are two reasons why this trend will also continue:

The subsumed approach for the small-to-medium system yields a clean, compact look. The DD/DS is treated just like any other DBMS application.

The subsumed architecture provides better opportunities for execution-time binding and dynamic capture of performance and operational metadata.

12.3.2 Reliance on DBMS for Support

As discussed in Chapter 7, there are very practical reasons why commercial DD/DS vendors (and in-house implementors) have often chosen the path of using the DBMS to support their DD/DS packages. The DBMS is used in this case to support an architecturally separate component. Thus, although we have a dependent DD/DS (on some DBMSs), the DD/DS is considered to be separate from the DBMS in the database environment.

The basic reasons for the dependent approach are as follows:

It is necessary if the metadata is to be shared on a parallel basis.

It is conducive to building an integrated product line.

It is the easiest, cheapest, and fastest way to implement the metadatabase.

These practical reasons will cause vendors and other implementors alike to continue to enhance and support dependent DD/DSs. Thus, vendor pressures will continue to create the momentum for the dependent DD/DS.

12.3.3 External Technological Trends

When the DD/DS resides within a database environment, it is naturally affected by the technological trends that surround it. There are two general areas which will impact the technological development of the DD/DS in the 1980s. These are:

DBMS-related developments, including database computers, distributed databases, and associative memories.
Language development, focusing on efforts for standardization.

These issues are discussed in the following paragraphs.

12.3.3.1 DBMS-Related Developments

The DBMS is closely related to the DD/DS, so it is not surprising that changes in DBMS technology affect the DD/DS. Specifically, the DD/DS of the future will be impacted by the following developments.

1. *Database Computer.* The development and acceptance of the *database computer* (also referred to as the *back-end computer*) impacts the DD/DS in terms of where the metadatabase should reside. It seems clear that the metadatabase will be partitioned with some portions in the host and others in the back-end. Conceptually, one might expect that dictionary metadata will be in the host and directory metadata in the back-end.
2. *Distributed Database Management.* Requirements for supporting databases in a distributed processing environment will lead to the development of a Network DataBase Management System (NDBMS). The relationship between the NDBMS and the DD/DS function of locating data across nodes of the network must be sorted out in the evolutionary development of this state-of-the-art technology.
3. *Associative Memories.* A major technological breakthrough in storage technology is the introduction of associative memories. The ability to retrieve data using only the values of keys and other data elements holds enormous potential if it can be done at random access speeds. The time is very near when this technology will be in widespread use.

From the perspective of the DD/DS and its small but extremely complex metadatabase, associative memories hold the potential for storing this metadatabase on a device which can offer almost unlimited capability in manipulating the complexity of inter-entity-attribute relationships. The late 1980s may bring some exciting new DD/DS capabilities using this new technology.

12.3.3.2 Language Development

The future development of DD/DSs will include the establishment of a comprehensive declarative language for the specification of data and systems. While these efforts have been underway for many years, they are just beginning to bear fruit and to gain wider acceptance. Perhaps by 1990, the industry will have a truly comprehensive declarative specification language. This language should in turn be the user's interface to the DD/DS.

Current activities in the standardization arena may have impact on the development of languages for the DD/DS. Specifically, two standards development efforts, both of which were organized in 1979 and gained momentum in 1980, are addressing the issues of a data definition language for the DD/DS as part of their overall task. The standards organizations and their development projects are:

1. *American National Standards Institute* (ANSI), which approved a project to develop a standard for an Information Resource Dictionary System. A formal technical committee, X3H4, was established to do the development. The standard which X3H4 will produce in 1984 will include the specification for an IRDS intrinsic language. The ANSI standard is national in scope and requires only voluntary compliance.

2. *National Bureau of Standards* (NBS), which established a formal project to develop a standard for a Federal Information Processing Standard Data Dictionary System. This standard will also include specifications for a DDS definition language. This standard is for Federal agencies and will require mandatory compliance, in connection with Federal procurements.

Obviously, these two efforts to formulate dictionary standards are similar. Close coordination between the two efforts exists. Constant exchange of information between the two projects ensures that the two resulting standards are not divergent.

Another factor that might influence the future development of DD/DS languages is the standardization activity in the area of DBMS data definition language. Currently, ANSI has an ongoing project in one of its technical committees, the Data Definition Language Committee (X3H2), which was chartered to use as a basis the language specifications developed by another committee, the Conference on Data Systems and Languages (CODASYL), and prepare a draft proposed American National Standard (dpANS). The relationship between

ANSI/X3H2 and CODASYL-DDLC is very complex, and there is little purpose in sorting out the political and organizational nuances of the intercommittee relationships. The various committee chairpersons know of each other's endeavors, and communication lines are open.

From a future development perspective, it is important to note that establishment of a standard DDL for DD/DSs would have a tremendous impact on the market. The impact may be so great that despite all the good reasons for a standard, only voluntary compliance can be expected.

12.4 DD/DS TRENDS IN THE COMMERCIAL MARKET

The commercial market for DD/DSs originated in the early 1970s with introduction of two independent DD/DSs. LEXICON (Arthur Andersen & Co.) and Data Catalogue (Synergetics Corp.) were the first commercial DD/DSs, as they are known today. LEXICON was developed by Arthur Andersen & Co., one of the "big eight" accounting firms, to support its practice, and evolved into a commercial venture; Data Catalogue was designed and marketed as a DD/DS package.

Since those early years, there have been many changes in the commercial DD/DS marketplace. Noticeably, Arthur Andersen no longer markets LEXICON, and there are now over fifteen widely used commercial DD/DSs. Figure 12.5 contains a list of these vendors according to the taxonomy for DD/DSs established in Chapters 7 and 8. This same taxonomy is used as the framework for the discussion of trends which follows.

12.4.1 DBMS-Dependent DD/DSs

IBM's DB/DC Data Dictionary is probably the most widely used hardware vendor-supplied DD/DS package. Called IMS Dictionary in earlier years, DB/DC, as it is affectionately called today, has achieved parity in IBM's line of DB/DC software. In the years to come, users can expect a strong commitment to enhancement and further development of this package as a tool for the DBA.

Other hardware vendors have begun to note this market penetration, and are developing systems of their own. Of particular note is Texas Instrument's DD-990, which released its product announcement in the fall of 1981. Farthest along in development is probably Burroughs Corp., where DMSII will be used to support a dependent DD/DS. UNIVAC, which had previously relied on independent vendors (Synergetics and Haverly Systems, Inc.) to supply the DD/DSs for its users,

DD/DS TRENDS IN THE COMMERCIAL MARKET

DBMS-dependent DD/DSs

   Hardware vendors

      International Business Machines (IBM) – DB/DC Data Dictionary
      Burroughs – under development
      Honeywell – under development
      Sperry UNIVAC – DDS-1100 (Level 1R1)
      International Computers Limited – ICL Data Dictionary System

   DBMS Vendors

      Cullinane – Integrated Data Dictionary
      INTEL – Integrated Data Dictionary
      CINCOM – Data Control System
                 TIS
      Software ag – ADABAS Dictionary
      Applied Data Research – DATACOM DATADICTIONARY
      INFODATA – EDICT
      Computer Corporation of America – The Model 204 Data Dictionary

   Independent Vendors

      University Computing Company (UCC) – UCC-10 Data Dictionary/Manager
      Haverly Systems – Data Control System (1100)

DBMS-independent DD/DSs

   Hardware Vendors

      Control Data Corporation (CDC) – under development
      Digital Equipment Corporation – under development
      Texas Instruments – DD-990 (first release announced)

   Independent Vendors

      Arthur Andersen – LEXICON (withdrawn from market)
      Haverly Systems – Self Generating Dictionary (SGD)
      M. Bryce & Associates – PRIDE/Logik
      MSP, Inc. – DATAMANAGER
      TSI – DATA CATALOGUE 2

Figure 12.5 Vendor offerings of DD/DS packages.

is now also involved in the development of data dictionary systems. UNIVAC has released a first version of its dependent data dictionary, DDS-1100, which works with UNIVAC's DBMS, DMS-1100.

The DBMS software vendors also hold a strong position in the DD/DS commercial market. In the late 1970s, virtually every DBMS vendor added a DD/DS to its product line. Many of the vendors (e.g., Cullinane, CINCOM, ADR, INTEL, Software ag, and others) have introduced integrated product lines driven by their DD/DS.

DBMS vendors (independent or otherwise) will continue to enhance and support architecturally separate DD/DS packages which are dependent on their respective DBMSs.

12.4.2 DBMS-Independent Vendors

For much of the 1970s, there were three major competitors in the market for commercial DD/DSs which were independent of any DBMS, but could still provide interfaces (generate metadata) for major DBMS packages. These vendors were Arthur Andersen & Co., Synergetics, and MSP, Inc. In 1980 Arthur Andersen & Co. bowed out of the market. Independent vendors will remain strong in the market due to existing market share penetration, wider range of metadata generation, (ability to generate across DBMS vendor lines) and the ability to support non-DBMS users.

Two of the original three independent vendors continue to be very active in this market, because both these packages have strong user bases. DATA CATALOGUE 2 claims in excess of 250 users, while DATAMANAGER claims in excess of 500 users. This established clientele, and the demand for mulit-DBMS support, as well as non-DBMS support, will insure the viability of the market for independent DD/DSs.

MSP's DATAMANAGER is noted for its wide-range metadata generation capabilities for DBMSs. It can support five of the major DBMS packages. In recent years, the vendor has made a concerted effort to support new and innovative uses of DATAMANAGER, such as using it in support of database design and as an audit tool.

TSI's DATA CATALOGUE 2(DC2) is based upon Synergetics' original product, named DATA CATALOGUE. The new DC2 was almost a complete rewrite of the original package. Enhancements to DC2 have been added at regular intervals since the rewrite. This is expected to continue in the 1980s. DATA CATALOGUE 2 is noted for its implementation on more diverse hardware configurations (than just IBM's hardware), and its richness and robustness of meta-entities which serve to support a wide range of system definitions and control problems. For example, DC2 users utilize their DD/DS to support forms control functions, and others use DC2 to do structured analysis.

Another DBMS-independent vendor is the developer of PRIDE/Logik. M. Bryce and Associates recently renamed the product. Information Resource Management System (IRMS). Logik was originally designed to support the system development/management methodology, PRIDE. Recently, M. Bryce and Associates have enhanced the product. This product, Information Resource Management System, has its strength in its software engineering principles, and provides strong support for control of system development life cycle activities.

---

*Note: TSI bought the Synergetics Operation in early 1982.

12.4.3 Small Computer System Vendors

As noted earlier, some of the vendors of computer system products in the small- to medium-range will continue to use the subsumed approach. These include IBM's System 38 and Tandem's offering.

12.5 SUMMARY

The future of DD/DSs in the 1980s can be expected to be a logical evolutionary progression of the developmental years of the 1970s. Users and developers of DD/DSs should recognize that the DD/DS is still evolving and will change in the years to come. Nevertheless, there is a well established and stable market of vendors and users, which will tend to temper the forces of change.

The following characteristics of DD/DSs hold true for the 1970s as developmental years, and the 1980s as evolutionary years.

> DD/DSs are necessary for disciplined and controlled development of database environments.
>
> Future trends indicate that the DD/DS will be a permanent component of system architectures.
>
> DD/DS vendors have been, and will continue to be, generally responsive to user needs.

APPENDIX

Hypothetical Case Study

BACKGROUND AND ORIENTATION
LAST NATIONAL BANK

The Last National Bank (LNB) of New York is a medium-to-large ($900 million in assets) commercial bank in one of the counties of upstate New York. Due to changes in New York's banking laws during the 1970s, the mammoth New York City banks were allowed to expand into LNB's market area, which several have done. Up to that time, LNB was a complacent institution, with unaggressive marketing, poor services, a small professional staff, and the minimum automation required to maintain, rather than expand, their customer base. In the face of extensive competition, and after fending off acquisition by one of the largest banks, LNB embarked on a multifaceted expansion plan. These plans included:

1. Ten small ($10–120 million in assets) banks in nearby counties were acquired, mostly for stock. This expansion was quite rapid, in part because of Federal Reserve pressure. As a result, the new banks, now branches of LNB, have been poorly assimilated, at best.
2. Three of the ten acquired banks had branches of their own, and four had some computerization. Only one of the four had hardware compatible with LNB's IBM 370 configuration.
3. Major additions and upgrades of professional staff occurred at all levels. In particular, the Operations Division has seen explosive growth. The EDP department expanded to the Information Services Group, under a Vice President, reporting to the Operations Division head.
4. LNB's senior management engaged management consultants to perform long-range strategic and tactical planning. One of their findings was that LNB had to anticipate customer information needs, rather than reacting to advances by their competitors. They could no

Source: This material is extracted from a comprehensive case study used by The Plagman Group.

longer afford to copy the major New York City banks, now that these were in their own area. Accordingly, an EDP Steering Committee was appointed at the senior management level, to assess and direct data processing needs. They have instituted a significant upgrade of hardware and software, and are committed to making LNB a leader in banking systems in their market area (see Figure A.1)

5. LNB's efforts to date have been rewarded. Starting with 100,000 accounts and $550 million in assets in 1974, they now have 200,000 customers with nearly half a million accounts, and $900 million in assets.

Year	Hardware	Software	Organization
1960			First automation, using a service bureau for DDA posting
1962	IBM 1401 Magnetic Ink Character Recognition (MICR) check reader	DDA application purchased from the same vendor who supplied the service bureau.	40,000 accounts EDP Supervisor and two programmer/operators, reporting to the Cashier
1966	2 IBM 1401s	DDA and commercial loan and DDA processing offered to other client banks.	50,000 accounts. Added 2 data-entry clerks, two computer operators, one programmer. EDP staff now numbers 8.
1968	IBM 360/40 and one IBM 1401. Burroughs 3500 rejected because of MICR reader incompatibilities.	DDA under 1401 emulation. Savings is first native 360 application. Commercial loan on 1401.	60,000 accounts. EDP staff is 12.
1970	Two IBM 360/40s, One IBM 1401, IBM 1419 MICR reader. 16 IBM 2314 disk drives	DDA converted to ANSI COBOL from Autocoder. Two-year effort, with several missteps requiring restarting project. For this reason, commercial loan is continued on 1401. Operating system is DOS	EDP Manager made Assistant Cashier; EDP department formed reporting to VP, Accounting. Total EDP staff now 18. Significant promotions and salary increases for EDP staff.

Figure A.1 Last National Bank development of data processing.

Year	Hardware	Software	Organization
1972	IBM 360/50 and IBM 360/40	DDA converted to ISAM organization, permitting online teller inquiry by Audio Response. Retail Loan on 360. Commercial Loan under 1401 emulation. Operating System is DOS with Power	Significant turnover in EDP causes slowing of expansion in the function. Three department heads in two years, the latest is AVP, EDP department
1974	IBM 360/50, IBM 360/40 Burroughs 3500 and MICR reader, IBM 1440	With acquisitions there is a wide range of incompatible software. Assimilation efforts fail, local systems continue in operation	First acquisitions. Now 100,000 accounts. Combined EDP staff is 30.
1977	IBM 370/145, IBM 360/50 retained, as is Burroughs 3500. DASD in main center is 32 IBM 2319's.	8 banks now acquired; none of the new banks have computers. These banks are rapidly assimilated into LNB's existing application systems. Operating system converted to OS/MFT.	300,000 accounts. Consultant report on the long-range plan (see summary below).
1979	2 370/158s, 32 3330 disks, and 10 3350's, 3890 MICR reader	DD/DS installed, DBMS undergoing conversion. DDA is pilot application for DB environment	IS Group numbers 45. 475,000 accounts. Data Administration split off from Technical Support.
1980	2 IBM 370/158's, 1 IBM 3032. IBM 2305 DRUM added for paging	Retail DDA is running under DBMS, conversion of Corporate DDA underway. Plans to convert other applications being studied. MVS running on the 3032.	Growth slowed. 500,000 accounts. Total IS staff is 50, largely due to high turnover, mostly in Technical Support

Figure A.1 (*Continued*)

LNB offers a complete spectrum of commercial banking services. The heart of their operation is retail banking, though they have a significant number of major corporate customers. Their major product lines are:

Retail	Corporate
DDA (checking)	DDA (checking)
Savings	Trust
Retail loans	Funds transfer
Mortgages	Commercial loans
Credit card	

These applications are supported operationally in a variety of ways. Retail DDA is fully automated, with a DBMS-supported system, and CPCS to clear checks, but corporate DDA is only semi-automated: computer-sorted checks are posted to corporate accounts by hand on a posting machine. Increasing corporate volume is making this untenable. Savings and retail loans are computerized, but mortgage and trust operations are totally manual applications. Funds transfers are accomplished by terminals attached to the Bankwire network, and credit card transactions are done on a specialized credit card service bureau in another state. Commercial loans are essentially a 1401 application run under emulation on the S/370.

Senior management at LNB is considering a number of new services. They were forced in 1978 by new state laws to offer interest on checking accounts. They accomplished this by a "bridge" between retail DDA and savings, which applied interest as a DDA adjustment once a month on average daily balances. With other customer adjustments and backvalues, interest is frequently in error, subjecting LNB to both customer and regulatory pressure. LNB is currently working on a separate interest-bearing checking (IBC) application system. Also under consideration is a 24-hour teller plan, providing customers with the ability to obtain money 24 hours a day from special machines at each LNB branch. Three options of this plan are under study: use Master Charge and have the cash advance bill to Master Charge; use Master Charge but have cash advances deducted from the customer's DDA; use a specially prepared bank card and have cash advances deducted from the customer's DDA. At present, additional electronic funds transfer (EFT) options are under consideration, but only for planning purposes; LNB is committed to a slow, orderly assimilation of new banking practices.

For preferred customers, a trust department and brokerage department provide specialized financial services. LNB arranges credit for Master Charge, but only forwards these credit card applications to the large regional processing center for approval and processing.

Funds transfer activities are accomplished by an online interface to the Bankwire II network. Bankwire II is a private telecommunications system for third-party transfers. At this time, LNB utilizes Bankwire via a telex machine, with data on a punched-paper tape. Debits and credits to LNB accounts are processed manually with advice slips. One copy is sent to the customer, two others are retained. One of these is held in Funds Transfer, with the offset processed via Decoding and CPCS.

HARDWARE/SOFTWARE ENVIRONMENT FOR LAST NATIONAL BANK

Progressive hardware upgrades have characterized Last National Bank for the past 20 years. Starting with a single 1401 in the early 1960s, the current hardware configuration includes three IBM mainframes. Specifically, the current hardware at this bank includes:

IBM 3032, 8 meg.
2 IBM 370/158-3s, 4 meg each.
IBM 3330 and 3350 disk drivers.
IBM 2305 drum.
IBM 3420 tape drives.
IBM 327x terminals.
IBM 3660 banking terminals.
IBM 3890 MICR reader/sorter.

A 3031 is on order, to be used as a testing machine, and for additional backup. When this is installed, all LNB's computers will be loosely coupled. For now, there is limited shared DASD, but no shared spooling.

VS1 is running on the two 370/158s, though one of these is scheduled for replacement by a 4331, which will be used only for testing. LNB expects to loosely couple the 3031, 370/158, and the 3032 in the next few years. Currently, MVS is running on the 3032, with plans for that operating system to be the standard at LNB in several years.

DBMS and DD/DS

The DD/DS has been installed since 1978 though its use was primarily for documentation until the DDA conversion. The DDA conversion is proceeding in four stages.

1. Conversion of retail DDA accounts to database, featuring online non-dollar inquiry and updates of existing accounts.

2. Conversion of retail DDA transaction processing, including all accounting functions.
3. Creation of a logical view of the database for Marketing which will allow products and services to be analyzed separately for profitability and marketability.
4. Conversion of corporate DDA to the centralized database system.

The first three stages are currently completed, and conversion of the corporate DDA accounts is under way.

THE DATA ADMINISTRATION CENTER

With the installation of a DBMS decided on in 1977, LNB hired an individual with prior database experience. Because the bank's senior management recognized the need for database skills, they relocated a database programmer from a New York City bank, paying him the highest salary ever given a new employee at LNB. He was assigned to the Technical Support Center, and he rapidly acquired a staff of eight, through new hires and internal transfers. His first salary adjustment, in mid-1978, put him in the position of earning considerably more than his manager, the AVP, Technical Support. For that reason, the Data Administration Center was created as of January 2, 1979, at which point retail DDA was already under conversion.

The Data Administration Center has six staff personnel, plus the AVP and his secretary. The area has responsibility for the development and control of the database environment, but installation and maintenance of all software, including the DBMS and the DD/DS, remain with the Technical Support Center. Functional descriptions of the AVP of Data Administration's responsibilities and the Center's three departments follow (see Figure A.2):

AVP, Data Administration reports to the VP, Information Services. Responsible for departmental management, the determination of LNB's data needs, interface with LNB Senior Management, and the maintenance of control over all LNB's database activities. These include:

1. Presentation of database-related proposals to the EDP Steering Committee.
2. Determination of the need for an execution of database reorganizations.
3. Development of training plan for LNB data processing personnel in database concepts and technology.
4. Consultation with users, analysts, programmers and operational personnel in the areas concerning database concepts and technology.

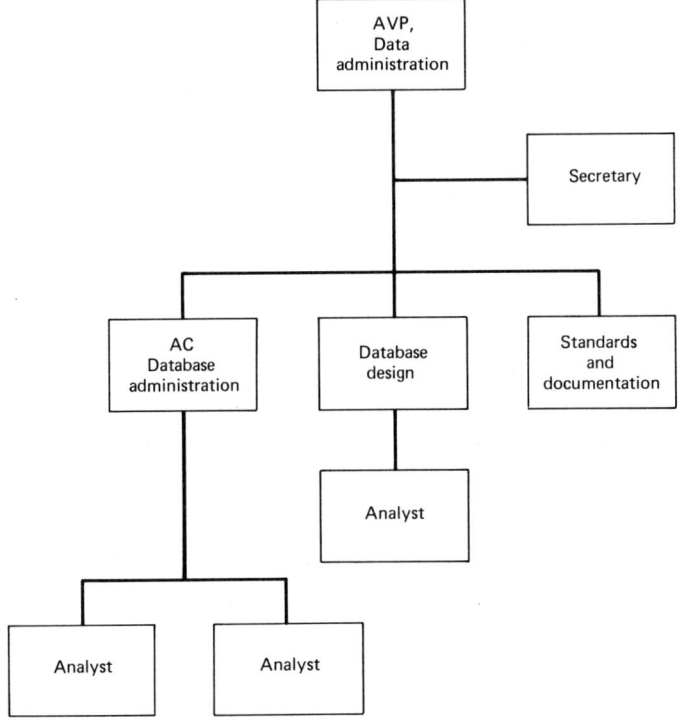

Figure A.2 Data administration center.

Assistant Cashier, Database Administration reports to the AVP Data Administration. Responsible for development and maintenance of database control procedures, interface with technical support, implementation of user's data needs, and quality assurance for new application systems. Two analysts report to the DBA.

1. Assistance to user departments in exploring the applicability of database technology for data needs, including integration with existing databases.
2. Development and testing of restart/recovery procedures.
3. Creation and maintenance of test databases and development of data validation and completeness criteria. Where appropriate, development of procedures to utilize vendor supplied utilities for the verification process.
4. Development and monitoring of backup procedures, including the authority to alter or override such procedures, as required.
5. DBMS and database performance measurement and subsequent tuning activities.

Database Designer reports to the AVP, Data Administration, Responsible for the design and documentation of all LNB's databases, interface with applications programming, and the maintenance of interface software with on-line software and the operating systems.

1. Interpretation of user requirements as expressed through system analysis into effective database design.
2. Generation of logical and physical database descriptions and program logical views.
3. Assistance to programming project teams in utilizing database and data dictionary technology.

Standards and Documentation reports to the AVP, Data Administration. Responsible for the development of database standards and guidelines, interface with data center operations, maintenance of the DD/DS, and the review function for new systems, to see that they conform to LNB standards.

1. Development and administration of procedures for data collection and documentation.
2. Development of procedures for utilization of the DD/DS as a data collection and documentation tool.
3. Development of procedures to insure the security and integrity of databases. This responsibility includes suggestion of security measure for the teleprocessing environment.
4. Maintenance and dissemination of the Data Base Standards Manual.

SYSTEMS DEVELOPMENT LIFE CYCLE (SDLC) AND RELATED PROCEDURES

Upon creation of the Information Services Group in 1976, the Vice President was charged with quality assurance and budgetary control over all new systems. Accordingly, he created the Systems Assurance Committee (SAC) made up of himself and his three (later four) AVPs. The EDP auditor has requested to be put on the committee, but thus far is invited to each SAC review as an observer. SAC must give formal approval of every new system at four checkpoints;

Feasibility (SAC 1).
Systems Requirements (SAC 2).
Detailed Specification (SAC 3).
Conversion (SAC 4).

Although, in theory, no project may progress until SAC approval is granted, SAC 1 is frequently waived, and SAC 2 and SAC 3 approval

SYSTEMS DEVELOPMENT LIFE CYCLE 289

is usually given after the fact. This is caused by senior management pressure for speedy development of systems, combined with time pressures on the AVPs, leaving them little time to read system documentation for review. SAC 4, however, is never waived nor are systems ever converted without approval. In particular, the DDA system conversion to database has proceeded with SAC approval only at conversion. Due to the perceived need to justify the investment in DBMS and DD/DS software, conversion costs, and additional personnel, the DDA conversion was given overwhelming priority, and nothing was allowed to slow its speedy implementation.

The following describes the SDLC of LNB. It is an overview of the procedures manual used to guide SDLC activities.

I. *FEASIBILITY*

No procedures currently exist for this phase of the SDLC. Currently, LNB programming projects are initiated by directives from the board of directors and senior vice presidents. However, a general consensus exists by corporate management of LNB that an EDP planning function must be implemented after the DBMS-supported DDA system is converted.

A. *Initial Investigation* All activities are initiated by requests for EDP assistance. Investigation covers possible EDP assistance and the determination of whether a current or proposed EDP system covers such a request.

Primary responsibility: Applications programming.
Secondary responsibility: None.

B. *Feasibility Study* If the request passes initial investigation, then a formal feasibility study begins. Such a study includes integration considerations with existing systems and databases, overall cost estimates, time estimates, and general development schedules.

Primary responsibility: Applications programming.
Secondary responsibility: Data administration and user.

II. *SYSTEMS REQUIREMENTS*

A. *Definition of Current Systems* Once SAC has accepted in principle the results of the feasibility study, definition of current EDP and manual systems in the area of the proposed project begin. All documentation, even of strictly manual systems, is to be placed on the DD/DS, the control of which is under data administration.

Primary responsibility: User, applications programming.
Secondary responsibility: None.

B. *Detail of User Requirements* Based on extensive interviews with appropriate user representatives, Applications Programming and the user liaison complete the definition of the user's requirements. Analysts have extensive pre-interview instructions and post-interview checklists to capture information regarding all aspects of the user's needs including data requirements, processing requirements, security, recovery and restart considerations. The DD/DS is used as the documentation tool for all data and process related information.

Primary responsibility: Applications programming, user.
Secondary responsibility: Data administration.

C. *Alternatives for Problem Solution* After the user requirements have been formulated and documented, various alternatives for an EDP supported system are fully detailed. Cost, time and resource requirements (both in development and implementation) are developed for each.

Primary responsibility: Applications programming.
Secondary responsiblity: Other I.S. centers, as needed.

III. *DETAILED SPECIFICATION*

Systems development on any major project proposal (referred to as "major" if time and resource estimates exceed six man/months) is predicated on formal approval and resource commitments by SAC, and further approved by the EDP Steering Committee.

A. *Logical Data Base Design* This step is a separate continuous process conducted by data administration to include conceptual database design as well as logical and physical database design. (Work on Application Design proceeds concurrently). Logical and physical designs are documented in the DD/DS and the generation capabilities of the DD/DS are used to create the DBMS control blocks from the metadata.

Primary responsibility: Data administration.
Secondary responsibility: Applications programming.

B. *Application Design* In this step, all transactions, programs, reports, and traditional files are designed and documented on the DD/DS. The user specifications are translated into programmatic terms, and HIPO diagrams are used to document system flow. Data requirements, in the form of data elements, are determined with the aid of database administration and the user.

Primary responsibility: Applications programming.
Secondary responsibility: Data administration, user.

SYSTEMS DEVELOPMENT LIFE CYCLE 291

C. *Programming and Testing* This step includes application coding as well as unit test procedures. All data division descriptions, except certain constants and accumulators, are defined in the preceding step and generated into the COBOL Copylib using the metadata generation capabilities of the DD/DS. Database administration's involvement with program coding of DBMS programs is sometimes desirable. Database administration is also responsible for creation and maintenance of test databases to be used by programmers in unit testing.

Primary responsibility: Applications programming.
Secondary responsibility: Data administration.

D. *Creation of User and Operational Procedures* Clerical procedures, Data Center Run Books, and detailed transaction instructions are included in this step. Special needs are also addressed, including implementation of procedures regarding security backup, recovery and restart. If the system is DBMS-supported, database administration is responsible for creation and testing of appropriate procedures. Internal audit's involvement is required in the testing and final approval of these procedures.

Primary responsibility: Applications programming, user.
Secondary responsibility: Data administration, auditing.

E. *User and Operational Training* This step includes training in the use of new computerized systems. Data administration's involvement is required for training of data center operations staff in use of DBMS utilities, restart of on-line software, and DBMS concepts.

Primary responsibility: Applications programming, user.
Secondary responsibility: Data administration, data center operations.

F. *Conversion Planning* This plan includes user conversion considerations, data conversion concerns, and database integration plans. Database administration may be required to develop data conversion and integration plans for DBMS supported systems. Internal audit's approval is required on all conversion plans.

Primary responsibility: User, auditing.
Secondary responsibility: Applications programming, data administration, data center operations.

G. *Systems Testing* This step consists of string and system tests of the new applications plus integrated testing of this component with existing systems. Database administration involvement is required with creation of test databases and test scenarios. Internal audit's and data administration's approval of test results is required.

Primary responsibility: Data center operations.
Secondary responsibility: Data administration, auditing.

IV. *IMPLEMENTATION*

Formal sign-offs are required of applications programming, DBA, and internal audit for the conversion plan and for systems testing, before a system is implemented.

A. *Conversion and Tuning* Actual conversion is based upon the conversion plan. Database administration and technical support constantly monitor database and online activity. As required, tuning efforts are employed to improve systems that do not perform at acceptable levels. Response times for online systems are compared to required service levels. Such tuning efforts might require changes to application code.

Primary responsibility: Data administration.
Secondary responsibility: Data center operations, applications programming.

B. *Review* Periodic formal review points, each month for the first six months and once again six months thereafter in the first year, are defined to review user problems, integration problems, tuning considerations, integrity and security problems. SAC, Internal audit and user representatives are present at each session.

Primary responsibility: All IS centers, user, auditing.
Secondary responsibility: None.

C. *Maintenance* All maintenance activities of application systems including corrections of errors and enhancements, are included here. Maintenance of all metadata descriptions is also required of the maintenance group. In the case of emergency fixes, next-day maintenance of metadata documentation is required. All program changes to production programs are controlled by data center operations personnel and copies of change logs are distributed daily to the AVP, Programming Systems, and the AVP, Data Administrator.

Primary responsibility: Applications programming, data center operations.
Secondary responsibility: Data administration.

THE CASE STUDY APPLICATIONS:

- DEMAND DEPOSIT ACCOUNTING (DDA) SYSTEM
- OTHER APPLICATIONS
- DD/DS LISTINGS
- GENERATED META DATA

The Demand Deposit Accounting (DDA) System

Last National Bank is nearing completion of the conversion of DDA into an integrated, DBMS-supported application system. As indicated previously, this is a four-phase project, the first three of which are completed.

1. Conversion of retail DDA accounts to database, featuring online nondollar inquiry and updates of existing accounts (see Figure A.3).
2. Conversion of retail DDA transaction processing, including all accounting functions.

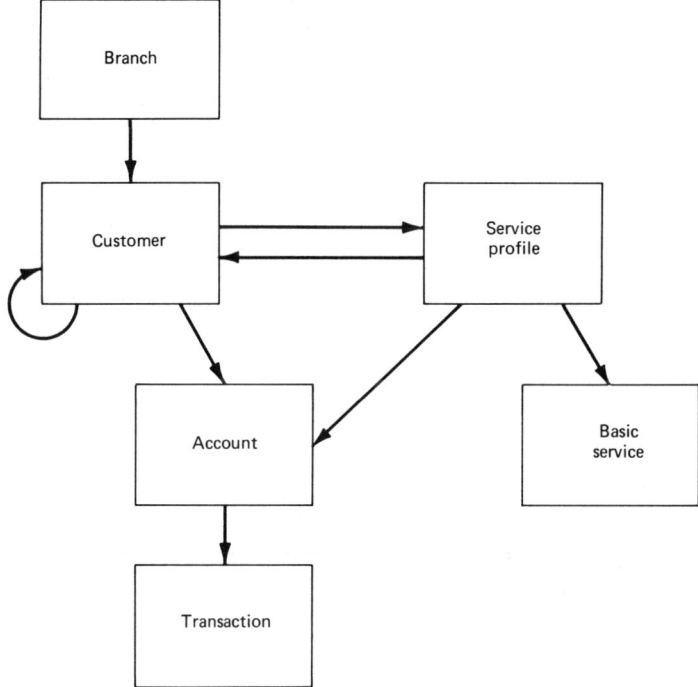

Figure A.3 Conceptual data structures.

3. Creation of a logical view of the database for marketing which will allow products and services to be analyzed separately for profitability and marketability (see Figures A.4 and A.5).
4. Conversion of corporate DDA to the centralized database system.

In the current, partially converted environment, financial updating of customer accounts follows two paths. Transactions come to LNB in three forms:

1. Checks (both retail and corporate).
2. Mail and cable (exclusively corporate).
3. Wire transfers over Bankwire II (primarily corporate, though some are retail).

Items other than checks are converted manually to check-equivalent MICR forms and are fed along with the checks into CPCS (Checks Processing Control System). The output of this is a temporary disk file (backed up on tape prior to posting) which is accumulated all day. At night, the disk file is split into retail and corporate, with retail updating done in batch with the DDA and marketing databases, while corporate transactions are listed out in order by branch and account, for manual posting between 4A.M. and 8A.M. Summary postings of balances, transaction totals, adjustments, and so forth, are made to the appropriate product type. (personal checking, small business accounts, line of credit accounts, IBS (interest-bearing checking accounts, etc.) When the corporate conversion is completed, it will be possible to post similar summary figures to a corporate master account.

Non-dollar status changes are received from customers by direct contact, mail, or cables. Such changes (name and address, credit line, statement date, etc.) are converted to a multi-purpose standard update form. Retail updates are then made online to the DDA database. Corporate updates were formerly made directly from customer advices, but for purposes of control, consistency and to ease conversion to the database system, corporate status changes are also put on the standard update form before changes are made to the ledger cards.

Teller and platform inquiries are made online to the DDA database for retail accounts. Opening day balances are given, although stops and holds can be placed online. For corporate accounts, an inquiry unit is available by telephone. They pull the appropriate ledger card and give balances over the phone. Intra-day balances for the largest, most active accounts are kept on T-accounts, and the most current balance is given to inquiries. It is suspected by those in the inquiry unit that some officers in some branches are allowing their best customers to call directly to the inquiry unit.

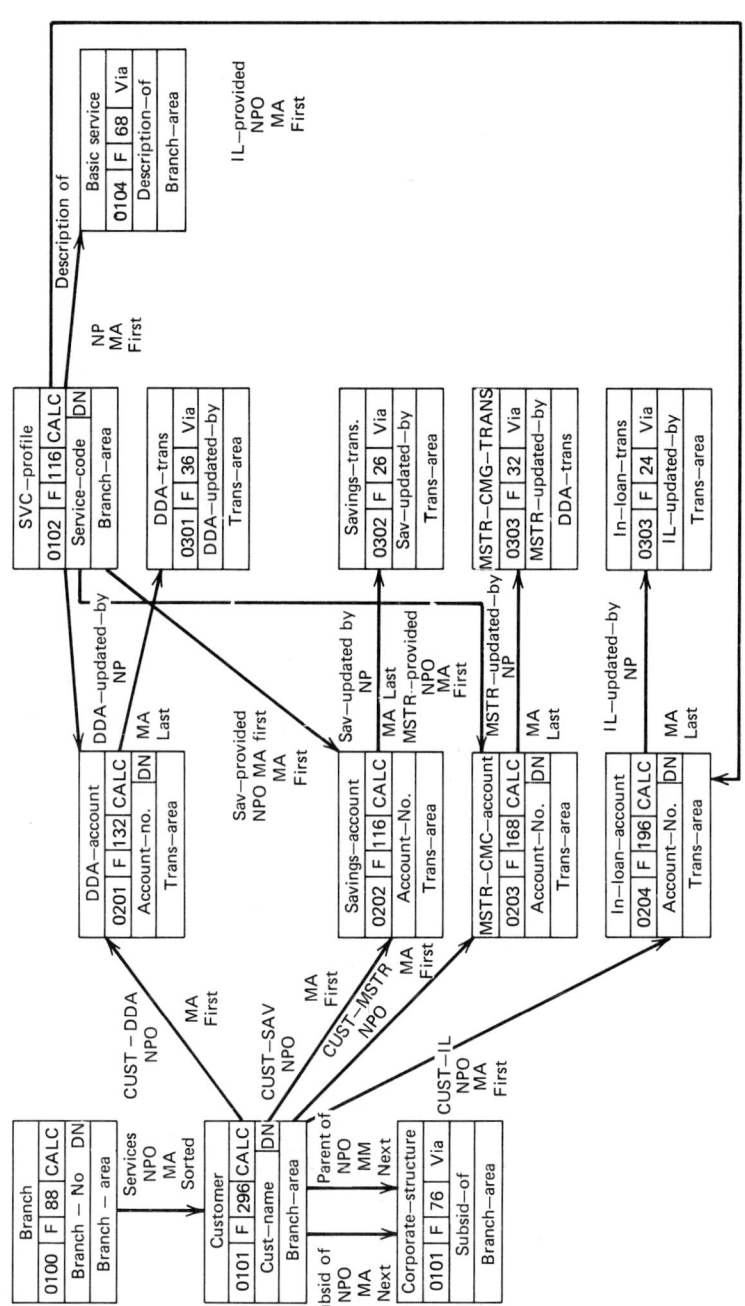

Figure A.4 Logical data structure diagram (IDMS)

```
REPORT NO. 59                    INTEGRATED DATA DICTIONARY REPORTER           12/15/80 PAGE   1
                                       RECORD REPORT - SUMMARY
*****************************************************************************************************
                                                                                    ---- D A T E ----
RECORD NAME          VER DESCRIPTION          LGTH RECORD STORAGE  OCCURRENCES   UPDATED    CREATED
*****************************************************************************************************
BASIC-SERVICE        0001                       60                                          12/13/80
BRANCH               0001                       72                                          12/13/80
CORP-STRUCTURE       0001                       52                                          12/13/80
CUSTOMER             0001                      228                                          12/13/80
DDA-ACCOUNT          0001                       92                                          12/13/80
DDA-TRANS            0001                       28                                          12/13/80
EMPL-HIST            0001                       16                                          08/08/80
EMPL-REL             0001                        4                                          08/08/80
EMPLOYEE             0001                      280                                          08/08/80
IN-LOAN-ACCOUNT      0001                      156                             12/15/80     12/13/80
IN-LOAN-TRANS        0001                       16                             12/15/80     12/13/80
INST-LOAN-ACCOUN     0001                      128                                          12/13/80
INST-LOAN-TRANS      0001                      128                                          12/13/80
MSTR-CHG-ACCOUNT     0001                      128                                          12/13/80
MSTR-CHG-TRANS       0001                       24                                          12/13/80
SAVINGS-ACCOUNT      0001                       76                                          12/13/80
SAVINGS-TRANS        0001                       20                                          12/13/80
SAVINGS-TRANS        0002                       28                                          12/13/80
SVC-PROFILE          0001                       68                                          12/13/80
```

Figure A.5 DD/DS listings from Cullinane's Integrated Data Dictionary.

REPORT NO. 08　　　　　　　　　　　　INTEGRATED DATA DICTIONARY REPORTER　　　　　　　　　　12/15/80 PAGE 1
　　　　　　　　　　　　　　　　　　　　　　　　RECORD REPORT

```
*************************************************************************************************************
                       RECORD                RECORD                              --- D A T E ---
RECORD NAME            LENGTH  BUILDER        TYPE            OCCURRENCES        UPDATED   CREATED
*************************************************************************************************************

BASIC-SERVICE              60     S                                                          12/13/80
   IN SCHEMA      BANKSCHM         VER                    VER   1           AREA     BRANCH-AREA
   IN SCHEMA      BANKSCHM                                VER   2           AREA     BRANCH-AREA
   IN SCHEMA      BANKSCHM                                VER   3           AREA     BRANCH-AREA
   IN SCHEMA      BANKSCHM                                VER   4           AREA     BRANCH-AREA
   IN SCHEMA      BANKSCHM                                VER   5           AREA     BRANCH-AREA
   IN SCHEMA      BANKSCHM                                VER   1   S       AREA     BRANCH-AREA
   RECORD         BASIC-SERVICE
      100  02  SERVICE-CODE                 99                                        COMP
      200  02  SERVICE-DESC                 X(50)                                     DISPLAY
      300  02  MEM-BALANCE                  S9(9)                                     COMP-3
      400  02  SERVICE-CHG                  S9(3)V99                                  COMP-3

BRANCH                     72     S                                                          12/13/80
   IN SCHEMA      BANKSCHM         VER                    VER   1           AREA     BRANCH-AREA
   IN SCHEMA      BANKSCHM                                VER   2           AREA     BRANCH-AREA
   IN SCHEMA      BANKSCHM                                VER   3           AREA     BRANCH-AREA
   IN SCHEMA      BANKSCHM                                VER   4           AREA     BRANCH-AREA
   IN SCHEMA      BANKSCHM                                VER   5           AREA     BRANCH-AREA
   IN SCHEMA      BANKSCHM                                VER   1   S       AREA     BRANCH-AREA
   RECORD         BRANCH
      100  02  BRANCH-NO                    99                                        DISPLAY
      200  02  BRANCH-NAME                  X(20)                                     DISPLAY
      300  02  BRANCH-LOC                   X(25)                                     DISPLAY
      400  03  BRANCH-ADDR1                 X(25)                                     DISPLAY
      500  02  BRANCH-MGR                                                             DISPLAY

CORP-STRUCTURE             52     S                                                          12/13/80
   IN SCHEMA      BANKSCHM         VER                    VER   1           AREA     BRANCH-AREA
   IN SCHEMA      BANKSCHM                                VER   2           AREA     BRANCH-AREA
   IN SCHEMA      BANKSCHM                                VER   3           AREA     BRANCH-AREA
   IN SCHEMA      BANKSCHM                                VER   4           AREA     BRANCH-AREA
   IN SCHEMA      BANKSCHM                                VER   5           AREA     BRANCH-AREA
   IN SCHEMA      BANKSCHM                                VER   1   S       AREA     BRANCH-AREA
   RECORD         CORP-STRUCTURE
      100  02  CUST-RELATION-DESC           X(50)                                     DISPLAY
      200  02  FILLER                       XX                                        DISPLAY

CUSTOMER                  228     S                                                          12/13/80
   IN SCHEMA      BANKSCHM         VER                    VER   1           AREA     BRANCH-AREA
   IN SCHEMA      BANKSCHM                                VER   2           AREA     BRANCH-AREA
   IN SCHEMA      BANKSCHM                                VER   3           AREA     BRANCH-AREA
   IN SCHEMA      BANKSCHM                                VER   4           AREA     BRANCH-AREA
   IN SCHEMA      BANKSCHM                                VER   5           AREA     BRANCH-AREA
   IN SCHEMA      BANKSCHM                                VER   1   S       AREA     BRANCH-AREA
   RECORD         CUSTOMER
      100  02  CUST-NO                      9(8)                                      DISPLAY
      200  02  CUST-NAME                    X(25)                                     DISPLAY
      300  02  CUST-BUS-ADDR                                                          DISPLAY
```

Figure A.5 *(Continued)*

INTEGRATED DATA DICTIONARY REPORTER
RECORD REPORT
12/15/80 PAGE 2

```
RECORD NAME                     RECORD   RECORD                          ---- D A T E ----
                                LENGTH   BUILDER           TYPE    OCCURRENCES    UPDATED    CREATED
         400  03 CUST-BUS-ADDR1                          X(25)                               DISPLAY
         500  03 CUST-BUS-ADDR2                          X(25)                               DISPLAY
         600  03 CUST-BUS-ADDR3                                                              DISPLAY
         700  04 CUST-BUS-CITY-ST                        X(20)                               DISPLAY
         800  04 CUST-BUS-ZIP                            X(5)                                DISPLAY
         900  02 CUST-HOME-ADDR                                                              DISPLAY
        1000  03 CUST-HOME-ADDR1                         X(25)                               DISPLAY
        1100  03 CUST-HOME-ADDR2                         X(25)                               DISPLAY
        1200  03 CUST-HOME-ADDR3                                                             DISPLAY
        1300  04 CUST-HOME-CTY-ST                        X(20)                               DISPLAY
        1400  04 CUST-HOME-ZIP                           X(5)                                DISPLAY
        1500  02 CUST-TYPE                               99                                  DISPLAY
        1600  02 SSN-TAX-ID                              9(9)                                DISPLAY
        1700  02 DATE-OPENED                             9(6)                                DISPLAY
        1800  02 DATE-PURGED                             9(6)                                DISPLAY
        1900  02 LAST-MAINT-DATE                         9(6)                                DISPLAY
        2000  02 SHORT-NAME                              X(8)                                DISPLAY
        2100  02 CREDIT-RATING                           X(5)                                DISPLAY
        2200  02 FILLER                                  XXX                                 DISPLAY

DDA-ACCOUNT                                                                                           12/13/80
    IN SCHEMA    BANKSCHM  VER   1                               VER  1        AREA    TRANS-AREA     DISPLAY
    IN SCHEMA    BANKSCHM                                        VER  2        AREA    TRANS-AREA     DISPLAY
    IN SCHEMA    BANKSCHM                                        VER  3        AREA    TRANS-AREA     DISPLAY
    IN SCHEMA    BANKSCHM                                        VER  4        AREA    TRANS-AREA     DISPLAY
    IN SCHEMA    BANKSCHM                                        VER  5        AREA    TRANS-AREA     DISPLAY
    RECORD       DDA-ACCOUNT                92       S           VER  1   5                           DISPLAY
         100  02 ACCOUNT-NO                              9(8)                                DISPLAY
         200  02 ACCOUNT-TYPE                            9(8)                                DISPLAY
         300  02 MAIL-CODE                               9                                   COMP-3
         400  02 DATE-OPENED                             9(6)                                DISPLAY
         500  02 DATE-PURGED                             9(6)                                DISPLAY
         600  02 ACCOUNT-STATUS                          X                                   DISPLAY
         700  02 CURRENT-BAL                             S9(9)V99                            COMP-3
         800  02 LAST-TRANS-DATE                         9(5)                                DISPLAY
         900  02 LAST-DEPOSIT-DATE                       9(5)                                DISPLAY
        1000  02 LAST-DEPOSIT-AMT                        S9(9)V99                            COMP-3
        1100  02 LAST-STATEMENT-DATE                                                         DISPLAY
        1200  03 BRANCH-CTY-ST                           X(20)                               DISPLAY
        1300  02 LAST-STATEMENT-BAL                      S9(9)V99                            COMP-3
        1400  02 STATEMENT-CYCLE                         X(3)                                DISPLAY
        1500  02 DAYS-OD-YTD                             999                                 COMP-3
        1600  02 TIMES-OD-YTD                            999                                 DISPLAY
        1700  02 SERVICE-CHG                             S9(3)V99                            COMP-3
        1800  02 FILLER                                  XX                                  DISPLAY

DDA-TRANS                                                                                             12/13/80
    IN SCHEMA    BANKSCHM  VER   1           28      S           VER  1        AREA    TRANS-AREA
```

Figure A.5 *(Continued)*

REPORT NO. 08   INTEGRATED DATA DICTIONARY REPORTER   12/15/80 PAGE
                                      RECORD REPORT

```
                              RECORD      RECORD                      ----D A T E----
RECORD NAME                   LENGTH  BUILDER    TYPE   OCCURRENCES   UPDATED  CREATED
  IN SCHEMA      BANKSCHM                        VER 2     AREA       TRANS-AREA
  IN SCHEMA      BANKSCHM                        VER 3     AREA       TRANS-AREA
  IN SCHEMA      BANKSCHM                        VER 4     AREA       TRANS-AREA
  IN SCHEMA      BANKSCHM                        VER 5     AREA       TRANS-AREA
  RECORD         DDA-TRANS                       VER 1  S
      100  02 TRANS-CODE          99                                             COMP
      200  02 TRANS-DATE          9(5)                                           DISPLAY
      300  02 TRANS-AMT           S9(9)V99                                       COMP-3
      400  02 TRANS-SOURCE        9(5)                                           DISPLAY
      500  02 TRANS-REF-NO        X(10)                                          DISPLAY

EMPL-HIST                                                                                 08/08/80
  SYSTEM         CORPDB          VER    1        16   S
  EMPLOYEE       SET                              VER 1                EMPLOYEE-EHIST
                 CORPDBEM
  IN SCHEMA      CORPDBEM                         VER 1     AREA       EMP-REGION
  COMMENT      100 EMPLOYEE HISTORY (SALARY) INFORMATION

EMPL-REL                                                                                  08/08/80
  SYSTEM         CORPDB          VER    1        4    S
  EMPLOYEE       SET                              VER 1                EMPL-EXPL
                 CORPDREM
  IN SCHEMA      CORPDREM                         VER 1     AREA       EMP-REGION
  COMMENT      100 EMPLOYEE JUNCTION FOR ORGANIZATIONAL CHART

EMPLOYEE                                                                                  08/08/80
  SYSTEM         CORPDB          VER    1        280  S
  IN SCHEMA      CORPDBEM                         VER 1     AREA       EMP-REGION
  COMMENT      100 CULLINANE EMPLOYEE RECORD

IN-LOAN-ACCOUNT                                                                 12/15/80  12/13/80
  IN SCHEMA      BANKSCHM        VER    1        156  S
  IN SCHEMA      BANKSCHM                         VER 2     AREA       TRANS-AREA
  IN SCHEMA      BANKSCHM                         VER 3     AREA       TRANS-AREA
  IN SCHEMA      BANKSCHM                         VER 4     AREA       TRANS-AREA
  IN SCHEMA      BANKSCHM                         VER 5     AREA       TRANS-AREA
  RECORD         IN-LOAN-ACCOUNT                  VER 1  S
      100  02 ACCOUNT-NO          9(8)                                           DISPLAY
      200  02 ACCOUNT-TYPE        9(8)                                           DISPLAY
      300  02 MAIL-CODE           9                                              COMP-3
      400  02 DATE-OPENED         9(6)                                           DISPLAY
      500  02 DATE-PURGED         9(6)                                           DISPLAY
      600  02 LAST-MAINT-DATE     9(6)                                           DISPLAY
      700  02 ACCOUNT-STATUS      X                                              DISPLAY
```

Figure A.5 (*Continued*)

299

REPORT NO. 03   INTEGRATED DATA DICTIONARY REPORTER   12/15/80 PAGE 24
                                                    RECORD REPORT

```
                                    RECORD          RECORD                          ---- D A T E ----
RECORD NAME                    LENGTH  BUILDER       TYPE       OCCURRENCES         UPDATED   CREATED

        800 02 CURRENT-BAL                          S9(9)V99                        COMP-3
        900 02 INTEREST-YTD                         S9(9)V99                        COMP-3
       1000 02 LAST-PAY-DATE                        9(6)                            DISPLAY
       1100 02 LAST-PAY-AMT                         S9(9)V99                        COMP-3
       1200 02 PAST-DUE-AMT                         S9(9)V99                        COMP-3
       1300 02 LOAN-TERM                            999                             DISPLAY
       1400 02 NO-PAYMENTS                          999                             DISPLAY
       1500 02 CURR-PAY-DUE                         S9(9)V99                        COMP-3
       1600 02 PAY-DUE-DATE                         9(6)                            DISPLAY
       1700 02 LOAN-PRINCIPLE                       S9(9)V99                        COMP-3
       1800 02 LOAN-INTEREST                        S9(9)V99                        COMP-3
       1900 02 LOAN-TYPE                            999                             DISPLAY
       2000 02 LATE-CHG-CURR                        S9(3)V99                        COMP-3
       2100 02 LATE-CHG-YTD                         S9(5)V99                        COMP-3
       2200 02 LOAN-OFFICER                         X(20)                           DISPLAY
       2300 02 COLLATERAL-DESC                      X(30)                           DISPLAY

IN-LOAN-TRANS                   16    S                                                        12/15/80  12/13/80
   IN SCHEMA          BANKSCHM  VER   1                          VER    2     AREA   TRANS-AREA
   IN SCHEMA          BANKSCHM  VER   1                          VER    3     AREA   TRANS-AREA
   IN SCHEMA          BANKSCHM  VER   1                          VER    4     AREA   TRANS-AREA
   IN SCHEMA          BANKSCHM  VER   1                          VER    5     AREA   TRANS-AREA
   IN SCHEMA          BANKSCHM  VER   1                          VER    1     AREA   TRANS-AREA
   RECORD    IN-LOAN-TRANS                                                           S
        100 02 TRANS-CODE                           99                               COMP
        200 02 TRANS-DATE                           9(5)                             DISPLAY
        300 02 TRANS-AMT                            S9(3)V99                         COMP-3
        400 02 FILLER                               XXX                              DISPLAY

INST-LOAN-ACCOUN                128   S                                                                  12/13/80
   IN SCHEMA          BANKSCHM  VER   1                          VER    1     AREA   TRANS-AREA

INST-LOAN-TRANS                 128   S                                                                  12/13/80
   IN SCHEMA          BANKSCHM  VER   1                          VER    1     AREA   TRANS-AREA

MSTR-CHG-ACCOUNT                128   S                                                                  12/13/80
   IN SCHEMA          BANKSCHM  VER   1                          VER    1     AREA   TRANS-AREA
   IN SCHEMA          BANKSCHM                                   VER    1     AREA   TRANS-AREA
   IN SCHEMA          BANKSCHM                                   VER    2     AREA   TRANS-AREA
   IN SCHEMA          BANKSCHM                                   VER    3     AREA   TRANS-AREA
   IN SCHEMA          BANKSCHM                                   VER    4     AREA   TRANS-AREA
   IN SCHEMA          BANKSCHM                                   VER    5     AREA   TRANS-AREA
   IN SCHEMA          BANKSCHM                                   VER    1     AREA   TRANS-AREA
   RECORD    MSTR-CHG-ACCOUNT                                                        S
        100 02 ACCOUNT-NO                           9(8)                             DISPLAY
        200 02 ACCOUNT-TYPE                         9(8)                             DISPLAY
        300 02 MAIL-CODE                            9                                COMP-3
        400 02 DATE-OPENED                          9(6)                             DISPLAY
```

300

```
REPORT NO. 08              INTEGRATED DATA DICTIONARY REPORTER                    12/15/80 PAGE   5
                                     RECORD REPORT

***************************************************************************************************
                                                                                    --- D A T E ---
RECORD NAME                        RECORD    RECORD                                 UPDATED CREATED
                            LENGTH BUILDER   TYPE        OCCURRENCES
***************************************************************************************************
         500 02 DATE-PURGED                  9(6)                                           DISPLAY
         600 02 LAST-MAINT-DATE              9(6)                                           DISPLAY
         700 02 ACCOUNT-STATUS               X                                              DISPLAY
         800 02 CURRENT-BAL                  S9(9)V99                                       COMP-3
         900 02 LAST-TRANS-DATE              9(5)                                           COMP-3
        1000 02 LAST-STATEMENT-DATE          X(20)                                          DISPLAY
        1100 03 BRANCH-CITY-ST               S9(9)V99                                       COMP-3
        1200 02 LAST-STATEMENT-BAL           X(3)                                           DISPLAY
        1300 02 STATEMENT-CYCLE              S9(9)V99                                       COMP-3
        1400 02 INTEREST-YTD                 S9(9)                                          COMP-3
        1530 02 CREDIT-LINE                  9(6)                                           DISPLAY
        1630 02 LAST-PAT-DATE                S9(9)V99                                       COMP-3
        1730 02 LAST-PAT-AMT                 S9(9)V99                                       COMP-3
        1830 02 PAST-DUE-AMT                 S9(9)V99                                       COMP-3
        1930 02 CARDS-ISSUED                 99                                             DISPLAY
        2000 02 EXP-DATE                     9(6)                                           DISPLAY
        2100 02 CURR-PAT-DUE                 S9(9)V99                                       COMP-3
        2200 02 PAT-DUE-DATE                 9(6)                                           DISPLAY
        2300 02 FILLER                       XXX                                            DISPLAY

MSTR-CHG-TRANS                   VER    1     24      5                                       12/13/80
IN SCHEMA         BANKSCHM                                     AREA      TRANS-AREA     COMP
IN SCHEMA         BANKSCHM                                     AREA      TRANS-AREA     DISPLAY
IN SCHEMA         BANKSCHM                                     AREA      TRANS-AREA     COMP-3
IN SCHEMA         BANKSCHM                                     AREA      TRANS-AREA     DISPLAY
IN SCHEMA         BANKSCHM                                     AREA      TRANS-AREA     DISPLAY
RECORD            MSTR-CHG-TRANS
         100 02 TRANS-CODE                   99                                             COMP
         200 02 TRANS-DATE                   9(5)                                           DISPLAY
         300 02 TRANS-AMT                    S9(9)V99                                       COMP-3
         400 02 TRANS-REF-NO                 X(10)                                          DISPLAY
         500 02 FILLER                       X                                              DISPLAY

SAVINGS-ACCOUNT                  VER    1     76      5                                       12/13/80
IN SCHEMA         BANKSCHM                                     AREA      TRANS-AREA     DISPLAY
IN SCHEMA         BANKSCHM                                     AREA      TRANS-AREA     DISPLAY
IN SCHEMA         BANKSCHM                                     AREA      TRANS-AREA     COMP-3
IN SCHEMA         BANKSCHM                                     AREA      TRANS-AREA     DISPLAY
IN SCHEMA         BANKSCHM                                     AREA      TRANS-AREA     DISPLAY
RECORD            SAVINGS-ACCOUNT
         100 02 ACCOUNT-NO                   9(8)                                           DISPLAY
         200 02 ACCOUNT-TYPE                 9(8)                                           DISPLAY
         300 02 MAIL-CODE                    9                                              COMP-3
         400 02 DATE-OPENED                  9(6)                                           DISPLAY
         500 02 DATE-PURGED                  9(6)                                           DISPLAY
         600 02 ACCOUNT-STATUS               X                                              DISPLAY
         700 02 CURRENT-BAL                  S9(9)V99                                       COMP-3
         800 02 LAST-TRANS-DATE              9(5)                                           DISPLAY
         900 02 LAST-STATEMENT-DATE                                                         COMP-3
```

Figure A.5 (*Continued*)

REPORT NO. 08   INTEGRATED DATA DICTIONARY REPORTER   12/15/80 PAGE 6
                                                  RECORD REPORT

```
                                             RECORD                              ---- D A T E ----
RECORD NAME              LENGTH  BUILDER      TYPE       OCCURRENCES             UPDATED   CREATED

       1000 03 BRANCH-CITY-ST                  X(20)                             DISPLAY
       1100 02 LAST-STATEMENT-BAL              S9(9)V99                          COMP-3
       1200 02 STATEMENT-CYCLE                 X(3)                              DISPLAY
       1300 02 INTEREST-YTD                    S9(9)V99                          COMP-3

SAVINGS-TRANS                                                                              12/13/80
  IN SCHEMA           BANKSCHM   VER  1
  IN SCHEMA           BANKSCHM                VER  2      AREA   TRANS-AREA
  IN SCHEMA           BANKSCHM                VER  3      AREA   TRANS-AREA
  IN SCHEMA           BANKSCHM                VER  4      AREA   TRANS-AREA
  IN SCHEMA           BANKSCHM                VER  5      AREA   TRANS-AREA
  IN SCHEMA           BANKSCHM                VER  1      AREA   TRANS-AREA
RECORD                SAVINGS-TRANS                 20    S
       100 02 TRANS-CODE                      99                                 COMP
       200 02 TRANS-DATE                      9(5)                                DISPLAY
       300 02 TRANS-AMT                       S9(9)V99                           COMP-3
       400 02 TRANS-SOURCE                    9(5)                                DISPLAY
       500 02 FILLER                          XX                                  DISPLAY

SAVINGS-TRANS         BANKSCHM   VER  2             28    S                               12/13/80
  IN SCHEMA                                  VER  1      AREA   TRANS-AREA

SVC-PROFILE           BANKSCHM   VER  1             68    S                               12/13/80
  IN SCHEMA           BANKSCHM                VER  1      AREA   BRANCH-AREA
  IN SCHEMA           BANKSCHM                VER  2      AREA   BRANCH-AREA
  IN SCHEMA           BANKSCHM                VER  3      AREA   BRANCH-AREA
  IN SCHEMA           BANKSCHM                VER  4      AREA   BRANCH-AREA
  IN SCHEMA           BANKSCHM                VER  5      AREA   BRANCH-AREA
RECORD                SVC-PROFILE                         S
       100 02 SERVICE-CODE                    99                                  COMP
       200 02 SERVICE-DESC                    X(50)                               DISPLAY
       300 02 MIN-BALANCE                     S9(9)                               COMP-3
       400 02 INTEREST-DISC                   SV9999                              COMP-3
       500 02 SERVICE-CHG                     S9(3)V99                            COMP-3
       600 02 CREDIT-LIMT                     S9(9)                               COMP-3
```

Figure A.5 (*Continued*)

INTEGRATED DATA DICTIONARY REPORTER
ELEMENT REPORT

ELEMENT NAME	VERSION	LGTH	USAGE	PICTURE	J B S	UPDATED	CREATED
ACCOUNT-NO	VER 1	8	DISPLAY	9(8)	D		12/12/80
ACCOUNT-STATUS	VER 1	1	DISPLAY	X	D		12/12/80
ACCOUNT-TYPE	VER 1	8	DISPLAY	9(8)	D		12/12/80
BRANCH-ADDR1	VER 1	25	DISPLAY	X(25)	D		12/12/80
BRANCH-ADDR2	VER 1	5	GROUP		D		12/12/80
BRANCH-CITY-ST	VER 1	20	DISPLAY	X(20)	D	12/12/80	12/12/80
BRANCH-LOC	VER 1	5	GROUP		D		12/12/80
BRANCH-MGR	VER 1	25	DISPLAY	X(25)	D		12/12/80
BRANCH-NAME	VER 1	20	DISPLAY	X(20)	D		12/12/80
BRANCH-NO	VER 1	2	DISPLAY	99	D		12/12/80
BRANCH-ZIP	VER 1	5	DISPLAY	X(5)	D		12/12/80
CARDS-ISSUED	VER 1	2	DISPLAY	99	D		12/12/80
COLLATERAL-DESC	VER 1	30	DISPLAY	X(30)	D		12/12/80
CREDIT-LIMT	VER 1	5	PACKED	S9(9)	D		12/12/80
CREDIT-RATING	VER 1	5	DISPLAY	X(5)	D		12/12/80
CURR-PAY-DUE	VER 1	6	PACKED	S9(9)V99	D		12/12/80
CURRENT-BAL	VER 1	6	PACKED	S9(9)V99	D		12/12/80
CUST-BUS-ADDR	VER 1	5	GROUP		D		12/12/80
CUST-BUS-ADDR1	VER 1	25	DISPLAY	X(25)	D		12/12/80
CUST-BUS-ADDR2	VER 1	25	DISPLAY	X(25)	D		12/12/80
CUST-BUS-ADDR3	VER 1	5	GROUP		D		12/12/80
CUST-BUS-CTY-ST	VER 1	20	DISPLAY	X(20)	D		12/12/80
CUST-BUS-ZIP	VER 1	5	DISPLAY	X(5)	D		12/12/80
CUST-HOME-ADDR	VER 1	5	GROUP		D		12/12/80
CUST-HOME-ADDR1	VER 1	25	DISPLAY	X(25)	D		12/12/80
CUST-HOME-ADDR2	VER 1	25	DISPLAY	X(25)	D		12/12/80
CUST-HOME-ADDR3	VER 1	5	GROUP		D		12/12/80
CUST-HOME-CTY-ST	VER 1	20	DISPLAY	X(20)	D		12/12/80
CUST-HOME-ZIP	VER 1	5	DISPLAY	X(5)	D		12/12/80
CUST-NAME	VER 1	25	DISPLAY	X(25)	D		12/12/80
CUST-NO	VER 1	8	DISPLAY	X(8)	D		12/12/80
CUST-RELATION-DESC	VER 1	50	DISPLAY	X(50)	D		12/12/80
CUST-TYPE	VER 1	2	DISPLAY	99	D		12/12/80
DATE-OPENED	VER 1	6	DISPLAY	9(6)	D		12/12/80
DATE-PURGED	VER 1	6	DISPLAY	9(6)	D		12/12/80
DAYS-OD-YTD	VER 1	3	DISPLAY	999	D		12/15/80
EXP-DATE	VER 1	6	DISPLAY	9(6)	D		12/15/80
FIL 0001	VER 2	1	DISPLAY	X	S		12/13/80
FIL 0002	VER 2	2	DISPLAY	XX	S		12/13/80
FIL 0003	VER 2	3	DISPLAY	XXX	D		12/13/80
INTEREST-DISC	VER 1	3	PACKED	SV99999	D		12/12/80
INTEREST-YTD	VER 1	6	PACKED	S9(9)V99	D		12/12/80
LAST-DEPOSIT-AMT	VER 1	6	PACKED	S9(9)V99	D		12/12/80
LAST-DEPOSIT-DATE	VER 1	5	DISPLAY	9(5)	D		12/12/80
LAST-MAINT-DATE	VER 1	6	DISPLAY	9(6)	D		12/12/80
LAST-PAY-AMT	VER 1	6	PACKED	S9(9)V99	D		12/12/80
LAST-PAY-DATE	VER 1	6	DISPLAY	9(6)	D		12/12/80
LAST-STATEMENT-BAL	VER 1	6	PACKED	S9(9)V99	D		12/12/80
LAST-STATEMENT-DATE	VER 1	6	GROUP		D		12/12/80
LAST-TRANS-DATE	VER 1	5	DISPLAY	9(5)	D		12/12/80

Figure A.5 (*Continued*)

```
REPORT NO. 09                    INTEGRATED DATA DICTIONARY REPORTER                    12/15/80 PAGE   1
                                            ELEMENT REPORT
****************************************************************************************************
*                                                                                                   *
ELEMENT NAME                                                                      BUILD ---- D A T E ----
                                                                                  CODE  UPDATED  CREATED
****************************************************************************************************

ACCOUNT-NO
  PICTURE        9(8)       VER 0001         DISPLAY LENGTH-  8                                          12/12/80
  ELEMENT NAME   ACCOUNT-NO
  RECORD NAME    DDA-ACCOUNT                 VER 1 IDD BUILT                                      D
  RECORD NAME    DDA-ACCOUNT                 VER 1 IN SCHEMA BANKSCHM VER 2
  RECORD NAME    DDA-ACCOUNT                 VER 1 IN SCHEMA BANKSCHM VER 3
  RECORD NAME    DDA-ACCOUNT                 VER 1 IN SCHEMA BANKSCHM VER 4
  RECORD NAME    DDA-ACCOUNT                 VER 1 IN SCHEMA BANKSCHM VER 5
  RECORD NAME    SAVINGS-ACCOUNT             VER 1 IDD BUILT
  RECORD NAME    SAVINGS-ACCOUNT             VER 1 IN SCHEMA BANKSCHM VER 2
  RECORD NAME    SAVINGS-ACCOUNT             VER 1 IN SCHEMA BANKSCHM VER 3
  RECORD NAME    SAVINGS-ACCOUNT             VER 1 IN SCHEMA BANKSCHM VER 4
  RECORD NAME    SAVINGS-ACCOUNT             VER 1 IN SCHEMA BANKSCHM VER 5
  RECORD NAME    MSTR-CHG-ACCOUNT            VER 1 IDD BUILT
  RECORD NAME    MSTR-CHG-ACCOUNT            VER 1 IN SCHEMA BANKSCHM VER 2
  RECORD NAME    MSTR-CHG-ACCOUNT            VER 1 IN SCHEMA BANKSCHM VER 3
  RECORD NAME    MSTR-CHG-ACCOUNT            VER 1 IN SCHEMA BANKSCHM VER 4
  RECORD NAME    MSTR-CHG-ACCOUNT            VER 1 IN SCHEMA BANKSCHM VER 5
  RECORD NAME    IN-LOAN-ACCOUNT             VER 1 IDD BUILT
  RECORD NAME    IN-LOAN-ACCOUNT             VER 1 IN SCHEMA BANKSCHM VER 2
  RECORD NAME    IN-LOAN-ACCOUNT             VER 1 IN SCHEMA BANKSCHM VER 3
  RECORD NAME    IN-LOAN-ACCOUNT             VER 1 IN SCHEMA BANKSCHM VER 4
  RECORD NAME    IN-LOAN-ACCOUNT             VER 1 IN SCHEMA BANKSCHM VER 5

ACCOUNT-STATUS
  PICTURE        X          VER 0001         DISPLAY LENGTH-  1                                          12/12/80
  ELEMENT NAME   ACCOUNT-STATUS
  RECORD NAME    DDA-ACCOUNT                 VER 1 IDD BUILT                                      D
  RECORD NAME    DDA-ACCOUNT                 VER 1 IN SCHEMA BANKSCHM VER 2
  RECORD NAME    DDA-ACCOUNT                 VER 1 IN SCHEMA BANKSCHM VER 3
  RECORD NAME    DDA-ACCOUNT                 VER 1 IN SCHEMA BANKSCHM VER 4
  RECORD NAME    DDA-ACCOUNT                 VER 1 IN SCHEMA BANKSCHM VER 5
  RECORD NAME    SAVINGS-ACCOUNT             VER 1 IDD BUILT
  RECORD NAME    SAVINGS-ACCOUNT             VER 1 IN SCHEMA BANKSCHM VER 2
  RECORD NAME    SAVINGS-ACCOUNT             VER 1 IN SCHEMA BANKSCHM VER 3
  RECORD NAME    SAVINGS-ACCOUNT             VER 1 IN SCHEMA BANKSCHM VER 4
  RECORD NAME    SAVINGS-ACCOUNT             VER 1 IN SCHEMA BANKSCHM VER 5
  RECORD NAME    MSTR-CHG-ACCOUNT            VER 1 IDD BUILT
  RECORD NAME    MSTR-CHG-ACCOUNT            VER 1 IN SCHEMA BANKSCHM VER 1
  RECORD NAME    MSTR-CHG-ACCOUNT            VER 1 IN SCHEMA BANKSCHM VER 2
```

Figure A.5 *(Continued)*

REPORT NO. 03   INTEGRATED DATA DICTIONARY REPORTER   12/15/80 PAGE   2
                                         ELEMENT REPORT

****
                                                                              BUILD ---- D A T E ----
ELEMENT NAME   CODE UPDATED   CREATED
****
          RECORD NAME   MSTR-CHG-ACCOUNT   VER   1 IN SCHEMA BANKSCHM VER   3
          RECORD NAME   MSTR-CHG-ACCOUNT   VER   1 IN SCHEMA BANKSCHM VER   4
          RECORD NAME   MSTR-CHG-ACCOUNT   VER   1 IN SCHEMA BANKSCHM VER   5
          RECORD NAME   IN-LOAN-ACCOUNT   VER   1 IDD BUILT
          RECORD NAME   IN-LOAN-ACCOUNT   VER   1 IN SCHEMA BANKSCHM VER   2
          RECORD NAME   IN-LOAN-ACCOUNT   VER   1 IN SCHEMA BANKSCHM VER   3
          RECORD NAME   IN-LOAN-ACCOUNT   VER   1 IN SCHEMA BANKSCHM VER   4
          RECORD NAME   IN-LOAN-ACCOUNT   VER   1 IN SCHEMA BANKSCHM VER   5

ACCOUNT-TYPE   VER 0001   D   12/12/80
     PICTURE   9(8)   DISPLAY LENGTH=   8
     ELEMENT NAME   ACCOUNT-TYPE   VER   1 IDD BUILT
          RECORD NAME   DDA-ACCOUNT   VER   1 IN SCHEMA BANKSCHM VER   1
          RECORD NAME   DDA-ACCOUNT   VER   1 IN SCHEMA BANKSCHM VER   2
          RECORD NAME   DDA-ACCOUNT   VER   1 IN SCHEMA BANKSCHM VER   3
          RECORD NAME   DDA-ACCOUNT   VER   1 IN SCHEMA BANKSCHM VER   4
          RECORD NAME   DDA-ACCOUNT   VER   1 IN SCHEMA BANKSCHM VER   5
          RECORD NAME   SAVINGS-ACCOUNT   VER   1 IN SCHEMA BANKSCHM VER   1
          RECORD NAME   SAVINGS-ACCOUNT   VER   1 IN SCHEMA BANKSCHM VER   2
          RECORD NAME   SAVINGS-ACCOUNT   VER   1 IN SCHEMA BANKSCHM VER   3
          RECORD NAME   SAVINGS-ACCOUNT   VER   1 IN SCHEMA BANKSCHM VER   4
          RECORD NAME   SAVINGS-ACCOUNT   VER   1 IN SCHEMA BANKSCHM VER   5
          RECORD NAME   MSTR-CHG-ACCOUNT   VER   1 IDD BUILT
          RECORD NAME   MSTR-CHG-ACCOUNT   VER   1 IN SCHEMA BANKSCHM VER   1
          RECORD NAME   MSTR-CHG-ACCOUNT   VER   1 IN SCHEMA BANKSCHM VER   2
          RECORD NAME   MSTR-CHG-ACCOUNT   VER   1 IN SCHEMA BANKSCHM VER   3
          RECORD NAME   MSTR-CHG-ACCOUNT   VER   1 IN SCHEMA BANKSCHM VER   4
          RECORD NAME   MSTR-CHG-ACCOUNT   VER   1 IN SCHEMA BANKSCHM VER   5
          RECORD NAME   IN-LOAN-ACCOUNT   VER   1 IDD BUILT
          RECORD NAME   IN-LOAN-ACCOUNT   VER   1 IN SCHEMA BANKSCHM VER   2
          RECORD NAME   IN-LOAN-ACCOUNT   VER   1 IN SCHEMA BANKSCHM VER   3
          RECORD NAME   IN-LOAN-ACCOUNT   VER   1 IN SCHEMA BANKSCHM VER   4
          RECORD NAME   IN-LOAN-ACCOUNT   VER   1 IN SCHEMA BANKSCHM VER   5

BRANCH-ADDR1   VER 0001   D   12/12/80
     WITHIN GROUP   BRANCH-LOC   VER   1
     PICTURE   X(25)   DISPLAY LENGTH= 25   PRIMARY GROUP
     ELEMENT NAME   BRANCH-ADDR1   VER   1 IDD BUILT
          RECORD NAME   BRANCH   VER   1 IN SCHEMA BANKSCHM VER   1
          RECORD NAME   BRANCH   VER   1 IN SCHEMA BANKSCHM VER   2
          RECORD NAME   BRANCH   VER   1 IN SCHEMA BANKSCHM VER   3
          RECORD NAME   BRANCH   VER   1 IN SCHEMA BANKSCHM VER   4
          RECORD NAME   BRANCH   VER   1 IN SCHEMA BANKSCHM VER   5

Figure A.5 (*Continued*)

```
REPORT NO. 09                    INTEGRATED DATA DICTIONARY REPORTER                 12/15/80 PAGE   3
                                            ELEMENT REPORT
************************************************************************************************************
                                                                                      BUILD ---- D A T E ----
ELEMENT NAME                                                                          CODE  UPDATED   CREATED
************************************************************************************************************

BRANCH-ADDR2                     VER 0001
    SUBORDINATE ELEMENT   BRANCH-CTY-ST                  VER   1                        PRIMARY GROUP    D      12/12/80
    SUBORDINATE ELEMENT   BRANCH-ZIP                     VER   1                        PRIMARY GROUP
    PRIMARY GROUP                                        DISPLAY LENGTH= 25

BRANCH-CTY-ST                    VER 0001
    WITHIN GROUP          BRANCH-ADDR2                   VER   1                        PRIMARY GROUP    D      12/12/80
    WITHIN GROUP          LAST-STATEMENT-DATE            VER   1                        PRIMARY GROUP
    PICTURE               X(20)                          DISPLAY LENGTH= 20
    ELEMENT NAME          BRANCH-CTY-ST
    RECORD NAME           DDA-ACCOUNT                    VER   1  IDD BUILT
    RECORD NAME           DDA-ACCOUNT                    VER   1  IN SCHEMA  BANKSCHM  VER  1
    RECORD NAME           DDA-ACCOUNT                    VER   1  IN SCHEMA  BANKSCHM  VER  2
    RECORD NAME           DDA-ACCOUNT                    VER   1  IN SCHEMA  BANKSCHM  VER  3
    RECORD NAME           DDA-ACCOUNT                    VER   1  IN SCHEMA  BANKSCHM  VER  4
    RECORD NAME           DDA-ACCOUNT                    VER   1  IN SCHEMA  BANKSCHM  VER  5
    RECORD NAME           SAVINGS-ACCOUNT                VER   1  IDD BUILT
    RECORD NAME           SAVINGS-ACCOUNT                VER   1  IN SCHEMA  BANKSCHM  VER  1
    RECORD NAME           SAVINGS-ACCOUNT                VER   1  IN SCHEMA  BANKSCHM  VER  2
    RECORD NAME           SAVINGS-ACCOUNT                VER   1  IN SCHEMA  BANKSCHM  VER  3
    RECORD NAME           SAVINGS-ACCOUNT                VER   1  IN SCHEMA  BANKSCHM  VER  4
    RECORD NAME           SAVINGS-ACCOUNT                VER   1  IN SCHEMA  BANKSCHM  VER  5
    RECORD NAME           MSTR-CHG-ACCOUNT               VER   1  IDD BUILT
    RECORD NAME           MSTR-CHG-ACCOUNT               VER   1  IN SCHEMA  BANKSCHM  VER  1
    RECORD NAME           MSTR-CHG-ACCOUNT               VER   1  IN SCHEMA  BANKSCHM  VER  2
    RECORD NAME           MSTR-CHG-ACCOUNT               VER   1  IN SCHEMA  BANKSCHM  VER  3
    RECORD NAME           MSTR-CHG-ACCOUNT               VER   1  IN SCHEMA  BANKSCHM  VER  4
    RECORD NAME           MSTR-CHG-ACCOUNT               VER   1  IN SCHEMA  BANKSCHM  VER  5

BRANCH-LOC                       VER 0001
    SUBORDINATE ELEMENT   BRANCH-ADDR1                   VER   1                        PRIMARY GROUP    D   12/12/80 12/12/80
    PRIMARY GROUP                                        DISPLAY LENGTH= 25
    ELEMENT NAME          BRANCH-LOC
    RECORD NAME           BRANCH                         VER   1  IDD BUILT
    RECORD NAME           BRANCH                         VER   1  IN SCHEMA  BANKSCHM  VER  1
    RECORD NAME           BRANCH                         VER   1  IN SCHEMA  BANKSCHM  VER  2
    RECORD NAME           BRANCH                         VER   1  IN SCHEMA  BANKSCHM  VER  3
    RECORD NAME           BRANCH                         VER   1  IN SCHEMA  BANKSCHM  VER  4
    RECORD NAME           BRANCH                         VER   1  IN SCHEMA  BANKSCHM  VER  5

BRANCH-MGR                       VER 0001
    PICTURE               X(25)                          DISPLAY LENGTH= 25                               D      12/12/80
    ELEMENT NAME          BRANCH-MGR
    RECORD NAME           BRANCH                         VER   1  IDD BUILT
```

Figure A.5 (Continued)

```
IDMSNPTS 5.51                                                           DATE        TIME     PAGE
RNGMAP              --------- RANGE MAP LISTING ---------            12/15/80      202942      1
                     FOR SCHEMA BANKSCHM VERSION   5


                      NAME                    LOW PAGE    HIGH PAGE
                                              NUMBER      NUMBER
AREA.........
      RECORD...       BRANCH-AREA             50001       50050
      RECORD...       BRANCH                  50001       50050
      RECORD...       CUSTOMER                50001       50050
      RECORD...       SVC-PROFILE             50001       50050
      RECORD...       BASIC-SERVICE           50001       50050
      RECORD...       CORP-STRUCTURE          50001       50050

AREA.........
      RECORD...       TRANS-AREA              60001       60030
      RECORD...       DDA-ACCOUNT             60001       60030
      RECORD...       DDA-TRANS               60001       60030
      RECORD...       SAVINGS-ACCOUNT         60001       60030
      RECORD...       SAVINGS-TRANS           60001       60030
      RECORD...       MSTR-CHG-ACCOUNT        60001       60030
      RECORD...       MSTR-CHG-TRANS          60001       60030
      RECORD...       IN-LOAN-ACCOUNT         60001       60030
      RECORD...       IN-LOAN-TRANS           60001       60030

                   --------- RANGE MAP LISTING --------- END
```

Figure A.5 (*Continued*)

```
IDMSRPTS 5.51                                                                    DATE       TIME    PAGE
SUBREC                     - SUBSCHEMA RECORD DESCRIPTION LISTING -              12/15/80   202942    1
                   FOR SUBSCHEMA BANKSUB2 IN SCHEMA BANKSCHM VERSION   5

RECORD NAME........ BRANCH
RECORD ID.......... 0100
RECORD LENGTH...... FIXED
LOCATION MODE...... CALC USING                BRANCH-NO
WITHIN............. BRANCH-AREA    FROM PAGE  50001  THRU  50050
PRIVACY LOCK IS 'YES' FOR.......:  ERASE     FIND   GET   CONNECT    MODIFY    DISCONNECT STORE
DATA ITEM.......... REDEFINES...:  USAGE.....  VALUE....  PICTURE.........................
02 BRANCH-NO                       DISPLAY    SET CONTROL ITEM FOR ------    99                                STRT  LGTH
                                              SET CONTROL ITEM FOR ------    CALC        DUP NOT ALLOWED         1    2
                                              SET CONTROL ITEM FOR ------    CALC        DUP NOT ALLOWED
                                              SET CONTROL ITEM FOR ------    CALC        DUP NOT ALLOWED
                                              SET CONTROL ITEM FOR ------    CALC        DUP NOT ALLOWED
                                              SET CONTROL ITEM FOR ------    CALC        DUP NOT ALLOWED
02 BRANCH-NAME                     DISPLAY                                    X(20)                              3   20
02 BRANCH-LOC                      DISPLAY                                    X(25)                             23   25
03 BRANCH-ADDR1                    DISPLAY                                    X(25)                             23   25
02 BRANCH-MGR                      DISPLAY                                    X(25)                             48   25

*****                                                                                                                 *****

RECORD NAME........ CUSTOMER
RECORD ID.......... 0101
RECORD LENGTH...... FIXED
LOCATION MODE...... CALC USING                CUST-NAME
WITHIN............. BRANCH-AREA    FROM PAGE  50001  THRU  50050
PRIVACY LOCK IS 'YES' FOR.......:  FIND      GET    CONNECT    MODIFY   DISCONNECT STORE
DATA ITEM.......... REDEFINES...:  USAGE.....  VALUE....  PICTURE.........................
02 CUST-NO                         DISPLAY    SET CONTROL ITEM FOR ------    9(8)                              STRT  LGTH
02 CUST-NAME                       DISPLAY                                   SERVICES    DUP NOT ALLOWED         1    8
                                              SET CONTROL ITEM FOR ------    X(25)                              9   25
                                              SET CONTROL ITEM FOR ------    CALC        DUP NOT ALLOWED
                                              SET CONTROL ITEM FOR ------    CALC        DUP NOT ALLOWED
                                              SET CONTROL ITEM FOR ------    CALC        DUP NOT ALLOWED
                                              SET CONTROL ITEM FOR ------    CALC        DUP NOT ALLOWED
                                              SET CONTROL ITEM FOR ------    CALC        DUP NOT ALLOWED
02 CUST-BUS-ADDR                   DISPLAY                                                                      34   75
03 CUST-BUS-ADDR1                  DISPLAY                                   X(25)                              34   25
03 CUST-BUS-ADDR2                  DISPLAY                                   X(25)                              59   25
04 CUST-BUS-CIT-ST                 DISPLAY                                   X(25)                              84   25
04 CUST-BUS-ZIP                    DISPLAY                                   X(20)                              84   20
02 CUST-HOME-ADDR                  DISPLAY                                   X(5)                              104    5
03 CUST-HOME-ADDR1                 DISPLAY                                                                     109   75
03 CUST-HOME-ADDR2                 DISPLAY                                   X(25)                             109   25
03 CUST-HOME-ADDR3                 DISPLAY                                   X(25)                             134   25
04 CUST-HOME-CIT-ST                DISPLAY                                   X(25)                             159   25
04 CUST-HOME-ZIP                   DISPLAY                                   X(20)                             159   20
02 CUST-TYPE                       DISPLAY                                   X(5)                              179    5
02 SSN-TAX-ID                      DISPLAY                                   99                                184    2
02 DATE-OPENED                     DISPLAY                                   9(9)                              186    9
                                                                             9(6)                              195    6
```

Figure A.5 *(Continued)*

```
IDMSRPTS 5.51                                                                                    DATE       TIME    PAGE
SUBREC            FOR SUBSCHEMA BANKSUB2 IN SCHEMA BANKSCHM VERSION    5                       12/15/80    202942    2

  02 DATE-PURGED                     DISPLAY                       9(6)                                    201      6
  02 LAST-MAINT-DATE                 DISPLAY                       9(6)                                    207      6
  02 SHORT-NAME                      DISPLAY                       X(8)                                    213      8
  02 CREDIT-RATING                   DISPLAY                       X(5)                                    221      5
  02 FILLER                          DISPLAY                       XXX                                     226      3

*****

RECORD NAME......: SVC-PROFILE
RECORD ID........: 0103
RECORD LENGTH....: FIXED
LOCATION MODE....: CALC USING
    WITHIN.......: BRANCH-AREA
PRIVACY LOCK IS 'YES' FOR
DATA ITEM........: SERVICE-CODE
  02 SERVICE-CODE                                              FROM PAGE    50001    THRU    50050
                                     FIND                      GET          CONNECT         MODIFY         DISCONNECT STORE
                                     COMP                      VALUE....                    PICTURE                                    STRT   LGTH
                                                                                            99                                            1      2
                                                               SET CONTROL ITEM FOR ------  CALC                 DUP NOT ALLOWED
                                                               SET CONTROL ITEM FOR ------  CALC                 DUP NOT ALLOWED
                                                               SET CONTROL ITEM FOR ------  CALC                 DUP NOT ALLOWED
                                                               SET CONTROL ITEM FOR ------  CALC                 DUP NOT ALLOWED
                                                               SET CONTROL ITEM FOR ------  CALC                 DUP NOT ALLOWED
  02 SERVICE-DESC                    DISPLAY                                                X(50)                                        3     50
  02 MIN-BALANCE                     COMP-3                                                 S9(9)                                       53      5
  02 INTEREST-DISC                   COMP-3                                                 SV99999                                     58      3
  02 SERVICE-CHG                     COMP-3                                                 S9(3)V99                                    61      3
  02 CREDIT-LINE                     COMP-3                                                 S9(9)                                       64      5

*****

RECORD NAME......: BASIC-SERVICE
RECORD ID........: 0104
RECORD LENGTH....: FIXED
LOCATION MODE....: VIA SET
    WITHIN.......: BRANCH-AREA
PRIVACY LOCK IS 'YES' FOR
DATA ITEM........:  DESCRIPTION-OF                              FROM PAGE   50001    THRU    50050    DISPLACEMENT            0000 PAGES
                                     ERASE                     FIND         GET          CONNECT         MODIFY         DISCONNECT STORE
                                     USAGE                     VALUE....                                 PICTURE                                STRT   LGTH
                                     COMP                                                                99                                        1      2
  02 SERVICE-CODE                    DISPLAY                                                X(50)                                        3     50
  02 MIN-BALANCE                     COMP-3                                                 S9(9)                                       53      5
  02 SERVICE-CHG                     COMP-3                                                 S9(3)V99                                    58      3
```

Figure A.5 (*Continued*)

```
IDMSRPTS 5.51                    - SUBSCHEMA RECORD DESCRIPTION LISTING -                              DATE       TIME      PAGE
SUBREC                    FOR SUBSCHEMA BANKSUB2 IN SCHEMA BANKSCHM VERSION  5                       12/15/80    202942      3

RECORD NAME.......  SAVINGS-ACCOUNT
RECORD ID.........  0202
RECORD LENGTH.....  FIXED
LOCATION MODE.....  CALC USING      ACCOUNT-NO     FROM PAGE  60001    THRU    60030
WITHIN............  TRANS-AREA                     FIND       GET      CONNECT     MODIFY     DISCONNECT   STORE
PRIVACY LOCK IS 'YES' FOR.......:   ERASE
DATA ITEM.......... REDEFINES     USAGE.......    VALUE.....                                            PICTURE.............                  STRT     LGTH
02 ACCOUNT-NO                     DISPLAY                     SET CONTROL ITEM FOR ------                9(8)                                   1        8
                                                              SET CONTROL ITEM FOR ------                CALC                    DUP NOT ALLOWED
                                                              SET CONTROL ITEM FOR ------                CALC                    DUP NOT ALLOWED
                                                              SET CONTROL ITEM FOR ------                CALC                    DUP NOT ALLOWED
                                                              SET CONTROL ITEM FOR ------                CALC                    DUP NOT ALLOWED
                                                              SET CONTROL ITEM FOR ------                CALC                    DUP NOT ALLOWED
02 ACCOUNT-TYPE                   DISPLAY                                                                9(8)                                   9        8
02 MAIL-CODE                      COMP-3                                                                 9                                     17        1
02 DATE-OPENED                    DISPLAY                                                                9(6)                                  18        6
02 ACCOUNT-STATUS                 DISPLAY                                                                9(6)                                  24        6
02 CURRENT-BAL                    DISPLAY                                                                X                                     30        1
02 LAST-TRANS-DATE                COMP-3                                                                 S9(9)V99                              31        6
02 LAST-STATEMENT-DATE            DISPLAY                                                                9(5)                                  37        5
03 BRANCH-CTY-ST                  DISPLAY                                                                X(20)                                 42       20
02 LAST-STATEMENT-BAL             COMP-3                                                                 S9(9)V99                              62       20
02 STATEMENT-CYCLE                DISPLAY                                                                X(3)                                  62        6
02 INTEREST-YTD                   COMP-3                                                                 S9(3)V99                              68        6
                                                                                                                                               71        6

*****

RECORD NAME.......  SAVINGS-TRANS
RECORD ID.........  0302
RECORD LENGTH.....  FIXED                                          DISPLACEMENT        0000 PAGES
LOCATION MODE.....  VIA SET          SAV-UPDATED-BY FROM PAGE  60001    THRU    60030
WITHIN............  TRANS-AREA                     FIND       GET      CONNECT     MODIFY     DISCONNECT   STORE
PRIVACY LOCK IS 'YES' FOR.......:   ERASE
DATA ITEM.......... REDEFINES     USAGE.......    VALUE.....                                            PICTURE.............                  STRT     LGTH
02 TRANS-CODE                     COMP                                                                   99                                     1        2
02 TRANS-DATE                     DISPLAY                                                                9(5)                                   3        5
02 TRANS-AMT                      COMP-3                                                                 S9(9)V99                               8        6
02 TRANS-SOURCE                   DISPLAY                                                                9(5)                                  14        5
02 FILLER                         DISPLAY                                                                XX                                    19        2

         - SUBSCHEMA RECORD DESCRIPTION LISTING - END
```

Figure A.5 (*Continued*)

```
IDMSRPT3 5.51                            -- SUBSCHEMA SET DESCRIPTION LISTING --         DATE      TIME    PAGE
SUBSET                        FOR SUBSCHEMA BANKSUB2 IN SCHEMA BANKSCHM VERSION    5     12/15/80  202942    1

SET...... SERVICES                      MODE IS CHAIN               ORDER IS SORTED
PRIVACY LOCK IS 'YES' FOR........ DISCONNECT CONNECT                FIND
OWNER.... BRANCH                  0100  LINKED NEXT PRIOR
MEMBER... CUSTOMER                0101  LINKED NEXT PRIOR OWNER     MANDATORY AUTOMATIC ASC CUST-NO    DUP NOT ALLOWED

SET...... CUST-SAV                      MODE IS CHAIN               ORDER IS FIRST
PRIVACY LOCK IS 'YES' FOR........ DISCONNECT CONNECT                FIND
OWNER.... CUSTOMER                0101  LINKED NEXT PRIOR
MEMBER... SAVINGS-ACCOUNT         0202  LINKED NEXT PRIOR OWNER     MANDATORY AUTOMATIC

SET...... SAV-PROVIDED                  MODE IS CHAIN               ORDER IS FIRST
PRIVACY LOCK IS 'YES' FOR........ DISCONNECT CONNECT                FIND
OWNER.... SVC-PROFILE             0103  LINKED NEXT PRIOR
MEMBER... SAVINGS-ACCOUNT         0202  LINKED NEXT PRIOR OWNER     MANDATORY AUTOMATIC

SET...... DESCRIPTION-OF                MODE IS CHAIN               ORDER IS FIRST
PRIVACY LOCK IS 'YES' FOR........ DISCONNECT CONNECT                FIND
OWNER.... SVC-PROFILE             0103  LINKED NEXT PRIOR
MEMBER... BASIC-SERVICE           0104  LINKED NEXT PRIOR           MANDATORY AUTOMATIC

SET...... SAV-UPDATED-BY                MODE IS CHAIN               ORDER IS LAST
PRIVACY LOCK IS 'YES' FOR........ DISCONNECT CONNECT                FIND
OWNER.... SAVINGS-ACCOUNT         0202  LINKED NEXT PRIOR
MEMBER... SAVINGS-TRANS           0102  LINKED NEXT PRIOR           MANDATORY AUTOMATIC

                                     -- SUBSCHEMA SET DESCRIPTION LISTING -- END
```

Figure A.5 (*Continued*)

The marketing system was added to DDA in 1979. It was felt, for competitive reasons, that the marketing staff needed to know more about LNB's customer base, customers' use of LNB's service, and the activity and profitability of both existing and proposed services. Products were described in "service profiles" and these profiles were added to the database. A logical view was created to enable marketing personnel to determine the accounts that fell into each service profile. The logical view consisted of access capability into customer, account, and transaction data elements (see Figure A.4).

In early 1980, the marketing effort became cost effective. Credit cards were offered to those DDA customers with a history of high activity and good balances. The results were so favorable that operational problems occurred in getting the marketing staff timely reports of DDA customers who had credit cards. To ease this situation, an *attach* transaction was created, that would allow marketing personnel to associate existing DDA customers to a new credit-card service profile. For this purpose, the *add* and *change* functions were added to the logical view used for analytical purposes.

The overal objectives of the DDA conversion, as stated by the EDP Steering Committee, are:

Improved customer service, including new products and extension of corporate-level service to retail customers.

Standardization of retail and corporate DDA.

Improved management control over product and customer profitability.

Timely online inquiry into all accounts.

Improved branch audit and control procedures.

Reduction of mispostings, adjustments, and the necessity for carrying excessive reserves due to late closings of corporate accounts.

Conceptually, DDA has four major components: status (non-dollar) maintenance, dollar (financial transaction) posting, inquiry (including stops and holds), and marketing (summary processing). Each component has associated transactions, which are described functionally to users, but are maintained internally by transaction codes. A description of each transaction follows below.

Transaction Code	Description
Status	
S01	*New Accounts* When an account is opened, it is opened at a particular branch and

Transaction Code	Description
	associated with that branch thereafter. Retail accounts are opened online in the branch, but a dollar transaction must be posted that day or the account will be removed from the database.
S02	*Account Closing* When a customer decides to close an account for any reason, he or she must notify the branch at which the account was opened. LNB suggests written instruction, to avoid lengthy telephone conversations, and verification between the customer and the branch. Formal account closing processing is processed online by the branch that houses the account.
S03	*Daily Balancing* Each branch is responsible for balancing of all financial transactions against cash on a daily basis. Shortages/overages of cash must be reconciled by branch personnel and transmitted to the central bank daily.
S04	*Account Status Changes* As with account closings, any change relating to nonfinancial account information is handled by the branch that houses the account.
Dollar	
D01	*Credits* All credit items are posted to each account prior to debits. Each item is handled as a separate transaction, though the account totals are maintained for the trial balance report.
D02	*Debits* Debits are handled like credits, but are "smallest items posted first," to reduce the number of overdrafts. Overdrafts and nonsufficient funds produce customer advices and are maintained separately for DDA posting purposes.
D03	*Interest Posting Debit* This is an internally

Transaction Code	Description
	generated transaction that takes interest on the average daily loan balance of online credit accounts. Interest posting is done once a month.
D04	*Interest Posting Credit* This is also an internally generated transaction in which interest is posted to IBC accounts. The average daily balance is the basis for the update, posted once a month.
Inquiry	
I01	*Status Inquiry* Inquiries into nondollar information are separated from balance inquiries because some personnel are authorized for one function but not another.
I02	*Balance Inquiry* This online transaction gives tellers and platform officers drawable, book and collected balances, as well as the last ten debits and three credits posted to the account.
I03	*Stops and Holds* These may be placed online. In the batch system debit processing checks for stops and holds before posting.
Marketing Summary	
M01	*Product Line Summary* This internally generated transaction posts key transaction and balance figures to the service profile of each account type.
M02 (proposed)	*Customer Master Account Summary* This internally generated transaction will post the same figures as for M01 to a master account record for major corporate accounts.

OTHER APPLICATIONS

Transaction Code	Description
MO3	*Service Profile Analysis* This parameterized transaction allows listing of DDA customers, accounts, and/or transactions that match the service profile of certain product types.
M04	*Service Profile Maintenance* This transaction allows the marketing staff to add, delete or modify a service profile.
M05	*Service Profile Attach* This transaction allows the association of existing customers with new or altered service profiles.

OTHER APPLICATIONS

Conversion of the *commercial loan* application from 1401 emulation is considered a high priority. It was only put behind DDA in priority because retail checking volume had made this application only marginally profitable under existing operations. It is scheduled for conversion in 1981, incorporating the same database as used for DDA. Ninety percent of commercial loan customers also have a DDA account at LNB.

Mortgage is currently being computerized, using a purchased package. This package does not use database and will be extensively modified to interface with the DBMS.

Retail loan and *savings* will be converted after DDA conversion is complete, following the same pattern as DDA conversion. A study is currently underway to determine whether *trust* should be automated. Factors being considered include:

1. Eighty-five percent of trust customers have at least one other relationship with the bank, usually DDA.
2. There are few trust customers — fewer than 1000 — but a staff of 20 professionals and 37 clerical personnel is required to service these accounts.
3. Trust is a very volatile market, particularly in face of the incursions of the major New York City banks. It is possible that LNB will no longer have substantial trust operations by the mid-80s. However, improved services would probably protect LNB's existing customer base.
4. Trust is a complex financial application with numerous customer relationships and special instructions.

There are no plans to convert the *credit card* or *funds transfer* applications.

Glossary

Active DD/DS A DD/DS is said to be *active* with respect to a program or a process *if and only if* that program or process is dependent on the DD/DS for its metadata.

Activity The relative control that the DD/DS exerts over a program or a process. (Also referred to as *activeness.*)

Application Program Application of computer technology to an operational function such as payroll, customer billing, or personnel management. An application program is a computer program that automates one or more functions within an operational area.

Attribute A characteristic, property, or description of an entity or a relationship.

Attribute Expansibility The ability of users to add their own attributes to an already established entity, based on specific enterprise needs.

Automated Interface An automated link between two software components that may perform one or more functions, such as translation and formatting.

Automated Tool *See* Software tool.

Binding Time The instant in time when the data description is "assigned to" or "bound to" the procedural code. The data description was previously separated (i.e., defined independently). Binding time has a direct effect on the level of control because, once data descriptions are bound to a program, the program is no longer dependent on the DD/DS for its metadata. Thus the longer the binding time can be delayed, the greater the level of control for the DD/DS.

Clone This facility allows new entity type names to be created from existing entity types. This is a DATA CATALOGUE 2 feature.

Communication Facilities A collection of processes and physical facilities that interconnect nodes.

Conceptual Data Model *See* Conceptual schema.

Conceptual Schema A model of the "real world" operations and applications. A conceptual schema should not be dependent on a particular DBMS. A description of the data required to support the "business" functions of an enterprise.

Copy Library Also known as Copylib. Contains stored data descriptions or segments of code that are often used and have been successfully compiled.

Customization The ability to design outputs according to user-specified parameters, unique to an enterprise.

Data Administration (DA) Function The DA function has the overall responsibility for the enterprise's data resources and for the administration, control, and coordination of all data-related activities. DA has the responsibility for planning and defining the conceptual framework for the overall database environment.

Database A repository for stored data that is shared and integrated. A data collection so organized for computer processing as to optimize storage and improve the independence of the stored data structure from the processing programs.

Database Administration (DBA) Function The enterprise's leading technical expert on database-related activities. The DBA usually has the technical responsibility over the day-to-day operations of all database related activities. These activities include definition, design, control, organization, documentation, protection, integrity, and efficiency of the database.

Database Management System (DBMS) (a) An integrated set of computer programs that collectively provide all the capabilities required for centralized management, that is, organization, access and control of a database that is shared by diverse users. (b) Provides an integrated source of data for multiple users while allowing each to obtain a different view appropriate to their requirements.

Data Cluster A named collection of data items.

Data Definition Language (DDL) The language used for defining the schema (or the data model) for the user database.

Data Dictionary/Directory System (DD/DS) (a) A DD/DS is a system that is designed to support comprehensively the logical centralization of data about data (metadata). (b) The DD/DS is an automated facility that supports the data administration function. (c) The DD/DS provides a logically centralized repository of all definitive information about the relevant data in an enterprise, including characteristics, relationships, usage, and responsibility.

Data Dictionary/Directory System Data Definition Language (DD/DS DDL) The language used for defining the entries for the metadatabase. The DD/DS DDL has both syntax and semantics — that is, the language has a grammar that prescribes a basic format for its statements, and each syntactical rule has an associated semantic rule that assigns meaning to the syntax.

Data Entities Data entities are a class of entities that describe or represent objects or entities that are units of data or aggregates of data, for example, element, record, files, and reports. *See* Metadata entities.

Data Independence The ability of various users (or applications) to have different views of the same data. Specifically, the way data is logically defined (and utilized) does not depend on a specific application, storage structure, or access strategy.

GLOSSARY

Data Integrity The ability to preserve the completeness, currency, and accuracy of the data without unintentional changes; the ability to produce results that are correct to a predefined level and to maintain data availability.

Data Item The most elementary unit of data in a user database.

Data Manipulation Language The command language that allows for accessing and processing of the content of the database.

Data Resources A critical concept which implies that data has the same characteristics as other more familiar resources, such as manpower, real property, and machinery. Like the better known resources, data resources have such characteristics as cost and value. This concept is critical to the study of data dictionary/directory system as an enterprise tool.

Data Sharing The ability of a number of users to access common data. This ability helps in reducing unwanted duplication, and inconsistencies, reducing storage requirements, and speeding up processing.

Degree of Activity The relative *operational* control that the DD/DS exerts on other processing components. This concept is closely tied to the binding time of the data definition to the procedure or code. The later the binding occurs, the higher the degree of activity.

Dependent DD/DS A DD/DS that uses DBMS facilities to implement the structure and organization of the metadatabase and its support functions.

Dictionary Metadata Addresses the "what" aspects of a data description, that is, what the data is, what it means, and what exists.

Directionality of Interfaces The direction in which the metadata flows though an interface, that is, either from the dictionary to an external component or from the external component to the dictionary.

Directory Metadata Describes where the data is located, how it can be accessed, and how the data is internally represented.

Distributed Databases The placement of a database, or portions of a database, in a network environment. The logical integration of an enterprise's related databases, which are physically stored in a network of geographically dispersed computers.

Distributed Database Management Database management functions (i.e., organization, update, retrieval, and control) that are performed at geographically dispersed locations and linked via computer communication network such that the user process is unaware of the dispersion.

Element The most basic unit of data that can be identified and described in the DD/DS. *See also* Data item.

End User Person or group of people who are the consumers of information and have little or no experience with data processing technology but have a need for data processing.

End User Facility A tool or a capability designed to assist the end user in applying or using data processing facilities.

Entity A generic term referring to any concept, person, event, or thing that may be the subject of a data collection.

Entity Expansibility The ability of the user to define their own entities, based on enterprise needs.

Expansibility The ability to expand both the structure and the functionality of the DD/DS. In this vein, there can be entity expansibility, attribute expansibility, and, in some cases, relationship expansibility. This capability must also be extended to the processing functions to allow expansibility to occur. (Also known as Extensibility.)

External View External view is the terminology for subschema used by the ANSI/X3/SPARC/Database Management Systems Study Group Interim Report. *See* Logical view.

Environment Entities *See* Physical entities.

Extensibility *See* Expansibility.

Free-Standing DD/DS When the management activities of the DD/DS (i.e., organization, access, and control functions) are performed by software built into the DD/DS itself, the DD/DS is said to be free-standing, or independent.

Front-End Processor A processor that performs certain activities *before* a main process occurs.

Independent DD/DS An independent DD/DS does not require other general purpose software systems (e.g., a DBMS) to perform its metadata management functions. *See* Free-standing DD/DS.

Integrated DD/DS An implementation of the parallel metadata sharing concept.

Interface A link between two processing components. *See also* Automated Interface.

Internal View *See* Physical view.

Keyword A word designated as being of importance for searching, accessing, or retrieving.

KWIC Keyword-in-context index or report is a listing of the keywords as they appear in the context of other text.

KWOC Keyword-out-of-context is a listing of all keywords arranged in some sorting sequence.

Logical Refers to a view or description of data that does not depend upon physical storage or computer system characteristics.

Logical View A model of, or representation of, the data as used in a particular user or application environment.

Meta A prefix used to indicate one level of abstraction "above" the user-data level.

Metadata Data about data, that is, the description of the data resources, its characteristics, location, usage, and so on. Metadata is used to identify, describe, and define user data. The content of the DD/DS is metadata.

Metadatabase (a) A collection of metadata that is managed and controlled as a unit. The metadatabase is a repository of stored metadata that is shared and integrated. The database for the DD/DS. (b) A collection of metadata so organized for processing as to reduce duplicative storage and improve the independence of the stored metadata structure from the processing components. (Also found as metadata database.)

Metadata Entities Meta-entities that represent data objects such as data element, record, and database.

Metadata Generation The ability to produce data descriptions for use by other processing components, based on stored definitions, maintained by the DD/DS. The automated metadata generation capability is the basic mechanism for implementing an active DD/DS.

Metadata Sharing The ability for more than one processing component or user to use the same metadata. This is one of the key principles of the database approach. There are two basic approaches to sharing metadata: parallel and serial. *See also* Parallel sharing and Serial sharing.

Meta-Entity (a) Represents objects that exist in the user data database, data processing, and user environments. Meta-entities are the basic building blocks of the metadatabase design. (b) A generic term used to denote entities or objects about which descriptions are stored in the DD/DS database.

Meta-System Entities Meta-entities that represent processes and components such as program, system, and module that exist as part of the data processing environment.

Natural Language The language spoken and/or used by the user (e.g., English or French), which is most "natural" for comprehension.

Network A computer network consists of a collection of circuits, data switching elements, and computing systems. The switching devices in the network are called communication processors. A network provides a configuration for computer systems and communication facilities within which data can be stored and accessed and DBMSs can operate.

Network Data Directory The directory function of the DD/DS, which provides data location for a node within the network.

Nodal Location Directory *See* Network data directory.

Node Technically, a point in the network at which data is switched. A node in a network consists of a computer processing facility, an operating system for executing user processes, and maybe a DBMS.

Parallel Sharing One of the approaches for metadata sharing. This approach allows **only one** physical representation of the metadatabase, while maintaining various logical views. Each software component gets the metadata it requires by sharing this one common source. Parallel sharing is only found in a highly active DD/DS. *See also* Integrated.

Partitioning A method of distributing data in a network whereby only a subset of the entire database is located at a user's node.

Passive DD/DS If a program or a process does not depend on the DD/DS for its metadata, that DD/DS is said to be passive. A passive DD/DS is defined with respect to the relative lack of control it exerts on other processes. The purely passive DD/DS registers metadata on an after-the-fact basis as a documentation facility.

Physical Refers to the representation and storage of data on media such as magnetic media, or to a description or view of the data that depends on such physical factors as length of elements and pointers.

Physical Entities Describes or represent objects or entities that are connected with the physical environment. Also known as Environment entities and Usage entities.

Physical View A model of, or representation of, the data as stored or as physically implemented.

Process An executing instance of a computer program, a software component, or a procedure with which a DD/DS interacts.

Processing Entities *See* Meta-system entities.

Program Subschema The way the program "sees" the data, that is, the program's logical view.

Query Language The means by which an end-user communicates and interacts with the information system. A language, usually English-like, that enables the user to interact directly with a DD/DS (or a DBMS) and to retrieve and possibly modify data stored in the metadatabase. Most query language processing is interpretive.

Query Processing The process that allows the user to retrieve selectively, based on some given criteria, in an impromptu manner.

Recursive The capability to nest an entity based on itself.

Relationship An association (relation) between two entities.

Replication A method of distributing data in a network whereby functionally identical copies of the data are stored at multiple nodes in the network.

Report Generation Facility to produce formatted, structured reports automatically. Often report generation is accomplished via a special purpose host-language application program or specialized software package.

Schema A complete description of the database, written in a data definition language, that is processed and stored by a DBMS (or DD/DS). A description of the data structure of the stored data. (Also known as a *data model*.)

Scope of Activity A measure of how active a DD/DS is; consists of the number of processing components that depend *solely* on the DD/DS for their metadata. A

GLOSSARY

wide scope of activity suggests a large number of processing components dependent on the DD/DS for their metadata.

Serial Sharing A strategy used in implementing sharing of the metadata. Under this strategy, each component can have its own independent mechanism for obtaining its metadata. Further, these components have the option to obtain their metadata from the DD/DS.

Software Tool Computer program, rules, and associated documentation that assist a data processing technologist in designing, developing, maintaining, and managing data and software. Under this definition, a DD/DS and a DBMS can be considered software tools.

Spectrum of Activity The range of activity of a DD/DS, which may vary from purely passive to purely active. Spectrum of activity is a function of the scope and degree of activity of a DD/DS.

Subschema A description of selected data elements and particular relationships among them as used by one or more application programs or processes.

Subsumed DD/DS An approach for implementing a DD/DS whereby the metadatabase is implemented as another user-database using all the existing facilities of a DBMS and other components of the database environment. With this approach, no architecturally independent component for the DD/DS is created in hardware or software. This approach is a variation on the dependent implementation approach.

System Development Life Cycle (SDLC) A collection of activities, usually devided into stages, that are necessary to develop and maintain a system. The SDLC consists of a predefined sequence of events and a discrete set of products. The SDLC starts when the need for creating a system is perceived through the time that the system actually produces the required results.

System or Processing Entities *See* Meta-system entities.

User A person (or a process) who uses the database. There are many kinds of users, depending on their technical background and knowledge. The end user is a special kind of user.

User Data Also known as operational data. Data maintained by an enterprise about its business operations and functions and used by an application program or a DBMS.

User Database A collection of user data which satisfies the definition of a database.

User Friendly Features in a system that assist a user in accessing (and using) a system without prior intensive training. Such features as online prompts, help-files, menu selection, and screen formats make the system easy to use.

User Interface The means by which a user communicates with the information system to obtain desired results. This is a generic term used to refer to tools that facilitate communication between the system and the user. Specifically, used to refer to such tools as a report generator and query processor.

Index

Pages in **boldface** refer to illustrations.

Access control, 15, 54, 106, 140-141, 216, 224, 250, 259
   facilities, 17
Access to data, 249
Active DD/DS, 1, 115, 117, 167, 176, 252-253, 257
   benefits of, 118-121, 128, 138, 142, 144, 149
   and parallel sharing, 157
   definition, 22
   metadata generation and, 116-121
Activity of a DD/DS, 22
   degree of, 118, 186
   scope of, 117, 185
   spectrum of, 117
ADABAS Data Dictionary, **76**, 122, 161, 177
ANSI, 69
   SPARC/DBS-SG, 32, 69
   X3H2, 101, 275
   X3H4, 101, 275
Application program, 116
   metadata generation for, 121-128
Attributes, 75, 80-86
   categories, 81
   control, 84
   identification, 82
   physical, 85
   relationship, 83
   representation, 82
   statistical, 83
   user-defined, 85

Audit:
   functions, 250-257
   software, 148, 266
Auditability, 249
Auditor, 250-272
Audit trail, 55, 249, 254-255, 256

Backup and recovery, 107
Binding, 117-118, 126
   to process, 118
   to program, 118
   time, 118, 125, 126

CODASYL, 101, 118, 144, 275
Conceptual Data model, 32
   detailed, 36, 39-41
   global, 36
Conceptual schema, 32
Control, 54
   concerns, 259, **260**
   functions, 250-260
   operational, 54
   tool, 54, 266
Controllability, 249
Conversion software, 148

DA/DBA, 155, 207-213, 216-217, 224, 243-245, 266
   DD/DS support of, 7, 213-217, **215**
   in distributed environment, 244
   functions of, 209-213, **210**

325

Data access, 46
Data administration (DA), 6, 13, 178, 195, 200
 center (case study), 286
Database, 10, 11, 202, 207, 208
 approach, 11, 61-64, 69, 156, 163
 centralized, 56
 design, 46, 47
 design aid, 145-146
 erosion, 257
 performance simulator, 147
Database administration (DBA), 15, 147, 195, 197, 198, 199, 250
 case study, 287
Database management system (DBMS), 10, 101, 116, 142, 156, 207, 273
 DD/DSs dependent on, 166-168
 DDL for, 143
 distributed, 229-230, 274
 and related developments, 274
 metadata generation for, 142-144
 for metadatabase, 153
 similarities with DD/DS, 10
Data Catalogue, 2, **76**, **88**, 97, 98, 99, 149, 167, **177**, 190, 276, **277**, 278
Data cluster, 31, 32, 35
Datacom/Datadictionary, **88, 177,** 189, 277
Data Control System (CINCOM), **76,** 166, 172, **177, 277**
 and SOCRATES, 129, 172
Data Control System (Haverly), **177, 190, 277**
Data definition language:
 characteristics of DD/DS, 95-96
 for DD/DS, 93, 94-99
 format types, 96-99
 keyword-oriented, 96-98
 preformated, 98-99
 semantics, 94-95
 syntax, 94-95
Data description, 184
Data dictionary/directory system (DD/DS), 1
 definition, 16
 distributed, 231
 foundation for design of, 61-73
 population of, 49, 221-224
 retrieval facilities, 16
Data Dictionary (ICL), **88, 177,** 277

Data Element Dictionary (DED), 17, 78
Data flow, 46
Data independence, 10, 69-70
Data integrity, 10
Datamanager, **72-73**, 76, 97, **120**, 121, **122, 123, 124, 125, 144,** 149, 161, 166, 172, 173, **177**, 190, 216, 222, **277, 278**
Data resources, 1, 4
 characteristics, 8
 management, 265
Data sharing, 10, 13
Data standardization, 195, 196, 200, 217-221
 lack of, 197
 program, 217
Data structures, 46, 143, 164
 network, 162
Data translation, 148, 235-236
 features, 240
DB/DC Data Dictionary System, **76,** 88, 97, 99, 149, 161, 166, 173, **177,** 276, **277**
Dependent DD/DS, 17, 165-167, 176, 273
Design, 46, 204
 logical, 46, 47, 48
 physical, 46, 47, 48
 system, 46
Dictionary metadata, 1, 18
 relationship between, 19
Directory function, 232
Directory metadata, 1, 19
Distributed database, 56-57, 231
 environment, 229, 232
 management, 229, 231
Distributed database management system (DDBMS), 229
Distribution alternative, 56, 233, 235, 240-243, **241**
 hybrid, 242
 for metadata, 240-243
 partitioned database, 233, 242
 replicated database, 233, 241-242
Documentation, 25, 49-51, 188, 205-206, 217, 250-251
 aid, 43
 application system, 50
 data, 51, 185
 program, 50

Ease-of-use, 170, 182, 187, 262
EDICT, **166, 177, 277**

INDEX

327

Editing rules, 52
Edit and validation, 139-140, 165, 185, 186
  programs, 139
  rules (EVR), 139-140, 224
End-user, 57, 128, 155
  interfaces, 57
End-user facilities, 116
  metadata generation for, 128-139
Entities, 8
  expansibility, 80
  metadata, 8, 66, 77, 78-79
  meta-environment, 68, 77, 79-80
  metasystem, 8, 67, 77, 79
Expansibility, 80, 86, 185
Extensibility, 86

FIPS 101, 275

Identifier, 50
Independent DD/DS, 17, 165, 167-168, 177, 273
Information hierarchy, 4, 6
Information requirements, 28
  definition and analysis, 41
Information resource dictionary system (IRDS), 101
Information system, 26, 27, 61, 136
  planning, 27, 29
Input facilities, 93-104
  batch, 102
  code scanner, 103
  database definition scanner, 103
  online, 102
  reference definition, 103
  special feature, 103
Integrated Data Dictionary (Cullinane), 76, 86, 88, 97, 110, 156, **158**, 159, **163**, 166, **177**, 190, **277**
Integrated Data Dictionary (INTEL), 76, 88, 122, 166, **177, 277**
Integrity function, 93, 116, 186
  integrity criteria, 105
  metadata, 104-107
  metadata generation for, 139-144
Interface, 115
  directionality of, 117
  software, 225-226
  user, 170-173, 186-187
  user-friendly, 271-272

Keyword-in-context (KWIC), 33, 185

Keyword-out-of-context (KWOC), 185

Last National Bank (LNB):
  case study, 25, 26, 33-34, 44-46, 48-49, 52-53, 55, 58, 281-315
Lexicon, **76,** 127, 128, 129, **130-135,** 142, 166, **177,** 216, 276, **277,** 278
Logical centralization, 16

Metadata, 1, 8, 115, 119, 127, 136, 137, 140, 143, 147, 148, 154, 156, 157, 159, 170, 184, 191, 197, 202, 203, 204, 205, 216, 221-222, 233, 234, 252, 272
  consistent, 121
  control, 165
  definition, 18
  management, 16, 166-167, 176, 177
  input, 101-103, 216
  input approaches, 102-103
  needs, 121
  types of, 17
Metadatabase, 9, 154, 169, 184, 186, 234
  characteristics of, 10
  database management of, 162, 185, 189
  requirements, 162-164
  services, 164-165
  software, 164
  design of, 61
  conceptual, 64-66
  management system, 10, 162-165, 166
Metadata generation, 53-55, 115-150, 185-186, 204, 257-259, 269-271
  and active DD/DS, 116-121
  for application programs, 121-128
  for DBMS, 142-144
  for end-user facilities, 128-139
  for integrity functions, 139-142
  multi-purpose, 149
  serial, 143
  for special purpose utilities, 144-149
Metadata sharing, 153, **162,** 186
  objectives, 156
  parallel, 156-159, 176
  serial, 159-162, 176, 177
  strategies for implementing, 154-162

Meta-entities, 66, 75-80
  categories of, 66
  hierarchical structure, 69
  network structure, 71
  relationships, 69
  structure, 69-73, 184
  sample, 72

Network, 56
  definition, 230
  backup-and-recovery, 239
  node, 56, 230
  schema, 240
  subschema, 240
  dominant node, 237
  hierarchical, 238
  ring, 239
  star, 237
Network data directory (NDD), 56, 233
Nodal location directory (NLD), 233
Node, 236

Output facilities, 93, 107-112
  ad-hoc, 112
  batch, 109
  characteristics, 109
  forms of, 109-110
  online, 108-109

Passive DD/DS, 1, 117, 176
  definition, 22
Password, 106, 140-141, 224, 225
Potentially active DD/DS, 22, 117
PRIDE/Logik, **177**, 190, **277**, 278

Query language, 136
Query language processor (QLP), 136
  and end-user, 136
  metadata generation for, 137

Recovery techniques, 165
Reorganization/restructuring, 47-205
Report generators, 129, 185
  interface, 170
Requirements definition, 26, 34

Schema, 48, 143, 168, 224, 258
Security, 53, 185, 186, 196, 211, 224-226
  codes, 106
  and control, 53, 106-107, 165
  DBMS-dependent, 107
  requirements for output, 111
  locks, 224
  profile, 140-141, 224
  status level, 106, 225
Selection:
  criteria, 182-189
  methodology, 179-182
  requirements for, 179
  team, 178
Self-generating dictionary, **177, 277**
Software tools, 148
Standards, 51-52
  data definition, 51
  data format conformance, 51
  for DD/DS, 100-101
Status, 106, 185, 216
  and security, 225
Subschema, 47, 48, 143, 168, 259
Subsumed DD/DS, 169-170, 190, 273
System development life cycle (SDLC), 25, 26, 27, 195, 202-206, **206**, 267-269
  case study, 288-292
  phases of, 26

Test data generator, 147, 185, 205
TIS, **172, 173, 177, 277**
Training, 201, 213, 226
Transaction, 32, 256
  impact analysis, 256

UCC-10, **76.** 160, **177, 277**
Univac Data Dictionary System, **177**, 190, **277**, **277**
User data, 9, 142
User facilities, 153
User/system interface, 11, 15, 170-173
  requirements for, 170, 171
  strategies for, 172

Version, 204
  checking, 126
  control of, 185
Views, 68-71
  logical, 63, 69
  physical, 69

IV